FRIENDSHIP WITHOUT BORDERS

Friendship without Borders

Women's Stories of Power, Politics, and Everyday Life across East and West Germany

Phil Leask

berghahn
NEW YORK · OXFORD
www.berghahnbooks.com

First published in 2020 by
Berghahn Books
www.berghahnbooks.com

© 2020, 2023 Phil Leask
First paperback edition published in 2023

All rights reserved. Except for the quotation of short passages for the purposes of criticism and review, no part of this book may be reproduced in any form or by any means, electronic or mechanical, including photocopying, recording, or any information storage and retrieval system now known or to be invented, without written permission of the publisher.

Library of Congress Cataloging-in-Publication Data

Names: Leask, Phil, 1947– author.
Title: Friendship without Borders: Women's Stories of Power, Politics, and Everyday Life across East and West Germany / Phil Leask.
Other titles: Women's Stories of Power, Politics, and Everyday Life across East and West Germany
Description: New York: Berghahn, 2020. | Includes bibliographical references and index.
Identifiers: LCCN 2019053840 (print) | LCCN 2019053841 (ebook) | ISBN 9781789206555 (hardback) | ISBN 9781789206562 (ebook)
Subjects: LCSH: Women—Germany—Schönebeck (Schönebeck)—Biography. | Schönebeck (Schönebeck, Germany)—Biography. | Female friendship—Germany—Schönebeck (Schönebeck) | Women—Germany (East)—Social conditions. | Women—Germany (East)—Biography. | Germany (East)—Biography. | National characteristics, German.
Classification: LCC CT3430 .L43 2020 (print) | LCC CT3430 (ebook) | DDC 920.720943—dc23
LC record available at https://lccn.loc.gov/2019053840
LC ebook record available at https://lccn.loc.gov/2019053841

British Library Cataloguing in Publication Data

A catalogue record for this book is available from the British Library

ISBN 978-1-78920-655-5 hardback
ISBN 978-1-80539-118-0 paperback
ISBN 978-1-80539-365-8 epub
ISBN 978-1-78920-656-2 web pdf

https://doi.org/10.3167/9781789206555

Contents

List of Illustrations	vi
Acknowledgments	vii
List of Abbreviations	viii
The Schönebeck Women and Where They Went	ix
Introduction	1
Chapter 1. From Schoolgirls to Young Women	27
Chapter 2. Grown Up: The Long 1950s	65
Chapter 3. No Longer Young: The 1960s	124
Chapter 4. Turning Fifty: The 1970s	169
Chapter 5. Toward Retirement: The 1980s	203
Chapter 6. Reunited? The 1990s and Beyond	245
Conclusion. The Schönebeck Women and Their Group	292
Bibliography	302
Index	315

Illustrations

1.1. The Schönebeck women as schoolgirls, 1937	28
1.2. Irma and Franz, 1950	51
1.3. A "new teacher" at work: Marianne and her class, Schönebeck, 1956	57
2.1. Marianne and Johannes in Thuringia, 1950	72
2.2. Marianne with her baby, catching the train to the Harz, 1951	75
2.3. Else in the directors' collective preparing for *Martha*	103
2.4. Hertha and her children, 1957	108
2.5. Lisa Liebmann: "Wow, that was just fabulous!"	112
2.6. The sixth book	114
3.1. Else (*back left*) with her fellow potato harvesters	140
4.1. Else's apartment in Prenzlauer Berg	182
4.2. Hertha's family: Klaus with his wife; Hertha; Kerstin; Wilfried's wife	185
4.3. The self-censored letter, Book 17, 1977	190
5.1. Arriving in Hamburg in 1987 for the first joint reunion	208
5.2. Jutta, Maria, and Edith in the United States, 1989	236
6.1. Fifty years on: class reunion, Burg Wilenstein, 1 September 1990	254
6.2. Class reunion, Schönebeck, 4 May 1996	267
6.3. Irma and Franz in Austria, winter 1994	271
6.4. Else reading from Book 1 at the 1998 reunion	275

Acknowledgments

Particular thanks are due to the Gerda Henkel Stiftung, who funded the research for this book, and to the Arts and Humanities Research Council for their earlier funding that led me to discover the Schönebeck letters. I am also grateful to the women who were happy to be interviewed and who were so full of energy and enthusiasm; the various archivists in the Akademie der Künste in Berlin, the Deutsches Tagebucharchiv in Emmendingen, and the Stadtarchiv in Schönebeck; and the anonymous peer reviewers, for their willingness to give their time and consideration to such a long manuscript. Special thanks are due to Andrew Bergerson for his support, observations, and recommendations.

The translations of letters, publications, documents, and interviews into English are my own, unless otherwise noted.

Abbreviations

BDM	Bund deutscher Mädel (League of German Girls)
DFD	Demokratischer Frauenbund Deutschlands (Democratic Women's League of Germany)
FDGB	Freier Deutscher Gewerkschaftsbund (Free German Trade Union Federation)
FRG	Federal Republic of Germany
GDR	German Democratic Republic
KPD	Kommunistische Partei Deutschlands (German Communist Party)
LPG	Landwirtschaftliche Produktionsgenossenschaft (agricultural cooperative)
MTS	Maschinen-Traktoren-Station (Machine and Tractor Station)
NÖS	Neues Ökonomisches System (New Economic System)
NÖSPL	Neues Ökonomisches System der Planung und Leitung (New Economic System of Planning and Management)
PDS	Partei des Demokratischen Sozialismus (Party of Democratic Socialism)
RAF	Rote Armee Fraktion (Red Army Faction)
SBZ	Sowjetische Besatzungszone (Soviet Occupation Zone)
SED	Sozialistische Einheitspartei Deutschlands (Socialist Unity Party)
SMAD	Sowjetische Militäradministration in Deutschland (Soviet Military Administration in Germany)
SPD	Sozialdemokratische Partei Deutschlands (Social Democratic Party of Germany)
UFV	Unabhängiger Frauenverband (Independent Women's Association)
VEB	Volkseigener Betrieb (state-owned firm)
ZBN	Zentraler Bühnennachweis (central agency for development and recruitment of performing artists and support services)

The Schönebeck Women and Where They Went

	Location in Schönebeck area	Moved within East	Moved to West (incl. West Berlin)	Occupation/ activity
Anna Siebert	Staßfurt		West Berlin; Hamburg	Engineer
Anni Lange	Schönebeck		Hamburg	Opera singer
Astrid Greiswald	Schönebeck		Braunschweig; Bad Bergzaben; Sinzig	Mostly not employed
Barbara Meier	Neugattersleben			Kindergarten director
Brigitte Hansen	Staßfurt	Pirna	Heilbronn; left FRG for Zürich	Operations nurse
Carla Brunner	Glinde			Farmer
Charlotte Krüger	Schönebeck		Dierdorf	Various; orchid grower
Edith Friebe	Schönebeck		Rösrath-Kleineichen, near Cologne (during the war)	Dressmaker
Elena-Luise ("Leni") Baumann	Staßfurt	Halle	Kiel; Braunschweig	Professor (psychology)
Elfriede Berger	Schönebeck		Cologne (during the war)	Mostly not employed; part-time administrative assistant
Elly Haase	Schönebeck (Bad Salzelmen)			Carpenter

	Location in Schönebeck area	Moved within East	Moved to West (incl. West Berlin)	Occupation/ activity
Else Hermann	Schönebeck	Magdeburg; Plauen; Brandenburg; Erfurt; Berlin; Schönebeck area		Theater costume designer; teacher; theater talent developer
Erika Krämer	Calbe	Rostock; Berlin; Calbe	Hamburg; Essen; Kassel	Partly "housewife"; administrator
Erna Walter	Schönebeck		Schleswig-Holstein: Kronsgaard; Kappeln	"Housewife"
Frieda Möller	Barby			Nurse
Gerda Höpfner	Schönebeck			Administrator, shoe factory
Gisela Riedel	Schönebeck			Pharmacy assistant; laboratory assistant
Heidi Kempf	Schönebeck (Bad Salzelmen)			Hospital laboratory manager
Hertha Pieper	Calbe			Farmer
Hilde Brenner	Schönebeck		Uhry (Lower Saxony)	Conference organizer
Ilse Klein	Schönebeck		Bad Oeynhausen (during the war)	"Housewife"; massage therapist; clerical assistant
Inge Fischer	Schönebeck		West Berlin	Unclear
Irma Kindler	Schönebeck (Bad Salzelmen)		Braunlage; Hanover; Hamburg	Interpreter; "housewife"; administrator
Käthe Sommer	Schönebeck	Magdeburg; Schönebeck	Bad Münstereifel	Clinic manager

	Location in Schönebeck area	Moved within East	Moved to West (incl. West Berlin)	Occupation/ activity
Lisa Liebmann	Dodendorf	Bad Suderode; Wismar		Teacher
Maria Stein	Schönebeck			Unclear
Marianne Schneider	Schönebeck			Teacher; "housewife"
Martha Jäger	Schönebeck			"Housewife"; part-time business manager
Sabine Kleber	Schönebeck	Bitterfeld	Kaiserslautern	Teacher
Susanne Becker	Schönebeck	East Berlin	West Berlin; Essen; Seligenstadt	Dental technician (initially in East Berlin)

Map. Divided Germany, with inner-German border, 1945–1990. © Berghahn Books.

Map. Area around Schönebeck/Elbe. © Berghahn Books.

Introduction

A Meeting in Magdeburg

It was 1 September 1940, the first anniversary of the start of World War II. In the small town of Schönebeck in central Germany, a group of schoolgirls—mostly thirteen years old—wondered what would become of them as the war progressed. There were problems already: lessons canceled when their teachers were drafted into the army; the school itself too cold in the winter as coal supplies dwindled. Soon it would be the boys from the neighboring school, their dancing partners, being put into uniform and taken off to the front. Some of the girls were moving away with their parents; others thought they would be evacuated; and there was talk of the rest being scattered around other schools.

What the girls valued most was their close-knit group of friends; what they most feared was the group falling apart. Desperate to prevent this, they made a solemn promise: come what may, they would meet up again in the Cathedral Square in Magdeburg ten years later, at three o'clock on 1 September 1950. Looking back in 1955, one of the group recalled how they had felt when making this promise: "But what was it we actually said in 1940? I believe, that we would find a way to make it to the class reunion, whether we should turn out to be in Africa or on the moon!"[1]

For the girls, Magdeburg was the big city, and Schönebeck no more than a provincial town. Magdeburg was twenty minutes away on the train, a different world, with its theater, opera, restaurants, its diverse population (including a substantial Jewish community), its streets full of shops and people and fascinating buildings from the late middle ages, its busy waterfront on the river Elbe, its quiet corners to meet or enjoy being anonymous. Many years later, Else Hermann, one of the Schönebeck women featured in this book, wrote of a visit to Magdeburg in 1939 with her friend, Charlotte Krüger, another of the Schönebeck women:

> I went to my first opera, *Freischütz*, with Charlotte. I can still see the two of us—we were twelve years old—at my house, sitting on the sofa with my father

as we read through the libretto. We had heard that no one understands what is being said in an opera because it is all sung. We insisted we would understand everything, so learned the text off by heart. In the Stadttheater in Magdeburg, we felt very special, particularly in the foyer during the interval, Charlotte in her best red dress, me in my best blue dress.[2]

At the end of the war, Magdeburg was in ruins, its theaters, its beautiful baroque center, and much of the rest of the city destroyed by British and American bombing and by artillery in the final battles of April 1945. Five years later, the ruins remained. Nevertheless, the miracle happened: at three o'clock on 1 September 1950, the rain cleared, the sun came out, and fourteen of the girls from the class of 1940—now women in their twenties—gathered in the square, in the shadow of the damaged cathedral. Some brought apologies from others who could not make it. Hardly able to believe what was happening, they drank coffee, swapped ten years of stories, and resolved to hold an annual reunion and to start a *Rundbrief* (round letter).

For young German women, establishing a *Rundbrief* at the end of their time at school or university was common enough. The process involved one person taking the lead, gathering all the addresses, and entering them in a notebook. The organizer then wrote the first letter, addressed to all of them, and sent the book to the next on the list, who wrote her letter and sent it on again, until the final person on the list sent the book back to the organizer. In the second and subsequent years, the organizer circulated the full book and the new book together, so that those who had written early letters in the first book could read the entries from those who followed and take them into account in their new letters.

It was rare for a *Rundbrief* to last long, but the women I call the "Schönebeck women" carried on meeting and writing from 1950 to 2000. In 2001, growing old, feeling they no longer had much to say, and seeing their children and grandchildren embracing the world of computers and emails, they decided to end both the *Rundbrief* and their reunions. They voted to archive the thirty-one notebooks, containing around a thousand letters and several hundred photos, in the Kempowski Biographienarchiv, now in the Akademie der Künste, Berlin. I refer to this set of letters as the "Schönebeck Letters." They offer us a unique collective image over time of the experience of women who lived through the Nazi Third Reich, then either stayed in the East or moved to the West when Germany was divided, and eventually experienced German reunification.

The Schönebeck women's determination to keep on writing stemmed partly from the fact that half of them eventually came to live in the West in the American, British, and French Occupation Zones and subsequently the Federal Republic of Germany (FRG), while the other half remained in the East in the Soviet Occupation Zone (SBZ), which later became the German Democratic

Republic (GDR). By repeatedly asserting the unity of their group, they sought to convey a view that at some level Germany itself remained united and that this was in part thanks to them.

Schönebeck and the Schönebeck Women

This book looks at the everyday lives of a group of women who explicitly defined themselves as nonpolitical and tried to distance themselves from what was being done by the authorities in the world outside their group. It considers how they experienced, understood, accepted, rejected, or countered the exercise of power, predominantly by men, across different regimes in Germany, from the 1930s to the end of the twentieth century. It seeks to draw out, from their letters and a number of interviews, the women's assumptions about what their place was and should be in society. It asks how their assumptions, and the words and actions that expressed them, changed as the society around them changed. In doing so, it looks at the way the group itself functioned and how it, too, exercised a form of power. How and why did the women create group norms and values that they expected one another to follow? How did they interact with the society and its structures as they sought to meet these expectations? How and why did their individual actions sometimes fail to conform to the expectations of the group?

This study takes in part a microhistorical approach: that is, an approach that involves assembling and analyzing stories of otherwise unknown or disregarded people's individual lives and their fragmentary events, anomalous behavior, patterns, and repetitions, along with their connections to the structures and frameworks within which such people operate.[3] As Sigurður Gylfi Magnússon and Davíð Ólafsson note, describing their microhistorical approach, "Somewhere between the two poles of social structures and individual agency, we propose a view exploring the 'in-between spaces,' where interaction and communication took place."[4] In this study, the in-between spaces are particularly complex. One of them is the group itself, which the women created partly to cope with what they saw as problematic external social structures, such as the division of Germany after the war into two states with conflicting ideologies.

The book takes as its subjects a group of women, born in 1926 or 1927[5] in a small provincial area of Germany, who were at school together in Schönebeck-on-the-Elbe, south of Magdeburg. Schönebeck had a population in the 1930s of almost forty thousand. It was a long-established market town for the fertile agricultural area around it. In the Middle Ages, it had flourished through the production of salt and its distribution up and down the Elbe. In the nineteenth century, like the nearby towns Staßfurt and Calbe, it developed a substantial industrial base and became a stronghold of the Social Democratic Party.[6]

By the late 1920s, there were serious clashes between the Social Democrats, a smaller number of Communists, and the National Socialists. When Hitler took power in 1933, the Nazi Sturmabteilung (SA) under Walter Karpe brutally attacked the Social Democrats and sought to enforce a boycott of Jewish businesses in Schönebeck. In 1938, the SA led the November Pogromnacht (or Kristallnacht) attacks on the tiny Jewish population, arresting many of them and forcing them to emigrate or be imprisoned in concentration camps, which few survived.[7]

These years of violent political conflict and repression, during which the industrial base of Schönebeck was increasingly turned toward war-related production, formed the backdrop for the girls' time at school. The girls themselves were pressured to join the Bund Deutscher Mädel (BDM), the female branch of the Hitler Youth, as a way of building support for Nazi policies. After the pogrom in November 1938, they were strictly forbidden even to acknowledge their Jewish former classmates and friends if they passed them in the street.[8] In their English classes at school, one of their set texts was *Why I Believe in Hitler*, by A. J. Macdonald.[9]

Everyday Life and Power

Scholars are engaged in an ongoing discussion about the nature of the dictatorship and the nature of everyday life first under the Nazis and then under communism in eastern Germany. They contrast these dictatorships with the attempts to construct and entrench a democratic system in western Germany after the war. In all cases, they are looking at the construction and exercise of power. Against this background, what can analysis of the Schönebeck letters tell us that is new about how power was exercised in everyday life? What do the letters reveal not only about denial, dissent, and resistance, but also about agreement, assent, or various forms of accommodation to the regimes and to others using power? In all of these societies, formal power was exercised predominantly by men. What can we learn about how women experienced their lives as women under these political systems with the regimes' different commitments to women's contributions and rights, and what can we learn about how women constructed their own ways of seeing the world and asserting their position in it?

To answer these questions, this study looks at the women's lives in terms of their own experience of the joys and difficulties of growing up into adulthood, moving toward middle age, and finally growing old. In terms of historical events and ruptures they had to contend with, their lives have as their backdrop the Nazi years to 1945; the periods of Allied occupation leading to the establishment in 1949 of both the GDR and the FRG, with the capitalist and communist systems competing with each other until the end of the 1980s; and the Wende and post-Wende period from 1989 to 1990, with German reunification in 1990. This study treats the various political ruptures as important, as well as looking for evidence of continuity during times of transition.[10] It also considers the significance of personal ruptures in the women's lives, looking particularly at ruptures caused by acts of humiliation, a specific way of exercising power that brings with it serious long-term consequences.[11] One of the advantages of focusing on humiliation is that, as discussed later in this introduction, memories of humiliation are relatively fixed and vivid, so that responses in interviews are likely to be more reliable and to help with the interpretation of incidents referred to in the letters.

Men and Women in the Nazi Period

The Nazi regime explicitly asserted the power of men and set out its policies accordingly. It promoted a vision that involved a strong man who went out into the world and was prepared to fight and die for his country, along with a revered wife who stayed at home, managed the household, and brought up their children to think and behave as good National Socialists. The Nazis sought to reduce the opportunities available to women in education and the labor force and excluded women from virtually all significant positions of political and administrative power.[12] Jewish women, of course, were fully excluded from the *Volksgemeinschaft*, the term the Nazis applied to the supposedly racially pure society they were creating. As the historian Ute Frevert says, the paradise for women that Hitler said he was creating "meant public humiliation, enforced sterilisation, torture, removal to concentration camps, murder" for those not German, Aryan, healthy, and politically loyal.[13]

The Nazis often had difficulty turning policy into practice in the face of conflicting demands. As they proceeded with rearmament in the late 1930s, they needed more, not fewer, single and married women to work in the factories. Similarly, during the war the authorities strongly urged women to work outside the home, but held back from conscripting them because of resistance from women and because conscription would clash too overtly with the regime's propaganda about women.[14]

Girls growing up in the Nazi period were faced with a clash of values and attitudes between those of the female branch of the Hitler Youth, the BDM, and those passed down by parents who had been born at the end of the nineteenth century and lived through World War I, the overthrow of the monarchy, and the years of the Weimar Republic.[15] Girls often enjoyed the activities of the BDM, which they saw as a way to escape from the constraints of the family and especially from their controlling mothers.[16] This matched the regime's wish to limit the influence of the family and to inculcate Nazi values through activities outside the home and outside the school. Dagmar Reese, whose work includes the extensive use of interviews and local studies, points to the substantial long-term impact of out-of-school education of girls through the BDM.[17]

The Nazi authorities used organizations like the BDM to give power at a very local level to hundreds of thousands of young women who were group leaders. As Frevert notes, these young women, often hardly more than girls, were figures of state authority, and "as miniature Führers they were enmeshed in a meticulously designed system both of duties and responsibilities, and of rights and privileges, which the Nazi regime employed to make its *Volksgemeinschaft* loyal and disciplined."[18] This was power at a very local level, however, and the Nazi authorities were successful in keeping women out of higher positions of power. At the same time, their approach to building a group or community ethos among girls and young women would have given the girls at school in Schönebeck precisely the expertise needed to build and sustain their own group long after the end of the Nazi regime.

The End of the War

By the end of the war, some of the Schönebeck women were already living in what would become the American or British occupation zones. Others were making their way home through either or both of the American and Soviet controlled areas. Schönebeck itself was occupied initially by the Americans, then by the British, and from July 1945 by the Soviet forces.

The historian Richard Bessel, looking at this period, says that "in 1945 Germans were transformed from active protagonists to passive observers of their fate."[19] However, neither the actions nor the words of the Schönebeck women suggest that they lost their sense of being able to act in their own right with some control over their lives at this time. Nor do they suggest that the women experienced the formal end of the war as a major rupture between one regime and another or between what would later be defined as West and East.

Having had the relatively smooth progress of their lives interrupted by their *Reichsarbeitsdienst* (a form of national service), and by their dramatic journeys home, the Schönebeck women were keen to take up where they had left off, with education, jobs, and getting together with young men. As far as they were concerned, there was not rupture but continuity. In terms of time, there was continuity both with the Nazi and pre-Nazi past and with the future opening up in front of them. In spatial terms, there was continuity as they still viewed Germany as a single entity, even if they accepted the loss of the eastern territories. Since Schönebeck, Staßfurt, Calbe, and the smaller settlements in the area had not suffered significant war damage, the young women had homes and families to return to and had their friends around them. Schönebeck, therefore, represented continuity in both temporal and spatial terms. If there was a moment of rupture in their lives, it was not Germany's defeat and the end of the war in 1945. Rather it was, as their letters suggest, the rupture caused by the *Reichsarbeitsdienst* itself, which transformed them from schoolgirls into young women and cast them out into the world to fend for themselves.

Generations and Their Significance

It is here that historians' consideration of generations is significant. The Schönebeck women belong to a very specific generation, the one Mary Fulbrook looks at in her discussion of the trajectories of men and women who were born in the late 1920s or early 1930s. In the FRG, people from this generation became prominent among intellectuals and in the media but less so in political, administrative, and economic structures. In the GDR, they were the "long-term carriers of communism" and were disproportionately represented in these structures, though not at the top of them. In both cases, people of this age were "available for conversion to an entirely new, even 'brave new,' world." Similarly, Hartmut Zwahr talks of the generation born between 1920 and 1929 as attracted by the new opportunities in the GDR and most likely to stay there.[20]

Considering much the same cohort, Mark Roseman and others look at youth revolt, with assessments of the formation and impact after the war of the "Hitler Youth generation" and specifically the "BDM generation."[21] As Roseman notes, within this generation, it was not just class and social background that shaped people's experiences of the war and its end, but also where they were and what had happened there, in that specific location. He points to the differences "between being bombed out or having an intact home, between staying at home and being evacuated, . . . between town and country," to which could be added the different experiences of men and women at this time.[22] It is here that the Schönebeck letters are helpful, offering detailed insight into a group who were "29ers," were women, were not directly affected by bombing or the loss of the family home, and did not become either intellectuals in the West or anything more than indirect representatives of the state in the GDR.

Hester Vaizey, considering the West, and Donna Harsch, the East, both raise questions about the extent to which women could shape their lives in the context of the different structures and expectations of the different regimes after the war.[23] Vaizey points to the "extraordinary resilience of the nuclear family and the emotional ties that bound its members together, under the extreme pressures of Nazism, war and reconstruction." Vaizey's nuclear families were often led by women, since the men were fighting the war or in prisoner-of-war camps.[24] Harsch's work highlights the unexpected actions and power of women who took the male-dominated GDR state organizations at their word. Women demonstrated, without necessarily attempting to do so, their ability to move elements of the state in the direction of women and their "domestic agenda" and away from the state's "productivist agenda."[25]

According to these accounts, which describe the context for the postwar lives of the Schönebeck women in both East and West, women developed real strengths of their own, as well as influence over their and their families' lives. However, as Gisela Helwig discusses, what the two regimes shared was a set of assumptions about the traditional or natural responsibilities of women. Whether the society or their husbands expected them to go out to work, or expected them not to go out to work, women would be responsible for the home and the family, including meeting the needs of the husband. Where women did work outside the home, they would be more likely to be in jobs seen as traditionally done by women, even in the GDR.[26]

Women and the History of Everyday Life

Given the formal commitment of both the FRG and the GDR to the equality of women with men, and the claim of the ruling Socialist Unity Party (SED) to have solved the "woman question" in the GDR, it is important to look both at the issues of formal power and its exercise in relation to women, and at the everyday experience of women in relation to power. It is here that *Alltagsgeschichte*, the history of everyday life, with its emphasis on the significance of the actions and behavior of ordinary, apparently or supposedly nonpolitical people, helps to bridge the gap between those seen as the rulers and those over whom they sought to exercise power.

Historians wrestle with the meaning and content of "everyday life" and what it means to write a history of it.[27] "Everyday life" takes place in a particular society and a particular period within a set of given structures that influence but are also influenced by the conduct of ordinary people. For Andrew Bergerson and Leonard Schmieding, "Everyday life is fragmented, multivocal, ambiguous, dynamic, and contradictory. It is the locus of complex interactions between elites and masses, micro and macro, public and private, the ordinary and the extraordinary. It contains a confusing mix of structure and agency, myths and experience, propriety and unruliness."[28] Approaching the history of postwar Germany from the point of view of the history of everyday life involves moving away from a primary focus on "big structures, large processes, [and] huge comparisons"[29] in the FRG, or on the SED, the Ministry for State Security (commonly known as the Stasi), and repression in the GDR, while not overlooking the significance of these for people's everyday lives.

Of relevance to studies of everyday life is the much-used concept of "agency," which microhistorians Magnússon and Ólafsson call "the capacity of individuals to act within the social structure that seems to limit or influence the opportunities individuals have." They consider that the restraints of the social structure are not just the formal agencies or activities of the state but also "come in the form of categories like class, gender, and ethnicity on the one hand, and social institutions on the other, such as the state, the church, and the educational system."[30] To these can be added the structures people construct for themselves, such as the group the Schönebeck women formed and which helped to shape the way they acted toward one another, and their attitude and responses to other external constraints.

It is here that the concept of "microsocial interactions" becomes helpful.[31] In order to understand what is happening in everyday life and what it might tell us about perceptions and self-perceptions, and about how power is being exercised, accepted, colluded with, resisted, or ignored, we can look at a very detailed level at the interactions between people in groups they belong to, or between them and their partners, children, friends, colleagues at work, and others they come across in society. In all regimes, but particularly in dictatorial regimes, some of the people with whom they interact at a relatively informal level will be actual or virtual representatives of the state or the ruling party (or parties, in the case of the FRG). Such detailed consideration can start to convey a new picture of the complexity of relations within and between the two states that were created in Germany after the war. Fulbrook, using her concept of "the honeycomb state," describes the specific, if changing, form of dictatorship that emerged in the GDR:

> The boundaries of the state in the GDR are harder to define than one might at first think.... What is really quite remarkable about the GDR is the way in which extraordinarily large numbers of people were involved in its functioning, who were implicated in a complex web of micro-relationships of power in every area of life, serving to reproduce and transform the system. Very large numbers of people acted as honorary functionaries in a wide range of organizations, in a manner that, by the 1970s and 1980s, was more or less taken for granted by a very significant proportion of the population.[32]

The stories that come out of the Schönebeck letters are in part, whether the women intended them to be or not, stories of this "complex web of micro-relationships of power" across several regimes, both dictatorial and democratic.

Women's Stories

Once again it needs to be emphasized that the stories told here are women's stories and that gender issues were complex within all the regimes considered here. The Nazi regime asserted that society should be male-dominated, and it shaped its policies toward women accordingly, even if there were difficulties turning these policies into practice. In the FRG until the late 1960s and the GDR until the 1980s, the male leaders were not challenged to look at their approach and assumptions. They did not consider, at least openly, that their way of seeing the world and defining possibilities for human interaction and development might arise from a set of concepts and frameworks drawn up specifically by men or with a male bias. They were not open to arguments—made in the West, at least—that their view of the world was constantly reinforced over long periods by theory and action that depended on the same concepts and frameworks. Nor did they see or want to see that such ways of thinking and acting had become so "naturalized" that even the majority of women found themselves only partially conscious of the limitations imposed on them. Nor did they concede that men, too, might be disadvantaged and condemned to lead unfulfilled lives by such ways of understanding and acting upon the world.[33]

After the Wende in 1989/90, women appeared to be the principal losers in the former GDR. They were often the first to lose their jobs and suffered from the reduction of childcare provision.[34] However, women in the former East have often shown great initiative in adapting to the new conditions and building new and successful lives. Some studies suggest that women used the strength and independence they had developed in the GDR to good effect in the newly united Germany.[35] For the Schönebeck women, the picture is more complex. Their letters and interviews suggest that their generation found the transition difficult and that this was not helped by the lack of support from some of the group in the West.

Despite the extensive literature on the position of women in the various regimes considered here, there is still a lack of accounts that analyze at the micro level over such a long period the letters, photos, and later interviews of a specific group of supposedly nonpolitical German women. It is this gap that this work seeks to fill. What I am concerned with is the position of women and how it was created, shaped, and reshaped across different periods; the agency of ordinary women individually and in groups; and what we can learn about these concerns through a detailed study of the Schönebeck women. Central to the study is the nature of the group itself, and its successes and failures as it sought to hold together a disparate group of women across many years and different regimes, and as its individual members sought to make distinctive, individual lives for themselves in ways that potentially threatened the unity of the group.

The Schönebeck Letters

This book is based principally on the thousand letters of the Schönebeck women. They are an invaluable and, until now, unused source of commentary on everyday life in Germany from the late 1930s to the late 1990s. "Egodocuments" of any sort, such as these letters, as well as diaries and autobiographies, are written with a number of different aims: self-justification, self-presentation, persuasion, or the imposition of a particular line of argument. However, personal letters have the advantage of usually being a single draft written without detailed planning and aimed at a specific recipient or set of recipients. In this respect, the Schönebeck letters are straightforward. Nevertheless, there are problems of interpretation that need to be borne in mind.

In each book of letters, each writer addressed around thirty recipients, women of roughly the same age who had in common their time at school in Schönebeck. Their task was to keep everyone in touch with one another and up to date with what was happening to each of them, and to follow the rules for writing the letters. The explicit rules were straightforward: the books had to be properly looked after and sent on within a short time to the next woman on the list.[36] The implicit rules were complex and restrictive and grew out of a set of myths that the women established for themselves and which did not match the foundation myths of the new German states. The GDR's foundation myths declared it to be the anti-fascist part of Germany, based on communist resistance to the Nazis and to the KPD's activities during the Weimar years. The FRG's myths stressed freedom, democracy, and anti-communism, and also harked back to the Weimar years.[37]

The first of the Schönebeck women's foundation myths was that Schönebeck was their *Heimat*, the place they would always remain emotionally connected to, no matter how far away they were, or how long they were prevented from visiting it. They were not explicit about what they meant by the term *Heimat*, whether it was backward-looking toward an ideal past, or forward-looking—a secure base that would help them move forward as their lives developed. It could be both or either, according to what was helpful at different times.[38] Implicitly, *Heimat* meant a place where they had all been united and where they had been happy. Its accidental location in the East when Germany was divided ensured that the women living in the West would have an acute sense of the way the FRG and the GDR were permanently entangled.

This set of attitudes required an emotional commitment to the group, which was to be reflected in their writing. Optimism and cheerfulness were to be expressed whenever possible; achievements were to be reported and admired; and the pleasures of one were to be the pleasures of all. When one of the women experienced difficulties or problems or reported on negative aspects of the society around them, the responsibility of the group was to provide comfort and reassurance, helping them all to cope with suffering and to manage uncertainty and disorientation.

The second of the myths was that their shared memories of happiness in their *Heimat* would ensure friendship and loyalty that would bind each of them to the group. The third myth involved an assumption of innocence: whatever had taken place around them and whatever terrible things might still happen all took place outside the group, and those within the group bore no responsibility or blame for them. The fourth myth was that just as the group itself was forever united, so also, at some fundamental level, Germany remained united. The letters were therefore expected to contribute to maintaining a sense of the group as unable to be divided by the division of Germany.

Differences and Divergence

There were, however, many things that threatened the unity of the group, which was certainly not homogeneous. Though many of the women came from relatively comfortable backgrounds, there were significant differences in terms of class, religion, education, jobs, aspirations, and, even if it was not spelled out, sexual orientation. When the women were growing up in the Schönebeck area, some of their parents were small farmers, while others were teachers, pharmacists, opticians, or carpenters; one family owned a soap factory; another, a construction company. As young adults, the women could expect to benefit from their parents' position. However, the extent of the destruction, disruption, and destitution at the end of the war meant that many had to make their own lives for themselves, starting with very little. These lives were inevitably influenced by decisions made by the different occupying powers and subsequently the two different German states. Where the women found themselves or moved to after the war was critical in determining their future.

In the GDR, all of the women went out to work, though with breaks to have and look after their children. Some became teachers or health workers (but were stopped from becoming doctors); one became a costume designer in the theater and later worked for an organization linked to the Ministry of Culture, where she was responsible for cultivating new talent throughout the GDR. Some took on family businesses that were subsequently taken over by the state; some continued to run tiny professional businesses; and some worked on farms and later became members of the agricultural cooperatives that took over their land. Only one of them ever worked in a factory, and she was in an administrative position. Most of those who stayed in the GDR remained in the Schönebeck area. One (the costume designer) moved to Berlin after positions in different regions in the GDR, but eventually returned to the Schönebeck area. Another moved because of her husband's job to Wismar, a GDR port on the Baltic coast.

Of those who lived in the West at the end of the war, or who moved there over the years—mostly before the Berlin Wall was constructed in 1961—many became comfortably well-off and tended not to work outside the home once they were married. Sometimes they worked part time and sometimes they acted as office managers for their husbands. One became a successful opera singer, one a civil engineer in a senior position, and one a professor of psychology (after doing her early studies in the GDR). Two of them lived in Hamburg, three in smaller cities (Braunschweig, Kassel, and Kaiserslautern), and the rest in small towns.

Some of the women were strongly religious and remained so, both in the FRG and in the officially atheist GDR; some were already nonbelievers or atheists; others ignored any discussion of religion.

The women attempted to overcome the differences between them by engaging in a process of communication and self-narration, describing their lives as they saw them while responding to the demand for assertions of unity. The result was that each letter was also in a way a position statement, setting out the writer's current perception of herself in relation to the others and to the world around them. Each position statement contributed to creating a shared, accepted record, a collective narrative, one which changed as the women and the circumstances in which they lived changed, but which also stressed the continuity of their lives over the decades and the way the women sought to feel part of a single, united Germany.

At the same time, the women in the GDR implicitly created subsidiary myths about their lives under communism. These sometimes appear as a defense against the state's attempts to shape their lives. Asserting that their lives were just as enjoyable as those of the women in the West, they tended to look out for and highlight the positive—the guarantee of a job, the childcare support (later, at least), and an emerging sense of the collective and of support from the collective. Such an approach allowed them to look away from many of the structures that surrounded and restricted them. With their observations and comments, the women in the FRG sometimes accepted these myths and helped to perpetuate them, and sometimes rejected them.

The Photos

The Schönebeck letters are written in a set of notebooks and are often illustrated by photos pasted into the books. The photos open up the letters to us, exposing different ways of seeing and understanding events and the individual women's lives. The photos are deliberately chosen but help us nonetheless to understand something about the women, about local conditions, and about the letters they accompany. For the women themselves, the photos had an important function: they reminded the others who they were and what they looked like, something that was increasingly important over time, since some of the women did not get to the reunions or see many of the others for years or even decades.

What we find in the notebooks are usually photos of people, but almost always of people in a landscape. In the East we see young women in forested, snowy landscapes; a woman with a baby waiting for a train near derelict railway coaches; a teacher in an overcrowded classroom; a group of husbands sitting drinking, with Erich Honecker on the wall in the background; the women and their husbands sunning themselves on the Baltic coast; and views of Budapest, the Caucasus, or the Black Sea. In the West we see similar forested and snowy landscapes, as well as comfortable, modern houses, and images of the women traveling in France, Austria, Turkey, and Greece.

The photos contribute to the creation of the group myth of unity. They also point to another way of interpreting the letters, as an assertion of individuality, of being more than just a member of a group. This can be seen by the personal nature of what is displayed: the ways individual women have of standing to one side or looking away in group photos; the way one dresses differently from the others, reinforcing points made in their letters; photos of themselves in different contexts, at work or in other groups that contrast sharply with the Schönebeck group and its self-image; photos of press cuttings put in by someone other than the woman featured in them; and photos that, inadvertently or not, compare conditions between East and West. The photos are also a declaration: this is how I see myself and how I want you to see me at this particular time in my life.

Self-Censorship

When analyzing the Schönebeck letters, another area of concern is the issue of self-censorship. The women knew the books might be intercepted by officers of the Stasi within the GDR, or by the GDR's border guards as they went into or out of the FRG.[39] They were mostly careful not to implicate themselves or anyone else by voicing opinions that might be considered hostile to the GDR or too complimentary about the FRG. It is also clear that they were careful about what they said both in their letters and at their class reunions, because they understood that no matter how well they knew one another and how important mutual trust was, there might still be someone in the group who was reporting on them to the Stasi. In the midst of what often comes across as nothing but friendly chatter, we find gaps and silences. In at least some cases, these indicate what could not be said or what the writer—being more political than she ever realized—chose not to say.

The Use of Language

These challenges to interpreting the letters make it necessary to treat what is written circumspectly, recognizing the defenses used, the strategies of avoidance and denial, the self-censorship and the special pleading. No one among the Schönebeck women is writing a detailed narrative account of life in whichever regime they are discussing, and only rarely are they recounting how state power and external structures impinged on them. Despite this, the way the letters are written does convey a picture of society and a picture of their own lives in it. Although the letters are often low-key, banal, even trite, the choice of language is frequently a useful clue. Certain words, ironic phrases, metaphors, and other figures of speech, as well as techniques of balancing events or activities against one another, combine to give vivid if fragmentary images of everyday life. In a close reading of the letters, we are forced to puzzle over individual words, phrases, sentences, and paragraphs, an approach from literary studies that is particularly productive.

Lutz Niethammer describes a similar approach, where comprehension begins with the response to what one does not understand. One of his key methodological concepts is *"Irritation prägnanter Unverständlichkeit,"* which he describes as

> the sense of puzzlement the investigator feels when confronted with some element that is highly suggestive, significant yet obscure: a sentence, a basic theme, a trauma, a constellation that taxes and challenges the previous knowledge of the interpreter, who then proposes hypotheses which must be examined in the light of the text of the entire life history. Such work discloses a deep structure of new relations and more general insights, whose specificity and generality can be more tightly defined and closely checked by ethnographic and group-biographical approaches.[40]

In doing so, Niethammer is describing important techniques that are used here to help understand everyday life through an analysis of the Schönebeck letters.

The Interviews

In this study, I complement the Schönebeck letters with interviews I conducted over the period 2012–2016 with some of the surviving Schönebeck women, in both the former East and the former West. By then they were all in their mid- to late eighties, so they were often talking about events from fifty to sixty years earlier. The interviews were semi-structured, based on a set of questions I sought to ask all of them.

Out of the thirty-two women who had been most involved in the group, it was clear that at least twenty-two had already died, and my eventual interviewees told me they believed that a number of the others had died too; or, as they put it, *"heimgegangen"* (gone home). It was possible to track down six of those who remained.[41] I was able to record interviews with Else Hermann and Hertha Pieper, who had always lived in the East, and Anna Siebert and Irma Kindler, who had lived in the West from around the end of the war. Each interview lasted between two and three hours. As is common with such interviews, it was impossible to keep them semi-structured: the women were enormously pleased to see me and determined to tell me everything they could think of about themselves and the other women in the group. I was able to intervene at various times to ask questions, but they were keen to just keep talking.

I interviewed Anna Siebert twice in Hamburg, once with Irma Kindler and once on her own. Irma Kindler asked me to write to her with further questions, then answered these extensively in letters to me. I interviewed Hertha Pieper in the Schönebeck area with her children: one in her late fifties and three in their mid-sixties. Else Hermann was the last organizer of the *Rundbrief* and was keen to wrestle with the meaning of the life she had led under both Nazism and communism, and with the significance of the group. She invited me back again and again and each time had new things to say. She died in October 2016, leaving me with over twenty hours of recordings of our conversations, letters she had written to me to clarify matters, and other documents, including a diary account by her father of the occupation by the Americans of the family house in Schönebeck in April 1945.

The interviews and the associated documents are in themselves not necessarily an accurate record, with details emphasized in a highly selective manner and some events apparently forgotten. At times the women were shocked when I quoted things they had written years or decades earlier—and never read since—as opposed to what they were remembering at the time of the interview. Sometimes they were clearly reinterpreting events and their actions in the light of their current position and the changes in society that had taken place over the preceding decades.

Despite these reservations, the interviews helped me to understand the written record of the women and the nature of the group, and to identify their shared myths, by allowing me to cross-check between the written and photographic record and the historical record. Several of the women referred independently to events and periods in ways that confirmed one another's accounts and that matched and then expanded on what was written in the letters. Their oral accounts made it easier to understand what was being said at the class reunions and some of the oblique references in the letters to these conversations. In the interviews, the women felt confident enough and far enough removed from the events to be able to give examples of how they had censored themselves and one another, and how the internal rules of the group encouraged this censorship.

A Spatial Assessment

Using an urban geographer's approach, I supplemented my understanding derived from both the letters and the interviews with a spatial assessment, something that is crucial to an understanding of actions in or arising from a specific place. The location, size, topography, layout, and social and economic structure of Schönebeck and its surrounding area are all relevant to the women's perception of who they were, what they were doing, and what was being done to them. Their stories would have been different if the women had come from a small village or been at school together in a large city.[42]

In the former East Germany, I visited where the women had worked, lived, or had their holidays. Sometimes I could check that what they described had been physically possible at the time. I looked at their houses and their specific location, their distance from those of the other women, the public transport connections from one to another and to where they had worked, the traces of the border, and the earlier and later paths through the woods across it. My aim was to understand the rhythms of their everyday lives and what kept them together or, at times, stopped them visiting one another. Concerned by silences in the letters and interviews, I looked at the locations of former Buchenwald subcamps and the routes their prisoners took to work toward the end of the war; I wanted to see whether it would have been possible for the young women to remain unaware of what was happening in their midst. These visits made it easier to understand what the women were expressing in their letters and how it was inextricably bound up with the circumstances in which they lived. The visits were part of the process of matching up what was conveyed by the letters, photos, and interviews both with one another and with the public record of historical events.

The Significance of Humiliation

To build on these approaches, a different and novel way of interpreting the letters is to apply the concept of humiliation to a number of events and experiences the women describe. This can help to understand the long-term significance of these events, and the meaning of letters that may be decades apart.

I am referring here to humiliation as a specific way of exercising power, with a set of common elements and predictable consequences.[43] Victims of an act of humiliation have a sense that an injustice has been perpetrated, one that is against all they could have expected, and for which there is no remedy. One of the consequences involves feelings of rage, but usually of impotent rage, where the desire for revenge clashes with a realistic perception of helplessness. Such an act of humiliation is almost always felt as traumatic. It covers a wide range of actions, such as those of the German state against the German Jewish population (and against Jews elsewhere), or of representatives of the United States in Iraq against prisoners in Abu Ghraib or at Guantanamo Bay; the use of rape as a weapon of war; the sexual abuse of children by priests and others across the world; violence, abuse, or controlling behavior within families; and, increasingly, bullying and other abuse made possible by the internet and social media. The use of humiliation as a way of exercising power has a long history and spreads far and wide across the world.[44]

Neuroscience and psychological studies suggest that nontraumatic and traumatic events are experienced differently not just immediately but also in the long term, and that what we tend to refer to as memories of them are separated out by the brain and respond differently to certain signals. On the one hand, nontraumatic memories can be renarrated, reinterpreted, and perhaps reconstructed over time, and depend on us thinking about and seeking to remember things.[45] On the other hand, a traumatic event leaves traces that are not so much memories in the narrative sense as sets of emotions and sensations that are, in a technical sense, "persistent" and can, in certain circumstances, be suddenly triggered and immediately re-experienced.[46] Victims of humiliation may suppress or avoid for many years the feelings the act of humiliation has caused and their anger at the irreversible act of injustice that they still cannot believe happened to them.

In the letters of the Schönebeck women, sudden expressions of anger or frustration, along with unexpected defenses and evasions, sometimes point toward memories of much earlier episodes of humiliation. The consequences of these episodes can then be tracked over time, even if the writer has sought to forget, deny, obscure, or ignore the memory of the humiliation. Using the concept of humiliation in this way can help us to look for meanings that are otherwise inaccessible in the letters.

The concept also becomes useful when we look at how individual women dealt with the expectations of the group. Sometimes they were aware that their actions or attitudes conflicted with the group's norms and values. They feared exposure and censure, which would have amounted to humiliation, and found creative ways to save themselves from this treatment and from the resulting sense of rejection and exclusion. Anticipating humiliation and taking steps to preempt it was part of the ongoing struggle for position and status within the group. Looking at both the internal and the external cases through the lens of humiliation can give us insights that we otherwise would not have into the way power was exercised, along with its long-term consequences.

A Clash of Myths

The Schönebeck women, writing to one another over fifty years, established and tried to live by a set of myths. Considering their letters and photos, and analyzing the interviews, we can perceive the myriad "microsocial interactions" among the women themselves and with others in the wider society. We see the women struggling to live for themselves, for one another, and at times against one another. We see them happily perpetuating traditional attitudes and values and reaching out toward new ways of thinking and acting. We see them asserting and reacting to power and acting as if external power does not exist.

What we witness in the slowly emerging pattern is a complex clash of myths, centered on the long period of their adult lives when Germany was formally divided. This clash sets the women's personal and group myths against the founding myths of the FRG and the GDR. It also leads the women in each part of Germany to express, however ambivalently, their loyalty to their own state, and puts them in opposition to their friends on the other side of the inner-German border. Additionally, the myth of friendship and loyalty that would bind each of them to the group made no allowance for the impact of individual or societal change. The reality of change and separation gives an occasional air of wistfulness and melancholy to the letters, and a sense of loss and isolation. In response, for those who slip out of the heart of the group or threaten to, there is always someone reaching out to bring them back in, at the price of reining in the errant woman's individuality and distinctiveness. Just as the external forces in society exercise power, so the group itself has its own power that has to be accepted, rejected, or ignored. It is this complex interplay of myths and power that is at the heart of the stories of the Schönebeck women.

The Shape of the Book

In considering these issues, this book is organized both chronologically and thematically. Chapter 1 starts with the period when these women were young girls. It covers the Nazi period before and during the war; the end of the war and the occupation of Germany in 1945; and the emergence of the Cold War, leading to the establishment of both the German Federal Republic and the German Democratic Republic in 1949. This chapter considers the impact of propaganda, actions, and structures on the attitudes and values of the Schönebeck group of girls as they grew into young women. It looks at the women's implicit attempts, individually and as a group, to establish and maintain a position out of reach of those with power over them. It suggests that by looking at attitudes regarding family, work, study, and the authorities, we can construct a picture of a group determined to remain united but already divided in ways they themselves did not recognize.

In this and subsequent chapters, a number of the women are mentioned and quoted, either from their letters or from interviews. The most prominent of these have their stories told throughout the book: Else Hermann from Schönebeck, Irma Kindler from Schönebeck/Bad Salzelmen, Anna Siebert from nearby Staßfurt, and Hertha Pieper from Calbe. Of these, Else and Hertha would stay in the Soviet Occupation Zone and then the GDR, while Irma and Anna lived in the West. Their stories are referred to as the "principal stories."

Chapter 2 explores the period in the women's lives when they saw themselves as active young women, growing up in new societies that were different but closely connected. In terms of historical events, it extends from the birth of the FRG and the GDR to the building of the Berlin Wall in 1961, the period that confirmed the SED's determination to build socialism on the Soviet model, and ended with the physical separation of the two parts of Germany. This chapter looks at homes, families, and the "woman question"; interactions with the state; the significance of role models for the group; and travel, leisure, and holidays. It highlights tensions between earlier values and those that the new states and some of the women themselves wanted the group to espouse. The letters show the women continuing to enjoy their lives and their personal development, as well as struggling to come to terms with both the subtlety and the viciousness of external power, most particularly in the GDR.

We can also see that the women felt that what connected them was stronger than anything that those exercising power from the outside might impose upon them. This gave them a feeling that they could look to the group and one another for sustenance in the face of difficulties, and for confirmation that, as young, enthusiastic women embarking on adult life, the pleasures and opportunities the world had to offer were theirs for the taking. The letters for this period make clear that the GDR, where their *Heimat* was located, would be the focus of attention for many of the women from both the East and the West and would help to shape much of what they wrote in the *Rundbrief* over the next fifty years, even after the GDR had ceased to exist.

Chapter 3 adopts a similar thematic approach for the period from 1961 to the early 1970s, as the women move toward middle age. This was a period of rapid economic, cultural, and social change in both the FRG and the GDR, with an ever-widening gap between the two in terms of the standard of living. There was also significant political change. In the West, Willy Brandt, the first postwar Social Democratic chancellor, promoted the idea of agreements with the Soviet Union, Poland, and the GDR. In the East, a decade of consolidation and modernization, with an emerging economic crisis at its end, culminated in Erich Honecker replacing Walter Ulbricht at the head of the SED in 1971, with promises of some liberalization and "consumer socialism."

In this period, as the women become aware of their own vulnerability and find themselves caring for their aging parents, they introduce an additional theme: health, illness, and dying. In the GDR, the political leaders' concession to women, while urging them to participate fully in the building of socialism, is to increase preschool and out-of-school care for children and provide extra facilities in the workplace to make women's lives easier. They do not ask men to share the work women have traditionally done. While most of the women in the group still display traditional attitudes to their husbands and families, there are comments in the letters from the East that indicate resistance to these attitudes and resentment of the burden women are expected to bear. It also becomes clear that women in the GDR are internalizing the SED's view of the importance of working outside the home, while those in the West remain happy with their position as mothers not expected to go out to work. As the gap widens further between East and West, any underlying resentment tends to be expressed as frustration about the different opportunities for travel and leisure, for which the GDR state can take the blame.

Once again, news of the authorities' arbitrary and unjust treatment of one of the families—a clear case of humiliation—is transmitted by the *Rundbrief*, highlighting its role as a conveyer of news and a creator of consensus within the group.

The same themes are considered in Chapter 4, covering the 1970s. The women in the East are increasingly inward-looking as they move into their fifties, while those in the West are lively and outward-looking, benefiting from the opportunities and consumer comforts of the prosperous FRG, despite social problems they see emerging there. Neither side makes any reference to the arguments set out by the women's liberation movement in the West.

The letters from the East confirm a shift in attitude in the 1970s, involving frustration and disappointment with the lack of improvement in conditions in the GDR. However, this is counterbalanced by the women's continued enthusiasm regarding their jobs, their families, and the trips they make to other eastern European countries and the Soviet Union.

Chapter 5 covers the 1980s, when the women reach retirement age. This, the final decade of the GDR, was a time of international and internal tensions that affected both East and West and caused significant social upheaval. In the West, there was a huge peace movement, the Green Party grew substantially, and the *Rote Armee Fraktion* (RAF) continued its attacks on state or senior business figures. In the East, independent women's, environmental, and peace groups grew but were infiltrated or repressed by the constantly expanding Stasi, and the SED made clear its opposition to the changes in the Soviet Union under Mikhail Gorbachev. For the Schönebeck women there is, at first glance, little sense of this in their letters. They have other preoccupations: what is happening to their children and grandchildren; illness and death; the traveling they are allowed to do; and, late in the 1980s when they have all turned sixty, meeting up again in their first joint reunion in the West. Nevertheless, the long-term consequences of an act of humiliation in 1950 threaten the group's unity.

This period exposes the fragility of the GDR's founding myths. Several of the women in the East who had expressed satisfaction at what had been achieved now write about the way things are decaying in the GDR, and about the first of their children seeking to move to the West.

Chapter 6 covers the years when the women retired and felt themselves growing old as they looked back on their youth. This is the period from 1989/90—the Wende, when the SED lost power and the GDR ceased to exist—to the start of the new millennium. What emerges from the Schönebeck letters is that the women in the East were enthusiastic about the Wende but often found it difficult to adapt to the sudden changes and the different forces that were now affecting their lives. Some had to leave their jobs before they wanted to; many were anxious about how much money they would have in their retirement; some missed the sense of the collective they had absorbed over the previous forty years; most felt disoriented by the loss of the old certainties.

At this time, the question of gender confronted them. Women, they saw, often lost their jobs before men. They were isolated and pushed back into the home, and they could no longer see how to find a purpose in their lives. Looking beyond their own generation, they saw many of their daughters and granddaughters fearing for their jobs and worried by the threatened closure of childcare centers.

At this point, the group as a whole should have helped them, but initially failed to. As a subgroup within it, the women in the East felt suddenly distanced from those in the West. Some of the letters from the West display ignorance, insensitivity, and a feeling of superiority, which angered those in the East. Attempts were made to overcome the damage. The *Rundbrief* and the reunions continued, and individual friendships flourished between East and West. In the end, it was growing old, along with the shock of illness and death, that kept them united, rather than a common understanding of what had happened to them in their years of separation and of how significant the rupture of the Wende and reunification had been for all of them.

It is here that their stories bring us full circle, back to their time as girls at school. Earlier attitudes reappear for some of them in the East—attitudes from the Nazi time, suddenly and brutally expressed, as if forty-five years of antifascist propaganda and education had had no impact on them. Earlier stories are also told for the first time. Most strikingly, overlapping from comments in 1989, two of the women give an account of what happened to one of the Jewish girls who was originally in their class. A serious question arises here about the limits of empathy: if it is so powerful within a group such as the Schönebeck women, does this mean it is more likely not to be applied to those outside the group? If so, is this something that they learned so many years earlier as girls socialized in the Nazi period and retained throughout their subsequent lives? We are forced at this point to look again at the nature of the group itself, to see whether its myth of unity was one that always depended on the exclusion of the "other," not just the Jewish girls in their class but also the women seen as too capitalist or too communist, too arrogant, too assertive, or too compliant. If this is so, then the clash of myths is much more than a story of conflicting ideologies; it is also a story of self-deception and of the difficulties we face, as individual people living under different regimes, as we try to live with integrity and create hope, confidence, and enduring friendships in our everyday lives.

Notes

1. Lisa Liebmann, 20 February 1955, in "31 Originalbände Klassenrundbriefe von ehemaligen Schülerinnen einer Oberschule in Schönebeck an der Elbe. Jahre 1950–2001" (hereafter "Schönebeck Letters"), Akademie der Künste, Berlin, Kempowski-Biographiearchiv (hereafter AdK Kempowski-BIO) 6383. "Lisa Liebmann" is a pseudonym, as are the names of all the women discussed, in order to preserve their anonymity and protect their families from intrusion.
2. "Schönebeck Letters," 26 September 1995.
3. Sigurður Gylfi Magnússon and Davíð Ólafsson, *Minor Knowledge and Microhistory: Manuscript Culture in the Nineteenth Century* (New York, 2017), 6. See also Sigurður Gylfi Magnússon and István M. Szijártó, *What is Microhistory? Theory and Practice* (London, 2013); Carlo Ginzburg, "Microhistory: Two or Three Things That I Know about It," *Critical Inquiry* 20/1, 1993; Carlo Ginzburg, *Threads and Traces: True, False, Fictive* (Berkeley, 2012); Matti Peltonen, "What is Micro in Microhistory?" in Hans Renders and Binne de Haan, eds., *Theoretical Discussions of Biography: Approaches from History, Microhistory and Life Writing* (Leiden, 2014).
4. Magnússon and Ólafsson, *Minor Knowledge*, 3.
5. The one exception was Hertha Pieper, born in 1925.
6. Kreisleitung der SED Schönebeck, eds., *Zeittafel der Chronik der Kreises Schönebeck (Elbe), Teil 1, 1945–1949* (Schönebeck, 1985).
7. Michael Viebig and Daniel Bohse, *Justiz im Nationalsozialismus. Über Verbrechen im Namen des Deutschen Volkes. Sachsen-Anhalt* (Magdeburg, 2013); Personalakte: Walter Karpe, PA 23, Stadtarchiv Schönebeck (Elbe); Günter Kuntze, *Juden in Schönebeck* (Schönebeck, 1991); Hans-Joachim Geffert, *Fragmentarische Nachrichten aus dem Leben jüdischer Mitbürger Schönebecks*, Stadtarchiv Schönebeck, 2012; "Schönebecker SA-Terroristen verurteilt," *Volksstimme Magdeburg*, 15 June 1948.
8. Kuntze, *Juden*, 54, quoting an eye-witness account.
9. *Cecilienschule zu Schönebeck/Elbe: Bericht über das Schuljahr 1939/40*, https://goobiweb.bbf.dipf.de/viewer/ppnresolver?id=101166545X_1940.
10. See the discussion about ruptures and continuity in Andrew Stuart Bergerson and Leonard Schmieding, lead authors for the ATG26 Collective, of which I was a member, in *Ruptures in the Everyday: Views of Modern Germany from the Ground* (New York, 2017), 22–4.

11. Phil Leask, "Losing Trust in the World: Humiliation and Its Consequences," *Psychodynamic Practice* 19/2, 2013.
12. Renate Bridenthal, Atina Grossmann, and Marion Kaplan, eds., *When Biology Became Destiny: Women in Weimar and Nazi Germany* (New York, 1984); Jill Stephenson, *Women in Nazi Germany* (London, 2001); Dorothee Klinksiek, *Die Frau im NS-Staat* (Stuttgart, 1982); Dagmar Reese, *Growing Up Female in Nazi Germany* (Ann Arbor, 2009); Dagmar Reese, ed., *Die BDM–Generation. Weibliche Jugendliche in Deutschland und Österreich im Nationalsozialismus* (Berlin, 2007).
13. Ute Frevert, *Women in German History: From Bourgeois Emancipation to Sexual Liberation* (Oxford, 1988), 207.
14. Frevert, *Women in German History*, 223–24, 229.
15. For different strands of the women's movement in the Weimar years, and the various organizations' relations with and attitudes to National Socialism, see Bridenthal, Grossmann, and Kaplan, *When Biology Became Destiny*, xiii; Frevert, *Women in German History*, 199–201, 209–11.
16. Stephenson, *Women in Nazi Germany*, 75–79, Frevert, *Women in German History*, 244.
17. Reese, *Growing Up Female*; Reese, *Die BDM–Generation*.
18. Frevert, *Women in German History*, 243.
19. Richard Bessel, *Germany 1945: From War to Peace* (London, 2009), 6.
20. Mary Fulbrook, *Dissonant Lives: Generations and Violence through the German Dictatorships* (Oxford, 2011), 8, 260; Dorothee Wierling, "How Do the 1929ers and the 1949ers Differ?" in Mary Fulbrook, ed., *Power and Society in the GDR, 1961–1979: The "Normalisation of Rule?"* (New York, 2009), 204–19; Hartmut Zwahr, "Die DDR auf dem Höhepunkt der Staatskrise 1989," in Hartmut Kaelble, Jürgen Kocka, and Hartmut Zwahr, eds., *Sozialgeschichte der DDR* (Stuttgart, 1994), 449–50.
21. Mark Roseman, ed., *Generations in Conflict: Youth Revolt and Generation Formation in Germany 1770–1968* (Cambridge, 1995), especially these chapters: Alexander von Plato, "The Hitler Youth Generation and Its Role in the Two Post-War German States"; Dagmar Reese, "The BDM Generation: a Female Generation in Transition from Dictatorship to Democracy"; Michael Buddrus, "A Generation Twice Betrayed: Youth Policy in the Transition from the Third Reich to the Soviet Zone of Occupation (1945–1946)."
22. Mark Roseman, "Introduction: Generation Conflict and German History 1770–1968," in Roseman, *Generations*, 32.
23. Hester Vaizey, *Surviving Hitler's War: Family Life in Germany, 1939–1948* (Basingstoke, 2010); Donna Harsch, *Revenge of the Domestic: Women, the Family, and Communism in the German Democratic Republic* (Princeton, NJ; Oxford, 2007). For the dangers facing German women at the end of the war, see Miriam Gebhardt, *Als die Soldaten Kamen. Die Vergewaltigung deutscher Frauen am Ende des zweiten Weltkriegs* (Munich, 2015); Norman M. Naimark, *The Russians in Germany: A History of the Soviet Zone of Occupation, 1945–1949* (Cambridge, MA, 1995), 69–140; Antony Beevor, *Berlin: The Downfall, 1945* (London, 2002), 409–15; Wolfgang Leonhard, *Die Revolution entlässt ihre Kinder* (Cologne, 1962).
24. On the tensions and difficulties when the men returned, see Christiane Wienand, *Returning Memories: Former Prisoners of War in Divided and Reunited Germany* (Rochester, NY, 2015).
25. Harsch, *Revenge*, 2, 14.

26. Gisela Helwig, "Einleitung," in Gisela Helwig and Hildegard Maria Nickel, eds., *Frauen in Deutschland, 1945–1992* (Berlin, 1993), 9–10; Frevert, *Women in German History*, 268, 276.
27. For a summary of the dispute among historians in relation to the FRG, see Geoff Eley, "Foreword," in Alf Lüdtke, ed., *The History of Everyday Life: Reconstructing Historical Experiences and Ways of Life* (Princeton, NJ, 1995), viii–xiii; for the GDR, see Andrew I. Port, "The Banalities of East German Historiography," in Mary Fulbrook and Andrew I. Port, eds., *Becoming East German: Socialist Structures and Sensibilities after Hitler* (New York, 2013).
28. Bergerson and Schmieding, *Ruptures*, 5.
29. Charles Tilly, *Big Structures, Large Processes, Huge Comparisons* (New York, 1984).
30. Magnússon, *Minor Knowledge*, 1–2.
31. Bergerson and Schmieding, *Ruptures*, 6.
32. Mary Fulbrook, *The People's State: East German Society from Hitler to Honecker* (New Haven, CT, 2005), 235.
33. See Joan W. Scott, "Gender: A Useful Category of Historical Analysis," *American Historical Review* 91/5, 1986; Judith Butler and Elizabeth Weed, eds., *The Question of Gender: Joan W. Scott's Critical Feminism* (Bloomington, 2011); Frevert, *Women in German History*, 4–5, 295; Fulbrook, "Gender," in *The People's State*, 141–75. For a longer-term view on how meanings of gender were historically constructed in Germany, see Ulinka Rublack, ed., *Gender in Early Modern German History* (Cambridge, 2002).
34. Fulbrook, *The People's State*, 174.
35. Dinah Dodds and Pam Allen-Thompson, eds., *The Wall in My Backyard: East German Women in Transition* (Amherst, 1994), 19. See also Angelika Griebner and Scarlett Kleint, *Starke Frauen kommen aus dem Osten: 13 Frauen, über die man spricht, sprechen über sich selbst* (Berlin, 1995); Martina Rellin, *Klar bin ich eine Ost-Frau!: Frauen erzählen aus dem richtigen Leben* (Berlin, 2004); Zentrum für Interdisziplinäre Frauenforschung der Humboldt-Universität Berlin, ed., *Unter Hammer und Zirkel: Frauenbiographien vor dem Hintergrund ostdeutscher Sozialisationserfahrungen* (Pfaffenweiler, 1995).
36. Marianne Schneider, 1 September 1950, in "Schönebeck Letters."
37. Alan L. Nothnagle, *Building the East German Myth: Historical Mythology and Youth Propaganda in the German Democratic Republic, 1945–1989* (Ann Arbor, 1999); Bill Niven, "The Sideways Gaze: The Cold War and Memory of the Nazi Past, 1949–1970," in Tobias Hochscherf, Christoph Laucht, and Andrew Plowman, eds., *Divided, but Not Disconnected: German Experiences of the Cold War* (Oxford, 2010), 48.
38. See the discussion of Heimat concepts in Caroline Bland, Catherine Smale, and Godela Weiss-Sussex, "Women Writing Heimat in Imperial and Weimar Germany: Introduction," *German Life and Letters* 62/1, 2019, 1–13.
39. Marianne Schneider, 1 May 1971, "Schönebeck Letters."
40. Lutz Niethammer, "Zeroing in on Change: In Search of Popular Experience in the Industrial Province in the German Democratic Republic," in Lüdtke, *History of Everyday Life*, 256, footnote.
41. There was one unsatisfactory interview with one of the women who had joined the group toward its end. She had been in a lower year at school and neither she nor most of the others seemed to feel she was a full member of the group. She half-heartedly answered my questions in the reception area of an optician's office, while also dealing with incoming clients. Another of the women was too ill to be interviewed.

42. This is demonstrated by the different preoccupations that show up in *Rundbriefe* written by women from Stuttgart (born around 1870): H. Jansen, *Freundschaft über Sieben Jahrzehnte. Rundbriefe deutscher Lehrerinnen, 1899–1968* (Frankfurt/Main, 1991); Dresden (born 1907 or 1908): Charlotte Heinritz, ed., *Der Klassenrundbrief* (Opladen, 1991); Erfurt (born 1915): Eva Jantzen and Merith Niehuss, eds., *Das Klassenbuch. Geschichte einer Frauengeneration* (Reinbek bei Hamburg, 1997); and Breslau (born 1925): Juliane Braun, ed., *Ein Teil Heimat seid Ihr für mich. Rundbriefe einer Mädchenklasse, 1944–2000*, 2nd ed. (Berlin, 2002).
43. Ute Frevert, *Die Politik der Demütigung. Schauplätze von Macht und Ohnmacht* (Frankfurt/Main, 2017); Leask, "Losing Trust"; Phil Leask, "Power, the Party and the People: The Significance of Humiliation in Representations of the German Democratic Republic," Ph.D. dissertation, University College London, 2012; Phil Leask, "Humiliation as a Weapon within the Party: Fictional and Personal Accounts," in Fulbrook and Port, *Becoming East German*.
44. Frevert, *Die Politik der Demütigung*, chapters 1 and 3. See also Karen J. Greenberg and Joshua L. Dratel, *The Torture Papers: The Road to Abu Ghraib* (Cambridge, 2005); Seymour M. Hersh, *Chain of Command: The Road from 9/11 to Abu Ghraib* (London, 2004); Michael Clemenger, *Everybody Knew: A Boy. Two Brothers. A Stolen Childhood* (London, 2012).
45. Alison Winter, *Memory: Fragments of a Modern History* (Chicago, 2012), 262–64; Victoria Pitts-Taylor, *The Brain's Body: Neuroscience and Corporeal Politics* (Durham, NC, 2016), 2–4.
46. Shane O'Mara, *Why Torture Doesn't Work: The Neuroscience of Interrogation* (Cambridge, MA, 2015), 23, 53, 117, 136–37; Winter, *Memory*, 266.

CHAPTER 1

From Schoolgirls to Young Women

Growing Up in the Third Reich

School, Family, Volksgemeinschaft

The Schönebeck women first met as girls at their school, the Cecilienschule, in the second half of the 1930s (see figure 1.1). Most of them were eleven years old. Surprisingly, in their class in 1938 there was also an English girl, an exchange student, with whom several of them became close friends. Writing from Hamburg more than fifty years later, on 18 May 1989, Irma Kindler copied into the *Rundbrief* a poem from her poetry album of that year, one chosen by their English friend:

> If you would hit the mark,
> You must aim a little above it;
> Every arrow that flies,
> Feels the attraction of earth.
> *A friendly Remembrance of the English girl Pauline W.*
> Schönebeck, Feb. 1938

The significance of this is not the trite nature of the verse.[1] Rather, it is that here is a young German girl, in a society pressed by its ideologically racist leaders to be more and more nationalist and hostile to its perceived foreign enemies, warmly embracing her English school friend and inserting a verse from an American poet as if everything around her was calm and unthreatening.

In fact, the school director's report for 1937–38 does give a picture of a calm and caring environment: there were music lessons, walks in the countryside, days off when the weather was too hot—seven of them in that summer— and visits from the dentist. At the same time, the girls were being taught to be young supporters of the National Socialist regime. On 20 April 1937, they celebrated Hitler's birthday; on 20 October, some of the classes, supposedly having a hiking day, were taken to visit a Hitler Youth exhibition in Magdeburg; on 29 January 1938, they celebrated the founding of the Third Reich and, after

Figure 1.1. The Schönebeck women as schoolgirls, 1937. Photo courtesy of "Else Hermann."

the special address, sang songs committing themselves to their German fatherland and the Führer; and on 2 February there were demonstrations of the uses of potatoes and bread in the kitchen, attended by representatives of the Nazi party and its women's organizations. The lessons themselves contributed too: required reading included textbooks on looking after babies, the mother in the home, and women in the service of the national community, the *Volksgemeinschaft*. Goethe, Schiller, Lessing, and Kleist were also on the list, but when it came to written exercises, the emphasis was on what the girls could learn from them for the new era: the depiction of women or the relationship between father and son in Goethe's *Hermann und Dorothea*, for instance. "Does Dorothea correspond to our ideal image of the true German woman?" they were asked. The girls also had to write about "the responsibilities of the German woman in the Third Reich" and answer the question: "How are the ideals of the Hitler Youth demonstrated in the exhibition in Magdeburg?"[2]

Much of the time, the school authorities were trying to loosen the grip of their families and their families' values on the girls and inculcate Nazi beliefs and values instead. They seem to have had some success. The girls joined the female section of the Hitler Youth, the BDM, and claimed later to have enjoyed the activities it provided and the chance to escape from their families. The historian Dagmar Reese argues that such girls "were influenced and shaped not by ideological content but by a *living practice* in the National Socialist organization."³ The pleasures of the BDM were not, of course, available to the girls' Jewish classmates, and the girls knew this.

Among the girls' friends and families, some went beyond mere membership of the BDM: during the war, both Else Hermann's sister and Hertha Pieper—one of the group of girls—had the rank of *Führerin* (group leader). Whether they intended to or not, they contributed to strengthening the "living practice" that reinforced the Nationalist Socialist message and the racial exclusion at its heart.

The letters and interviews give a sense of the success of the Nazi propaganda as well as the tension between families and the authorities. After the war, talking about what they had done, some of the girls—by then young women—displayed naivete or ignorance, at the very least. One of the Schönebeck women whose story will be followed throughout this book is Sabine Kleber. Writing of the period after leaving school in November 1944, Sabine says, "I had a pretty idle life at first. In order to reduce the boredom, I set off traveling with my father. I got to know Poland, which I really liked. In February 1945 I was finally installed in a job, sitting all day at an adding machine, but luckily you didn't have to apply any logical thinking to that!!"⁴ The most extraordinary sentence here is the passing comment about getting to know and liking Poland, at a time when the Red Army was taking control of much of Poland and the tragedy of the Warsaw uprising had already occurred. With the American and British armies rapidly approaching from the west, Sabine's lack of "logical thinking" in February 1945 is even more puzzling. She seems unwilling or unable to question the Nazi leaders' declarations about the war. Her comments suggest that the efforts of the school and the BDM had significantly influenced the attitudes of at least some of the group.

Else Hermann

Else Hermann's story shows how different influences pulled the girls in different directions. Else's father had clashed with the Nazis in 1933 when, as a senior teacher in a school in Magdeburg, he was denounced for making derogatory remarks about Hitler and the new regime.⁵ He was suspended from his post. After defending himself robustly, he was demoted to a minor position in provincial Schönebeck. Aware that he was being watched, he spent the rest of the Nazi period making as few concessions as possible. He was neither trusted by the authorities nor forced to prove his commitment to the regime. He was never required to give the address at the special school events celebrating Hitler, the Third Reich, or Nazi Party anniversaries. In an interview in 2015, Else talked about her father, the stubborn, principled schoolmaster who was also a linguist, poet, and later an environmentalist: "My father said in the thirties that Hitler would start a war that we would lose, and after that would come Bolshevism. And it would serve us right, he said." This seemed to have little effect on her own attitudes, however, even during the war. Only in 1945 did she realize for herself that Germany would lose the war.

Else's father was brought up on a farm in a village west of Magdeburg. As the older son, he was due to inherit the farm. His father, however, was relatively young, so Else's father was sent to study for five years in Leipzig, Munich, and Göttingen, coming back with a doctorate in philology. He wanted to teach, not to return to the farm. Else's mother, on the other hand, was from a privileged family. She learned to sew and knit but was not expected to have an occupation. She was very demanding and would smack Else whenever she felt she needed to. This was one of the reasons Else felt closer to her father who, she said, did not approve of smacking *girls*. Else also admired her father for his intelligence and interest in language and literature, and for his keenness to be involved in the world around him. She did not notice what her school friends laughed about: his haughty, cantankerous side.

The dynamics of the family were such, however, that even Else felt a need to rebel against her father as she moved toward adolescence. It was here that Nazi propaganda had some success in offering young people an alternative way of being in the world. To ensure she remained accepted by the group, and to provoke her father and assert her independence, Else joined the BDM.[6] Even at this age there was a sense that her friends at school represented the future, with access to a wider community, while the family represented the past and a set of outdated values to be rejected, just as the Nazis wished.

The Collapse of Routine

In 1939, even before the war broke out, teachers were in short supply as they were being called up for army service. By early 1940, coal shortages stopped the school being heated. Classes were often canceled or held in the meeting rooms of local factories or in the teachers' homes. Later in 1940, school holidays were extended at short notice because it was not possible to organize lessons or find somewhere warm for them, even if teachers were available. In September 1940, classes were sometimes canceled because of unspecified threats from the war—probably early bombing raids on the cities.[7]

By 1940, the girls were already good friends, a tight group determined to stay together. Despite their anxiety about things collapsing around them, some of their school life went on more or less as usual. Irma Kindler pasted into the *Rundbrief* in 1991 the program from an evening of Viennese music at the Cecilienschule on Sunday, 17 November 1940, at 2:30 p.m. This shows Else Hermann singing Schubert's "Du holde Kunst," and Irma and one of the other girls playing Schubert's "Tänze." The war continued to encroach, however. In 1941, the girls were moved to a much smaller school in the center of Schönebeck; their old school became a military hospital.

In 1942, Else's father decided that the Schönebeck school was not suitable for Else. There, she was being educated to be a housewife and mother in what was known as the "pudding stream," at the end of which she might not be allowed to go to university. He sent her back to Magdeburg to get a proper education. At first Else traveled by train each day. Later she lived with her maternal grandparents, studying literature and history and attending, with their encouragement, the theater and the opera. However, when the bombing raids became more threatening, the children from her school were evacuated to Wernigerode, at the foot of the Harz mountains. There they had lessons on alternate days and spent the other weekdays looking after and teaching the younger children, which Else said brought out her creative side. At the weekend there was music and dancing, as if the war were not happening. (But many of their dancing partners—boys her own age or a year or so older—never made it back from the war, Else said later in her interviews.)

In Wernigerode, they were still taught to be good Nazi citizens. Sometimes it seemed that the message had not been properly absorbed. There was a dispute over the celebration of Christmas, which Else interpreted as a clash between the atheism of the Nazis and the Christian beliefs of local people. Else also remembered a teacher being severely reprimanded for arranging a concert where works by the Russian composer Tchaikovsky were played; this was seen as support for the enemy. The dancing came to an end after the German defeat at Stalingrad and the declaration of total war, but the girls were still allowed to put on plays, provided these were acceptable to the authorities. This was the start of Else's enthusiasm for the theater.

Working for the Nazi State

In November 1944, the girls' lives were transformed. A year before they could gain their end-of-school certificate, the *Abitur,* they were required to leave at once and start their *Reichsarbeitsdienst,* national service with premilitary training in military-style uniforms that bore the Nazi swastika. They were given an emergency certificate, a *Notabitur,* and a promise that at the end of the war this would allow them to move on to higher education.

The *Reichsarbeitsdienst* was originally introduced to get unemployed men into productive activity. It was later used as a means of educating them in accordance with the Nazi ethos, to boost the economy after the Depression, and to help with rearmament and preparations for war. From the time of the invasion of the Soviet Union in 1941, male *Reichsarbeitsdienst* units became support units for the armed forces.[8] For women, the six-months *Reichsarbeitsdienst,* introduced in the late 1930s, had a similar Nazi ethos and became compulsory after the start of the war. As well as periods of training within the camps they were sent to, the women were used on farms to replace men who had been called up into the army. During the war, a further six-month period was made compulsory. Women would spend this in the *Kriegshilfsdienst*, the service directly helping the war effort, working in hospitals, social services, army offices, or armament factories.[9]

Irma Kindler in the *Reichsarbeitsdienst*

Irma Kindler lived in Bad Salzelmen, the small spa town that had merged with Schönebeck. Her stepfather ran the restaurant and dance halls of the Villa Bismarck in the *Kurpark* (spa park). In 1942, after he was called up into the army, Irma's mother could no longer manage the Villa Bismarck on her own but was offered a position running a guesthouse in Braunlage on the western side of the Harz mountains. This guesthouse, the Villa Rosa, had originally belonged to Irma's great-grandmother. By then, the family included two young children from the second marriage. (The first marriage, Irma said, was a victim of the Depression at the beginning of the thirties.) As there was no secondary school in Braunlage, Irma was sent to live in Halberstadt to finish her schooling. Halberstadt was another city terribly damaged by bombing late in the war, but by that time Irma was two hundred kilometers further north, doing her *Reichsarbeitsdienst* in a desolate part of the province of Hanover.

In the area surrounding her camp, Irma said in an interview, there was little work to be done on the land in the winter, so they spent their time learning home economics, which she appreciated, not having covered it in Halberstadt. In April 1945, however, the camp was suddenly closed and the young women had to fend for themselves. At a time of widespread fear and panic when millions of people were on the move in central Europe, many of them fleeing west to escape the Red Army, Irma had to take to the road to get home. Her account, written much later, has a self-effacing, matter-of-fact quality that underplays her achievement:

> We sewed our blankets up to make rucksacks in which we carried the things we most needed. I left with a friend who was originally from the Saarland and somehow or other we made it by train to Salzwedel. From there we had to go on foot, sleeping overnight in ditches by the side of the road—we were lucky it was a warm spring. But then we had a bit of luck: military vehicles came flooding back from the front and they picked us up and we finally made it to Braunlage. A few days after our arrival, the Americans marched in.

In April 1945, when Irma was walking home to the Harz, and the German lines were collapsing on every front, Hitler ordered the establishment of a "Harz fortress," an area to be defended to the death, not only by the army but also by everyone still living there. The Allied armies moved around the Harz but also had to bring some of their forces to fight the German 11th Army through the woods and across the mountains, a battle that lasted until 23 April. At the same time, the Germans were emptying the concentration camps in the area. Thousands of prisoners and forced laborers were taken on "death marches" through the Harz, trying to reach other main camps such as Bergen-Belsen, Sachsenhausen, or Ravensbrück, north of the Harz. Two of the columns passed through Braunlage and made their way east to Wernigerode. They were then caught up in the massacre at Gardelegen, where over a thousand prisoners were burned to death in a locked barn by the local Nazi leader, assisted by other local people, one day before the Americans arrived.[10] Irma's account, consciously or not, glides over the horror of what was going on around her, and the danger she was in at every stage of her journey home.

Anna Siebert in the *Reichsarbeitsdienst*

Anna Siebert lived in Staßfurt, an industrial town twenty-five kilometers southwest of Schönebeck. As a schoolgirl, Anna was one of the half dozen who traveled into Schönebeck each day from the surrounding towns of Calbe, Barby, and Staßfurt, or from isolated farms. Her father owned and managed a construction company with three hundred employees, and their house—used as a show house by the company—was a model of comfort and modernity, with all the conveniences then available, including Italian tiling, gas central heating, two bathrooms, and three toilets.

Anna's father wanted her to become a civil engineer—then unheard-of in Germany for a woman—so that she could take over the family firm. Even at nine years old, when her brother was born, she was greatly relieved that he could do this instead of her. Her father persisted with his wish, but their plans were disrupted by the war. Anna was required to undertake her *Reichsarbeitsdienst* in 1944 in Eichenbarleben, forty kilometers north of Staßfurt. Her experience in the camp was mixed. She suffered because of her privileged background, which had isolated her from much of what was going on around her. An interview with her in December 2012 gives a vivid picture of everyday life in the *Reichsarbeitsdienst*. It makes the war and the power of the Nazi state seem remote and hardly relevant, but also highlights class differences and the continuing success of the construction business despite, or perhaps because of, the war:

> Anyway, I did my *Reichsarbeitsdienst* in Eichenbarleben, it was a disaster for me, firstly because I was a very spoilt child, very spoilt, very sheltered, and when I went into the *Arbeitsdienst*, it was a disaster. I did nothing but cry.... And Erika Krämer from our class, whose story you have read—about being locked up—was with me in the *Arbeitsdienst*, but we were not in the same group, we were not allowed to sleep in the same room.[11]
>
> There were three large rooms, each of them with around 30 people, and my bed was up high where the rain came through.... But I was, even then, and still

am, good at organizing things, and so I said, "This can't go on, the rain coming through on to us," and I was allowed—I was the first one this happened to—to have special leave and go home, where I got hold of materials—that was something my father could do because of his construction firm—and came back and made the roof watertight.

But as I had come from school, from the *Abitur* class, another thing I was required to do in the *Arbeitsdienst* was housework. I had to get up in the morning and make a fire in the rooms of the camp leaders. And I had never made a fire in my life, since we didn't have a fireplace! My father had built the house as an advertisement, so that people could come and see what could be done, with parquet floors and tiling and such things, and we were the first to have gas heating. So I didn't know how to light the fire. I stood there by the fireplace and put in some damp, pretty large pieces of wood, and it didn't burn. And then someone else came along, someone who lived on a farm, and she was able to light the fire. So I realized that what you needed for a fire was paper and dry wood, and there was an old man there, in his early eighties ... (*Anna breaks off and she and Irma laugh: "Oh God, now here we are older than that!"*). We were not supposed to have any money there, but I had hidden some in my locker, so I gave the old man money and a note and asked him to go to the post office (we ourselves were not allowed out of the camp) to send a telegram, which said "urgently need kindling for fire." And so I was the first one in the camp to get a package—a huge package—and everyone thought there were cakes in it, but no, it was full of specially chopped, dry kindling, expensive, but not a problem for a construction firm. So now I was able to light the fire.

After her *Reichsarbeitsdienst*, Anna lived at home in the last months of the war while undertaking the *Kriegshilfsdienst* in a local hospital. In the chaos of the time, she and her family were lucky, she says. From her account, it can be seen that her relatively wealthy family benefited financially from the Nazi period: there are always contracts for large construction and civil engineering companies in a war, building or rebuilding roads, helping to get important buildings back in operation after bombing raids, and in this case, helping to build concentration camps and subcamps.[12] As if anticipating that her family could be seen as natural allies of the Nazis and opponents of the Allied forces, Anna says that her father was a Freemason and so could not be in the National Socialist Party. To reinforce her point, she tells the story of the forced laborers working for her father's firm.

"Naturally," she says, her father's firm had a number of foreign workers, forced laborers who lived in terrible conditions in the concentration camps—in this case, subcamps of Buchenwald. The Sieberts had a large garden, and in it chickens and a pig to help the family get enough to eat. Anna's mother discovered that the foreign workers were eating the food that was left out for the pig. Each day after that she made a large potato stew for them. Additionally, Anna's father had built an air-raid shelter for the family. Although Staßfurt was not bombed, there were frequent alarms, and the family took the foreign workers with them into the shelter. Word of this was apparently passed around in the foreign workers' camp, since, in the anarchic conditions as the camps were dissolved, nothing was stolen and there were no attacks on the Siebert family.

It is not possible to know whether Anna's account is just a defensive way of justifying her comfortable family's behavior during the war; there were indeed Germans who did their best for the forced workers, despite the sanctions they risked for this.[13] At the very least, her desire to tell the story indicates her closeness to and protectiveness of her family, or perhaps her belief, sixty-seven years later, that these were her feelings in 1945.

Else Hermann in the *Reichsarbeitsdienst*

Late in 1944, Else Hermann was sent home to Schönebeck to prepare for her *Reichsarbeitsdienst*. After a while, she seemed to have been forgotten, so—to her great shame, she said in an interview—she went to the administrative offices in Bernburg to tell them that she and two others in Schönebeck wanted to go; the others were outraged and stopped speaking to her. From this we get a sense of the impact on Else of the Nazi efforts at education and propaganda, the reluctance of others to commit themselves at this stage in the war, and the potential damage to the group of not having a single, agreed line to follow.

Else's *Reichsarbeitsdienst* camp was high up in the Erzgebirge, the mountains separating Saxony from what had been Czechoslovakia before the German takeover in 1938. Suddenly, in the depths of winter in early 1945, the mountain roads winding across steep, exposed ridges and down deep, wooded valleys were full of refugees from the east fleeing the Red Army—the Russians, as Else called them. As well as the refugees, there were young girls like her whose camps had already been closed, and soon there were soldiers too, German soldiers, disorganized, retreating, desperate like all the others to get down into the cities, to reach somewhere safe. That was when she truly realized what was happening, she said, that the war was lost, the Russians would soon be there, and everything would be different. In the meantime, there was the small matter of staying alive.

Else described a particular problem in the everyday lives of women toward the end of the war: surviving the winter and the threat of starvation—here in an area with a meter of snow on the ground.[14] There was mining and industry in the towns scattered along the narrow, wooded valleys, but where Else was, near Cranzahl, farming was important despite the steep slopes and the long, hard winters. Like many of the others doing their *Reichsarbeitsdienst*, Else was sent to work on a farm:

> On the farm they had cattle that gave them milk, and fields that gave them nothing at all until early summer. The husband was away at the war, the woman and

her very old mother ran the farm with the help of a Yugoslav prisoner, a forced laborer, I guess, who went back to his camp every evening. There was also an ancient grandfather. He was always hungry. There wasn't much to do but I did what I could and they liked me, which would turn out to be useful, as it happened.

In 1945, the war that had seemed so far away suddenly reached them:

> The mountains were full of retreating soldiers. Sometimes they were given refuge in one of our barracks, then after a bit they moved on down towards Chemnitz. But it wasn't just soldiers. We had great waves of Germans from Upper Silesia, trying to keep ahead of the Russians, mostly passing through, and young women from other *Reichsarbeitsdienst* camps who were put up in the barracks until our camp was overflowing. They slept everywhere, even on top of the lockers.
>
> There came a point when we couldn't feed so many of them any more, so they were sent off on a train—probably one of the last trains—to Chemnitz, where they could be more use in supporting the war. But Chemnitz was full of factories producing things for the war. So it was a target for the bombers. As their train arrived, it was hit by bombs and every single one of them was killed.

When the camp was closed in April 1945 and the camp leaders disappeared, Else knew she would not be able to get home. She put on her civilian clothes and went back up to the farm. Since she brought potatoes and sugar from the camp on her bike, they were happy to see her, as everyone was close to starving. Nothing had grown in the winter and nothing new could be brought in because the roads were blocked and the trains were no longer running. The Yugoslav forced laborer had disappeared. One of Else's jobs was to churn the cream into butter, hard work that was done by hand and had its own complications. When she talked about it, her hands made strong, churning motions, part of an ancient body memory: "One day I went down to start on it and there was the old grandfather scooping the cream out of the pail and eating it before anyone else could get it, just to keep himself alive."

With the spring, the snow thawed, filling the streams, flooding the valleys, and washing away the roads and the railway line. Work on the farm started up again:

> They had horses for the hardest, heaviest jobs, and it was so hard to stop them slipping or trying to bolt down the hillsides. (I was just eighteen, I weighed possibly fifty-five kilos, so you can picture the fun I had!) It was also unbelievably tedious, utterly back-breaking, planting the new season's crops. You can't imagine how primitive it all was! Each seed was put in by hand and covered by a stone, row after row, up and down the hillsides. Why? Well, to protect the new plants from the frost and to stop the soil just heading off down into the valley. And then a bit later, when the weather was warmer and the plants could fend for themselves, each stone had to be carefully moved to one side. Still, somehow I

did manage to enjoy being there and I knew I was safer in the mountains than down in the towns and cities. We heard enough about what was happening there to know that.

Meanwhile, the war was reaching its end and the mountains were suddenly full of columns of starving prisoners from concentration camps with their SS guards, on their "death marches" toward supposed safety in Bohemia. Some of these prisoners had been forced to walk the hundreds of miles from their barracks in Schönebeck and Staßfurt.[15] Shortly after, the "Russians" appeared from the east and the Americans from the west, and the war was over. Else hid on her farm, waiting to feel safer, having heard the accounts of rape and theft.

In the curious no-man's-land that emerged between the Russian and the American lines, just where Else's farm was located, "anti-fascist committees" emerged, made up of former Social Democrats and Communists, mostly older men, who had kept themselves under cover during the war. These took charge and prevented starvation. They helped to clear up the remaining SS and other Nazi forces who were hiding in the forests and to get the refugees and former prisoners down into the cities. In July, the Soviet forces moved west to their designated boundary, occupied this area, and dispensed with the anti-fascist committees.

The historian Gareth Pritchard argues that in many ways the anti-fascist committees were extremely successful. However, in the face of apathy and hostility and a refusal to reject Nazi attitudes and habits, they resorted to increasingly authoritarian measures that alienated the local population. This, he says, was a contradiction that was to remain throughout the time of the GDR.[16] An idealized view of this "no-man's-land" comes from a novel by Stefan Heym, *Schwarzenberg*, named after the largest town in the area.[17] In Heym's account, the decent, idealistic Social Democrats and Communists are outwitted by the ruthless German representative of hard-line Soviet communism.[18]

In the meantime, Else Hermann was restless and homesick. She made two attempts to leave on her bicycle but was turned back at checkpoints where the Soviet zone met the American zone. She was shocked by the chaos she encountered, the millions of refugees and forced laborers—so many trying to go further west, away from the Soviet forces—people dying, and the railway stations packed with people with no chance to get anywhere.

After the adjustment of the borders in July, Else's whole route home was in the Soviet zone.[19] By this time, there was pressure from the authorities for all outsiders to leave the mountains so that local people would have enough food and shelter and be able to rebuild their lives:

> So I decided to try again. I packed what I could on the back of my bicycle and set off down the mountain, all the way from Cranzahl to Zwickau without once being challenged and without a foot on the pedals, a great bit of cycling! I car-

ried on past Leipzig and all the way to Halle, where I stayed a few nights with relatives before the last leg to Schönebeck. On the whole trip I only had one bad moment: coming around the corner pretty fast along the main road into a village, I saw a group of Russian soldiers ahead of me, maybe fifteen or twenty of them in the middle of the road. I put my head down, pedaled as hard as I could, and as I got up to them greeted them with a "good morning" (in my best German!) and drove straight through the middle before they had time to get hold of either me or the bicycle.

Once again, an epic and extremely dangerous journey is treated as an everyday event. At the end of it is a scene of domesticity from an earlier time:

When I got home, my parents were waiting for me as if they had known I would just turn up. And my sister was waiting too. She was getting married but had held off until I could be there, and so that I could sew her wedding dress for her! It was curious to be home, it felt like a return to how it had been years before. It was summer and the harvest was not going well, but there was still food from the countryside around Schönebeck. I had home comforts and felt safe at last. I didn't know what I would do next. Keep on with my education? I decided to wait and see what would happen, and in the meantime got on with making my sister's wedding dress.

Hertha Pieper and the BDM

Hertha Pieper had a very different experience of working for the Nazi state and of returning home. Almost two years older than many of the others, and nineteen years old at the end of the war, she had become a *Führerin*, a group leader, in the BDM. BDM leaders needed a range of practical skills and a commitment, at least in principle, to Nazi beliefs and policies.

Hertha, being so young herself, was responsible only for the younger grouping in the BDM, those aged from ten to fourteen. There was lots of singing, she said somewhat wistfully nearly seventy years later.[20] However, anyone who had been in such a position was suspect at the end of the war. Hertha was arrested and taken to a camp in Paderborn, in the British Zone. There she was held for eighteen months before being released. It was a hard time, a difficult time, she said, but she didn't wish it hadn't happened; she learned so much and met so many interesting people during her time in Paderborn.

In the meantime, the Americans who had occupied the Schönebeck area, stopping at the Elbe, and the British who had replaced them as the occupying power, withdrew to the agreed border to the west. With Schönebeck now in the Soviet Occupation Zone (SBZ), Hertha knew that if she went home and it was discovered she had been a prisoner in the West, she would be arrested by the Soviet army and imprisoned in one of the Soviet Special Camps. Just before Christmas 1946, she was so homesick that she decided to take the risk.

In Braunschweig, near the border with the Soviet Zone, she bought a false identity card and used this to return to her home in Calbe, getting a lift with the father of one of the other young women from her class.

Her family kept her hidden, but one evening Soviet soldiers came knocking at the door. Fortunately, they went to the apartment above to see if the teacher living there had information about suspect people hiding in the town. When they had gone, the teacher's wife came down and warned Hertha that it was too dangerous for all of them for her to stay any longer. Hertha's mother slipped out and arranged for the local milkman to take Hertha, hidden among the milk churns, to Schönebeck. From there, other relatives took her back over the border. Talking about this, she recalled a friend, another BDM group leader, who was arrested and taken to the former concentration camp at Buchenwald—by then being used as a Soviet Special Camp for former Nazis or alleged opponents of the Soviet occupation—and who died there. Returning after a pause to talk about herself, she said she came back eventually in 1948 and got married.

Into Adult Life

On the Move

Many of the Schönebeck women were on the move at the end of the war, making their way home to their families from their *Reichsarbeitsdienst*. They were not victims and did not see themselves as such, but many of their journeys were long and dangerous in terrible conditions. Home, they hoped, would be a place of safety and a base for starting again, building a new life as adults. Some of their families had moved during the war to areas that were now in the West, but most were still living in or around Schönebeck.

Schönebeck and its inhabitants were relatively fortunate at the end of the war. As the American army approached in April 1944, efforts were made by self-appointed representatives of the town, the Communist Richard Sparmann (emerging from the underground) and the Roman Catholic curate Vikar Jäkar, to surrender the town so that it would not be subject to an artillery bombardment. The German military commander would not agree, but one of the mayor's officials refused to sound the alarm as the Americans entered Schönebeck. This meant that the tank barriers were left open, the Americans could pass through, and night bombing of Schönebeck was prevented. A brief battle still took place, in which young boys and old men in the ill-trained and ill-equipped units of the Volkssturm were killed, including fifteen- and sixteen-year-olds from the Junkerswerke apprentice school who were forced to fight. The absurd but tragic battle—described in fictional form in the novel by GDR writer Erik Neutsch, *Der Friede im Osten*—was over by midday on 12 April 1945.[21] With the bridge over the Elbe blown up by retreating German forces, the German military commander escaped across the river in a small boat. He died soon after in a battle with the Red Army on the other side. His deputy killed himself with his own anti-tank weapon.[22]

The war and the consequences of Nazi rule had come to the Schönebeck area in other ways too, leaving the *Heimat* compromised, although the Schönebeck women did not seem to notice this. In the early 1940s, the authorities were sending transports of incurable, disabled, or mentally ill prisoners to be killed in six euthanasia centers across Germany. One such center was in Bernburg, another of the prominent towns in the Schönebeck area, where at least 9,385 people were murdered in 1940 and 1941. The Bernburg center was also used later to kill several thousand Jewish concentration camp prisoners.[23] Buchenwald concentration camp established a subcamp in Schönebeck, and others in Staßfurt for the factories being built in the old mines nearby. The subcamp in Schönebeck, set up in 1943, had around 1,200 prisoners at any one time in unheated wooden barracks just outside the town center. Every day, the prisoners were marched across the town to work in the factories producing parts for airplanes and rockets. When the camp was closed on 11 April 1945, some of the prisoners escaped or managed to hide. The rest were sent on death marches toward German-occupied Bohemia.

As the women made their way home to the relative safety of Schönebeck, and the war in Europe approached its end, millions of people were on the move, most particularly in Germany. These included concentration camp survivors, former forced laborers, and refugees from the territories to the east: Germans fleeing ahead of the Soviet forces or displaced and driven out of these eastern territories as a new Poland was created by the shifting west of the Soviet and German borders. Millions more Germans would soon be driven out of the restored Czechoslovakia.

Millions of refugees, particularly women and children in a desperate position, came first into the SBZ. Many stayed: by the beginning of 1949, 4.3 million refugees had settled in the SBZ, making up almost 25 percent of the zone's population. Over a million of these were in Saxony-Anhalt (the new administrative district, the *Land*, comprising the old Province of Saxony and the district of Anhalt). A further 7.3 million went to the Western zones, making up 20 percent of the population there.[24] Schönebeck became home to many refugees, and its population rose from 39,497 in 1939 to 46,426 in 1950. The regional newspaper reported that from February to the end of 1946, 508 trains with 900,000 "*Umsiedler*" or "resettlers" had arrived in Magdeburg, intending to go on to the British Zone. Of those, 9,705 changed their minds and sought refuge in Magdeburg, 6,831 of them from the new Poland, and 1,681 from Czechoslovakia.[25] The Communist authorities used the term *Umsiedler* to imply that the refugees had moved voluntarily rather than being driven out by the

Red Army or the new authorities in the Soviet-occupied lands.[26] In the West, the official terms were "expellees" for those forced out of the eastern territories or countries, and "refugees" for those who moved from the SBZ or GDR to the FRG.[27]

A further report in September described another 780 "resettlers" coming from the former German territories now in Poland to Schönebeck: 190 men, 447 women, and 143 children. By this time, 29,231 refugees had passed through Schönebeck, of whom 14,045 had remained there.[28] The new authorities were keen to be seen helping the refugees. The local women's committee and the anti-fascist committee, working with the office for women and young people, brought food and toys for 270 children in one of the refugee camps. Such work, it is clearly implied, was women's work.[29]

The Problem of Rape

Women suffered in huge numbers in every occupied zone at the end of the war through rape by the occupying soldiers, but particularly in the SBZ, where roughly three-quarters of the rapes took place.[30] Even the German Communists who were put in place to administer the territory were unable to persuade the Soviet authorities to take seriously what their soldiers were doing.[31] Walter Ulbricht, the leader of the German Communists in the SBZ, opposed abortion even after rape, despite there being thousands of deaths a year from illegal abortions. The law preventing abortions was partially suspended in the SBZ in the late 1940s, only to be reintroduced in the GDR in 1950.

As the historian Norman Naimark points out, the rapes by Soviet soldiers had serious consequences not just for the women but also for the Communists, whether German or Soviet: "The threat and reality of rape made many German women fiercely resistant to the appeals of communists on behalf of friendship with the Russians."[32] According to Miriam Gebhardt, a combination of factors was behind the rapes: hatred and the desire for revenge, access to alcohol, poor discipline, the constant arrival of new troops as others moved elsewhere, and the stationing of troops in people's houses. The fact that these led to rape, as opposed to any other violence, Gebhardt argues, has to do with the traditional power structures involving the dominance of men over women; only this explains why soldiers in the Allied armies were indiscriminate, raping not just their German enemies but also French and Polish women and victims of Nazi persecution.[33]

Neither in the interviews nor in the letters are there any hints from the Schönebeck women that any of them were raped. There are clear indications that they were aware of the threat of rape: Else Hermann's moment of fear as she had to cycle through the group of Soviet soldiers, for instance. Similarly, Anna Siebert and her family knew what was happening. Anna's story of this period is largely about the family's experiences with the Russian occupiers. It is a story of managing and making do, of accepting the occupiers and their power and of trying to remain safe.³⁴

Anna Siebert

Not surprisingly, the Sieberts' large, modern house was attractive to the incoming occupiers, first the Americans and then the Russians. When the Russians came, it was in the form of a group of elite troops headed by a major, a senior prosecutor. They were friendly and helpful, and insisted, in the face of the parents' fear for the safety of Anna and another young woman living in the house, that all would be treated as part of the family, the Russian family. They also stressed caution: "But if Russians knock at the door, don't open it—*don't open it!*" The major and his troops blocked the street with a barrier and only the family and the Russians living in the house were allowed through, with a password that was changed every day. The only others who came were women that the major brought home and entertained in his large bedroom, young women Anna knew. But, Anna insists, these were elite troops and didn't attack anyone. It was also the case that the Soviet military commander in Magdeburg, whose domain included Staßfurt, was known by his troops to be particularly severe in his punishment of soldiers arrested for raping German women. Gebhardt quotes an example from a village near Magdeburg of a Soviet officer personally beating one of his soldiers to death for raping a twelve-year-old German girl.³⁵

The family's anxiety remained, however. The Russians taught Anna to drink schnapps. Knowing, as the family did, of the rapes going on in Staßfurt, Anna's father taught her what to do if she was made to drink too much: put her fingers down her throat and bring everything up again: which worked, she discovered. Later, this group was transferred elsewhere and replaced by a group of doctors who treated the house shamefully and even fired their revolvers in the room. While they were there, Anna's parents were invited to a wedding outside Staßfurt. They contacted the previous officers, and the major and his captain returned and looked after the house and ensured the two young women were safe from the Russian doctors.

Staying Alive

Getting Enough to Eat

The Schönebeck women write in their letters about how hard it was to get enough to eat during the early period after the war. This was a huge problem across the whole of Germany; ordinary people's accounts in the archives constantly focus on it, and on their fears for their older family members or their children.³⁶ In all the zones, physical conditions were terrible, most of the cities were in ruins, and the economy had collapsed. Millions of German men were in prisoner-of-war camps. After a cold winter, there was little food, and the population depended on the occupying forces to keep them alive.

Neither the French nor the "Russians" (the term commonly used by Germans) were in a position to do this satisfactorily. The French were dependent on the Americans for aid, while the Russians had to contend with the failure of their own harvest and the way their land had been ravaged during the years of occupation and the battles as the Germans retreated.[37] Overall, the Allies aimed to ensure people had 1,550 calories per head each day. By early summer in 1945, the reality was 1,330 calories a day in the American sector, 1,083 in the Soviet sector, 1,050 in the British sector, and 900 in the French sector. A catastrophe was averted by imports of food, by the contribution of private organizations abroad, especially CARE (Cooperative for American Remittances to Europe), which sent more than eight million CARE packages, and by the black market.[38]

Cries for Help

In Schönebeck, the new circumstances of dire need were reflected in local newspapers, barely more than newssheets, which contained the orders of the military occupiers. The authorities instructed people not to steal fruit off trees, even in the woods or where it appeared no one owned them: all fruit had to be centrally delivered to make jam, so that there would be enough for everyone.[39] Meanwhile, black-bordered notices confirmed the deaths of fathers, husbands, and brothers, even as the months went by after the war. With three out of four pages filled with small ads, the newssheets also carried the cries for help of ordinary people: "Where can I track down refugees from Großräfchen?";[40] "Widow, 54, wants to meet decent man, 55–65, with a view to later marriage."[41] There were also older men with accommodation of their own looking for women. Knowing they could be choosy, they sought much younger women. At this time there were 7,300,000 more women than men living in Germany, and the disparity was greatest for those aged between twenty and forty.[42]

The Leading Role of Women

The everyday struggle to survive was led by women: older women who had for the most part not been involved in the war; younger ones working in jobs left empty by men; and even-younger women, often taken out of school prematurely to do their *Reichsarbeitsdienst* and *Kriegshilfsdienst*. Whether they had supported Hitler and the war or not, many of these women had suffered. They had been bombed and evacuated or had lived in the ruins in the cities. They had endured the battles as the Allied armies fought their way in from east and west. They had made their way home over hundreds of miles from their war service camps in the midst of fleeing soldiers and concentration camp prisoners on death marches. Many had fled from the east as refugees. Many of their husbands and fathers had been killed in the war or were now prisoners of war, their whereabouts unknown to their relatives.

By July 1945, the American and British forces had moved to the new boundary west of Schönebeck and were administering their zones, increasingly with the assistance of local Germans. Power in the SBZ was exercised primarily by the Soviet Military Administration (SMAD). Members of the German Communist Party, the KPD, had been brought back from Moscow by the Red Army to help set up a Communist-dominated administration. The KPD forced through a merger in the SBZ between the KPD and the Social Democratic Party, the SPD, to form the Sozialistische Einheitspartei Deutschlands or SED. The KPD and then the SED administered the zone on a day-to-day basis, developing and concentrating the party's power but remaining beholden to the Soviet authorities.

In the face of the terrible conditions in 1945, women in all zones formed groups to help one another and their children survive in the early difficult years, and to make it possible for the society to start to function again. These self-help groups were formalized as anti-fascist Women's Committees and were connected across the zones through what the historian Ursula Schröter calls the "peace consensus."[43] They had many Communist members in the SBZ. The SED wanted women to work to rebuild Germany in the SBZ and to show active political support for the party and its program. The women themselves wanted somewhere to live, safety from Russian attacks, abortions if necessary, food, clothing, security for their children, and a chance to communicate with their husbands or sons who had not returned from the war, if they were still alive.

With the immediate postwar crisis past and many of the men back from the war or their camps, the SED reasserted the primary importance of the class struggle, and downgraded the concerns and achievements of women. The SED was instrumental in setting up the Demokratischer Frauenbund Deutschlands (Democratic Women's League of Germany—DFD) in 1947. The independent women's committees were gradually marginalized or dominated by the DFD. As the SED sought to eliminate independent centers of power, the DFD became the only recognized women's organization once the anti-fascist women's committees were finally merged into it.[44] While theoretically independent, the DFD was the target of active intervention by the SED. In 1949, SED pressure apparently contributed to the DFD's decision to close its workplace branches and concentrate on local branches, greatly reducing the DFD's influence.[45]

The Winter of 1946/47

For the Schönebeck women, as for people across Germany, attempts to move on after the war were hampered by many things, not least the weather, which showed how close the economy and the social structure were to catastrophic collapse. In November 1946, anticipating another hard winter, the authorities in Schönebeck started a campaign called "Schönebeck in the battle against hunger and cold" and asked everyone to donate anything they could, whether it seemed useful or not. The newssheet announcing the campaign made clear the extent of the misery and deprivation that prevailed at the time. Articles to be collected included furniture, shoes, clothing, household goods, rags, paper, and wood. From the wood, beds and small pieces of furniture would be made, while the paper would be exchanged for roofing felt. People were to hand in damaged and apparently useless items, which would be transformed into something useful: the upper from one shoe and the sole from another would make a shoe fit for wearing. Likewise, cycling jackets, inner tubes from car tires, haversacks, and other sturdy fabrics would be used to make or repair footwear. The proclamation was particularly directed at women because of their supposed compassion for those in need:

> Housewives, mothers! Look through your whole place again, check whether in the attic or the cellar or in any odd corner there might be objects lying around that for you are worthless but for many a person in need could greatly ease the conditions they currently find themselves in; unfortunately, there are many among them who possess nothing but the clothes they stand up in.[46]

Once the winter arrived, the extreme cold—dry, with no snow—caused huge problems. The rivers and canals, which were vital for transport, froze; the winter-sown seeds lay unprotected on the frozen ground. When the snow came, it filled the streets and blocked the railway lines, severely disrupting transport, industrial production, and food distribution. At the local level, there were immediate shortages of bread since the bakeries had no coal to heat their ovens. The threat of overall food shortages and starvation was even more serious.

A proclamation by the mayor and chief of police in Schönebeck required both men and women to move the dangerous "mountains" of snow off the roads, pavements, and railway lines on to the fields adjoining the Elbe.[47] Because of the shortage of coal, public buildings for entertainment—including bars and restaurants—were no longer allowed to be heated, the one exception being approved canteens. These had been emergency classrooms for the girls at the start of the war; now they were emergency feeding stations.

In the West, conditions were similar. Frozen canals, roads, and railways, as well as the continuing shortage of working locomotives, prevented the distribution of vital goods. Food was hard to obtain, and hunger widespread. Coal for domestic heating and for industrial use was in extremely short supply because it could not be transported. The number of cases of diphtheria, typhoid, and tuberculosis doubled. As a result, tens of thousands of people were dying of cold, hunger, and disease. Industrial production dropped to the level of the previous year, only 32 percent of that of 1938.[48]

The problems in the West created further problems for the East. No coal was delivered from the Ruhr in the West, while the frozen earth meant that mining local brown coal became almost impossible. When trains from elsewhere did arrive in Schönebeck with coal, morale was so low and hunger so widespread that local people stopped the trains and stole the coal.[49] Similarly, people went out into the woods to collect firewood, or pulled down unused wooden barracks in order to have something to burn. With the temperature below minus twenty Celsius, neither appeals from the Communist authorities to be more socially minded nor threats of strong police measures had any effect on people's behavior.[50]

After the long months when everything was frozen, the thaw in mid-March 1947 and the collapse of a dam brought widespread flooding that swept away railway lines and caused yet more problems for industry and agricultural production throughout the area.

Families, Study, and Work

When the women came home to their families in Schönebeck in 1945, they found the town almost undamaged, although there was no longer a bridge across the river. However, there was little food, not enough fuel to heat their homes, and too little housing to cope with the influx of refugees. Economic activity had declined, and there were few opportunities to get a job. The factories had survived, and the machines could still operate, but there was no longer any demand for armaments and airplanes. It was difficult to get hold of materials to produce anything else, even though restarting production was vital to provide for the needs of the population.

The Schönebeck women were enthusiastic about the future and, for the most part, keen to play their part in rebuilding their society. Many of the remaining or returning men—often former industrial workers—also wanted to do what they could to improve the everyday lives of their families. In the face of rapidly changing demands by the Communist authorities, this was not easy. One of the principal factories in Schönebeck, Metallindustrie Schönebeck AG, produced the famous "Weltrad" bicycles in the 1880s and motorcycles from 1903. It expanded into general engineering and machine-tool production, but in World War I produced grenade cases, bayonets, and other munitions. After returning to its traditional production, it shifted again in 1936 into the production of machine guns and other war-related items.

Arms production ended with the end of the war. In September 1945, the firm started to produce prams, metal beds, and generators for vehicles. By the end of October, it had 387 workers, and the number was constantly increasing.

There was already a severe shortage of welders. In an attempt to be socially conscious and meet people's immediate needs, the firm planned to produce 24,000 prams, 6,000 handcarts, and 10,000 bicycles in 1946.

Such plans came to nothing in the face of the Soviet decision to dismantle war-related factories and move them to the Soviet Union. By order of the Soviet Military Administration, production ceased on 13 March 1946, and the machinery and vehicles were all taken away.[51] The workers were dismissed, except for those dismantling the machinery. Surprisingly, production started again soon after, since a number of workers, initially unpaid, helped reassemble machines taken from the ruins of factories in Magdeburg. Metallindustrie Schönebeck reemerged and was renamed FAMO (Fahrzeug- und Motorenwerke; Vehicle and Motor Works). In July 1946, following a decree on the confiscation of the property of war criminals, the firm was taken over by the state. It started to make a significant contribution to providing employment for local men and women and the waves of refugees. It would eventually become a huge tractor factory, helping the modernization of agriculture in the GDR and exporting widely to the rest of Eastern Europe; it would be vital to the GDR and also to the local economy and the prosperity of Schönebeck. Many of the other factories in Schönebeck developed similarly in the planned economy that emerged, growing steadily and providing employment for people across the wider region.

The shape of the Schönebeck women's lives for the next forty years would be largely determined by two things; first, where they happened to be living; and, second, the decisions they made in 1945 about what they would study and the work they would do, in accordance with the opportunities available to them. What is clear for virtually all of them is that, regardless of the chaos and dangers of the end of the war and the immediate postwar period, they were energetic, active, optimistic, and outward looking. As far as they were concerned, the new world was theirs, and they would help to shape it. Unfortunately, the emergency *Abitur* certificate the girls had been given in 1944 was not recognized by the new authorities. The young women had to choose: return to school to complete their *Abitur* or go straight out to work.

Official attitudes to women working differed between the East and West after the war, though the concept of the family was strongly supported by the authorities in both parts of Germany. In the Western zones, it would become clear that women were expected to be part of supposedly traditional families, stopping work when they had children and taking care of the home while the husband went out to work.[52] In the SBZ, the family would be seen as central to the development of a stable society. However, both a principled commitment to equality by the Soviet administration and the SED and a need for more women to enter the labor force meant that women were encouraged to go to work and to remain in work whether they had children or not.[53] In theory, everything would be made easy for them. Regulations guaranteed equal wages and a number of other benefits, such as childcare. In practice, the new regulations were widely ignored.[54]

In the West and in the East, a number of the young women chose to go back to school before going to work or on to further study, but even that choice was not without its problems. In Schönebeck itself, it was not until the beginning of October 1945 that the schools reopened—only to be closed again a week later because of an outbreak of typhus.

Else Hermann

While Else Hermann was at home in July 1945, wondering what to do next, her family decided for her: she needed a ration card so would have to go to work. Else took a job with a dressmaker to fill in time until the schools reopened. However, Else says in her *Rundbrief* letter of 27 November 1950, she enjoyed it so much that instead of doing her *Abitur*, she decided to do a three-year apprenticeship and get a qualification in tailoring. Talking about this in 2013, Else said that when she started her apprenticeship in 1945, she was paid less than was due to her. Her father said they were now in a time of socialism, so she should join the union; she did and was paid at the proper rate.

Else was caught up in the process of "denazification" in Schönebeck. All who had in any way been members of the Nazi party had to report to the authorities, who would decide what punishments were warranted. The Nazi party had automatically incorporated into membership anyone who was in the BDM. Else duly presented herself. She was not sanctioned but remembers vividly the Soviet translator looking at her and shaking his head as he said, "So young, and fascist already."

Other memories come from the terrible winter of 1946/47. There was only crumbly brown coal and not enough of it, while the gas supply was intermittent. At work, Else would sit with a hot iron in her lap to keep her warm enough to sew. At lunchtime she would run home for something to eat, only to find the potatoes were not cooked because the gas had not come through for long enough. At her job, they were making uniforms for the Russians, who gave her employer, the *Meisterin*, food in return. Else was given potatoes to take home and was so hungry she tried to eat them on the way. Some people, she says, caught fish. The river was frozen so that, even with the bridge not yet replaced, it was possible to cross it. People went across to fish where there was a patch of open water, as well as to catch things in the woods. In 2014, Else recalled those times:

> Yes, I knew about stealing coal from the trains. It was mostly the young people; I knew them all. It was in the worst days, when trains with coal for somewhere

else passed through Schönebeck. They all ran out on to the lines, changed the signals, stopped the trains and simply stole the coal. People had to do it to heat their houses and keep themselves alive.

The threats had no effect since "everyone knew it was happening and nobody thought it was wrong."

For Else, work was enjoyable in itself. It was also a way of escaping from the control of her mother. Increasingly Else became involved with other people her own age outside work. Ironically, after her earlier membership of the BDM in the Nazi period, Else found herself pushed into joining the SED-controlled youth group, the Freie deutsche Jugend or FDJ. In the late 1940s, she was part of a group of young people who composed and performed songs. They were invited to be on a radio program in Halle, south of Schönebeck, but first had to be members of the FDJ. They joined, she says, adding—as if embarrassed by the evidence of her commitment to the new state—that the FDJ was not very active in Schönebeck.

After her initial examinations, Else worked for a year in tailoring in Magdeburg, then for six months unpaid in the costume department of the Magdeburg Theater. She worked with the *Gewandmeisterin*, the head of the costume department whose responsibilities included deciding on the sketches and patterns that would be required and overseeing turning these into costumes that met the artistic needs of the production. For Else, this was a wonderful experience that made her want to spend her life working in the theater.

She still had to do further training, however. In 1949 she was given a place in the specialist school for higher-level skills in fashion design in Weimar, where she herself became a *Gewandmeisterin*. The range and quality of the theaters in Weimar opened her eyes to what might lie ahead of her. The new state, in one way so harsh and arbitrary, was also pushing her forward, opening up opportunities she had never thought possible.

Irma Kindler

After the war, Irma Kindler was back in Braunlage, where her family also faced the challenge of surviving. Writing in 2013, Irma describes the early months in what was by then the British Occupation Zone:

> Life gradually became more normal. Trying to get hold of food and other necessities of life was exceedingly difficult. A lot of what we got—if we were able to get anything at all—came after long periods of standing in queues, but the feeling of no longer being in danger from bombing or other effects of the war, or fearing the loss of your relatives (insofar as they had not died already), led to a general sense of relief. We just had to try, with any tricks at our disposal, to make ends meet. My parents had chickens, later even a cow, and on the lawn around the

house they planted potatoes and so on. Then the "CARE Packet" program got started: we had relatives in the U.S. who provided us with all sorts of unimaginable delicacies, so we were in pretty good shape and stayed optimistic.

Relatives in the right place, help from the Americans: in a way it prefigured much that would happen as the two parts of Germany grew apart over the years to come.

Young, intelligent, and restless, Irma enjoyed trying out her English—learned for eight years at school—on the Americans and then the British, despite the ban on "fraternization." She also longed to visit Schönebeck and her friends there. Between Braunlage and Schönebeck, however, was the border with the SBZ. The border ran along the middle of a stream, two kilometers away through the woods that backed on to the Villa Rosa. At this stage, it was not fortified, but was patrolled by Soviet troops. It was strictly forbidden to cross the border without permission. Nevertheless, Irma on a number of occasions walked down through the woods at night, crossed the stream, and set off up through the hills toward the nearest railway station in order to go on to Schönebeck. This was not always so easy: "On one of my night-time crossings, I walked straight into the arms of a Russian soldier patrolling the border. With others who had crossed border illegally, I was taken to Wernigerode and locked up, but after a few hours let go again, unscathed."[55]

Irma refers to this as the "Sturm und Drang" period of her life, when her mother was too preoccupied with the fate of Irma's stepfather in a Soviet prisoner of war camp, with looking after two young children and coping with an overflowing house full of refugees, to attempt to control her daughter. In the context of the mass rape of German women toward the end of the war and in the subsequent months, and with casual violence an everyday event, Irma was not only adventurous but also very lucky.

Despite Irma's attachment to Schönebeck, the only opportunities open to her were in the West. However, Irma's account suggests that access to higher education (and to housing) could be at least as difficult in the West as in the East. It is notable that, talking of this period many years later, she still thinks it was "natural" for men to have precedence over women after the war:

> And now it was important for me to think about my own future. For a long time, I had wanted to be a journalist, and for that I wanted to do German studies and art history. But there was no chance of getting started on that with the certificate we had been given on leaving school. In the meantime, a lot of secondary schools had set up special *Abitur* classes. There was a great need for these, since many young men had had to leave school early during the war to become soldiers. I managed to get accepted into one of these classes in the secondary school in Duderstadt (a lovely medieval town south of the Harz), and I found myself as

a nineteen-year-old young woman back in a classroom with nobody around me but men: fighter pilots, U-boat captains and so on. Despite feeling hugely ill at ease, I managed to get through successfully. Then I had to start looking for a university place, which proved to be pointless since so many young men whose studies had been interrupted by the war were back from the prison camps and wanted to start up again, and naturally they had priority. Many universities had been damaged or destroyed during the war and were only now starting to be rebuilt. I applied in vain to virtually every university and just got nowhere.

By this time, English was greatly in demand as Braunlage was in the British occupation zone. Having studied English for eight years at school, Irma became a translator and interpreter. Her work involved many difficult journeys; often she slept in railway missions or, if she was lucky, in friends' armchairs. This was not a good time, she says, though it was also when she met her future husband (see figure 1.2). Irma finally realized she needed a professional qualification: "I enrolled in one of these year-long courses and acquired a profound knowledge not just of the English language but also of English literature and history, and

Figure 1.2. Irma and Franz, 1950. Photo courtesy of Akademie der Künste, Berlin.

finished with a qualification as an interpreter. In the meantime, I had got to know a nice young man."

Irma's "nice young man" was studying in Hanover to be a civil engineer when he was called up and trained to be a pilot in the Luftwaffe, the air force. However, Irma says, the training was so long that happily, by the time he had finished, the Luftwaffe was no more. He was released after a short time as a prisoner of war. As he could not get a place to resume his university studies, he trained as a bricklayer.

Irma and Franz married a few days after the currency reform in 1948, and started their new life together in Hanover with forty marks each. Then, she says, things started to happen quickly. Franz was given a place at a university; she finished her course and got a job with the British occupation forces; and Franz, with the help of a former colleague, set about rebuilding an apartment in a bombed-out ruin:

> It was all terribly primitive, no bath, the toilet on the half landing, but we were ecstatic, just to have a roof over our heads, even if it wasn't completely waterproof. At that time there were no student grants, so it went without saying that I would be the one bringing in the money for the household.[56]

Anna Siebert

After first going back to school in Staßfurt in 1945 to do her *Abitur*, Anna finally followed her father's wishes and studied to become a civil engineer.[57] Since he thought Anna would be safer in the West, he sent her to live and study in the British sector of Berlin. This decision led to her living in the West for the rest of her life, while her parents remained in Staßfurt.

By this time, it was clear there would be no family firm for Anna to come back and run. As private businesses were taken over and their owners often victimized, Anna's father transformed his construction business into a small services company. He offered access to expertise that was useful to the new authorities, a safer option than running a large firm on capitalist lines.

In her *Rundbrief* letter of 12 May 1951, Anna says more about the early years after the war and her studies:

> As you know, my father has a construction firm, and because of that I came to what for you all might seem a somewhat mad idea. First I had to get some practical experience, which I did in the family firm, but it was still not an easy six months. I had never before heard such a collection of dirty jokes and foul comments. Certainly that at least is better now I am in Charlottenburg, but the work is no easier. Not to mention enduring the Blockade by candlelight in a cold room, and all the associated exam anxieties. Despite that, in the meantime I have almost got as far as being a qualified engineer which—touch wood—I will be in the autumn.

Anna would, in fact, be the first and for some time the only female civil engineer in the West, something that singled her out for attention throughout her career.

In mentioning so briefly the Berlin Blockade, which caused real suffering for many West Berliners and confirmed the gap that the new Cold War was opening up between East and West, Anna plays down the impact on her life and her studies. As a university student, Anna would have benefited even in the difficult years from extra food rations.[58] However, during the Blockade, she would have had to contend with food shortages, disruption to power supplies, and problems with public transport.

The blockade from June 1948 to May 1949 arose partly from increased economic and political cooperation among the Western zones, a separate economic approach in the SBZ, and increased political tension between West and East. It was precipitated by the Western currency reform of 1948, which helped transform economic conditions and end the black market in the Western zones but was a breach of the Allies' agreement to treat Germany as a single, undivided economy.[59] The SBZ authorities responded with a currency reform of their own, attempted to ban the use of the Western currency in the Western sectors of Berlin, and blocked the movement of goods in and out of these sectors. People in the Western sectors were then supplied through American and British planes landing at its small airports, particularly Tempelhof, which led to the Western occupiers increasingly being seen as allies of the Germans against the Soviet forces. In March 1949, the Western allies declared their Mark to be the only legal currency in the Western sectors of Berlin, thus confirming the political division of the city. Paul Steege's history of everyday life in Berlin for this period highlights the many ways local people found to get around the blockade and reduce their suffering. It also demonstrates the complications arising from, for instance, the whole of the rail system for Berlin being under Soviet jurisdiction but having its headquarters in the American sector and many thousands of its workers in the Western zones. These workers demanded to be paid in West Marks. When a strike took place, the SED and the FDJ brought in workers from the East to try to break the strike, which further undermined the SED's attempt to appeal to the population in the Western sectors.[60]

Hertha Pieper

After her difficulties with the occupying forces after the war, Hertha Pieper's life-shaping decision was to marry the son of a farming family. Hertha became not just a farmer's wife but also a committed farmer in her own right on an exceptional farm near Calbe.

Hertha's father-in-law had studied mathematics and music and started out as a teacher. After World War I, with children to support, he found it hard to manage financially. As his parents were farmers, he decided to take over the farm, but wanted to avoid the backbreaking work that was usually involved. He planned and organized the running of the farm so that by 1928 he had mechanized everything that could be mechanized. This was highly unusual. Although he had relatively little land, he had as many machines as the owners of the large estates.[61]

To understand Hertha Pieper's subsequent life, it is necessary to look at land reform in the SBZ.

In the early years after the end of the war, different policies established a pattern that would lead the two parts of the new Germany to move far apart, politically, economically, and socially. In the East, these included the state seizure of private industry, the emergence of a Leninist "party of a new type" on the model of the Soviet Communist Party, and land reform. The land reform represented a clear break with previous German agricultural policies and was not followed in the Western zones, despite the Western allies' hostility to the Junkers, the owners of the largest estates.

On 11 June 1945, the KPD published an *Aufruf*, a call for action to the German people. In this relatively conciliatory document, the KPD declared that it would not seek, with its anti-fascist partners, to replicate the Soviet system in Germany. The *Aufruf* included a demand for land reform, based on the "liquidation" of the large estates of the Junkers. Their property, land, and animals would be given to the provincial governments and distributed to small farmers ruined by the war, or to other landless agricultural workers. Such a demand was in line with the Communist tradition of seeking an alliance between the workers and peasants against the other social classes. It was moderated, however, by a commitment to not taking away the land of other large landowners.[62] A further *Aufruf* from the KPD on 12 September 1945 pointed to the Hitler regime as the cause of the destruction of the livelihood of agricultural workers, small farmers, and tenants, and to the particular needs of farming families driven out of their homes as a result of Hitler's war.

If the KPD—later the SED—was to be accepted by the population as a legitimate ruler, not just a puppet of the Soviet Union, it had to offer a vision of the future that was attractive and that made present suffering worthwhile. Rebuilding the cities was a heroic but slow and difficult process with few immediate rewards. Rebuilding the factories was made difficult by the Soviet requirement that many of them be dismantled and removed. Redistributing the land, on the other hand, could be implemented easily and presented as proof that everyone could benefit from the party's actions. As it set the land reform in motion, the party claimed to be responding to the demands of such people: it would satisfy the age-old dream of the peasants, to see *"Junkerland in Bauernhand"*—the Junkers' lands in peasants' hands.[63] This aspect of the land reform had widespread political support. It had been promoted by all the Allies during the war as necessary to break support for German militarism.[64]

It was significant for Hertha Pieper and her family that the land reform started in the Province of Saxony and therefore applied at once to their area. According to the SED, the first calls for land reform in the Province of Saxony came from farmers in an area between Schönebeck and Barby, in August 1945, ahead of the KPD's formal announcement in September. Progress was rapid: an early report in September 1945 noted that in the Calbe area (including Schönebeck), 16,460.92 hectares had already been redistributed to 356 farmers with small landholdings under five hectares, 1,735 farmers and agricultural workers with no land, and 191 refugees and "resettlers."[65] The land confiscated from the large estates came in principle from those of more than a hundred hectares, amounting to more than a third of all agricultural land. Two-thirds of this was distributed to private persons; the rest was given to the provincial governments.[66] In the Soviet Zone as a whole, around 7,000 large landowners had 2.5 million hectares of land confiscated without compensation. Additionally, 600,000 hectares of land belonging to the Nazi state or to leading Nazis were confiscated. This amounted in total to 35 percent of agricultural land in the SBZ. Around 500,000 people, including 83,000 "resettlers," were allocated land.[67]

Agricultural policy in the SBZ after the land reform was based on the concept of the *Soll*: a quota that every farmer had to hand over to the state authorities at a certain price before being allowed to sell anything on the open market. The quota was often difficult or impossible to meet, since even where the land was classified as poor, the quota was based on what could be expected from more productive land. The initial punishment for failing to meet the quota was confiscation of any spare grain found, which was treated as being hoarded. The authorities could also evict farmers and their families without notice and expel them from the area.[68]

Government representatives went from farm to farm collecting the quota. Often the results were absurd. In one account, the egg collectors tried to take the eggs that were being used to feed the extra workers who were there for the harvest. Because the farmer resisted, the collectors seized the farm's chickens and geese as a replacement, despite the farmer pointing out that these were too small and thin to be any use for food and that after a few more weeks on the farm they would be far more suitable.[69] There were similar problems in the West, where the difficulty of getting farmers to put their supplies on the open market led to soldiers accompanying German officials trying to collect what was due, often without success.[70]

For many of the new owners of land in the East, and even for existing farmers, conditions in the late 1940s remained difficult: they had little experience and not enough land. Many were dependent on the larger farmers, from whom they had to hire machinery. The authorities supported the smaller producers by establishing mutual aid groups and by bringing machinery and equipment from the disbanded estates into *Maschinenausleihstationen* (MAS), places where they could hire the machinery on terms that made them less dependent on larger producers.

At the end of the 1940s, Hertha Pieper's family had sixty *Morgen*—about fifteen hectares—of fertile land on which they mainly grew vegetables. This was made up of land they had owned for many years, land from the large landowners that was given to them in 1946 during the land reform, and some they leased. In the early days at least, it was not too difficult for them to produce the amount required. Nevertheless, the authorities continued to struggle to feed the population and were continually threatening to reorganize agricultural production further.

The only other one of the Schönebeck women involved in farming was Carla Brunner. Carla left school in 1943 and worked on her parents' farm, so did not have to go into the *Reichsarbeitsdienst*. She continued to work there after the war and loved it. Since they were close to the Elbe, she was an avid swimmer in the river in the summer at the end of the day's work, an unexpected image for the hard years of the SBZ.[71]

Interaction with the State

In the occupied zones and then the two new German states, many choices were made in overtly political circumstances, whether the women recognized this or not. In the East, becoming a teacher involved a commitment to the new state. Running a private business raised questions about one's class position and loyalty. Farming, however much land the farmer had, meant being faced with politically inspired demands to feed the people, in the West and in the East.

Leftover Attitudes from the Nazi Years

Astrid Greiswald's father was one of the girls' teachers before the war, a prominent Nazi who often appeared at school in uniform. When Astrid returned to Schönebeck in 1945 after her *Reichsarbeitsdienst*, she discovered that her father had been taken away "towards an unknown destination." She adds (1 March 1951), "Thank God, in a westerly direction." By this time, she herself was in Braunschweig, in the West, and would soon join her father in the far southwest of Germany. In January 1946, he started working for an oil company but was never allowed to return to teaching. At no time does Astrid make even an implied criticism of Nazism or of her father's beliefs.

For some of the other Schönebeck women living in the West in the early years, attitudes were similar. Elfriede Berger, writing from Cologne on 19 March 1951, says that she did her *Reichsarbeitsdienst* in the Südetenland, then worked very happily as a nurse in a military hospital in the "Protectorate," the rump Czech state that was occupied by the Germans. Particularly enjoyable, she says, were her excursions to Prague, the "golden city on the Moldau."

More common in the letters is a tendency for the women to be opaque about what happened during the Nazi period, particularly in relation to their parents. Carla Brunner hints that her father and Marianne Schneider's father were prisoners of war: "Because of the shared fate of our fathers in the postwar period, I found there was still a strong bond between Marianne and me" (see figure 1.3).[72] Only much later—in the letters from the West, in the interviews with the women, and in their subsequent letters in connection with the research for this book—are there specific references to fathers or husbands having been involved in the war or returning from prisoner-of-war camps. These are considered in subsequent chapters.

It is notable that nowhere in the letters and only once in the interviews— with Anna Siebert—is there any mention of the Buchenwald subcamps and the forced laborers. In both Staßfurt and Schönebeck, it is inconceivable that the girls and their parents were not aware of them. In Schönebeck, the most obvious route to work each day would have led the prisoners past the school the girls were moved to, between Breiteweg and Böttcherstrasse; the camp itself was just a few minutes away. In 1945, the barracks were still there and were used to house refugees.[73]

Over the decades, it would have been politically safe on both sides of the inner-German border for the women to reflect on what they had seen and experienced, and to condemn the actions of the Nazis. To do so, however, would

Figure 1.3. A "new teacher" at work: Marianne and her class, Schönebeck, 1956. Photo courtesy of Akademie der Künste, Berlin.

have meant wondering about the actions of their husbands and fathers as well. This could have been a threat not only to their personal relationships but also to the cohesion of the group.

State Power and Options in the SBZ/GDR

In Schönebeck, Elly Haase was one of those who suffered from having the wrong class background: her father ran his own carpentry business and was a capitalist employer, not a worker. Elly was bright, mathematically gifted, and had done well at school. Since, like Else Hermann, she had to do something to make a living immediately after the war, she did an apprenticeship in her father's firm, an unusual choice for a woman. Three years later, she took a break and set out on an astonishing journey around Germany, covering 1,800 kilometers by rail. On her return, she went back to school and completed her *Abitur*, then applied to go to university. While waiting for an answer, she did another even longer and more wonderful journey around Germany. When her application was rejected, Elly found herself lazing around at home, intellectually and emotionally frustrated. She was left supporting her ill mother and helping her father in the business while waiting to see what the future would bring.[74]

The other Schönebeck women chose a wide variety of occupations. Some, having been back to school to finish their *Abitur*, took up the opportunity to become a *Neulehrerin*—a "new teacher." The new teachers replaced the ideologically suspect teachers in the GDR, many of whom had been members of the Nazi party. The new Communist state expected to be able to rely on the new teachers to inculcate the values of socialism in the next generation.

Two of the women who stayed in the East wanted to become doctors but were not admitted to study medicine. They had to settle for what they saw as lesser positions, Brigitte Hansen as an operating theater nurse, Heidi Kempf as a technician in a medical laboratory. While this might appear as discrimination against them as women, the pattern emerging over the years suggests that, as with Elly Haase, it was more to do with their perceived class position. Brigitte Hansen, whose father owned a textile firm, notes in her letter of 17 December 1950 that it was "external circumstances" that prevented her becoming a doctor or going to university at all. In the eyes of the SED, Brigitte was the class enemy, part of the old bourgeoisie. Positive discrimination favored the children of workers, and the GDR authorities were proud of the social mobility resulting from this.

Gerda Höpfner was the group's only real "worker" and therefore in a relatively privileged position under communism. She left school in 1943 for health reasons and was excused from her *Reichsarbeitsdienst*. She did an apprenticeship in Magdeburg at the firm of Schäffer und Budenberg (manufacturers of pressure measuring devices) and passed her examination shortly before the end of the war. Late in the 1940s, she moved to one of Schönebeck's major manufacturing companies, VEB Schönebecker Gummiwerke, which had been taken into state ownership. The factory would have felt familiar: some of the girls' classes had taken place in the warmth of its canteen in 1939/40. Gerda's new job was in the technical development section of the factory, which produced rubber shoes and rubber soles for shoes. Gerda would remain at the Gummiwerke until 1990.

Conclusion: From Schoolgirls to Young Women

As girls at school, Else Hermann, Irma Kindler, Anna Siebert, Hertha Pieper, and their friends were pulled back and forth between the demands, values, and attitudes of their families on the one hand and those of the National Socialist authorities on the other. Although not all the teachers were members of the Nazi party, many of them were, and the organization and direction of the school was closely tied up with the demands of the Nazis. What the girls read, wrote, discussed, sang, or had imposed on them through official functions and visits was oriented toward shaping them as women who would do what was expected of them for the Führer and the Nazi state. They were encouraged to join the BDM, and it appears that most, if not all of them, did so—except the Jewish girls, who are not mentioned in any of their early accounts. At the same time, even in their early years the girls demonstrated a certain individualism and their own unique personalities. They were close friends with the English girl in their class; they threw themselves into music, dancing, writing and quoting poetry; they read with enthusiasm some of the German classics on their reading list, even when they were expected to give a Nazi interpretation to these.

The *Reichsarbeitsdienst* and the chaotic end of the war turned them from schoolgirls into women. Their direct and indirect experiences of the war and of their long journeys home seemed both sobering and exhilarating, and fragmentary references to this period appear in the *Rundbrief* over many years. Only one of them was held in a camp because of her involvement in the war. Returning home provided them with a base from which they could look outward, beyond hunger and the distress of millions, toward the life they wanted for themselves. In this, they had the advantage of returning to homes that had not been destroyed by bombing, and to families who, in many cases, were relatively privileged.

In the first years after the war, there was already a gap opening up between the women who were in the Western zones and the majority in the Soviet zone. The women in the West did not necessarily feel better off. They had the same problems with shortages as those in the East, and if they lived in the cities could find only the most basic accommodation. Some of them, like Anna Siebert, lived through the Berlin Blockade. Those in the East, in and around Schönebeck, were able to go back to school and move on to education or training more easily than those in the West. In the towns, they could get jobs; on the farms, they could get more land. They were also able to exercise freedoms that seem astonishing: traveling around the whole of Germany as if the war had never happened.

There are few indications that in the early years the Schönebeck women thought much about what the Nazi regime had entailed or how much their own values and attitudes had been shaped by it. For some of the women, casual remarks demonstrated how much they had internalized the Nazi propaganda and the lessons learned at school.

At the same time, the women did not appear to sense that things in the SBZ would become radically different and that they as young women growing up in a new society would be forced to reconsider their values and attitudes and to make some kind of accommodation with the new authorities. Across the zones, they appear to have little sense of a "good" pro-American, capitalist West and a "bad" pro-Soviet, Communist East, despite the much greater incidence of rape in the SBZ. There is very much a feeling of life going on, of them having a chance at last to spread their wings, get out into the world, and participate in society as young, lively, enthusiastic women in both the West and the East. For them, this was a land where things were much the same as before, apart from the need to rebuild the cities, transport links, factories, and ports, and start producing food again: a huge task, which seemed not to deter or intimidate them. Without perceiving it, however, they were emerging into a world of rapid change and modernization, with an increasing emphasis on individuality and on individual rewards and satisfaction. This shift would be likely to draw them away from the values and attitudes of their parents. In the East, it would conflict with the SED's promotion of the collective and collective action.[75]

Notes

1. Henry Wadsworth Longfellow, "Elegiac Verse," XI, *Poetical Works* (London, 1916), 780.
2. *Cecilienschule zu Schönebeck/Elbe: Bericht über das Schuljahr 1937/38*, https://goobiweb.bbf.dipf.de/viewer/image/101166545X_1938/1/LOG_0003/.
3. Reese, *Die BDM–Generation*, 8. In "The Path of the German Girl," 22–24, Reese describes the procedures and activities the Schönebeck girls would have been involved in at this time.
4. "Schönebeck Letters," 6 November 1950.
5. Dr O. H., "Bericht über meine Beurlaubung im Sommer 1933," typed manuscript (9 July 1934) given to the author by Else Hermann.

6. This is how Else remembered it. From 1936 there was a legal requirement to join; in practice many still did not. See Reese, *Die BDM–Generation*, 36, 40.
7. *Cecilienschule 1939/40*.
8. Kiran Klaus Patel, *Soldaten der Arbeit. Arbeitsdienste in Deutschland und den USA, 1933–1945* (Göttingen, 2003), 416–17.
9. Wiebke Stelling and Wolfram Mallebrein, *Männer und Maiden: Leben und Wirken im Reichsarbeitsdienst in Wort und Bild* (Preußisch Oldendorf, 1979).
10. André Sellier, *Histoire du camp de Dora* (Paris, 2010), 348–53; *Magdeburg Volksstimme*, 17 October 1997.
11. Erika Krämer's story is told in chapter 2.
12. The website of the Amicale des Déportés à Neu-Stassfurt (Kommando de Buchenwald), drawing on the work of Max Gombert, *Historiographie du kommando de Neu-Stassfurt* (Paris, 2003), lists the family firm as one that was contracted to carry out surface works and the construction of huts at the Neu-Staßfurt subcamp of Buchenwald: https://sites.google.com/site/kommandodeneustassfurt/home/2-notre-histoire-1/la-vie--neu-stassfurt.
13. Geoffrey P. Megargee, ed., *The United States Holocaust Memorial Museum Encyclopedia of Camps and Ghettos, 1933–1945*, vol. 1 (Bloomington, IN, 2009), 298.
14. Interviews, February and May 2013.
15. Megargee, *Encyclopedia*, 383, 416–17, 422.
16. Gareth Pritchard, *Niemandsland: A History of Unoccupied Germany, 1944–1945* (Cambridge, 2012), 117, 178.
17. Stefan Heym, *Schwarzenberg* (Munich, 1984).
18. This theme was mostly eliminated from GDR writing by the censors; Heym's novel was published in the West.
19. As the German armies retreated from both the west and the east, the Western allies occupied the country at least as far as the Elbe in many areas, while the Soviet forces occupied the eastern section, including Berlin. The four allies agreed to divide Berlin into four sectors and in return the Western allies agreed to move back west of the Elbe and to evacuate areas in Saxony, Thuringia, the Province of Saxony (later Saxony-Anhalt), and western Mecklenburg and pass these over to Soviet control.
20. Interview, May 2013. Many aspects of her story, including her arrest and imprisonment, were also recounted in interviews with the other women. See also her letter of 15 January 1951.
21. Erik Neutsch, *Der Friede im Osten*, vol. 1 (Halle/Saale, 1974).
22. Vikar Jäker, "Über die Einnahme der Stadt Schönebeck (Elbe) durch die amerikanischen Panzertruppen am 11. und 12. April 1945," in Uwe Niedersen, ed., *Soldaten an der Elbe. US-Armee, Wehrmacht, Rote Armee und Zivilisten am Ende des Zweiten Weltkrieges* (Dresden, 2008); Kuntze, *Juden*, 74–76; Kreisleitung der SED Schönebeck, *Zeittafel*, 2.
23. Dietmar Schulze, *"Euthanasie" in Bernburg* (Essen, 1988), 124.
24. Matthias Uhl, *Die Teilung Deutschlands. Niederlage, Ost-West Spaltung und Wiederaufbau 1945–1949* (Berlin-Brandenburg, 2009), 64–67.
25. *Volksstimme Magdeburg*, 28 August 1947.
26. Joachim Klose, *Heimat in der Diktatur* (Leipzig, 2014), 7.
27. Tamás Vonyó, *The Economic Consequences of the War: West Germany's Growth Miracle after 1945* (Cambridge, 2018), 33.
28. *Volksstimme Magdeburg*, 6 September 1947.

29. "Kinderfest im Umsiedlerlager," *Volksstimme Magdeburg*, 28 August 1947.
30. Gebhardt, *Als die Soldaten Kamen*, 8, gives figures of 860,000 overall, of which at least 160,000 were in the Western zones; Naimark, *The Russians in Germany*, 69–140; Nothnagle, *Building the East German Myth*, 146; Beevor, *Berlin*, 409–15.
31. Leonhard, *Die Revolution*, 372, 382–83, 482–83.
32. Naimark, *The Russians in Germany*, 129.
33. Gebhardt, *Als die Soldaten Kamen*, 113, 144–52.
34. Interviews, December 2012, May 2013.
35. Nina Willner, *Forty Autumns: A Family's Story of Courage and Survival on Both Sides of the Berlin Wall* (New York, 2016), 23; Naimark, *The Russians in Germany*, 85; Gebhardt, *Als die Soldaten Kamen*, 15.
36. See, for instance, E. S., *Zwei Leben müsste man haben* (Berlin, self-published, 2007), DTA 2160: in 1946 when she thought they would all die of starvation, E. S. had a photo taken of herself, her husband, and their two children, so that her relatives would have a reminder of them. In *Lebenslauf* (Berlin, 1964), AdK Kempowski-BIO 6168, a woman notes simply, "My father was in Berlin from 1945 to 1947, where he died of malnutrition." Similarly: J. T., *Aus meiner Zeit. Autobiographie* (Bremen, self-published, 1993), AdK Kempowski-BIO 6599; S. K., *Briefe und Erinnerungen 1939–1946*, AdK Kempowski-BIO 6779.
37. Naimark, *The Russians in Germany*. Naimark, 65, comments on the dissension caused, even among German Communists, by "the Soviets' use of grain confiscated from the hungry farmers to make vodka for their troops."
38. Uhl, *Die Teilung Deutschlands*, 38–40; Wehler, *Deutsche Gesellschaftsgeschichte*, vol. 5: *Bundesrepublik und DDR* (Munich, 2008), 951–52.
39. *Amtliches Mitteilungsblatt, Schönebeck (Elbe)*, no. 7, 3 July 1945.
40. *Schönebecker Nachrichten. Mitteilungs-Blatt des Militärbefehlshabers und der Behörden der Stadt Schönebeck*, no. 4, 16 June 1945.
41. *Schönebecker Zeitung. Mitteilungs-Blatt des Militärbefehlshabers und der Behörden der Stadt Schönebeck*, no. 2, 28 May 1945.
42. Frevert, *Women in German History*, 264.
43. Ursula Schröter, "Die DDR-Frauenorganisation im Rückblick," in Ursula Schröter, Renate Ullrich, and Rainer Ferchland, *Patriarchat in der DDR: nachträgliche Entdeckungen in DFD-Dokumenten, DEFA-Dokumentarfilmen und soziologischen Befragungen* (Berlin, 2009), 13.
44. Naimark, *The Russians in Germany*, 129–32; Schröter, "Die DDR-Frauenorganisation im Rückblick," 16–17.
45. Schröter, "Die DDR-Frauenorganisation im Rückblick," 18–21; Corinnne Bouillot, "Mouvement des femmes' ou rejet du 'séparatisme féminin': De la création des comités féminins antifascistes en zone d'occupation soviétique à la transformation de l'organisation des femmes de RDA en un relais du pouvoir socialiste," in Corinne Bouillot and Paul Pasteur, *Femmes, féminismes et socialismes dans l'espace germanophone après 1945* (Paris, 2005), 70.
46. *Amtliche Bekanntmachungen der Stadt Schönebeck (Elbe)*, 13 November 1946, Stadtarchiv Schönebeck.
47. "Bekanntmachung!," 24 February 1947, in Gerd Cramer, *Schönebeck (Elbe), Plakate von 1945–1954*, Stadarchiv Schönebeck, Bl.3786.
48. Christian L. Glossner, *The Making of the German Post-War Economy: Political Communication and Public Reception of the Social Market Economy after World War II* (London,

2010), 121; Vonyó, *The Economic Consequences*, 42–43; there is a vivid description of this winter in Hamburg in Cay Rademacher's novel *Der Trümmermörder* (Cologne, 2011).
49. This was common in the West too. See Glossner, *The Making*, on the moral debate about it.
50. "Aufruf vom Rat der Stadt," 21 February 1947, in Kreisleitung der SED Schönebeck, *Zeittafel*, 9; and a second "Bekanntmachung!," 24 February 1947, in Cramer, Bl.3786.
51. Rainer Karlsch, *Allein bezahlt?: die Reparationsleistungen der SBZ/DDR 1945–53* (Berlin, 1993). Karlsch, 59–60, and Naimark, *The Russians*, also give examples of British and American dismantling of industry in areas they occupied that were later passed to Soviet control. Naimark, 237, notes that the Americans took substantial quantities of uranium from Staßfurt in order to hold back the Soviet attempts to get the atomic bomb. A report in the *Volksstimme Magdeburg*, 11 April 1974, condemns the Americans for the "theft" of a thousand tons of uranium in April 1945, and says that the Americans held back from bombing Staßfurt because they were determined to get hold of the uranium they knew was there.
52. Vaizey, *Surviving*, 3.
53. Fulbrook, *The People's State*, 149.
54. Harsch, *Revenge*, 45–50.
55. Letter to the author, 7 April 2013.
56. Letter to the author, 2013.
57. The German term is *Bauingenieur*. In English there is a distinction between civil and construction engineering that does not apply in Germany. Anna would be both a civil and a construction engineer. As the term "civil engineer" signals a higher technical and design level, it is not appropriate to call her a construction engineer, even though that is what her father wanted for her.
58. Paul Steege, *Black Market, Cold War: Everyday Life in Berlin, 1946–1949* (Cambridge, 2007). In October 1947 in the American and British sectors, "normal" consumers had an official ration allowing for 1608 calories per day, though estimated consumption for the first seven months of 1947 was only 1,287; Berlin University students received special rations, believed to be around 2,000: Steege, *Black Market*, 46.
59. Glossner, *The Making*, 126.
60. Steege, *Black Market*, 241–42, 248, 270–71.
61. Interview with Hertha Pieper, May 2013.
62. Hermann Weber, ed., *Der deutsche Kommunismus. Dokumente* (Cologne, 1963), 431–38.
63. Weber, *Der deutsche Kommunismus*, 609–11.
64. Naimark, *The Russians in Germany*, 142.
65. Kreisleitung der SED Schönebeck, *Zeittafel*, 4.
66. Joachim Grube, and Diethard Rost, *Dorferneuerung in Sachsen-Anhalt. Alternative Siedlungsentwicklung* (Schönebeck, 1995), 19.
67. Hermann Weber, *Die DDR 1945–1990*, 3rd ed. (Munich, 2000), 13.
68. Armgard zur Mühlen, "Kein Platz für 'Junker,'" in Hildegard Baumgart, ed., *Briefe aus einem anderen Land: Briefe aus der DDR* (Hamburg, 1971), 13–22.
69. *Lebenserinnerungen Friedrich K. 1939–1956*, AdK Kempowski-BIO 7043, 252–54.
70. Vonyó, *The Economic Consequences*, 48–49.
71. "Schönebeck Letters," 17 July 1951.
72. "Schönebeck Letters," 17 July 1951.

73. Megargee, *Encyclopedia*, 414–17: many of the prisoners worked in the Junkers factory adjoining the nine unheated barracks in the Barbyerstrasse; others were marched across town to the NARAG factory (Nationale Radiatoren AG) to produce parts for the V1 program; the factory was taken over by Volkswagen, which was decentralizing to avoid the bombing raids, but the old name was kept to disguise what was happening; production expanded into cellar vaults below the nearby brewery, Kaiserbrauerei Allendorf.
74. "Schönebeck Letters," 18 February 1951, and interviews with Else Hermann.
75. On the tensions between collective approaches and modernizing pressures in different regimes, see Moritz Föllmer, *Individuality and Modernity in Berlin: Self and Society from Weimar to the Wall* (Cambridge, 2013).

CHAPTER 2

Grown Up
The Long 1950s

The "Woman Question"

The Context

By the start of the 1950s, two separate German states existed, each limited in what it could do by occupying powers with contrasting ideologies. As separate economic and social policies were implemented, so separate attitudes emerged, notably concerning women.

Optimism was obligatory in the GDR, where most of the Schönebeck women were still living. The SED promised a glorious future: its Marxist-Leninist ideology "proved" that the party was correct and that in creating a new and historically inevitable classless society, it would make life better for everyone. The "woman question" had been resolved, the party asserted, by the working class having state power: Article 7 of the GDR's 1949 constitution declared that men and women had equal rights, and revoked all laws and regulations to the contrary.[1] Women, freed from exploitation by men, would henceforth work outside the home alongside men to build a socialist society, and the socialist society would in turn promote further opportunities, particularly through paid work, for women's fulfillment.

In practice, as well as having to endure the problems caused by the Soviet authorities and their soldiers, women in the SBZ were badly treated by the new German Communist authorities, both inside and outside the newly formed SED. Regulations encouraging the employment of women were widely ignored, and women continued to be discriminated against. The role of the "rubble women" in clearing the ruins after the war was subsequently held up as a model by the GDR authorities, but when this hard work was over, women were forced out of the construction industry, and women's participation rates in the economy declined in the late 1940s.[2]

Overall, there was no suggestion that traditional gender roles would change. Even if women went out to work, they would still be responsible for all domestic matters. Men, on the other hand, would work in their jobs and then carry out the time-consuming political tasks the SED and its mass organizations imposed upon them: attending meetings, organizing events, undertaking further training, traveling as delegates to conferences elsewhere, or building support for and taking part in demonstrations to promote peace and socialism.

SED Attitudes

The SED's attitudes were heavily influenced by its origins in the Social Democratic Party in the nineteenth century and by the long history of the labor movement in Germany. Marxist social democratic activity clashed with or emerged into communist revolutionary struggles during and after World War I and through the Weimar era. Although there had been strong, prominent women, such as Rosa Luxemburg, Clara Zetkin, and Ruth Fischer, in the socialist and communist movement, the revolutionary struggles were dominated by men. The earliest years of the KPD established a pattern whereby issues concerning the position of women were consistently seen as relatively insignificant.[3] Historian Ben Fowkes says that early party congresses removed the "woman question" at the last moment from the agenda in order to discuss "more urgent" matters.[4]

It had not always been self-evident that women would play only a minor role in the revolutionary struggles. The efforts and writings of August Bebel, Friedrich Engels, and Clara Zetkin, with their commitment to the full emancipation of women, were matched by the increasing activism of working-class women around the end of the nineteenth century. This mixture of theory and practice brought significant political, economic, and social gains for women and some shift in gender relations, at least within the SPD. However, the patriarchal attitudes of both the state authorities and male party members ensured that women remained in an inferior position, working both inside and outside the home. They were expected to subordinate their demands as women to the requirements of the class struggle and the political views of their husbands within what had become the traditional nuclear family.[5]

Going beyond traditional explanations of the role of the patriarchy, the historian Ralf Hoffrogge attributes some of the ways men and women separated out politically and socially to trends early in the nineteenth century. Following the emancipation of the serfs in 1808, the Junkers developed the production of schnaps as a significant new industry, financed by payments the peasants made for their emancipation. Schnaps was then used to desensitize the workers in new factories where work was interminable and conditions terrible. By the mid-nineteenth century, when quality became an important issue in the factories, schnaps was largely replaced by beer, which was drunk more slowly and without immediate effect. Schnaps continued to be provided for the worst-off workers, leading to chaotic spontaneous actions, difficulties organizing such workers into unions, a lack of solidarity, and extensive antisocial behavior. Leading socialists, such as Kautsky, declared schnaps to be the enemy of the worker. They spoke in favor of beer and of the local pub as a place to meet, talk, organize, and escape from overcrowded conditions at home, particularly as free time emerged as a concept and possibility. This reinforced the gender divide: women stayed home to look after the household and the children, while men used their time and the family's money in the pub. Since women then tended to turn away from socialism—because of their exclusion from the location that bound men together, and because of the domestic work they were left with— they were criticized for their lack of involvement in the activities of the labor movement and for showing little solidarity with the men.[6]

There are clear echoes in postwar Germany of such debates. In the GDR, men were often required to spend many hours after work on activities outside the family, whether they wanted to or not. Long meetings took place over beer and cigarettes—an image constantly repeated in GDR films and novels. In both the GDR and the FRG, the political culture was one of extensive evening meetings and opportunities for establishing the necessary networks of contacts, and women with children were far less able to be involved.[7] This spatial separation reinforced the gender separation in the home and in the workplace, since men were at the center of what was happening and could take advantage of opportunities for advancement that arose. It also made it likely that the political parties would promote policies and ways of thinking that were largely shaped by men to meet the needs of men.

Another problem in the East was the nature of the KPD/SED. Was it an independent German party promoting the interests of the German working class, or was it an internationalist party promoting revolutionary struggles across the world? Almost from the beginning, it became impossible for the KPD to present itself either as a truly national German party or as an internationalist party. The political context ensured that its primary commitment would be to the survival and growth of the new Soviet Union, the unexpected home of Communism, and that it would be subject to the Soviet-dominated Communist International, the Comintern. National parties, as Comintern members, could seek to influence decisions but had to follow the line laid down by Moscow, even when the line changed dramatically from one moment to the next. This perceived lack of independence disconnected both men and women members from many of the everyday concerns of the people among whom they lived and whose interests they claimed to represent.

The contradictions and ambiguities in the KPD's position in its first two decades showed up many times: in the early discussions about membership of the Comintern; in the attempts at insurrection during the Weimar years; in the battles with both the Social Democrats and the Nazis; and in the crushing defeat by the Nazis in 1933, even as the Comintern changed its line and required cooperation with the Social Democrats. The time of working underground or going into exile during the Nazi years was not straightforward either, dominated as it was by events in the Soviet Union. Stalinism gave rise to the show trials and purges in the late 1930s that threatened not just millions of Soviet citizens and old Bolshevik leaders but also the lives of every Communist exile in Moscow. It also led to mistrust in the Soviet Union of the Germans in exile in the West. The final shock at this point was the Nazi-Soviet pact in August 1939, which overnight left Communists everywhere no longer able to criticize or act against the Nazis until Germany invaded the Soviet Union in June 1941.

Revolutionary struggles over this long period required a full-time commitment and absolute dedication, as well as the readiness to radically modify one's position at a moment's notice in order to survive. The men involved paid little attention to the question of women, their demands, position, or physical and emotional needs, let alone to the view that men, too, should be responsible for shopping, cooking, cleaning, and looking after children. The KPD leaders who would eventually come to rule and shape the GDR learned their trade as professional revolutionaries during these decades, forever waiting to realize their vision of a communist society in Germany. When their chance came after the war, issues to do with women *as women* were not seen as significant in themselves or as relevant to the class struggle.

A further problem facing the SED was the need to change the attitudes and values of its citizens who were children during the Nazi period, such as the Schönebeck women. Without this, the new society would be unlikely to see one of the developments the SED most desired, the emergence of the "socialist personality":

> an all-round, well-developed personality, who has a comprehensive command of political, specialist and general knowledge, possesses a firm class outlook rooted in the Marxist-Leninist world view, is notable for excellent mental, physical and moral qualities, is thoroughly imbued with collective thoughts and deeds, and actively, consciously and creatively contributes to the shaping of socialism.[8]

It is hard to read this definition as anything but a program conceived for men by men. The words used are those used for decades in Communist meetings, conferences, public declarations, and newspaper articles to bring working-class men into the party or into the demonstrations and street battles; they were not words designed to appeal to women.

"I'm Very Grateful to Our Government"

It is helpful, when considering the position of women in the GDR, to see what was being said in the press. The GDR newspapers were an important way for the SED to relay its messages to the population, since the party could determine what went into different, apparently independent papers. Expressions of gratitude by ordinary people featured strongly whenever there was a policy change or a new initiative the party wished to promote:

> One of our new citizens, Frau Emmi Badziura from Schönebeck, expresses her joy over the new price reductions with the following words: "It's barely a week since we housewives so gratefully welcomed the significant reduction in the price of margarine in the state shop. Today our government has once again added even more to our housekeeping money in the form of a reduction in the price of eggs. Equally to be welcomed is the price reduction that has just come into effect for stockings and socks, something that takes away from us as women so many of our worries. We are grateful to our government for that, and of course to all the working men and women on the land and in industry, but most particularly to our activists and innovators there. For us housewives, what goes hand in hand with that is the obligation to commit ourselves ever more actively to the struggle for peace and German unity."[9]

On one level, this expression of gratitude comes across as absurd propaganda, with the leaden prose echoing the set phrases the SED repeatedly pressed upon its people. It also demonstrates the tendency of the party to treat ordinary people as children, to be encouraged or chastised. Beyond the obvious intention to see apparently spontaneous praise heaped upon the government, however, there are other aspects worth noting. First, the writer is referred to as a "new citizen" to avoid admitting that she had probably been driven out of territory that many Germans—East and West—still thought of as theirs. Second, it is made clear that it is women, not men, who notice the cuts in prices, since they have control of the "housekeeping money" and have to make ends meet for their families. Similarly, women are alleged to be interested in stockings and socks, while men have more serious concerns. The women are grateful to the activists and innovators, most of whom are men, who provide a model for the women to follow. Finally, the women are permitted to identify themselves only as "housewives"; they are not shown to be present or future "socialist personalities." For the SED, the importance of housewives is that they demonstrate their gratitude by endorsing the party line and publicly supporting the party's campaigns for peace and unity on Soviet terms.

Equality between Men and Women?

When the German Communists returned from exile in Moscow in April 1945 or emerged out of hiding in Germany and established themselves in the new Soviet Occupation Zone, they embarked on a strategy in line with the demands of the Soviet Communist party, to establish a joint anti-fascist movement in which they would occupy the key positions. Over the years leading up to the founding of the GDR in 1949, they were faced with a variety of responses from Germans in the SBZ: anger at the brutality of the Soviet forces toward both men and women; scorn for the Communists' dependence on these forces to keep them in power; outright hostility from Nazis or ex-Nazis or people who had accepted the Nazi propaganda about the Soviet Union or who could see a new dictatorship emerging; uncertainty and suspicion among many social democrats who were forced into the SED; and, in some cases, relief and enthusiasm, which might or might not have been politically based.

In the context of a resurgence of Stalinism and the emergence of the Cold War in the late 1940s, the position of women was clear to the Communists: women would help to build socialism in the form decided on by the men ruling them. For these men, the "woman question" was closely linked to questions about the nature of the family and the implications this had for work outside the home.

The Schönebeck women were too young for their marriages to be directly affected by the Nazis' demands, but their attitudes and expectations were formed at a time when the Nazi laws and institutions were promoting a twin approach to the family. First, one set of policies aimed to push women out of employment into homemaking based on the nuclear family. These policies, backed by the kind of education given to the Schönebeck women, soon clashed with the Nazi state's need for women to enter employment to support the war effort. The second set of policies allowed the state to intervene in what people had seen as the private sphere, and to shape the family and marriage as institutions that would help to create a supposedly racially pure national community.[10]

The Communist leaders in the GDR set out to transform society politically, economically, and socially, as well as in terms of attitudes and behavior. Their view of the family, however, was conservative, based on their image of the nuclear family from the time of the Weimar Republic. The family with a husband and wife, they asserted in the 1950s, was vital to provide a stable base for their other policies. Formal equality and the right to work would be accompanied by the expectation that women would return home after work and take care of their household, their husband, and their children. There was no suggestion that eventually, when the most urgent battles were won, the SED would reconsider the balance of power between men and women, the nature of the family, or alternative ways of living or of managing the society, which might involve changing the roles not just of women but of men too.

Ironically, in promoting this traditional, patriarchal form of the family as a vital structure in society, the SED made it more likely that women would cling to their earlier values and less likely that they would look to develop a specifically socialist way of being in the society, one that would demonstrate a commitment to building socialism.

Homes and Families

Marianne Schneider: Shaping Attitudes

In the early 1950s, most of the Schönebeck women were still in the GDR. Did they show an interest in building socialism, or wonder what it might mean in practice to live as equals to men? Their letters suggest they had other things on their minds.

Out of the meeting in Magdeburg on 1 September 1950 came the annual *Rundbrief* and the annual reunions. Out of the first of the *Rundbrief* volumes came an implied sense of values, attitudes, and expectations of how the women should behave and what they should be aiming for. Marianne Schneider, the first organizer of the *Rundbrief*, was socially conservative. As she grew older, she became more willing to look at the political and social context they were living in and to be more relaxed about social change. However, her letter of 1 October 1950 from Schönebeck set the tone by stressing that marriage was a target, perhaps the primary target, for all of them.

To get the *Rundbrief* going, Marianne bought a small notebook, hardbound with a cloth cover like old-fashioned curtain material, patterned with squares and rectangles: orange and brown lines across, blue and brown from top to bottom. Over sixty years later, the threads are coming apart and the spine is threatening to break. As if there can never be enough pages, her writing is tiny and fills every possible space.

In Marianne's view the women, now in their early to mid-twenties, are hungry for love. Life and love, however, are to be contained within traditional frameworks and shaped by traditional attitudes to the family and the role of women. Marianne, one of the "new teachers," goes to work happily. After work, "running the household is a lot of fun and brings me great joy. Even if it sometimes seems a bit too much for me, I still manage to make a perfectly good job of it." She is married, and pastes into the book a photo of herself and her husband, Johannes (figure 2.1).

This photo says a lot. We are in the early, difficult days of the GDR. Inviting the women to the next class reunion, Marianne says she can supply the coffee but adds "Please bring your own cakes!" Yet here is a picture of everyday life, of two young people out in the open air, apparently bursting with love and confidence, on a walking trip in the mountains a hundred and fifty miles from where they live. It is just as if all the old German traditions remain and there will never be anything to worry about.

Marianne's letter starts a conversation about marriage. The women respond immediately and over many years. The model Marianne offers becomes the one the women seek to follow, whether they want to or not. She advises them to look out for "the right man," since only when they are linked to someone else

Figure 2.1. Marianne and Johannes in Thuringia, 1950. Photo courtesy of Akademie der Künste, Berlin.

can they really fulfill themselves. However, she adds, "If anyone has a different view, then please feel free to contradict me." In response, the majority say how wonderful it is to be married; some from both East and West say they want to remain independent; a few imply they are looking out for the right man; and one says confidentially, as if ashamed, that she is now divorced.

There are three notable responses to Marianne's urgings. The first, from Leni Baumann, suggests that love and romance are all very well, but that sex is also important. Leni, writing on 6 December 1950 from Halle/Saale, is now a student. Like Marianne, Leni trained as one of the "new teachers" and taught in Staßfurt. She enjoyed it but, as "the problem of mankind, the world, and God became ever more insistent," she grew restless and wanted to carry on studying.

Since September 1947, she has been at university in Halle. She is studying psychology and already having articles published. In case they think she is just a bookworm, deserving their pity, she reassures them:

> No, no, I too am engaged in student life ... You get to sample the delights of decadent literature and enjoy maxims such as these: "*Greife wacker nach der Sünde, denn aus der Sünde allein wächst Genuß*" [Go fearlessly after sin, since only out of sin can pleasure grow] (Frank Wedekind).

> Don't worry, I am not a complete abstainer! But it always really makes my blood boil when some representative of the stronger sex thinks that with a pair of nicely ironed trousers, a well-knotted tie and a fancy hairdo he has given me something to write home about. That makes me really hostile towards him! But still I haven't had just bad experiences but also some good ones; more explicit details than that I'm afraid I can't give you. I guess I'm still at the "experimental stage." Those among us who are married already have that behind them—or do they??

Leni displays a dismissive attitude to male pretention, and a carefree, uninhibited approach to sex and to talking about it. Her views are far from those of many of the other women and do not reflect the puritanical, controlling instincts of the SED leaders.

The second notable response is from Anna Siebert (12 May 1951). Anna gives her address as Berlin and Staßfurt, taking in both the East and the West. She refers to the often-quoted lines from Schiller (*Das Lied von der Glocke*):

> Looking at the experiences you have all had in relation to men, I must say I actually haven't thought about marriage yet. Although I am in fact almost exclusively around men (out of my 200 fellow students, only about four are women) and so really must have enough to choose from, I remain on my own. I still stick with the saying:

> Drum prüfe, wer sich ewig bindet,
> ob sich noch was Bessrs findet.

This injunction to look around if you are planning to tie yourself to someone forever, in case there may be someone better, is one Anna is keen to follow:

> Maybe I have missed out on something, but I don't think so. At the moment, my student life is absolutely enough for me. Although I live entirely independently in this den of iniquity that is Berlin, I can't go along with Leni. I haven't made Frank Wedekind's maxim my own, and nor have my fellow students, I believe. That comes, I think, from how hard we really do have to work.

Hard work and having to defend herself and her achievements in the face of rejection and ridicule by men in a profoundly male profession are themes that will recur throughout Anna's record of her life.

The most significant response to Marianne's letter comes from Else Hermann (27 November 1950, Weimar): "So here I have had the opportunity to get a closer look at the world of men than I ever had in Schönebeck, and must say, I don't find it all that bad. Unfortunately, I can't give you concrete details by letter!!"

Else's comment appears totally anodyne. It can be seen as comparable to the way men boast about their sexual exploits. However, there is more to it than that. The assumption within the group is that all of them can only be looking for a *man*. So powerfully is this presented, that it would be risky to challenge it. Future letters and interviews suggest that what Else has written here is little more than a cover for a reluctance to get involved with any man, and a wish to hide her reluctance from the rest of them. In order to remain accepted, she purports to share their views.

In my first interview with Else Hermann, she declared forthrightly that for her, at least, the letters were a fictional version of events, a "smokescreen." I interpreted this as meaning that they did not say what they meant in order to avoid political difficulties. This, it turned out, was only part of what she was trying to convey. It became clear over the years that she had used the smokescreen to hide herself and her ambivalence about her sexual orientation from the other women, for fear of being laughed at and rejected by them.

Children

During the 1950s, two thirds of the women had children—and there appeared to be little else they wanted to talk about. What is striking in the letters is their acceptance that it is natural for them to want a husband and children, and to look after them along with the home.

In her second letter (1 October 1951, Schönebeck), Marianne Schneider says that she now has a baby and loves being a mother (figure 2.2). Less than three years later (27 May 1954), she describes herself half-mockingly as a housewife, now that they have a second child, the twentieth their group has produced. By 1959, she has four children.

The desire of many of the Schönebeck women to have children can be seen to arise from a number of factors. First, there was a biological basis for it: they were young and fertile. More important were the social context and the social pressures which they experienced and reinforced across the group. The social pressures came from the attitudes of their own families, from the Nazi period with the state's demand that women produce children for the new society, and from the postwar societies of both West and East, which stressed the importance of having children in order to rebuild and rejuvenate the population and to guarantee the future labor force.

Grown Up: The Long 1950s 75

Figure 2.2. Marianne with her baby, catching the train to the Harz, 1951. Photo courtesy of Akademie der Künste, Berlin.

In the West, in line with the prevailing ethos and the policies of the relatively conservative government, it felt natural for the Schönebeck women to marry, give up their jobs, and stay home to look after their children. At this time, equality between men and women was narrowly interpreted by the courts, leaving many laws in place and men in charge of the household. Sabine Schenk notes that as late as 1977 in the FRG, "the Marriage and Family Law contained the following principle: 'The wife is responsible for running the household. She has the right to be employed as far as this is compatible with her marriage and family duties.'"[11]

The Schönebeck women in the East also found it normal in the 1950s to leave their jobs when they were married and had children, despite the increasing pressure to stay in employment. Similarly, they gave no sign of expecting their husbands to take on any housework. Their letters helped to maintain an accepted group view that women's and men's roles were different and would remain so.

Some still challenged the group's expectations. On 9 December 1951, Leni Baumann says she is now qualified, working at Halle University, and happy to be there. Her specialism concerns children with learning difficulties but, "thank God, not mine!" Leni challenges them with her photos, too. We see her on the beach on the Baltic coast in a two-piece bathing suit. This is in sharp contrast with the conservative way most of them have dressed so far for their photos:

Frieda Möller, for instance, looking prim and proper in her nurse's uniform in Barby; Else Hermann, serious about life in Plauen. Another photo from Leni (11 November 1957) shows her sitting on her bed with several cushions—beside her a newspaper, to her left a large radio. Behind her is a wall-hanging displaying naked men and women, erotic scenes, and a chase taking place.

Over the years, the women's attitudes to what they could wear and present themselves in changed significantly. As early as 1952, a few were following Leni's lead: Lisa Liebmann for one, and Käthe Sommer's photo shows her on the beach, deeply tanned and either topless or wearing a strapless top. Eventually, such images became commonplace for them, in both the West and the East, and their daughters (and sons) appear in the photos wearing very little at all. While this may seem a minor point, it was significant for the women as they slowly emerged from their cocoon of provincial habits and attitudes. (Here they were ahead of their husbands, whose photos show them steadfastly wearing suits and ties to the reunions well into the 1970s.)

However, even Leni Baumann paid at least lip service to the pressure to have children. On 5 April 1955, Leni says she is working on her doctorate in Halle. She has neither a husband nor a fiancé but has adopted a new motto: "First I turn myself into a doctor, then I seek out a doctor for myself, and finally I start producing lovely little mini-doctors!"

Elly Haase is another without a husband, and in her letter of 20 February 1955 from Schönebeck, she jokes with the rest of them about their attempts to find her one. However, the light-hearted tone covers a serious concern that there are not enough men around for all of them:

> And now, as to the main theme: still nothing has happened. I'm pleased that you had such a good time here at my place in September 1954. To those of you who so regretted that my housewifely talents remain uncultivated, I'd like to ask that you seek out a man for me. Please bring any candidates with you to Barby, so that we can vote on them there—but do remember that I have a vote too! Maybe one of them will get enough votes, it'll be a Saturday and on top of that we'll already be in the rectory, so you could marry me off straight away. And then the party's on me.

Elly Haase often uses her wry sense of humor at her own expense. She also chooses her words and metaphors to convey more than she is apparently saying, a useful skill in the GDR. Here Elly uses *brach*, a rare word, to describe her housewifely talents. Its sense is agricultural, meaning fallow or uncultivated. It is unlikely she has done this without thinking. For the SED, which is always praising agricultural workers for their achievements, the key to a better future lies in not allowing the fields (or, therefore, Elly's talents) to lie fallow or remain uncultivated. In mocking herself, Elly is also mocking the party, but in a way they are unlikely to notice, even if they intercept the *Rundbrief* and read it.

Avoiding Humiliation: Ilse Klein

Ilse Klein was acutely aware of the norms and values the group sought to promote. From what she wrote, it is clear that she too supported them. Her actions, however, showed her diverging from these norms and values, so much so that she feared condemnation and humiliating rejection from the other women. Her response was to outflank them by seeking to make it impossible for them to criticize or push her away from them.

Ilse Klein's parents moved from Schönebeck to the spa town of Bad Oeynhausen (in what would become the FRG) in 1942. In 1948 she married but suffered terrible housing problems and unhappiness with her husband. Hinting at episodes of humiliation, she tells the women in her letter of 4 April 1951 that she was divorced and had returned to live with her parents in 1951. Conscious of the disgrace her new status carried with it, she asks the women in the Schönebeck group to keep her divorce confidential. She expects that they will be sympathetic, since she has done nothing they could see as wrong.

Her next letter (16 April 1952) takes up the question of men, as set out by Marianne. She thanks them for their kind thoughts about her divorce and tells them that she is okay. She does not have a husband, nor, she adds, does she have a child, since in "proper" relationships that is not the done thing. In any case, it is better to be alone, she says, than to add to the number of unhappy marriages. But—she is quick to reassure them—she is not in any way talking about their marriages.

However, Ilse's letter of 8 September 1953 contains news that would have astonished the other Schönebeck women: she is now the mother of a "sweet little daughter," but is neither married nor in a relationship. Many of them will find this "schoking [sic]," she says, but she is ecstatic about it. Her tactics here are clear: she will acknowledge their prejudices before they express them, and will refuse to allow them space to humiliate her; since she is so happy with what she has done, they have to be happy too. She says that as her father is to be the child's godparent, she feels that when people look at the morality of what she has done, they will not judge her too unfavorably.

She then appeals directly to the group for support, saying how important they are to her, how she longs to be in Schönebeck, and how sorry she is that the difficulty of getting a permit to enter the GDR made it impossible for her to attend the reunion there. She urges them to include photos of the reunion, and compares her happy memories of growing up with them in Schönebeck with her difficulties in the West: "It is after all our *Heimat*, and the people in Westphalia make it very hard to really settle in here, despite eleven years having passed." In contrast to her neighbors, she implies, all of them in the group will always be there for one another.

In the face of this approach, it is difficult for the others to be critical of Ilse's choice. In fact, no one does criticize her or even mention the new baby, which she might have seen as disapproval and an attempt at humiliation. Consciously or unconsciously, she appears to choose not to interpret their silence in this way. Her happiness and the confidence it has given her enable her to rise above their presumed moralistic concerns. Still, she makes things easier for them in her next letter (10 June 1955), telling them she has met "her one true love," and declaring that, "if everything turns out the way I imagine it will, I shall be content for the rest of my life." By 1956, she is married; by 1958 she has a son, and the family does then appear to live in a state of contentment for all the years that are left to them, making no distinction between the son and the daughter, and with Ilse never mentioning again her early decision to have a child by herself. Ilse becomes a strong presence in the group, no longer challenging it but helping to strengthen it: she attends the reunions in the East and, if she cannot, sends money to help them buy extra food for the day. Sometimes she sends real coffee, a welcome luxury for the women there. She also hosts reunions in the West, providing some of the energy and organizational skills that have been missing there. In doing so, she commits herself to the group ethos and values, including their emphasis on the importance of husbands and children in traditional nuclear families. Her actions may be seen as overcompensation, but they do put her in a powerful position in the group. This is a rare example of anticipating humiliation and acting in a way that prevents it happening.

Homes and the Housing Problem

Women after the war were expected to take charge of the home, the housework, and the children. The assumption was that they had a suitable home as a basis for this. However, in the years after the war, building or refurbishing enough decent housing continued to be difficult in both the GDR and the FRG. Problems arose because of the damage to the cities through bombing and artillery fire, the age of the surviving housing stock, and the need to house millions of refugees. Even in an undamaged area such as Schönebeck, the population increased initially through the settlement of refugees and later through the growth of the factories in the 1950s.

In what became the Soviet zone, around 14 percent of the housing had been destroyed or made uninhabitable, a total of 640,000 apartments or houses. In the Western zones, the figures were between 20 and 25 percent, with the loss of 4.75 million apartments or houses.[12] There were huge regional differences, some of which would benefit the GDR. In the West, Koblenz was around 82 percent destroyed, Kassel 80 percent, Cologne 70 percent, and Stuttgart 55 percent. Berlin was 50 percent destroyed. In the SBZ, Magdeburg and Dresden each suffered about 60 percent damage, but many of the industrially and culturally important smaller cities and larger towns suffered much less, including Halle, Naumburg, Eisenach, Erfurt, Gera, Fulda, Jena, and Gotha.[13]

The housing that was left in the West had more space per person than in the East, but still people shared beds or slept on floors and kitchen tables. Huge numbers slept in emergency accommodation, such as the 2,200 Nissen huts in Hamburg alone, where 250,000 apartments or houses had been destroyed. These temporary shelters had no kitchen or private areas and were freezing in the winter. By 1949, there were still more than a million people in emergency accommodation in the West.[14]

In the SBZ in 1947, there were three-quarters of a million people in emergency accommodation. The new authorities requisitioned housing and required people who had space to make it available to refugees.[15] These actions reduced the number in emergency accommodation to several tens of thousands by the end of 1949. However, there was still a shortage of a million and a half apartments at the time the new GDR constitution guaranteed decent accommodation to all its citizens.[16]

Looking at the GDR, Harsch notes how little investment there was in housing in the five-year plans during the 1950s, apart from demonstration projects like the Stalinallee in Berlin and the steelworkers' complex in Stalinstadt (later renamed Eisenhüttenstadt) near the Polish border. These projects were intended to show how ordinary people would live under socialism in modern, healthy, and attractive apartments. The SED could not resolve a number of contradictions, however. First, the construction costs were too high to make it practical to build such housing more widely, although there were modest attempts in the center of Magdeburg, which the Schönebeck women could see for themselves. The second problem was the style the SED proposed for furnishing and fitting out the new apartments. This was supposedly a German national style, rather than the ideologically suspect Bauhaus and Jugendstil approaches, but was in fact modeled on nineteenth-century "bourgeois" design. The reproduction Chippendale chairs and other items of furniture were too expensive for ordinary people, and GDR manufacturers were reluctant to make them.[17] Finally, the SED was caught between the promotion of Soviet neoclassicism, supported by Stalin, and pressure in 1954 from the new leader in the Soviet Union, Khrushchev, to move to a modernist style, which would allow much speedier building of the necessary housing.[18] Stefan Heym offers a fictional portrayal of this dilemma in *Die Architekten*, which was not published until after the end of the GDR. Ironically, in retrospect, his anti-Stalinist heroes can be seen to be promoting the shoddy, ugly *Plattenbau* (low-rise prefabricated buildings), which provided none of the close-knit, sociable urban features of traditional housing blocks or even of those in the Stalinallee. Politically, Heym's heroes were on the right side in terms of breaking with Stalinism, but in terms of urban design, what they supported was much worse than the model developments in the GDR.[19]

Harsch describes housing conditions at the end of the long 1950s: "In 1961, fifty-two percent of apartments and single houses in the GDR had one or two rooms ... Central heating could be found in 2.5 percent of homes. One third had a toilet, and twenty-two percent a bath."[20] Where there was investment, it was concentrated in the highly industrialized areas, such as the chemical complexes of Leuna and Bitterfeld. Even here, conditions were terrible: "four adults in one room, four adults and one child in one room, two adults and three children in one room plus a kitchen. In 1958, the women's dormitory at Leuna had no private rooms: mothers and their children bunked alongside women without children."[21]

In the West, the transformation of housing conditions was more rapid, with early investment coming from Marshall Plan credits.[22] At the beginning of the 1950s, there was still a need for five million homes. In 1951–52 alone, almost 900,000 were built. A fifth of these were financed by the state at various levels.[23] The economic historian Tamás Vonyó argues that the urban housing crisis undermined efforts to rebuild economic activity in the late 1940s and that the determined effort in the 1950s required the intervention of the new FRG state and the restoration of functioning capital markets. These, in turn, set the "economic miracle" in motion. Investment in housing directly stimulated production. It also overcame the problem of the labor shortages in the cities, providing accommodation for workers who were otherwise forced to live in smaller towns with few jobs. Vonyó says, in the impersonal language of economists, "The temporarily displaced labour reserves of the country were gradually absorbed as the urban housing stock was rebuilt in a gigantic national housing program between 1949 and 1957." In the longer period considered here, more than five million apartments or houses were built or substantially renovated, with social housing accounting for around 55 percent.[24] This program of house building ensured that the Schönebeck women already in the West, and those who moved there in the 1950s, were eventually able to find larger, more modern housing than was ever available to most who stayed in the East.

The women's letters, and the photos in them, show the way housing differed from West to East by the end of the 1950s, and made it plain to the group how great those differences were. Irma Kindler and Anna Siebert both had comfortable, modern apartments by then. Anna's was in one of a group of tower blocks, laid out in a modernist style that was totally different from the traditional, dense housing blocks in Hamburg. From her photo (5 May 1955) it looks, sixty years later, forbidding and cut off from the life of the city, with a major road alongside the development. It is, however, a good example of the amount of new housing going up in a short time and of the way this new housing transformed people's lives. Anna says their apartment is extremely comfortable and conveniently laid out and they are very happy there. Others in the West talk less about their housing, but photos throughout the *Rundbrief* show how comfortably they are living.

The picture varies in the East. Else's parents are comfortable in their home, while she often struggles to find somewhere to live (usually a rented room in a widow's apartment). Those with farms have enough space (even if it is shared with their parents), and Martha Jäger is proud of the changes they have made to their house, but others are barely making do, still sharing cramped apartments with their parents. Heidi Kempf (23 February 1952) describes living alone with her elderly mother:

> For the most part 1951 brought me nothing but trials and tribulations, and I'll spare you the details of those. But to be brief: on 20 July we had to move house yet again since we still had too many rooms. (That's twice in two and a half years!) Hopefully they'll leave us in peace now with our two rooms and the shared use of a kitchen!

Some years later, Heidi's husband of only five years died suddenly. Heidi (writing on 18 November 1959) was confronted by a shocking lack of compassion from the authorities: "Our apartment, which we moved into just a year before, has been taken back, which means we have to move out—because of underoccupation."

The women in the East know they are almost powerless when it comes to determining where and how they will live: the state will make decisions about investment and housing allocation, and they must accept the consequences. In the West the women are also affected by state decisions about investment, and about the economic system that will provide the necessary housing, through both the private and the public sectors. The difference is that the consequences for them have, by the end of the 1950s, been almost entirely beneficial.

In other areas of their everyday lives, too, the Schönebeck women are affected in major and minor ways by the decisions and actions of the state. At times state power is both destructive and irresistible, and all of them, through the exchange of letters, are forced to see that this is the case.

Interaction with the State

The Political Fights Back

During the 1950s, the separation of the West from the East was confirmed. Politically, the conservative chancellor Konrad Adenauer rejected the idea of neutrality for the FRG or for the whole of Germany and moved ever closer to the Western powers, with the FRG joining NATO in 1955. The FRG government was strongly anti-Communist; it referred to the GDR disparagingly as "the Zone" as a way of declaring that it was controlled by the Soviet authorities. (The government and press of the GDR referred to the FRG equally disparagingly as the "Bonn Republic.") In the first FRG elections in 1949, the KPD received 5.7 percent of the votes, taking fifteen seats in the federal parliament. At the next elections, its vote dropped to 2.2 percent and no Communists were elected. Following a decision by the constitutional court that the KPD's operations conflicted with the *Grundgesetz*, the FRG's constitution, the KPD was banned. It would re-emerge in 1968 as the DKP, and although it was insignificant in terms of membership, it was still seen by the authorities as a threat to democratic rule.[25]

Economically, conditions and prospects were transformed for ordinary people in the West by the Marshall Aid program, the currency reform in the late 1940s, and the pursuit of a social market economy. The theoretical basis for the social market economy was that the state, while endorsing capitalism, should accept responsibility for the economic and social wellbeing of the population, and should construct a framework that rejected both capitalist individualism and socialist collectivism, and "encouraged ordinary people to pursue their own interests together with the common good."[26] The FRG's "economic miracle" increasingly set the flourishing West apart from the economically struggling East throughout this decade and beyond. Of both political and economic significance were the moves during the 1950s toward integrating sectors of the FRG economy with those of France, in particular, and the other partners in what would become the European Economic Community.

Socially, the FRG was conservative, with the ruling Christian Democratic Union and Christian Social Union reflecting and helping to shape social attitudes and expectations. The legal equality given to women was accompanied by policies that made it likely women would have little direct involvement in the formal political structures, and that women with children would not work outside the home.

In the East, there was substantial repression, often involving terror and torture, as the SED made clear its determination to eliminate opposition to its hold on power. As well as carrying out show trials of Communist leaders and former Social Democrats in the GDR, the GDR and Soviet intelligence and security forces arrested anyone suspected of attempting to undermine the SED and the state. Key political moments were the 1952 Party Conference with its decision to build socialism, the events of 17 June 1953, the limited move toward "destalinization" in 1956, and further show trials of party leaders in the late 1950s.

At the local level, there were arrests and disappearances that ordinary people would have known about. One example is the mayor of Schönebeck during the Nazi period, Kurt Bauer. Bauer is portrayed by some commentators as an upright, principled man who kept his distance from the Nazis.[27] Other sources show a stronger commitment to the Nazi cause.[28] Nevertheless, he appears to have been instrumental in ensuring that Schönebeck surrendered without a serious battle. He was kept in post by the Americans and the British but arrested by the Soviet forces when they moved into Schönebeck. He then disappeared and only in 1949 was it clear that he had died of diphtheria in the Soviet Special Camp in Ketschendorf/Fürstenwalde. In the meantime, although his wife and children were harassed by the Soviet and local Communist forces, they maintained contact with many local people in Schönebeck, who understood what was happening to them.[29]

By 1951, mass show trials (the "Waldheim Trials") as well as individual trials of alleged opponents were being given extensive publicity as a way of making clear to the whole population what could happen if people expressed opposition.[30] In a number of villages, such as Dähre by the border with the FRG north of Schönebeck, there were show trials in 1951 to punish people allegedly seeking to undermine agricultural production.[31] Separately, there were many examples of people disappearing, being tried by Soviet military tribunals, sentenced to long terms of imprisonment, or executed in Moscow. These were secret trials. For the most part, even friends and family who knew of the disappearances did not know what had happened until the files were opened in Russia in the 1990s.[32]

These are the kinds of events the Schönebeck women would have heard about but which at first sight they appear to be ignoring. However, a careful reading shows something else: the letters are filled with incidental mentions, often critical, of the women's everyday interactions with the state and its various institutions.

Leni Baumann, for instance (6 December 1950, Halle/Saale), loves her life as a student and is fascinated by her studies. However, she is wrestling with concerns "about human nature, and our situation here today," declaring she is philosophically neither an idealist nor a materialist but a realist. This position would be seen as suspect by the authorities with their Marxist-Leninist commitment to the theory of dialectical materialism. Leni also says opaquely, "There is so much, so much that I could tell you, but unfortunately not things I can write down."

Barbara Meier (28 December 1952, Neugattersleben), after talking about the joys of family life and Christmas, writes one of the rare accounts of conditions worsening in 1952, the year of the SED's decision to build socialism. As well as political controls tightening significantly—expressed in harsh discriminatory acts and attempts to squeeze out the private firms that still existed—the economy started to perform worse, not better. Barbara tells them,

Reading what I have written, you will no doubt have noticed that everything I do and think revolves mainly around our boy. Life outside—I mean outside our family and our apartment—often brings little that is pleasant. My husband's college went through changes in the past year, and along with that, so did our boarding school here in Neugattersleben. Since then, there are no relaxed evenings, no musical recitals and so on—at least, nothing that takes place in private. It's a great pity, since in the village there is nothing cultural on offer *for us*. Prospects are not good for visits to the theater or concerts in Bernburg and Dessau either. For a start, I wouldn't want to leave our little one on his own, but also the petrol problem has recently become quite critical. So we make do with our much-loved radio as a substitute—as long as there's not a power cut. Unfortunately, that's a frequently recurring misfortune here, which sometimes really drives me to despair. We have no gas. There is little we can burn for heating. Who knows what we should do? You just have to use the evenings for ironing, preparing food and so on. In the meantime, we have acquired an oil lamp, which gives us a bit of light without any mess. It sits on top of our "Super" [radio]. Is that not progress?

Käthe Sommer (8 March 1953) and her family have also had a difficult time. She and her husband run an optical clinic but have been the victims of apparently arbitrary action by the authorities, who make no pretense of abiding by the rule of law in terms of property rights:

As you will have seen, I have finished up back in Schönebeck (the beloved!!!). Admittedly, rather unwillingly. Our place in the Wienerstrasse in Magdeburg was "needed" for some other purpose, so we had to clear ourselves out within a week. As we had previously set up our own practice in Schönebeck, we moved over to there. And there we were with all our goods and chattels for a good eight weeks, in a frightful mess among boxes and all possible bits of junk.

Gerda Höpfner was another who suffered over this period. Gerda worked at the shoe factory, the Gummiwerke, in Schönebeck. In her letter of 4 July 1952, Gerda says she is soon to be married to one of her colleagues. On 26 February 1954 she reports, "1953 brought us endless grief and trouble. In February 1953, my husband was arrested for agitation against the state and after twelve months is still not back home." Their daughter was born while her husband was in prison.

In her next letter (3 November 1955), Gerda reports that her husband came home in August 1954 after a year and a half of separation. Only those who have suffered long separations in such terrible circumstances can imagine the joy they felt, she says. She adds that their child, over a year old, had never seen her father and naturally could not understand at first what was happening. Gerda includes a photo of her husband looking older, his face lined. Two years later (8 December 1957), Gerda's photo of herself and her husband shows them both looking younger and more relaxed again, nearly five years after his arrest.

Frieda Möller is ambivalent about the GDR authorities. In her letter of 18 July 1952, she says that a serious illness has led her to appreciate the help she has had from the state: she was well looked after and spent five weeks in a rehabilitation center in the Harz. Her job in the local clinic was secure and she did not suffer financially by being off work. However, it is a different story in the months leading up to the events of 17 June 1953. In her letter of 5 May 1954, she says that her parents-in-law fled to the West after being forced out of their farm so that its sixty-eight hectares could become part of a cooperative. Immediately after they left, the police appeared and searched the house where Frieda and her husband lived, and confiscated their furniture. It was not until the brief relatively liberal period after the events of 17 June that their furniture was returned.

Martha Jäger in the 1950s

Martha Jäger was one of the Schönebeck women who never moved from the *Heimat*. Her story is told here and in subsequent chapters because she was exceptional in a number of ways. First, she was from a comfortable family with their own home and business. This meant she was, in the eyes of the SED and the GDR state, the class enemy. Second, her letters indicate that she was engaged in an almost constant tussle with the GDR authorities. Third, she only rarely realized that she was engaged in this tussle, and even more rarely attributed it to her class background and position.

If the SED insisted that the GDR's citizens should be optimistic, Martha Jäger was happy to comply. In her letter of 21 June 1951 from Schönebeck, happiness is her favorite word. She is happily married. She is, she says many times, so happy in herself. She is also very happy to stay at home and look after her young child (though "home" means they are living with her parents). She has no interest in going out to work: "I plunged into married life on 26 June 1948. Our Holger was born on 6 August 1949. I have been a housewife for three years now, am very happy and must say that I wouldn't want to be hanging around anymore without my 'other half.'"

On 17 June 1952, Martha is now doubly pleased as they have their own home in Schönebeck, rebuilt out of her parents' home to their own design, with a garden so that Holger can grow up outside. For the GDR, what she describes is a life of luxury, and she describes it with no apparent awareness of the political context:

> Since I last wrote, we have set up our own home. It was great fun fitting it out according to my own taste. Of course it took a lot of work, since all the tradesmen had to do their bit but now, thanks to that, it is really comfortable. Even in the garden I've been very active, though I must admit we have more lawn and fruit trees than vegetables growing.

By this time, the national and regional newspapers were full of the preparations for the SED's Second Party Conference, planned for July 1952. Their reports involved the constant repetition of formulaic phrases about U.S. aggression, German-Soviet friendship, the achievements of the industrial workers, and the sharpening of the class struggle. It can be seen—but not by Martha—that the whole family is vulnerable to charges of being petty-bourgeois class enemies.

In 1953, there was increasing pressure on people in Martha's position in the run-up to the events of 17 June that challenged the hold of the SED on power. Martha mentions neither these events nor the subsequent partial relaxation of pressure. However, in her next letter (12 February 1954), she says she has been allowed to go on her own from the GDR to visit her sister in the West. This was the result of a temporary relaxation of travel restrictions. Her visit demonstrated the GDR state's use of family members as hostages to guarantee the return of the person traveling to the West, since Martha's husband and child were not permitted to go with her.

Two and a half years later (8 August 1956), Martha is chatty and cheery as she talks about her family. Her older child has had lots of illnesses, including inflammation of the salivary glands or, as she says in German, "*Mundspeicheldrüsenentzündung. (Herrliches Wort, nicht wahr?* [Great word, isn't it?])." They are still living comfortably: in June they had a holiday on the Baltic coast; on Sundays they go for rides in her parents' car.

In September 1957, Martha and her husband hosted the reunion. By this time, since Martha's father was chronically ill, her husband had become a part owner of the family business. Other women describe the reunion as unforgettable, stressing the range, volume, and quality of the food, and how much of it they all ate. This is in stark contrast to the shortages at the beginning of the decade; by 1957 there is a sense that they are eating so much partly because food was once so scarce. In fact, by this time the authorities were concerned about increasing obesity in the GDR.[33] The photos in the *Rundbrief* over the years do show that some of the Schönebeck women are overweight, but this applies at least as much to those in the West as to those in the East.

The East-West connections at this reunion demonstrate how close they all still felt, despite the border. Astrid Greiswald and Ilse Klein, who could not be there, sent money from the West to buy food; and, as Marianne Schneider says in her letter of 22 September 1957, "At one o'clock in the morning there was another particular surprise. Martha's husband put on a tape on which we could hear Anni Lange singing. Thank you so much, dear Anni, for the pleasure you gave us!" Anni Lange, one of the Schönebeck women, was an opera singer in Hamburg.

In her next letter (25 October 1959), Martha notes a change in their class reunions: after they have met and talked on their own, the women now allow the husbands to join them for the second half. It becomes clear that the men have only a secondary role, with the women organizing the event and limiting the men's involvement. Regardless of what happens at home, in the group the women have collective power and can tell the men how to behave.

By 1959, Martha is working in the family business for two afternoons a week, not because they need the money, but "so as not to totally stagnate in the interminable sameness of household work." She is at last what the SED desired, a housewife and a working woman, though perhaps not in a way the party had envisaged.

Missing: Erika Krämer's Story

Looming over all these encounters between the women and the state is a story the Schönebeck women could not avoid hearing: the story of Erika Krämer. This starts with her letter of 2 August 1951 from Calbe.

After leaving school and doing her *Reichsarbeitsdienst* and *Kriegshilfsdienst* with Anna Siebert in 1944/45, Erika Krämer worked in the family business in Calbe. She then returned to school, completed her *Abitur* in July 1946, and went to Rostock University to study economics. From there she moved to Berlin—which she loved—to continue her studies. Though she studied in East Berlin, she lived in West Berlin, for some time in the same apartment as Anna Siebert:

> If I was going to report on my three years of studying in Berlin, I could write a whole book. Let's just say that despite the winter of the Blockade, the power cuts, the S-Bahn strikes and so on, it was a wonderful time, during which Berlin became my second home.
>
> In July 1950 I did my exam in economics at the Humboldt University in Berlin. But that wasn't the end of it, they were not going to give us our diplomas at that point. First we would have to work for six months in a state-owned business and demonstrate our political acceptability! But I took a bit of a break in Calbe and found a place for myself in our family firm—my father had died in the meantime. In December I got engaged, but right from the beginning we were plagued by bad luck, since my better half could find nothing better to do than to break two vertebrae, and had to be completely encased in plaster.
>
> On Easter Saturday (I had in the meantime started doing my placement in the local bank here), I was bringing him back in our car to Calbe so he could spend the rest of his recovery at our place when, as we arrived in Calbe, we were arrested, carted off to Potsdam and there immediately separated. Since then I have never seen my fiancé again. After I had been sitting in solitary confinement for four weeks like a hardened criminal, they let me go. But to this day there is not a trace of my Karl. The uncertainty is enough to drive me to despair, doubly so as I know the physical condition he was in when we were arrested.

Marianne, you ask if I'll come to the class reunion this year. I was enormously pleased when the *Rundbrief* got to me, and I would also really like to keep in touch with you all, but I've been so destroyed by this whole affair that I am not up to having so many people around me. Don't be cross, dear friends, hopefully next time I'll be there with better news. I shall think of you all on 1 September.

The Schönebeck women would inevitably have known about the repression of alleged opponents of the SED. Confronted in 1951 with Erika Krämer's very personal account, they would have had to decide how to respond: by acknowledging her suffering, by criticizing the SED and the Russians, or by looking away and implying this was not part of the everyday life they wanted to write about. Erika herself does not demand that they take a stand, but her tone suggests that she expects a response in the next *Rundbrief*.

Surprisingly, the first eleven entries in the next book make no mention of Erika's account. On 15 February 1952, Elly Haase is the first one to acknowledge it: "I would also like to wish all the best to our Erika, who must have had the worst time of any of us, and now whose mother has died as well, shortly before Christmas." Similarly, Astrid Greiswald (5 May 1952) sends her love, most particularly to Erika. Elfriede Berger (26 March 1952, Cologne) says, "I wish, dear Erika, that the sun will soon shine again for you and that through a happy stroke of fate your Karl will come back into your life."

In her letter of 11 August 1952, Erika says that she was very happy to receive the *Rundbrief*, which paints such a good picture of them all and makes her feel close to them again. She says, less than wholeheartedly, that she appreciates their concern, "even though up to now your good wishes haven't brought me much comfort." She continues her story:

> Because of all the upset I told you about in the last letter, my mother had a stroke and lost a lot of her mental capacity.... In the end she could not be looked after at home any longer and we had to take her into an institution. Our visits to her there for eight weeks belong among the most horrific impressions in my life, so we asked the doctor whether we could take my mother home, along with someone to look after her. On 1 December, we took her home and she sensed once more that she was back in her own house. But then things became steadily worse and we thank God that on 16 December—precisely on the anniversary of my engagement—he released her from her suffering. On top of that there was all the commotion about my fiancé—up to now, after more than seventeen months, there is still no trace of him. The condition I'm in is something only someone who has also been left dangling, knowing absolutely nothing about the fate of a loved one, could understand.

Erika spends her time running the household for her sister and working at the family firm in the afternoon, "so that my mind does not completely rot away. And so one day passes like the next—unfortunately I grow older in the process."

Erika updates them again in her letter of 17 March 1954. Her fiancé is missing as before, with everything "for so long totally unclear." Erika's tone is somewhere between caustic and bitter. She says she loves getting the *Rundbrief* and is happy to read all their accounts, mostly cheerful, satisfied letters, spoilt only by the unlucky few among them who have to torment everyone with their dreadful tales.

In one of the few indirect references to the months leading up to the events of 17 June 1953, Erika says that they had a hard time with the business in the first half of 1953, but now it is going better. They have to work very hard, but she is happy with that, since it leaves no time to think about other things. Without explaining how it was possible, Erika says she spent five weeks in Lübeck (that is, in the West) in the summer of 1953 and was able to fully relax. She is sorry that she did not have enough money to go and visit the others in the West. Perhaps she will be able to this year, she says.

In her next letter (3 January 1955), Erika says she would prefer not to have to report bad news to them:

> But it is also not my fault that my run of bad luck still hasn't come to an end! Now on top of everything I have managed to get tuberculosis. I have been here eight months already, and they are not yet ready to be rid of me. It is so lovely here in the sanatorium in Bennechenstein in the Harz: my every need is met, completely and totally!!!!

Eighteen months later (13 July 1956), Erika writes a very different letter. After a year in the sanatorium, she is completely over her tuberculosis, able to work again, and extremely happy with life. She has visited Anna Siebert several times in Hamburg, as well as Irma Kindler. Although she does not say so explicitly, the traumatic time dealing with the tuberculosis seems to have shifted her beyond her earlier troubles and she can now start life again. There is no mention of her missing Karl.

A further year later (28 September 1957), Erika Krämer has put her lost Karl and her tuberculosis behind her. She is married to an engineer and living in Hamburg. She says nothing about how she came to leave the GDR. Reading about the reunion, which she was not able to attend, she says she could really feel how close they all still are, despite the years of being apart. Anyone passing through Hamburg is welcome to visit or stay with her. Her only regret about having left Calbe is that her sister is now alone there. As if to confirm that recovering from tuberculosis enabled her to put her previous life behind her, she says, "Each day we are thankful all over again for the change, since who gets to have such a great beginning these days?"

Responding to this chapter in Erika's life, Lisa Liebmann (16 December 1957) comments, "I think we don't need to be sending our wishes for more happiness for Erika (Krämer); her happiness shines out of every word she writes."

Erika Krämer and Humiliation

How are we to understand Erika Krämer's tragic story with its apparently happy ending? It is certainly the most dramatic example of the GDR state intervening in the everyday lives of the Schönebeck women. Like her, we never hear what happened to her Karl and can only assume he was one of the many who were taken secretly to Moscow and executed. She does not give enough detail about him for this to be checked against the records that became available in the 1990s.

It is helpful to see what was done to Erika Krämer as an act of humiliation by the GDR or Soviet authorities. It has all the elements of humiliation:[34] it is a demonstrative exercise of power that was outside what she could have expected from those authorities; it was thoroughly demeaning and reduced her status in a direct, practical way, from someone apparently running her own life to someone for whom everything was decided by those above her; it involved a rejection of her as an ordinary, compliant, positive member of the society, or her exclusion from those seen as dependable; and it involved a clear injustice for which there could be no remedy, since she could not pursue the GDR authorities for false arrest and imprisonment.

Similarly, the consequences of this act of humiliation follow the model suggested, where "the victim tends to pass through different sets of responses, from a sense of bewildered helplessness to rage and from there to revolt, resistance or submission, which may also involve despair and self-destruction."[35] In each of these responses, there will often be defensive behavior as well, involving denial and self-deception, as a way of refusing to face up to the horror of what has happened. Here it is necessary to look carefully at the wording and tone of Erika Krämer's letters, since at times it appears that she is seeking to shrug off what was done to her (and of course to Karl, which had a direct effect on her too).

Erika addresses the group directly. She has terrible news but does not wish to sound self-important or to impose her own suffering on them. Early in her account, she adopts an amused, almost humorous tone. She refers to her fiancé as her "better half" and jokes that he "could find nothing better to do" than break his vertebrae. Her account of their subsequent arrest and separation is told in a very matter-of-fact way. To be kept for a month in solitary confinement, presumably being intensively and at the very least unpleasantly interrogated, must have been a truly shocking, life-changing experience. To then talk casually of simply being released reads like a highly defensive response, suggesting that they should not worry, that nothing significant happened to her. She does convey some of her deeper feelings: the uncertainty over what has happened to Karl has driven her to despair, and she feels too "destroyed" by what has happened to be able to face the other women at the class reunion.

When she says, "Don't be cross, dear friends," she acknowledges that they will be talking about her in a way that she cannot control. There is a sense that she now feels vulnerable, as if she has revealed too much about herself. Despite her attempt to be outward-looking, it is also clear that Erika is inward-looking and self-absorbed. She will not come to the reunion, not because she finds it hard to be among other people, but because she does not want so many people around her—that is, with her as the focus of their attention.

Between Erika's first and second letters, there has been a class reunion and another book of letters, many of them full of sympathy for her. As a group they gather around to embrace her. At the same time there is, significantly, no discussion of what actually happened and what might have become of Karl; even about him they have to remain optimistic. For Erika, this is not helpful; when she thanks them in her second letter, it is somewhat grudgingly, as if they could have done more to take away the cause of her suffering. This is common after humiliation: the victim seeks the impossible, to make it never have happened in the first place, or to reverse it now that it has happened.

Most significant in Erika's second letter is the suffering and death of her mother, which Erika attributes to what happened to her and her fiancé. One of her concerns appears to be the shocking experience of her mother being cared for in an institution. While it would be unfair to suggest that Erika thought this consciously, problems with her mother perhaps helpfully turned her away from her own misery. Only at the end of the letter is there a mention of her Karl, of whom she has still heard nothing. Her comment serves to distance the rest of the women from her: only someone in her very specific position, she says, could understand the position she is in. This, too, is a common response for the victim of humiliation: the sense of isolation and exclusion, of being cut off by her experience from those around her, whose sympathy and compassion cannot change how she feels about herself and her life. Her only effective defense is to work, and so stop her mind rotting away, she says. Shortly afterward, we learn from Marianne Schneider's letter that Erika was planning to attend the next class reunion but was prevented at the last minute.

In her third letter, Erika again stresses that work is a help to her. Her tone toward the group is close to sarcastic as she regrets that some of their stories, such as her own, have to disturb the otherwise happy accounts. The strangest thing in this letter is her unexplained trip to Lübeck in the West. How could Erika Krämer, an apparent enemy of the state, an associate of someone arrested and never seen again, and a representative of the old factory-owning "bourgeoisie," be allowed travel to the West, even in the brief period of relative liberalization after the events of June 1953? Why was she allowed back into the GDR? And how was she able to marry someone from the West and to move there herself in 1957, a time of renewed repression?

In the GDR, prisoners were sometimes released early because they had agreed to be Stasi informers. There is not the slightest hint that this was the case with Erika Krämer, but even the idea that it might have been possible would have been enough to unsettle the other women. The Stasi was skilled at spreading doubt and suspicion.[36] This might have been its reason for doing favors for Erika, without her being in any way implicated. Later examples will show that awareness of the actions of the Stasi was enough to undermine the trust that held the group together, even if the Stasi did nothing at all.

The Schönebeck Women and the Events of 17 June 1953

The events of 17 June 1953 are often described as an uprising against the SED and its government.[37] The SED, for its part, claimed the events were "the work of provocateurs and fascist agents of foreign powers and their accomplices in the German capitalist monopolies."[38] Either way, there was a huge outpouring of rage against the SED, caused by its dictatorial approach and repression and by the way day-to-day living conditions for ordinary people worsened after the decision in 1952 to build socialism. The conflict came to a head because the government could not fulfill its promise not to increase prices and because it raised the production "norms"—the targets that workers had to reach if they wanted to be paid a full salary—in an attempt to raise productivity. Additionally, the government announced that from 1 May ration cards would no longer be given to the class enemies: owners of private businesses, private sector professionals such as lawyers and accountants, property owners living mainly from rental income, and owners of derelict farms. This applied to their relatives as well, except for children under fifteen. The decision affected around two million people, among them a number of the Schönebeck women's families.

The Soviet authorities, seeing the increasing unrest in the GDR, put pressure on the SED leaders to slow down their efforts to build socialism and to stop their persecution of the churches and the "petty-bourgeois" sections of the population. On 9 June, the SED said it had made mistakes and announced a "New Course."[39] The price rises were to be reversed, ration cards would be returned, and confiscated property and full rights would be restored to people who had fled to the West and now came back. There would also be less pressure on private farmers, and credits would be available to encourage small businesses and small farmers. There would be more emphasis on the production of consumer goods and less on heavy industry. Travel between East and West for family members would be made easier. Discrimination on the grounds of religion would be stopped, and the prison population would be reduced. (It was not stated that this would be through the release of political prisoners, though that was what was meant.) Since they did not cancel the increases in the work norms, these changes were not enough to overcome the widespread frustration and anger. Strikes by building workers in Berlin—on the Stalinallee, the most prestigious construction project in the GDR—suddenly turned into strikes in many parts of the country, street demonstrations, and demands for the replacement of the government and an end to rule by the SED. A concession on the norms on the morning of 17 June came too late: across the GDR, demonstrators stormed buildings, tore down party flags, forced the release of prisoners, and threatened or attacked police and government ministers.

The SED and its government were saved by the intervention of the Soviet forces and their tanks. Around 125 people were killed (including seven police officers killed by demonstrators), and 368 seriously injured. Russian troops arrested three thousand people and the GDR authorities subsequently arrested thirteen thousand more. As an inner-party struggle took place, the SED leader Walter Ulbricht was saved by a shift in power in Moscow that brought the Soviet authorities down on his side.

After the events of 17 June, the SED strengthened its security apparatus and set up armed units of workers in factories in order to prevent such events ever happening again. Even so, it remained forever fearful of the workers and what they might do.[40] The general population, cowed by the Soviet intervention and the repression that followed, grew more resigned or found ways to leave the GDR.

In strictly economic terms, the party was correct to emphasize the need to raise productivity. Just as in a capitalist society, the GDR needed to accumulate capital to make improvements, and that meant producing more for the same wages. It was politically foolish of the SED, however, to think this could be done easily by raising the norms. After June 1953, the SED no longer felt able to argue that subsidizing goods and services or paying workers more than could be justified by levels of output would cause economic problems in the long run. There would, over the years, be constant emphasis on the need to raise productivity, but productivity would never reach the level needed to ensure a surplus was available to cover the cost of benefits provided to the population and to maintain investment in production.

Reunification in the 1950s?

The events of 1953 comprised the most dramatic episode in the GDR in the 1950s. What is curious is not just that they get so little mention in the *Rundbrief*, but also that several of the women, apparently deluded by their sense of ongoing personal connections between East and West, express the view in the 1950s that Germany could soon be reunited. Hilde Brenner (4 May 1952, writing from the West) writes as if what has happened since 1945 can be relatively easily sorted out: "Hopefully the day is no longer so far away when finally the borders will come down. Maybe my parents would go back to Schönebeck. After all, we still have our piece of land in Salzelmen, though unfortunately it has been taken over by someone else." Barbara Meier (27 June 1954, writing from the East) says with more ambiguity and less confidence about how soon changes will occur: "Before I end my epistle, I should like to address all of you who have been through hard times or still have to endure them: don't lose heart, keep yourselves strong. Some time there'll be a turnaround, and things will be good, or at least better in some way or other. That's how it has been for me in recent years."

Elfriede Berger (3 August 1955, Bergheim, near Cologne) asks the others, "Since at last there are serious hopes for reunification, could we not at short notice after it happens turn our intentions from 1950 into reality and all of us, from West and East, meet on the steps of the cathedral in Magdeburg?"

"Voluntary" Work

In the West, independent trade unions fought for shorter hours, better conditions, and higher pay for their members. This was not possible in the GDR, where the unions were not independent since, the SED declared, the workers already owned the means of production.

In the GDR, work was long, initially forty-eight hours a week spread over six days, and workers were hailed as heroes who embodied the values of the socialist society. These workers, it was declared, voluntarily turned up when their paid work was completed or during their holidays to ensure that reconstruction projects proceeded quickly and in a way that saved the state and its working people money.[41] Including free work in official calculations also made it look as though productivity was higher than it was in reality.

Supposedly voluntary work was a feature of the Schönebeck area, as it was elsewhere. Helping with the harvest was a recurring demand put upon local people. A report from summer 1953 for the Schönebeck area says that workers from the local explosives factory contributed 30,272 hours of voluntary labor in the fields over twenty-six days. This followed initial reluctance from some of the workers, but "after an in-depth discussion, it was possible to get widespread acceptance of the necessity of helping the agricultural workers."[42] Urban development also involved voluntary labor. A newspaper report in October 1954 discussed the building of 158 new houses in the Schönebeck area, as well as a whole new settlement with shops, a pharmacy, a nursery and a kindergarten. Progress was made possible by twenty thousand hours of voluntary labor by local people. As a result, there was a saving to the state of 17,000 Marks, which was used to fund a swimming pool.[43] Similarly, in 1956, a large new children's park and playing area was to be built, for which local people were willing to give thirty-five thousand hours of their time.[44]

For Gerda Höpfner and her husband in Schönebeck, the solution to their housing problem was to join a housing cooperative. Until their house is finished, Gerda says (8 December 1957), she has to work on a voluntary basis for four hours a day. She is happy to do so, but does not explain how she will combine this with working in the shoe factory and looking after her child. Of course, working like this was not unknown in the West either, particularly in the early 1950s: Irma Kindler described how she and her husband created their first home together out of the ruins of a building in Hanover. Nevertheless, the supposedly voluntary work in the GDR was not an example of self-help or spontaneous community building; it was an institutionalized way for the state to extract more labor from its population, and to do so without having to pay for it. In a state supposedly emancipating its citizens from the servitude of labor and allowing them time at last to fulfill themselves in line with Marxist theory, the result was a severe reduction in the time available for leisure and holidays, in contrast with conditions for many people in the West.

Pushed Out: Sabine Kleber

Clashing with the East German state, even at a very local level, could have long-term consequences. These highlighted the differences between East and West and made a mockery of the women's desire for unity. The case of Sabine Kleber is just one example of what was happening across the GDR in the 1950s.

Sabine Kleber became a teacher after the war and was soon teaching biology in Bitterfeld, noted for its highly polluting chemical industry, power station, and brown coal mining. In her letter of 6 November 1950, Sabine says she is off work with chronic hoarseness. Although she notes that Bitterfeld has "so much soot and grime" from the industry there, she does not make a connection between this and her health problems. On 31 October 1951, she says she is still in Bitterfeld, although the education authority had tried to transfer her to a village, where she would be for the rest of her career. "Thanks a lot for that!" she says. She managed to resist, since "the villages around here are dreadful, terribly isolated and without any decent train connections."

By 25 February 1956, Sabine is still teaching in Bitterfeld but would like to move, "since the town and its surroundings are really not attractive. The tiny bit of forest that we have is being swallowed up by the constantly spreading brown coal mines." In addition to teaching biology for twenty hours a week, she is also teaching literature, with a new writer to discuss every week: Grimmelshausen, Lessing, Shakespeare, Goethe, "and so on."

Suddenly, Sabine's next letter (7 January 1958) is from the West; she is now in Kaiserslautern in Rheinland-Pfalz, toward the French border. She alludes opaquely to the problems that caused her to leave, and is the first to openly refer to having to flee the GDR: "A year-long battle with a family of four (also teachers) gave me my first grey hairs.... After the trouble spread from where I was living to my work, it was clear I was going to have to leave. I went on a *Kur* [spa trip for health reasons], then fled across the border between the Zones and finished up, after a few places on the way, in Kaiserslautern." In Kaiserslautern she is being retrained to be able to teach in Rheinland-Pfalz. Then, she says, she will be "shipped off" to teach in some isolated village; her dread of the German village is a constant, in the West as in the East.

The Blindness of Power

In her first letter (27 June 1951), Gisela Riedel laughs about how they tormented some of their teachers at school and talks of the wonderfully carefree time she and Martha Jäger spent working in Weimar during the war. She wanted, like so many of the others, to do her *Reichsarbeitsdienst*, but, to her parents' relief, she was declared unfit because of a middle ear infection. She then had a long-lasting lung complaint, which forced her to endure many unpleasant times and procedures in a hospital. When she was well again, she became an apprentice in her father's pharmacy.

In the 1950s, the state set about taking over the pharmacies in the GDR, paying rent to the former owners and making the pharmacist a state employee. On the death of the pharmacist, his widow would be entitled to a large part of the higher pension that was given to people defined as members of the intelligentsia. The Riedels' pharmacy became a special case, however, as Gisela's father was already eighty when the pharmacy was due to be taken over. The officials responsible were hesitant about passing on special benefits to an old man who would die soon anyway, and whose pharmacy hardly made a profit. For the ministry in Berlin, however, the policy allowed for no exceptions, so the change of ownership took place in May 1960. Gisela's father died a year later. Gisela's mother, who otherwise would have had nothing but the rent from the pharmacy premises to live on, received the widow's portion of the intelligentsia pension.[45]

The photo Gisela chooses to accompany her first letter shows her standing smiling as she leans against a wall; behind her at a higher level, on the other side of a pit, stands a large black bear. Her note says this is Leipzig Zoo, 1949. In the context of her family's struggle with the new authorities, it is difficult not to see the photo as a reference, however unconscious, to the Russian bear and other Soviet imagery, and perhaps also to Nazi propaganda about the Soviet Union.

Role Models and the Principal Stories

One way the Schönebeck women held themselves together was to give some members the status of role models for the whole group. Since the role models were in both the East and the West, it was possible to admire achievements in the GDR just as much as those in the FRG. This helped to strengthen the myth that the unity of the group reflected the unity of Germany as a whole.

Comments in the letters point to an accepted view that several of the Schönebeck women were such role models, to be admired for what they were doing in their jobs and for demonstrating what women could achieve. In talking of their role models the women suggest, at least implicitly, that they do understand the restrictions men put upon them and are proud of those in their group who ignore them. At the same time, their comments sometimes convey a sense of frustration, envy, and even disapproval, as if they are forced to recognize their own choices, their own more limited achievements, and the way they have internalized male attitudes. The most prominent of the role models are Anna Siebert, Else Hermann, Leni Baumann, and Anni Lange, the opera singer. To these can be added Hertha Pieper, who is recognized for her warmth and emotional generosity; Irma Kindler, who is the only one from the West who almost always attends the reunions in the GDR, and therefore acts as a bridge between East and West; and Marianne Schneider, whose story is told elsewhere.

Anna Siebert

Anna Siebert's achievements and constant promotion in a man's world astonish them all. Addressing Anna on 10 July 1960, Elfriede Berger says, "Along with Anni Lange, Else Hermann and Leni etc., you have the most interesting profession. I often regret that I didn't study law, but really you never can know what the line of work will turn out to be for the man you get tied up with." Elfriede's husband is a successful, wealthy lawyer and she is now working part time in his offices. In an earlier letter (19 March 1951), she had mentioned that she dreamed of becoming a doctor, but gave up her dream when she got married. She often goes to court and enjoys it a lot, she says; the regret and wistfulness suggest that she envies Anna and the others who are so successful in their own right outside the home.

Anna Siebert followed the path her father had chosen for her, to become a civil engineer. It soon became her own path, and she was glad to be on it. After finishing her studies in Berlin, she undertook a number of professional courses. She got her first job, with the harbor authority in Hamburg, at a time when the authority was rapidly rebuilding and expanding its facilities after the war. In December 1953, she married a fellow engineer, six years older, who had fought on the Eastern Front, been taken prisoner in Bohemia, and spent four years in a prisoner-of-war camp in Siberia.

At the time of the class reunion in 1955, Anna is in the middle of her last exams, which will finally give her all the professional qualifications she needs. She apologizes (5 May 1955) for not being able to attend. On 2 December

1956, Anna pastes into the book a photo of herself and a brief description from *Die Welt* of her achievements in becoming the first fully qualified female civil engineer in Germany (by which is meant West Germany). She does her best to play down her achievements: "Attached is a picture of me out of the newspaper. Yes, I know, it makes me look dreadfully self-important, doesn't it? But that's not how it is, as there's nothing worse than having to appear in the paper like that, since you see yourself as completely stupid." Anna also tells them that, not having managed to have a baby, she is sometimes sad when she sees others with their babies. She also feels a sense of melancholy when she realizes that she would have to give up her beloved job if she did have a baby, since combining the two is so difficult to manage.

In her next letter (12 October 1957), Anna writes from a sanatorium, since working too hard has made her ill. She needs to learn to rest and take care of herself again, she says. She is enjoying herself in the beautiful countryside: relaxing, reading, bathing, and having massages for five weeks.

By 1960, Anna says (10 May) she has now achieved the professional status of a *Baurätin*: "that means, a permanent civil servant with entitlement to a pension." She is not planning to work until she is old, she tells them, but will certainly be there for a few more years as she enjoys it so much. She is now in the external works department of the harbor authority, heading four harbor districts and responsible for all the infrastructure and associated works, managing sixty skilled workers and eight civil engineers. She is out and about a lot, often by boat. The work is often hard, sometimes because there are still a lot of men who cannot cope with women working in technical areas and having an opinion of their own. They try to catch you out, so you always have to be on your guard, she says. It is possible to see in Anna's description here and in many subsequent letters her constant struggle to prove herself to men and to avoid being humiliated by them.

Irma Kindler

In the early 1950s, Irma Kindler is still living in Hanover and enjoying her varied and interesting job as an interpreter. By 1952, she is adding French to her repertoire. From her letter of 31 May 1953, it is clear that some of the GDR's problems are also problems in the West. In particular, the shortage of housing makes Irma's working life much more complicated. Her husband Franz has finished his training and will have a job in Hamburg from 1 June, but they cannot find anywhere for them both to live. Franz will move to Hamburg and she will carry on working, based in Hanover, instead of stopping in the autumn as they had planned.

However, Irma's letter also shows the possibilities that living in the West opens up. She entered and won a competition run by the Rank Organisation, the British film company, which involved devising a new ending for a film. The prize was a trip to England, with three days in London—the one place she had always longed to see—along with visits to film studios, cinemas, film premieres, and discussions with prominent actors and directors.

Irma's letter of 1 May 1955 says she is now living with Franz in a nice apartment they found in Hamburg at the end of 1953. In her new job she is responsible for foreign correspondence in one of Hamburg's import-export firms. How wonderful it is to get to know such a huge city, a gateway to the world, she says, noting that "after all, we're from the provinces."

By 1956, Irma and Franz have a son and Irma stops working. Two years later they have a daughter. In her letter of 6 April 1958, she compares the custom in the West of women staying home with their children with the tendency in the GDR for women to continue going out to work after having children. For women at home with children, she says,

> there is nothing left for us except to bask in the fame of our menfolk and to see our children as our collected works. Will our time come again, perhaps? But who would like to exchange the one for the other? To do both would be good, for sure, but if we can only have one, then let's take what is more natural: family and children, even when that inevitably comes with its share of work and worries.

In the group, Irma is admired for several reasons. First, like Marianne, she is full of energy and enthusiasm, and capable of doing so much that many of them would never dare to do. Her transformation of herself into a translator and interpreter for the British after the war is one example, along with her willingness to put herself in danger to come and visit them in Schönebeck. More important, however, is her commitment to ensuring the group always sees itself as a group that cannot be divided by the inner-German border, and to getting to the reunions in the East on almost every occasion. Like Marianne Schneider, she addresses many of them personally in her letters. At the reunion, she takes on the job of class photographer and includes photos in the *Rundbrief* so that those who were not there can get a sense of the event. In 1960, she does something that astonishes those in the East: produces the photos in color, giving them an altogether different image of themselves, one not otherwise available in the GDR.[46] It is Irma's role as cheerful, uncomplaining unifier of the group that is most important to the rest of the women.

Anni Lange

The other role model from the West is Anni Lange. She is rarely at the reunions, writes very little, and does not comment directly on her performances. Sometimes she appears at a mini-reunion for those living in or near Hamburg, but leaves early for rehearsals or performances. She is often away performing, in Bayreuth, for instance, or at the summer opera festival in Eutin (north of Lübeck), where she had twelve nights as a soloist, as well as in Berlin, Bergen, and Copenhagen. Nevertheless, Anni Lange is a significant presence, frequently referred to by the others. They love hearing tapes of her singing if they have a chance; Irma Kindler, at least, attends her performances in Hamburg; and they comment on her touring to places they would love to visit. There are occasional asides from Else Hermann in the theater to Anni in the opera; they sense they are kindred spirits operating in the same sphere, despite one being in the West and one in the East.

Anni Lange also helps to drag the group away from their conservative, puritanical attitudes. They accept this from her because she is the wild, free artist, throwing herself out into a world they do not share but find fascinating all the same. Anni's photo of herself as the waitress Jette in Carl Zeller's operetta, *Der Vogelhändler*, is deliberately provocative.[47] The five men in the picture are all gazing straight at her. The one sitting at the end of the table, a noble of some sort, is looking expectantly with twinkling eyes and pursed mouth and holding a bottle pointed toward her in his right hand, while tickling her chin with his left hand. Anni is smiling or singing, leaning slightly toward him, and has her hand around the neck of the very phallic bottle. This is who I am, this is what I do, she seems to be declaring to the rest of the Schönebeck women. Suddenly we are a long way from the Schönebeck of their childhood under the Nazis.

Else Hermann

In the 1950s, Else Hermann achieved what she had most wanted: a career in the theater. Throughout her letters in this decade, work and the people she works with are at the center of her life. She is not unaware of the political problems around her, but they rarely impinge on her. Of more significance is cultural development in the GDR, and her part in it. Even when there is a struggle between the theater and the state, she finds this curious, rather than threatening, and the idea of going to the West does not interest her.

In her letter of 27 November 1950, Else tells them she is studying at the specialist school for higher-level skills in fashion design in Weimar:

> I've already been in Weimar for three semesters now, and I really love it here. After the fourth semester, probably in July 1951, I'll be doing my final exams to become a master designer.... What I would most like to do is to become a fashion reporter, writing articles for a publishing house. But my secret desire is to be the master designer in the costume and outfitting department of a theater. We'll see! The school here is very good and I have already learned a lot. The highly varied program requires a wide range of work in every different discipline. These are some of the things we have to do: practical activities, fashion drawing, nude drawing, freehand drawing, pattern making, the theory of color, art history, cos-

tume history, calligraphy, perspective, anatomy, German correspondence, calculation, social sciences and contemporary social studies. To that they are planning to add Russian. Many evenings we are up studying until midnight, after eight hours of teaching. But on top of that we have a lot of fun. There are six of us in the third semester, all women, and we get along famously.

In one of her interviews, Else made a point of telling me that in Weimar she met Christof Grüger, an artist from Schönebeck, who was working with wonderful colors in glass, and with textiles, using wax, following the Balinese batik techniques. He would later make his living working on church windows across the GDR as well as a number in the FRG. He also worked on public buildings in the GDR. She showed me proudly a beautiful shawl he had made her.

Else's identification with Grüger is significant: she saw herself and Grüger as two young artists from Schönebeck who loved being in Weimar, the center of the world as far as she was concerned. During the war, the sculptor and painter Katharina Heise had returned from her bombed-out studio in Berlin to her family home in Schönebeck. After the war, other artists formed a group around her, the Schönebeck Circle. Christof Grüger was part of this group, and Else, through him, identified herself with it. It was important for her that Schönebeck should be seen as a center of creativity, not just as an industrial town being developed in the image of the SED. For this reason, she also identified with the GDR novelist Erik Neutsch, who was born in Schönebeck in 1931 and wrote about Schönebeck and the surrounding area in his four-volume *Der Friede im Osten*.[48]

A year later (26 November 1951), Else is writing from Plauen, at the foot of the Erzgebirge. She moved there to attend the school for the development of textiles but was disappointed to find it still being set up. Instead, she has taken a job in a firm making women's clothes, where the work is enjoyable. She is pleased to be making money at last but has mixed feelings about Plauen: "Plauen was badly damaged by bombing, though I am already used to that from Magdeburg. The truly magical surroundings make up for it, however.... Culturally, there is naturally not so much going on as in Weimar, not by a long way. The theater is a bit of an old barn." It will do her for a while, but Plauen will not be the last place she ends up, she says; it is time to gain some experience, above all in her profession.

In the important year of 1953, Else is still in Plauen and has been given further responsibilities. She is overwhelmed and exhausted by the experience of having a collection of clothes designed by her on display at the Leipziger Messe, the famous international trade fair. This was the one place in the GDR where people could see both what the GDR had to offer and what was being produced in Western countries. So great was the strain that she has had to rest for six weeks afterwards. To balance her work, she often goes walking or climbing in the wonderful area around Plauen. She is also starting to paint and would like more lessons in drawing and painting.

Else's letter of 11 July 1954 shows she has finally got where she wanted to:

> What a joy it was to receive our beloved *Rundbrief*. It came at exactly the right time, as I have news for you: since 15 June 1954, I have found my way into the theater! No, not as a clown (which would also be appropriate for me) but as costume designer and head of the design department. After so long, my dearest wish has been fulfilled.
>
> I only ever saw making clothes as an interim stage. I was able to learn a lot there, but for a year or so I was looking around for a way out. Since they decided the whole process was to be approached "scientifically," the work gradually became unbearable. The scientific approach brought with it the requirement to fill out three sides of A4 with countless columns for every model we designed!! Around Christmas I heard that they were looking for a costume designer in Brandenburg and I applied at once. I had a discussion with the theater manager and the set designer, and a few days later a telegram arrived: perfect match, contract follows.
>
> I gave in my notice at once and came back home to have some peace and quiet to prepare for my new career. I worked for three months in the Magdeburg theater and was allowed to design and make the costumes for Lessing's *Der junge Gelehrte* all on my own. Then I had to go to Brandenburg and take over everything that was there from my predecessor. I already have somewhere to live too.

On 15 March 1956, Else returns to the much-discussed topic of marriage. Her work has given her confidence, and she responds firmly to the recurring hints from the others: "Get married? No—I'm already too old for that." She was about to turn twenty-nine. She also swamps them with a long list of the productions she has worked on in the theater in Brandenburg, from Mozart to Schiller, to Verdi, as well as *Bunbury*, the German title for Oscar Wilde's *The Importance of Being Earnest*. She is enjoying the work and the challenge of her surroundings:

> We work damned hard here. My fellow workers "on the shop floor" are just as good and just as bad as any others; they get up to just as much—perhaps with a little more grace—as those living a so-called bourgeois life, that's all! . . . There is no such thing as private life in the theater; you have to throw yourself and your whole being into the task at hand, often to the point of physical exhaustion. But a successful premiere makes you forget all the effort and is the most wonderful reward.

In an aside, Else reveals more about herself when she declares that it is much easier to dress women than men: "I have ascertained that men are more difficult to satisfy than women; men can never be beautiful enough!"

Figure 2.3. Else in the directors' collective preparing for *Martha*. Photo courtesy of Akademie der Künste, Berlin.

The photo Else chooses to illustrate her work in Brandbenburg puts the emphasis on the collective she is part of (figure 2.3). However, the photo is composed to put her at the center, with the men grouped around her. Ironically, this follows the same model or set of stereotypes as the earlier photo from the West of Anni Lange in her opera. The difference is the earnestness of all involved: there is to be no frivolity here, no demonstration of sensuality, no sexual innuendo; this is serious art, demonstrating the seriousness of the theater in the GDR and the importance of collective effort to open it up to the people. The choice of the romantic opera *Martha* somewhat contradicts these implied assertions.

In letter after letter, Else makes little or no direct reference to the political context of her work; her enjoyment of what she is doing overrides everything else. To be allowed to go to the Leipziger Messe was a privilege given only to those seen to be committed to the state's approach; for her it is nothing but an important and prestigious professional achievement, so exhausting it needs to be walked off in the mountains. In 2013, Else mentioned that during her time in Brandenburg, she had several offers of theater jobs in the West. It would have been easy to accept one, she said, but she chose not to because her life—the life she wanted to lead—was in the GDR, and because her family was there.

In her next letter (31 May 1958), Else is writing from Erfurt. Here she has been caught up in the politics of the time whether she wanted to or not:

> For a year now, I have been the costume designer of the city theater in Erfurt. This is a category 1 theater (Brandenburg was category 3). It has been a good but difficult year. In terms of artistic creativity, it's been a great leap forward and it's great the way my theater colleagues and directors and I all work together. But there were difficulties at the beginning with the tailoring workshops. Conditions there were simply chaotic. It would take too long to give you a picture of that, but it was all to do with the sudden exit of the men's wardrobe director. In order to rescue the premiere, I had to jump into the breach, although I have little idea about men's tailoring. It was very taxing, but we did it. On 1 December I was released from this position I didn't want to be occupying and could breathe a sigh of relief. The theater management were very nice and sent me for two weeks to a trade union holiday home near Meuselbach in the Thüringer Wald. There in the sunshine and snow I could recover and return to being human again.

The key to this letter is in the words "sudden exit of the men's wardrobe director." Else cannot spell it out, but the implication is that the wardrobe director escaped to the West. She confirmed this interpretation in an interview. This was a widespread problem at the time in the GDR in any occupation, theater, factory, school, hospital, or local authority: with no notice, key workers would simply disappear, having gone to the West, yet the work had to go on.

Else also gives a good picture of everyday life for a woman in her position. She is enjoying Erfurt, which is sprucing itself up for the international flower exhibition in 1960. Would any of them like to come when that is on, she asks. She could put them up since has her own apartment now, and how wonderful it is "when you no longer have to get upset by the oddities of landladies and their often even odder furniture and pictures." She has managed to get furniture of her own and finally some curtains. She has a tiny built-in kitchen so feels a moral obligation to cook, which she has rarely done before because of the landladies. Her father's 1910 student cookbook is standing her in good stead, she says. However, Else is used to having work and life outside work feeding off each other. She regrets that the people in the theater in Erfurt are not so interesting, whereas "In Brandenburg it was different—like a large family." Without them, she feels more on her own, but is still single and happy to be so, she assures them.

When she writes on 5 March 1960, Else is near the end of her third year in Erfurt. She has signed up for a fourth year, then will need a change of scenery, she says. All is going well, with many successful theatrical performances, covering historically important moments and places. Describing these, she cannot avoid a reference to the GDR's travel restrictions: "We are always charging along through the history of the world: 1830, 1945, 1890, 1750, China, France and so on. What you have at least in part seen with your own eyes—I mean, foreign countries—I can only conjure up in my imagination and try to bring to life on the stage."

After five years in the theater, Else has done all the designing and fitting out for over a hundred productions, of which only three have been repeats. She is ecstatic over the variety of her working life. At a more prosaic level, she says she has moved on from the 1910 cookbook and is inventing things that have never made it into print. "Should I," she wonders, "maybe write a cookbook for women on their own?"

While in Erfurt, Else was invited to Berlin to help turn a play into a television film. She was given a room in the Adlon Hotel near the Brandenburg Gate and treated as a VIP. She does not seem overwhelmed by this, however; nor does she see herself as being in a privileged position. The whole process was different but interesting, she says, and hopefully another opportunity will come out of it for her. Once again, it is the work that gets her attention, not the political or social context that has made it possible.

Hertha Pieper

Hertha Pieper is mostly cheerful and energetic and helps to hold the women in the East together. It is more difficult to remain optimistic, however, in the face of constant pressure on independent farmers. In the 1950s, she lived through a whole chapter in the tortuous story of agriculture in the GDR.

Hertha and the Collectivization of Agriculture

By the time of the SED's Second Party Conference in July 1952, which declared that the task of the whole country was to build socialism, Hertha had already been complaining about the pressure being put on them. Independent farmers were constantly required to produce more but were denied access to or were charged more for the state-owned tractors and farm equipment intended to be used by state-owned farms. Hertha's farm had its own equipment, but still found the production demands hard to meet. The Second Party Conference decided to promote agricultural cooperatives, having previously opposed them.[49] Cooperatives were to be formed on a voluntary basis, but it was clear at once that the new policy was part of a political shift toward the collectivization of agricultural land, and that sooner or later it would be made impossible for farmers to operate independently.[50] Although Hertha's 1952 letter (1 February) preceded the party conference, the problems facing small farmers were clear for all to see, along with an awareness that complaining might only make things worse (which does not entirely stop her complaining):

What's new that I can tell you about? Little that's new has happened, and certainly nothing good. If I didn't get on so well with my "old man" and we didn't get such joy out of our children, then sometimes things would just be unbearable.

You know that we run a farm and that we have fifteen hectares. That is not a lot, but when you have to do everything—everything—on your own, with all the animals as well, then you get no pleasure out of it. At five in the morning I'm already in the cowshed and by ten at night I'm still not finished with patching and darning—and doing all the counting up. But all our work would not be so bad, if they weren't trying still to put a noose around our necks.

Still, I'll sing no song of woe here, for who might hear it? But if there is never, never, a moment's let-up, never something to look forward to, then it's impossible to see things differently.

Following the Second Party Conference, many small farmers abandoned their land and went to the West. After the end of the events of 17 June 1953 in the cities and towns, unrest carried on in the countryside. There were over five thousand LPGs (agricultural cooperatives) at the time, and more than five hundred of them dissolved themselves; in terms of members, around 22 percent left the LPGs.[51] By 1956, around a million hectares or 16 percent of agricultural land was not being farmed. This land was meant to be given to local LPGs, but they were so short of leaders, workers, machines, and spare parts that most could not accept more land.[52]

Attempts to solve this problem were focused on the "Schönebeck method," developed at a Machine and Tractor Station (MTS) in Schönebeck. The purpose of an MTS was to concentrate agricultural machinery at a central depot and send it, with skilled operators, out to the LPGs whenever it was needed. The MTS Schönebeck Nord observed that if the LPGs implemented the most advanced methods of agriculture and refined their way of using the MTS, the harvest would increase dramatically. For this to work, they said, each MTS had to have its own agitator, an agricultural expert who was also a political expert, so that LPGs would understand what they had to do and why it was so important. The SED decided that every MTS should introduce the Schönebeck Method, and heavily promoted it.[53] Little was gained and the term was quietly dropped, so ending Schönebeck's brief period of national fame.

In November 1956, with problems in the LPGs continuing, one of the SED's agricultural experts, Kurt Viewig, recommended softening the policies and allowing LPGs and private farms to operate side by side. Compulsion and norms for deliveries should be discontinued and single price levels introduced. Viewig was arrested and sentenced to twelve years in prison, making it clear that no criticism of the party's policies would be tolerated. (Viewig was released after six years and became a Stasi informer as well as a professor in Greifswald.)[54]

The SED continually sought to persuade the population that its policies were successful and that everyone must follow them. In April and May 1956, *Neues Deutschland* sent a team of reporters to Schönebeck and published twenty-two daily articles under the heading "A Schönebeck Diary." One of these looks at the behavior of individual farmers who, it says, produce what they have to but have no sense of what the republic as a whole needs from them; they have not made the necessary cultural shift toward a collective outlook. For this it blames local officials.[55]

Another article in the series looks at the role and position of women, particularly those working in agriculture. The night before an important day of planting turnips, says a woman working for an LPG, she has the household to organize: the potatoes for the next day have been peeled, and the children's dinner prepared. It is a good, if unintended, demonstration of the expectation that women will continue to do everything, while the men simply go out to work. When it rains and the work is delayed, the reporter notes patronizingly that there is now time to do some knitting—and to think about how the society and the lives of women are being transformed. The reporter cannot help noting, however, that in the Schönebeck area there are very few women in positions of leadership,[56] and in the LPGs a tiny proportion, even though around half the workers are women. Where there is a woman on the management board, she says, it is often as an afterthought. Despite that, she is impressed by the women's strength and determination, and concludes with one of the rare calls to men to change their attitudes: "We should all—above all, the men too—work more effectively to ensure that the women in our Republic make it into the positions they are entitled to."[57]

By 1957, the promise of more pressure on individual farmers has become a reality for Hertha's family. However, she and her husband are still working hard and independently on their farm and greatly enjoying their three children (see figure 2.4).

> Our children are blossoming. I'll introduce them to you in turn. Elka is already very sensible, now eight years old. She is well-behaved and hard-working. (Clearly doesn't take after her mother.) But maybe Wilfried does! He is seven and has mastered all our vehicles from the pushcart to the tractor! He does some mad things. Recently he raided the sparrows' nests and put the poor sparrows in the letter boxes all around our area. Klaus has often been ill and a bit of a mummy's boy up to now. But Wilfried is a good model for him and he is starting to grow up very nicely.[58]

She says (28 August 1957) that their work is made more difficult, however, by the political developments around them: "We have so much work and no one to give us any help. Despite that, our aim is to constantly improve the farm.

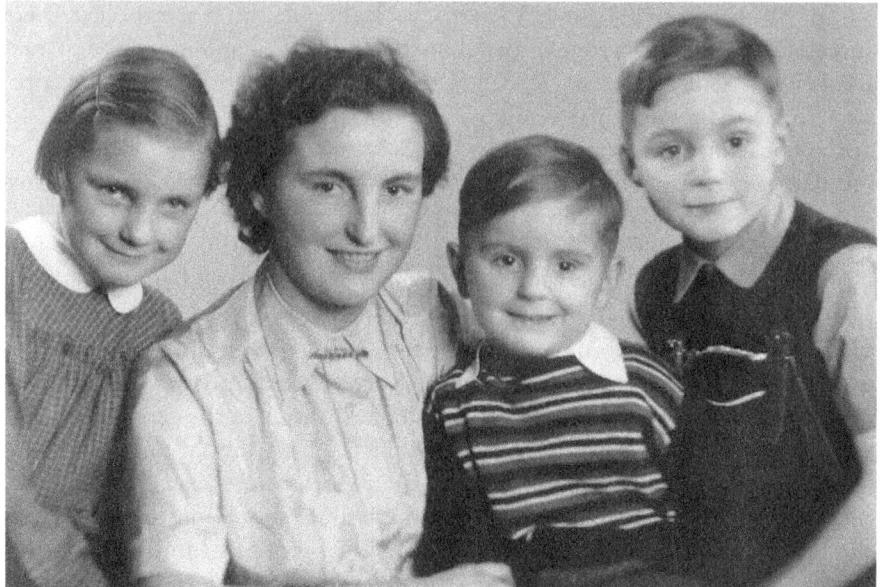

Figure 2.4. Hertha and her children, 1957. Photo courtesy of Akademie der Künste, Berlin.

We are not short of anything, and "certain people" have already cast their eye over us and sought to tell us what to do. However, our motto is to hold out stubbornly against any exercise of power against us."

In 1959, the SED decided that its program of building socialism would be extended to "the building of socialism on the land," a policy change intended to complete the collectivization of agriculture. Not surprisingly, Hertha's next letter (15 January 1960) has a resigned air to it: "You all know how things are for us farmers. We are all slowly heading toward the cooperative, and that's what will be in store for us this year." There is so much work to be done, and only the two of them to do it. Despite this, the children are healthy and growing up wonderfully, she says.

Hertha Pieper's story up to this point is dominated by her concerns over the farm and the political pressure she and her husband have to endure. A curiously different picture emerges from the letters of Carla Brunner. She and her husband have a farm adjoining the Elbe. Her letters stress how happy she is with her life there, their work on the farm, and her husband and children. The only mention of contact with outside institutions is a favorable one in her letter of 8 June 1958: on a hot, humid July day in 1957, their cowshed was struck by lightning. Thanks to the local fire brigade, the fire did not spread beyond the cowshed. On 29 January 1960, she makes no mention of pressure to join the LPG but reports on a benefit the state has brought them: "For a full year now, we have been able to watch television, which for us, in our isolated position, really means a lot."[59]

Collectivization and Its Consequences

In January 1960, starting in Rostock and moving across the whole country under the banner of the *sozialistische Frühling* (socialist spring), party agitators set out to convince around 400,000 individual farmowners of the need to collectivize the remaining 56.5 percent of the GDR's agricultural land. Those who continued to resist were labeled class enemies, publicly defamed, threatened, and arbitrarily arrested. Many left for the West, 12,634 with their families in the first three months of 1960. Some committed suicide.[60]

Even when farmers formally joined the LPGs, passive resistance often continued. At times, Schöne demonstrates, there was active resistance, with the value of damage up by a quarter in the first three months of 1960 compared with the same period the previous year: fires were lit, LPG machinery and equipment were destroyed, markings showing where fields had been consolidated were sabotaged, and there was a large increase in the number of cattle sent for rendering. Despite this, the process of collectivization was declared finished by 25 April 1960.

By the middle of 1960, there was a severe drop in production, and it was no longer possible to meet export commitments. Soon there were shortages of vegetables in the GDR, while fresh fruit was no longer for sale. Many people spent as little time as possible on LPG work and as much as possible cultivating their own residual plots (up to half a hectare for each household) and looking after the limited number of animals they were allowed. Productivity was much higher here.

The SED both recognized and denied the problems of food production at this time. A newspaper report in April 1961 on the two LPGs in Barby, near Schönebeck, sets out in detail the problems of poor discipline, workers not turning up, and key workers objecting to policies decided on by managers. The most expert milker, for instance, could not face the prospect of having some of "his" cows slaughtered; he was found sitting in the bar, drinking, and refused to return to his job. Ironically, when he was put back into his job after admitting his faults and doing his penance by working in the fields, a more principled worker refused to work with him, and so the problems continued.[61] By contrast, a report on the harvest around Schönebeck in summer 1960 says that six thousand volunteers helped to bring it to a successful conclusion, making clear that the LPGs lacked the capacity to do this.[62] Similarly, a report says that the workers of the gelatine works in Calbe carried out an average of eleven and a half hours of free work bringing in the harvest.[63]

110 *Friendship without Borders*

It took from 1952 to 1960 to collectivize agriculture in the GDR. By May 1961 there were 19,345 cooperatives covering 5.4 million hectares. There were 945,020 members, of whom two-thirds were people who had only become farmers through the land reform of 1945. One curiosity in the GDR, in contrast to collectivization in the Soviet Union, was that when people put their land and buildings into the LPG, they continued technically to own them, but the LPG had rights of use, including the right to put new buildings on the land.[64] Not surprisingly, the complications this might cause if the regime ever came to an end were not foreseen.

Leni Baumann

While Else Hermann's entry into the world of the theater has given her a fascinating life in the GDR, life has not been so straightforward for one of the other role models in the East, Leni Baumann.

In her letter of 5 April 1955, Leni says she is still teaching at the university in Halle. Like all the others where the new faculties were put in place in 1945, it has been turned upside down by a huge restructuring. Nevertheless, she is in a good mood and getting ready to start on her doctorate, so that they will be less able to push her around. She is proud of an article she has recently had published in an academic journal. In 1956 (writing on 10 April), she is still in Halle, working on her doctoral dissertation as well as writing a book. She is highly enthusiastic about her work on family pedagogy. By 1957, she is being ground down by conditions at the university and often asks herself "how much longer?" She does not go into detail about her difficulties but refers to someone, apparently her superior, as "der Dickschädel," the pigheaded one, who is becoming ever more pigheaded.[65]

Suddenly, on 10 July 1959, we hear from Marianne Schneider in her summary of events that Leni is now in Kiel, in the West. "Well, Elena-Luise (or may we still call you Leni, despite your resettlement?), are you aware of the loss the GDR has suffered through your relocation? We have made a note here of this affair!"[66] The ironic tone is clear, but there are other noteworthy points here too. Marianne uses the GDR's preferred word for a refugee, referring, to Leni's "Umsiedlung" or resettlement, as if her move was voluntary. In fact, to leave the GDR without permission—as Leni apparently did—was a crime, and the punishment could be severe. Marianne suggests that Leni's departure is a loss to the GDR as well as to the rest of the women still living there. This will be noted, she implies, not just by the group but also by the GDR authorities. There is also melancholy in the comment, since Leni will not be permitted to return to visit them or attend their reunions.

Leni's mood is quite different: she is overjoyed to be in the West, referring to the move as her "change of climate." She explains what happened: "Where I was working before, they simply threw me out, without even a chance for a final dotting of the '*i*'s and crossing of the '*t*'s!" She shed a few tears but now has no regrets. She had an offer of a good job in Düsseldorf, and then an opportunity to study sociology and do her doctorate in Kiel. Turning the GDR's ideology on its head, she says on 20 June 1960, "And there idealism conquered materialism: I said no to Düsseldorf and headed for Kiel. You just can't imagine how happy I am. . . . Do you know what's so great? Here you can read everything that you want!"

Travel, Holidays, Leisure

Between Desire and Reality

When the Schönebeck women were still girls at school, leisure and holidays meant escaping the clutches of their parents through school and BDM activities. During the early years of the war, it was evacuation to places such as Wernigerode that gave them excitement away from home. Later in the war, they experienced other parts of Germany and what had been Poland and Czechoslovakia during their *Reichsarbeitsdienst*. Travel, for some of them, had a surprising sense of indulgence, combined with blindness to what was happening around them. Sabine Kleber's observations about the pleasure of being in Poland, and Elfriede Berger's delight at her visits to Prague in late 1944 have already been noted. Martha Jäger and Gisela Riedel loved the time they spent in Weimar during the war, at the commercial college. Martha (21 June 1951) refers cheerfully to "the pranks we got up to!"

For many, however, travel at the end of the war meant long and dangerous journeys in terrible conditions just to get home: Irma Kindler leaving her camp in the Province of Hanover; Else Hermann cycling from the Erzgebirge to Schönebeck; Marianne Schneider, Elfriede Berger, and several others joining the rush to leave Upper Silesia and Bohemia and make their way back home through the Erzgebirge. Marianne recalls this vividly, more than twenty years later, in an aside to her letter of 3 January 1968: "(Can you still recall, dear Käthe Sommer, how we spent the night of 7 to 8 May in Karlsbad? I had battled to get a spot on the radiator of one of our army's vehicles, since there it was at least a bit warm. But enough of the past!)" What becomes clear is that Marianne and some of the others had already enjoyed a holiday in the Sudetenland in 1943, apparently on a school trip.

In the early years after the war, despite the problems throughout Germany of getting enough to eat, staying warm, and having somewhere to live in the ruined cities and overcrowded towns, there is still a certain restlessness among the women, and a desire to see the world. Elly Haase's two trips by rail around

Germany in the late 1940s are the most surprising example of desire turning into action.

In the 1950s, it becomes clear how important it is for the women to have time to travel and to enjoy holidays away from where they live. Marianne Schneider has a walking holiday with her husband in Thuringia in 1950. Else Hermann is entranced by Weimar and, when she moves on from there, explores the forests and mountains around Plauen. In 1955, Lisa Liebmann pastes in a photo of her winter sports holiday in Friedrichsbrunn in the Harz, with an extravagant caption (figure 2.5).

It is at this point that the differences between East and West become more obvious in the letters. Throughout the 1950s, it became ever easier for the women in the West to travel widely, and ever harder for those in the East.

The GDR was threatened economically, socially, and politically by the reluctance of many people to stay and help rebuild their part of Germany. The 1952 decision to push ahead with the building of socialism caused even more people to leave for the West. Ever-tighter controls over the inner-German border were put in place, and people living close to it were forcibly removed.[67] It became increasingly difficult for people from the GDR to get permission to travel to the West, even to see family members. This effectively confined their travel and holidays to the territory of the GDR itself. Gisela Riedel, qui-

Figure 2.5. Lisa Liebmann: "Wow, that was just fabulous!" Photo courtesy of Akademie der Künste, Berlin.

etly working away in her father's pharmacy and saying little enough about the world around her, cannot hold back from commenting in her letter of 20 February 1954:

> Before I finish my letter, I would just like to say to those in the West: do make sure you fully, consciously, enjoy the travels you get to undertake. I think you don't know—you really don't know—how well off you are in this respect. We here keep on patiently and persistently with our visits to the Harz, Thuringia, and—if we're lucky—the Baltic. Naturally this is *only* because we are fully conscious that one can never adequately know one's own homeland!

The events of 17 June 1953 were followed by a limited relaxation of the controls, and some of the women were allowed to travel to the West. In 1954, Martha Jäger traveled to the Saar region for three weeks with her sister. In 1956, Lisa Liebmann and her husband traveled with friends who had a car to the Federal Republic and, more surprisingly, to Austria, Liechtenstein, and Switzerland. A year later, Lisa Liebmann had a GDR holiday on the island of Usedom in the Baltic Sea, then a short visit to the FRG to visit her father in Aachen; she regretted (16 December 1957) not being able to visit the Schönebeck women in the West, but hoped to do so in 1958. As it happened, Lisa was not able to make this planned visit.

Despite the closure of the border and the establishment of border areas as prohibited zones, many people continued to find a way across from the GDR to the West. The GDR authorities responded in December 1957 with a new law that limited the allocation of visas, increased the penalty for leaving the GDR illegally to three years in prison, and made it a criminal offence to prepare to leave the GDR illegally or to help someone to do so.[68] The SED argued that the new approach was not directed against the citizens of the GDR but against the "rat-catchers" in the West who maliciously and as part of their Cold War tactics sought to get people to move there through a modern form of "people trafficking."[69] The new law reduced the numbers going to the West by around 40 percent, although the border remained permeable for those willing to take the risk of being caught. One of the Schönebeck women directly affected by the changes was Frieda Möller, from Barby. She says in her letter of 8 July 1958 that they were planning to visit her parents-in-law in the West but were prevented by the new law.

During this period there was a slow drift away from the GDR to the West among the Schönebeck women. By the start of Book 6 on 20 July 1957, fourteen of the thirty-two women whose addresses were listed were in the West (see figure 2.6). By the start of Book 7 on 10 July 1959, seventeen were in the West, and only fifteen in the East.

Those in the East still longed to travel beyond the GDR's borders. Before her move to the West, Sabine Kleber says how much she enjoys being in Schierke,

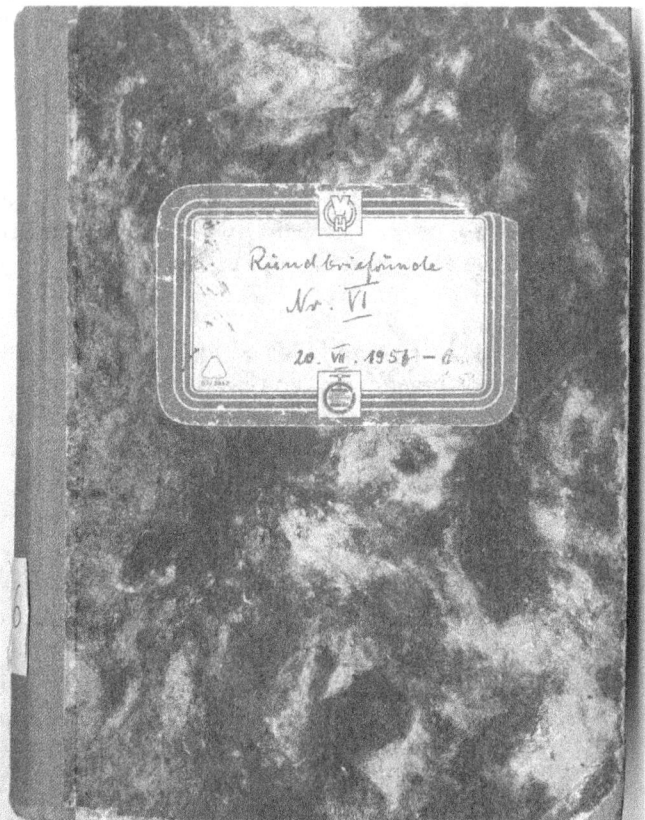

Figure 2.6. The sixth book. Photo courtesy of Akademie der Künste, Berlin.

in the Harz, for the winter sports, and her visits to Quedlinburg, Dresden, and the Baltic coast, but makes clear her deep desire to be able to go further.[70]

The accounts from the West show them what they are missing: more frequent and longer holidays, often much further afield. In 1953, Irma Kindler writes of winning her trip to England and talks enthusiastically of her time there. Later in the year (10 October), Hilde Brenner says she has been spending time in Switzerland and will probably be going to England. On 18 December 1955, she says she is back home after eight months of living with a family there and working on her English.

On 3 August 1955, Elfriede Berger stresses how much she loves traveling. She lists where she has been since she last wrote: in England in January, in Switzerland in February, and in Paris in May. Next spring in England, she hopes to see the apple trees blossoming in Kent, something their teacher, "Frau Doktor E.," always talked about. Elfriede adds that she will be "driving for the first time to the Tegernsee [Bavaria], to have four weeks relaxing with my husband. I have become, in the literal sense of the word, a travel addict." And all this in her Mercedes, which she finds "fiendishly" enjoyable to drive.

Travel, the Borders, and the Wall

With the GDR's borders tightly controlled by the late 1950s, it seems surprising that some of the Schönebeck women still found a way to move to the West. In the context of ever-increasing numbers seeking to escape a further round of repression, and farmers leaving to avoid seeing their property and animals forcibly collectivized, they were not exceptional.

For the GDR authorities, the problem was that Berlin was under four-power control. As long as there was no properly policed border between the Soviet zone and the three Western zones in Berlin, there was no way to stop people escaping to the West via West Berlin. Quite apart from those seeking to leave permanently, there was considerable cross-sector movement of people going to work, with possibly fifty thousand people from the East going to jobs in the West each day, and ten thousand to the East.[71]

One of the Schönebeck women, Susanne Becker, was in this position. She had moved to Berlin from Staßfurt and lived in the East. Later, when she was married and her husband was working in West Berlin, they moved to an apartment there. However, she still traveled to her job as a dental technician in East Berlin, in the hospital in Friedrichshain. For her, Berlin was always a single city and she loved being there, enjoying the theater, cinema, walking by the lakes, and swimming.[72] In 1961, Susanne says it is time to leave Berlin because her husband has a job in the FRG, near Frankfurt/Main, and her sister is living in Darmstadt. They will miss Berlin since it has so much to offer. When the move is complete, she will send Marianne Schneider her new address, she promises.

The Berlin question, which the Soviet Union wished to solve by incorporating the whole of Berlin into the GDR or by finding a way to establish West Berlin as a neutral city, led to crises in the late 1950s and early 1960s. By the middle of 1961, the loss of population and skills meant the GDR was faced with a threat to its very existence. For this it blamed the West, repeating its earlier charges of "people-trafficking." At the same time, it asserted that large numbers of refugees from the FRG were crossing into the GDR, with many of them having to be housed in a reception center, the old *Schloss* in Barby, near Schönebeck. *Neues Deutschland* used as evidence a report from the *Daily Express* in England, saying that in 1959 alone, fifty thousand people had moved from the FRG, intending to stay in the GDR. The *Daily Express* did indeed report this, but compared it with the figure of between two and a half and three million people leaving the GDR over the previous few years. The *Daily Express* also noted that probably two-thirds of the people crossing into the GDR were people who had moved West but were now returning. This part of the report was ignored by *Neues Deutschland*.[73]

On 10 August 1961, the *Volksstimme Magdeburg* published an article titled "How Dangerous is West Berlin?" It defined West Berlin as a "center of disruption and provocation in the heart of the GDR," and "the most dangerous trouble spot in world politics, and a potential cause of war breaking out." The account was dramatic, and the aim clear: to blame the Western allies and insist on finding a solution to the Berlin problem on the GDR's terms:

> For a twenty-Pfennig ride on the underground, they can despatch their secret agents deep into the heart of the GDR. Nowhere else in the world is it so cheap and convenient for them.... West Berlin's function is to disrupt the building of socialism in the GDR.... With the most barbaric methods, from promises to subtly threatening to make public intimate relationships, they attract to West Berlin both the weak-willed and those who are drawn to the capitalist morality of the jungle.
>
> ... Therefore, the Western powers must be forced to come to the negotiating table this year, and the long overdue peace treaty has to be agreed, establishing West Berlin as a demilitarized Free City.

Three days later, the GDR authorities chose a different solution, building the Berlin Wall around West Berlin to close off permanently the last relatively open border for people in the GDR.

Conclusion: Grown Up

From 1950 to 1961, the GDR and the FRG grew further and further apart in political and economic terms. The FRG oriented itself toward Western Europe, the United States, and other members of the NATO alliance; the GDR toward the world Communist movement, but in practical terms toward the Soviet Union and the other members of the Warsaw Alliance. Restrictions on travel and the criminalization of unauthorized attempts to leave the GDR made it difficult for the women in the West and those in the East to see one another. The physical separation was increased by the building of the wall around West Berlin.

In the FRG, the power of the state was demonstrated by the "economic miracle" and the housing boom, which helped transform the lives of the Schönebeck women living there. Similarly, the FRG's orientation toward the other Western allies was clearly politically based, helping to support the private sector and to impose anti-communism as a major theme in the FRG. In the GDR, however, power was used more overtly and more brutally. Two of the women were directly affected by this through apparently arbitrary arrest, or the arrest of their partners. Through the letters and the reunions, the group developed a shared awareness of such events. Their response was one of deep sympathy, but not overt condemnation of the dictatorship in the GDR. In this way, they could look away and try to make what was happening outside not matter in their everyday lives.

Such an approach was an assertion of their power to run their own lives, make their own decisions, and pursue their own interests, individually and as a group. Often their everyday lives were in fact full of small but important pleasures unconnected with the state and its structures. While Hertha Pieper and her family were subjected to great pressure to join the agricultural cooperative, Carla Brunner's story of life on the farm in the GDR was one of enjoying her work and her life outside, whether swimming in the Elbe on summer evenings or going to the theater in Dessau.

Socially, the West and the East grew apart as their separate economies offered different opportunities. However, the Schönebeck women, wherever they were, shared similar attitudes to families, husbands, and children; they expected to be the ones who ran the household and did all the domestic work, and in this period were equally likely to stop work when they had children. Even so, as the decade progressed, different expectations became evident, with the women in the East increasingly ready to follow official encouragement and go to work outside the home.

In the FRG, the opera singer Anni Lange and the engineer Anna Siebert were exceptions and neither, at this stage had children. Anna Siebert, who would have stopped work if she had had children, was forced to fight a constant battle against male expectations: women should not be engineers, and, if they were, should not be promoted into positions where they would be managing male engineers. In the GDR, Hertha Pieper was as active in work outside the house as any man, despite having three children; Else Hermann pursued a career in the theater with great enthusiasm, determination, and success; and Leni Baumann rejoiced at being in higher education and fought to make her mark in the academic world. Leni's career in the GDR was destroyed by those above her, apparently because of the perception that her ideas and approach differed from those that were acceptable. It can be speculated that her position as a strong woman in her field might have worked against her in the male-dominated academic world, but this cannot be demonstrated. She remained strong enough, however, to find her way to the West in order to continue with her work in psychology. These examples suggest that the group produced strong women who would have fought for what they wanted, whether in the West or in the East; this is certainly how the Schönebeck women as a whole interpreted their achievements.

The women in the West largely stayed at home after having children and were happy to see themselves as housewives. Most of the other women in the GDR returned to work relatively soon after having children: several of them were health workers in clinics or hospitals; others were teachers; one became a pharmacy assistant; another was a farmer alongside her husband; one was a technical worker in the shoe factory; and two helped their husbands in an optician's and a specialist eye clinic. What united the women with children across the two parts of Germany was a commitment to being housewives, whether or not they had jobs outside the home.

Other social attitudes and values seem to have been largely shared across the group at this stage. The historian Josie McLellan points to the SED leaders' hypocritical attitudes to sex and sexuality: behind the puritanism which they attempted to impose on ordinary people in the GDR, they used sex to sell: "Advertisements featuring semi-clad women appeared as early as 1952 and were to remain a constant feature of East German life." Similarly, "the first specifically erotic consumer good [*Das Magazin*] appeared on the market in the wake of the workers' uprising of June 1953."[74] After the early accounts of getting to grips with the world of men, the letters become more reticent about sex and sexuality, both East and West, even though dress became more casual and more revealing. What emerges is an agreed line that approves of monogamous marriages, the nuclear family, and heterosexuality, and that leaves no space for alternatives. In this period, remaining single or being divorced is seen as embarrassing for those concerned; they have to go along with the group's expectations. They are never given a chance to explain their position or set out alternative preferences, which is why Ilse Klein's assertiveness was so significant. The most persuasive excuse for not being married—since excuses were needed—was the absolute shortage of men in Germany at the time, but no one chose to use it. Even Else Hermann, who showed no inclination to get married, resorted to saying that she was already too old at the age of twenty-nine.

The group itself had a powerful influence on the lives of the women throughout this period, providing them with a framework for living, a particular view of themselves as women, comfort and reassurance when these were needed, and a belief that their joint strength would help them all to build a satisfactory future. The latest *Rundbrief* volume was always welcomed with great joy. As early as 1951, Hilde Brenner says, bringing in memories of their time together at school,

> You can't believe how overjoyed I was when finally, finally, the *Rundbrief* got to me!… When I had it in my hand, I almost danced for joy (as we used to do at school when we breathed on the thermometer to make it go up, and then we got the day off because it was too hot). But then it occurred to me that in the meantime I have grown up, I'm now 24, and that this wouldn't be appropriate any more at my age.

By the middle of the 1950s, the response started to read almost as self-parody: "How great was my joy!" they exclaim at the arrival of the book, sitting down to write their own letter and send it on.[75]

Nevertheless, there were tensions in the group. The effects of the *Rundbrief* were reinforced by the class reunions. With Marianne Schneider, the organizer, living in Schönebeck, and the women in the GDR unable to travel legally to the West, it was inevitable that the reunions would take place in the GDR. Many of the women from the West were unable to travel there because of practical difficulties: apart from anything else, for those living near the Rhine, it would have been an epic journey to Schönebeck, with several changes of trains, and long delays in both directions at the border as travelers and their belongings were searched and items confiscated.[76] There were also problems getting visas, especially for those who had left the GDR without permission. Many of them were content to read about the reunion and to study and comment on the photos. Sometimes they sent money to help pay for the refreshments.

The letters soon contained urgings from those in the East to those in the West: organize your own reunion and tell us about it. Gentle pleas evolved into exhortations, and from there into direct criticism, since the women in the West showed little inclination to organize a reunion. Eventually a few mini-reunions of three or four of the women took place in Hamburg, but these were more like a chat over coffee with two or three friends than the long, well-structured events in the East.

The divergence in the long 1950s is most obvious in attitudes to travel, holidays, and leisure. The women in the West had the freedom to travel, and the money to back it up. The women in the East wanted just as much to travel but were increasingly constrained by laws that forbade them to leave the GDR. They also had less money. The letters from the East show a gradual acceptance of these constraints. However, some of the comments from the West, such as Elfriede Berger's expression of delight about traveling around in her Mercedes, were insensitive, to say the least.

The building of the Berlin Wall—the "Anti-fascist protection wall," as the GDR authorities referred to it—demonstrated to the Schönebeck women still in the East that their options were now further limited and that they lived in a permanently divided Germany. Nevertheless, the group itself had built a certain strength by this point and continued to assert that its own unity reflected the underlying unity of Germany. The 1960s would test such assertions as an ever-wider gap opened up between the GDR and the FRG.

Notes

1. Hermann Weber, *Dokumente zur Geschichte der Deutschen Demokratischen Republik 1945–1985* (Munich, 1986), 158.
2. Harsch, *Revenge*, 44–50.
3. The KPD was influenced by developments in the Soviet Union, including the formal rejection of early experimentation promoted by Alexandra Kollontai around sexual re-

lations and the position of women. See Phil Leask, Sara Ann Sewell, and Heléna Tóth, "Families," in Bergerson and Schmieding, *Ruptures*, 82–83; Martin A. Miller, *Freud and the Bolsheviks: Psychoanalysis in Imperial Russia and the Soviet Union* (New Haven, CT, 1998), 94–96.
4. Ben Fowkes, *Communism in Germany under the Weimar Republic* (London, 1984), 183.
5. Ralf Hoffrogge, *Sozialismus und Arbeiterbewegung in Deutschland. Von den Anfängen bis 1914* (Stuttgart, 2011), 90–98; Richard J. Evans, "Politics and the Family: Social Democracy and the Working-Class Family in Theory and Practice before 1914," in Richard J. Evans and W. R. Lee, eds., *The German Family: Essays on the Social History of the Family in Nineteenth- and Twentieth-Century Germany* (London, 1981), 268–73, 279–80.
6. Hoffrogge, *Sozialismus und Arbeiterbewegung*, 106–13.
7. Sabine Berghahn and Andrea Fritzsche, eds., *Frauenrecht in Ost- und Westdeutschland: Bilanz, Ausblick* (Berlin, 1991).
8. Herausgeberkollektiv, eds., *Wörterbuch zur sozialistischen Jugendpolitik* (Berlin, 1975), 249. Quoted in English translation in Fulbrook, *The People's State*, 115.
9. "Ich bin unserer Regierung sehr dankbar," *Neues Deutschland* (the official SED newspaper), 3 April 1952.
10. Paul Betts, *Within Walls: Private Life in the German Democratic Republic* (Oxford, 2010), 92.
11. Sabine Schenk, "On Employment Opportunities and Labour Market Exclusion: Towards a New Pattern of Gender Stratification?," in Eva Kolinsky and Hildegard Maria Nickel, eds., *Reinventing Gender: Women in Eastern Germany since Unification* (London, 2003), 58.
12. Uhl, *Die Teilung Deutschlands*, 41–43.
13. Michael Gehler, *Deutschland. Von der Teilung zur Einigung. 1945 bis heute* (Vienna, 2010), 29.
14. Uhl, *Die Teilung Deutschlands*, 41–43.
15. Examples for Schönebeck are described in Neutsch, *Der Friede im Osten*.
16. Uhl, *Die Teilung Deutschlands*, 43–44.
17. Betts, *Within Walls*, 126–29.
18. Betts, *Within Walls*, 130.
19. Stefan Heym, *Die Architekten* (Munich, 2000). The modernist approach devastated many urban areas in the United Kingdom, the FRG, and elsewhere in Europe over the same period; the SED was following a trend as much as it was leading it. The "Stalinist" developments in the center of Magdeburg are now desirable places to live or work, while modernist blocks are being demolished and attempts made to bring life back to the prominent streets, such as the Breite Straße.
20. Harsch, *Revenge*, 175.
21. Harsch, *Revenge*, 176.
22. James C. Van Hook, *Rebuilding Germany: The Creation of the Social Market Economy, 1945–1957* (Cambridge, 2004), 199.
23. Gehler, *Deutschland*, 106.
24. Vonyó, *The Economic Consequences*, 10; see also 53–56, 76–77.
25. Michael Gehler, *Deutschland*, 110.
26. Glossner, *The Making of the German Post-War Economy*, 5.
27. Jäker, in Niedersen, *Soldaten*; Edda Ahrberg and Dorothea Harder, *Abgeholt und verschwunden*, vol. 2: *Nichtverurteilte Speziallagerhäftlinge aus Sachsen-Anhalt und ihre Angehörigen*. (Magdeburg, 2012), 130–47.

28. Letter from Dr. Kurt Bauer to Walter Karpe, 4 March 1935, in *Personalakte: Walter Karpe*, PA 23, Stadtarchiv Schönebeck.
29. Ahrberg and Harder, *Abgeholt und verschwunden*, vol. 2, 130–47.
30. Gary Bruce, *Resistance with the People: Repression and Resistance in Eastern Germany, 1945–1955* (Lanham, MD, 2003), 126–29; Karl Wilhelm Fricke, *Politik und Justiz in der DDR. Zur Geschichte der politischen Verfolgung, 1945–1968* (Cologne, 1979), 205–15, 274–76.
31. Jens Schöne, *Das sozialistische Dorf. Bodenreform und Kollektivierung in der Sowjetzone und DDR* (Leipzig, 2008), 91.
32. Jörg Rudolph, Frank Drauschke, and Alexander Sachse, *Verurteilt zum Tode durch Erschießen. Opfer des Stalinismus aus Sachsen-Anhalt 1950–1953* (Magdeburg, 2006); Arsenij Roginskij, Frank Drauschke, and Anna Kaminsky, eds., *"Erschossen in Moskau..." Die deutschen Opfer des Stalinismus auf dem Moskauer Friedhof Donskoje 1950–1953* (Berlin, 2008).
33. Neula Kerr-Boyle, "The Slim Imperative: Discourses and Cultures of Dieting in the German Democratic Republic, 1949–90," in Fulbrook and Port, *Becoming East German*.
34. Leask, "Losing Trust," 131.
35. Leask, "Losing Trust," 136.
36. Jens Gieseke, *Mielke-Konzern. Die Geschichte der Stasi 1945–1990* (Munich, 2001), 158; Clemens Vollnhals, "Das Ministerium für Staatssicherheit," in Kaelble, Kocka, and Zwahr, *Sozialgeschichte*, 513–14.
37. See, for instance, "A Failed Revolution? the Uprising of June 1953," in Mary Fulbrook, *Anatomy of a Dictatorship* (Oxford, 1995).
38. "Bekanntmachungen der Regierung der DDR," *Neues Deutschland*, 18 June 1953.
39. "KOMMUNIQUE des Politbüros des Zentralkomitees der SED vom 9. Juni 1953," *Neues Deutschland*, 11 June 1953.
40. One indicator of this is the change in the use of key words in the press. In the three national papers, *Neues Deutschland*, *Neue Zeitung*, and *Berliner Zeitung*, "Sozialismus" was in the first five months of 1953 mentioned 2,017 times—an average of 403 times a month. In the next seven months, the number dropped to a total of 504—averaging 72 times a month. This reflected the change of course by the SED from June 1953: from May, with 417 mentions, to June with 99 and July with 59. There were 161 references in the three national newspapers to "Normenerhöhungen" (raising the norms) in 1953, 134 of them in the three months of April, May, and June. For the rest of 1953 after June, there were seventeen such references; in 1954, thirteen; and only nine for all the remaining years of the GDR.
41. Martin Kohli, "Die DDR als Arbeitsgesellschaft?" in Kaelble, Kocka, and Zwahr, *Sozialgeschichte*, 42.
42. "In 26 Tagen 30272 freiwillige Arbeitsstunden,"*Neues Deutschland*, 1 August 1953.
43. "Aufbauhelfer wissen, worum es geht," *Neue Zeit*, 1 October 1954.
44. "Ein Park für die Kleinen," *Neues Deutschland*, 21 August 1956.
45. Karl Beyer, *Die Geschichte der Apotheken und des Apothekenwesens im Kreis Schönebeck* (Schönebeck, ca. 1980).
46. Germany had been a world leader in color photography before the war, through the AGFA plant in Wolfen, near Bitterfeld. When the Americans initially occupied the area, they removed indispensable materials and machinery from the plant: Bessel, *Germany 1945*, 377; Karlsch, *Allein Bezahlt*, 59.

47. "Schönebeck Letters," 30 August 1953.
48. Volume 1 (1974) contains an unflattering portrait of Else's father, which did not please him.
49. "Zur Frage der Produktionsgenossenschaften," *Volksstimme Magdeburg*, 12 July 1952. The party conference also abolished the upper tier of regional government, the *Land*, replacing it with the smaller *Bezirk*. Saxony-Anhalt ceased to exist, and the area centered on Magdeburg, including Schönebeck and its surrounding towns, became the Magdeburg *Bezirk* or district.
50. There is a minor tragicomic episode of humiliation that is based on this decision in Erwin Strittmatter's extremely popular novel, *Ole Bienkopp* (Berlin, 1965), 231. A loyal SED member has been trying to suppress a voluntary cooperative and is preparing to speak at the conference about his success, only to hear that party policy has changed without him being told, leaving him to be portrayed as a saboteur. His superior in the party sums up a problem that would face party members and ordinary people trying to work out what to think and how to act throughout the life of the GDR: "The world moves on. What was wrong yesterday can be right tomorrow." See also Leask, "Humiliation as a Weapon."
51. LPG was the common term for the *Landwirtschaftliche Produktionsgenossenschaft*, or agricultural cooperative, in the GDR.
52. Schöne, *Das sozialistische Dorf*, 119–20.
53. "Schönebeck für alle MTS Vorbild," *Neues Deutschland*, 24 December 1955.
54. Schöne, *Das sozialistische Dorf*, 120–23; Helmut Müller-Enbergs et al., eds., *Wer war wer in der DDR?* (Berlin, 2006).
55. Lieselotte Thoms, "Schönebecker Tagebuch XX: Die Einzelbauern und die Funktionäre," *Neues Deutschland*, 3 May 1956.
56. One of them, however, is the *Bürgermeisterin*, the mayor, of Schönebeck itself.
57. Lieselotte Thoms, "Schönebecker Tagebuch X: Die Frauen von Schönebeck," *Neues Deutschland*, 20 April 1956.
58. "Schönebeck Letters," 28 August 1957.
59. This is Carla Brunner's last letter. No one explains why she stopped writing, but she is still referred to in a friendly manner in other letters.
60. Schöne, *Das sozialistische Dorf*, 127–31; André Steiner, *The Plans That Failed: An Economic History of the GDR* (New York, 2010), 94–96. See also a vivid personal account: Rudolf Bentz, *Geschichte an der Havel. 1921–1991*, 98, DTA 1874.
61. "Barby," *Volksstimme Magdeburg*, 15 April 1961.
62. "Endspurt in der Ernteschlacht," *Volksstimme Magdeburg*, 27 August 1960.
63. "Kampf um Qualität bei Gelatine," *Volksstimme Magdeburg*, 31 October 1960.
64. Grube and Rost, *Dorferneuerung*, 19, 24.
65. 11 November 1957. The comment works better in German: "Der Dickschädel wird immer dicker," where "dick" can have the sense of thick or fat as well.
66. "Schönebeck Letters," 10 July 1959.
67. On the imposition of border controls in the 1950s, and the contradictions, humiliation, and absurdities resulting, see Inge Bennewitz, *Zwangsaussiedlungen an der innerdeutschen Grenze* (Berlin, 1994); Edith Sheffer, *Burned Bridge: How East and West Germans Made the Iron Curtain* (New York, 2011); Jason Johnson, Craig Koslofsky, and Josie McLellan, "Taking Place," in Bergerson and Schmieding, *Ruptures*, 235–34; Jason B. Johnson, *Divided Village: The Cold War in the German Borderlands* (London, 2017).

68. "Zur Änderung des Paßgesetzes der Deutschen Demokratischen Republik," *Berliner Zeitung*, 12 December 1957.
69. "Das Strafgesetz der sozialistischen Demokratie,""Republikflucht Verrat an der DDR," *Neues Deutschland*, 12 December 1957.
70. "Schönebeck Letters," 31 October 1951, 18 December 1952, 25 February 1956.
71. Rene MacColl, "Astonishing, This Trek Back behind the Iron Curtain," *Daily Express*, 27 July 1961.
72. "Schönebeck Letters," 16 September 1952, 14 December 1953.
73. "Existenzangst in Westdeutschland," *Neues Deutschland*, 29 July 1961; *Daily Express*, 27 July 1961; Zwahr, "Die DDR auf dem Höhepunkt der Staatskrise 1989," 440, gives a total of 2,738,572 refugees from the GDR (including East Berlin) between 1949 and the end of 1961.
74. Josie McLellan, "Even under Socialism, We Don't Want to Do without Love," in David Crowley and Susan E. Reid, *Pleasures in Socialism: Leisure and Luxury in the Eastern Bloc* (Evanston, IL, 2010), 222; Josie McLellan, *Love in the Time of Communism: Intimacy and Sexuality in the GDR* (Cambridge, 2011).
75. See, for instance, Martha Jäger, 8 August 1956; Carla Brunner, 4 September 1956.
76. There are detailed accounts of such journeys in Andreas Walter Kahlow, "... und hoffen, daß das Jahr 1964 eine Wende bringt und wir alle wieder zusammen kommen!" Fluchtberichte und Alltagsbriefe, die deutsch-deutsche Befindlichkeit betreffend, Mai 1961 bis Dezember 1989, letters of 22 April 1964, 18 May 1964, AdK Kempowski-BIO 6780.

CHAPTER 3

No Longer Young
The 1960s

Overview

The Lost Book

In the early 1960s, the Schönebeck women, so keen to have nothing to do with politics and the world of those in power, had to face a serious question: was it coincidence, carelessness, or something more sinister? The eighth book of the *Rundbrief*, covering the period immediately following the building of the Berlin Wall, had simply disappeared.

In the last entry in Book 7, on 22 June 1961, Susanne Becker promised to send on her new address when she moved away from Berlin. The eighth book started as normal and traveled around, filling up with entries and photos, until it was sent to Susanne Becker in the now completely divided Berlin, on the assumption that she was still there. And that is the last that is known of it. There were conflicting explanations: Susanne failed to send on her new address, so the book went to her old address and was discarded; Susanne received the book and mislaid it when she was packing to leave Berlin; or it was intercepted somewhere on its journey by the GDR authorities. There is no way of knowing which of these was correct. Years later, it becomes clear that a particular book has been opened and looked at by the authorities—where is not clear—then closed up and sent on its way again, as if it were not worth worrying about. However, a book from 1961 and 1962 that contained references to the Wall, no matter how guarded or indirect, or that talked about shortages and implied there was discontent in the GDR, might have been a different matter.

The women themselves believed, or made themselves believe, that it was simply a coincidence and that it might have been any book that was lost. Else Hermann in her interviews declared that Susanne was at fault. This was also Marianne Schneider's view, since Susanne did not send on her new address. Marianne asserts as a fact that the book was not taken by the authorities, though she presents no evidence for this. Marianne always chooses her words carefully, however. On 20 February 1964, she says that the book has "vanished without trace" (*spurlos verschwunden*). The expression is common enough, but in the GDR press it initially referred to Nazis who had disappeared after the war or who had caused large numbers of people to vanish without trace. Later it referred particularly to people supposedly involved with or acting for the Western powers: such people frequently "vanished without trace" before the GDR authorities caught them. (When they vanished after being arrested, like Erika Krämer's Karl, this was never mentioned.) Marianne would have used the term knowing this. She might well be hinting that something more sinister, some criminal act or state intervention, could have been behind the loss of the book.

There is another puzzling aspect to the disappearance of Book 8. With the exception of the first book, when Marianne sent the *Rundbrief* around, the new one never went on its own but was part of a pair. This was the only way for all the women to see the letters that were written in the previous book after they had written in it themselves and sent it on. Therefore, when Book 8 went to Susanne in Berlin, Book 7 went with it. Book 7, however, was *not* lost. So, if Book 8 was confiscated by the State Security forces or by officers at the border, why was Book 7 allowed to go on its way? In order to avoid suspicion, or because it was not so politically sensitive? Or if Susanne lost Book 8 or caused it to be lost, how did Book 7 find its way back to Marianne? How did Susanne or someone else come to send it back, and if it was Susanne, why did she send it alone? Whichever way we look at it, it appears that someone had both books and did not let Book 8 make its way back. It is hard to find an innocent explanation for this.

When it was clear that the book had been lost, Else Hermann wrote to everyone, asking them to write in again with what they had said before. Sadly, she said to me, no one responded. This raises further questions. Did the women think events at the time were too dangerous for them to trust to the post? Were they not sure they could absolutely trust all the others in the group? Did they have doubts about Else's reasons for wanting them to write about a politically sensitive time? There are certainly indications elsewhere that the women were not sure that what they said or wrote would always stay within the group.

The GDR after the Wall

The building of the Wall solved the SED's immediate difficulties, ensuring the survival of GDR. For the first time, the GDR was not apparently at the mercy of outside forces it could not control. (The continuing influence of the Soviet Union was seen as perfectly normal.) This new freedom obliged the SED to prove it could at last establish a stable state and a supportive society in line with its Marxist-Leninist ideology. For the first time, there could be no more excuses if it failed.

Else Hermann said later that the Wall did allow the GDR to have a life of its own, but that it caused it to be inward-looking and provincial. The SED declared that the Wall, with the associated militarization of the border with the FRG, was a necessary measure to defend the GDR. This line was constantly repeated, all the way down through the different levels of the state and its mass organizations and state-owned enterprises. If the women still living in the Schönebeck area hoped to see a softening of the official line at the local level, they were to be disappointed. The workers in the industrial complexes, such as the Traktorenwerk, declared their commitment to the party and described the Wall as justified. They talked of the need to prepare to defend the works against the imperialists and to maintain the gains made by the GDR in building socialism. One lesson they drew was the need to constantly raise productivity and reduce costs "within the framework of socialist competitiveness."

Workers exhorted one another to work extra hours voluntarily, in accordance with the slogan "Strike at the militarists with action to support socialist production," to which they all "spontaneously" responded.[1] Similarly, the senior doctor for the Schönebeck district, Wolfgang Fettback, said that building the Wall and securing the borders were important steps toward "normalizing conditions in Germany and in the whole of Europe. They are to be welcomed by every upright, honorable citizen. We want to work in peace."[2]

Such responses made it more difficult, but also more important, for the women to hold to their underlying myth that Germany remained a single, undivided entity. The growing divergence between the GDR and the FRG over the next decade—including different approaches to the "woman question"—would strengthen the founding myths of the separate German states and challenge the women's determination to maintain the integrity of the group.

The "Woman Question"

During the 1950s in the FRG, economic, social, and political forces combined to restore what had been seen as the "normal" family as a stabilizing factor, and "to return the woman to the domestic sphere and to make her role within the family both appealing and unavoidable."[3] However, by the 1960s, the pressure to buy more consumer goods and raise the family's quality of life meant that more women were going out to work, if only—as they saw it—to supplement the family income, provided mainly by the man. Women were frequently criticized for this by politicians and church leaders. Such pressure helped to reinforce a widespread commitment to gender-specific roles, although around 30 percent of women could not afford to stay home full time to look after their children.[4] It was often the grandparents who looked after the children, as in the GDR in the 1950s.

The 1960s were a time of slow change in social attitudes and corresponding legal frameworks in the FRG. In 1950, 26.4 percent of married women under sixty were in employment. This had increased to 36.5 percent by 1961 and 40.9 percent by 1970.[5] Economic expansion, the increased access of women to higher education, and the desire to be doing something with more social involvement made many more women choose to return to their jobs after having children. Often their work was still part time because schools and nurseries were open only in the morning. However, the attitudes and position of men were hard to shift; it was still the women who were expected to look after the house and the children, even if they went out to work.

By the mid-1960s, the existing women's organizations in the FRG were becoming more outspoken about the position and needs of women with children working outside the home.[6] Late in the 1960s, as male-dominated anti-authoritarian movements emerged, the new or second-wave feminist movement began to go further, making demands and carrying out actions specifically related to the position of women, and criticizing conventional assumptions about the roles of women and men. Although many of their early actions concentrated on the war in Vietnam, out of this grew demands that concerned the wider society, the structure and practices of the family itself, and the groups on the left and in the protest movements.[7] These demands appear to have had little direct impact on the Schönebeck women in the FRG.

In the GDR, the authorities had a very different view of the needs of women and were not prepared to have groups of women with their supposedly bourgeois concerns telling them what to do. At the end of 1961, the SED issued a major position paper concerning the position of women in the GDR. The Politburo (the group of men at the very top of the SED) declared in *Neues Deutschland* (23 December 1961) that the task for the nation was to ensure that women were more involved in the building of socialism and that their lives were thereby improved. This required, first, a number of political problems to be resolved, effectively by men since women did not have access to the top positions: "above all else, the conclusion of a peace treaty and a solution to the Berlin question in order to clear away what is left over from the war and, through disarmament, to secure peace in Germany, to strengthen the workers' and peasants' state." Only then would it be possible to "fulfill the economic aims leading to the victory of socialism, and to promote the new socialist ways for people to relate to one another." Women were praised for their newfound self-confidence and skills at work, for bringing up their children, and for connecting with and being involved in leadership positions in state institutions. This last point ignored the limited access women had to high positions in the state-run enterprises, the ministries, and the SED itself.

The SED did recognize that much remained to be done to ensure women had the opportunities that the constitution guaranteed to them. It criticized even leading comrades for requiring women to "prove" themselves, and for making disparaging remarks about women's capabilities or their reliability in the face of demands from family and children. It went some way toward recognizing the unequal burden of expectation placed on women: "Often women who are already carrying out leadership functions are overburdened with a surfeit of work, without any consideration of their duties as mothers and housewives. More is often asked of them than is asked of men in comparable positions." There was no questioning of who should be responsible for these supposedly women's duties, however. In this document, which the SED wanted to see widely discussed in all organizations throughout the society, there was significant criticism of men for discriminating against and undermining women at work, and of the education and training organizations who presided over a reduction of the number of women being given technical expertise. A key theme was that looking after the household and the children was the work of women, and only of women, and that special provision needed to be put in place to enable them to participate better in employment. This included, for instance, opportunities to do their shopping at work, to drop off their laundry there, and to be able to borrow high-quality appliances for cleaning the house.

The response of the industrial workers at Schönebeck's Traktorenwerk to the party's document on women was to claim great advances while demonstrating a similar lack of understanding about relations between men and women. They noted that, in January 1962, the women's committee in the works was ten years old, and that it had been fostered by the party at a time of shifting production from prams and bicycles (work suitable for women, it implied) to tractors (work normally done by men). There were two hundred women at the time who had to be retrained; some of these, they said, had since progressed to the lower level of management.

The reality of the position in 1962 looks worse than even such minor achievements suggest. A party-led history of the Traktorenwerk, published in 1989, contains ten photos in the first eleven pages, the section where the response to the 1961 document is narrated. Each of these photos portrays men but only one has women in it: a photo of a brigade with eighteen men and three women. Over the next twenty-five pages, there are fifty photos showing a total of one hundred and ninety men and eight photos showing twelve women, four of whom are not production workers but entertainers (singers or acrobats). Finally, there is a photo of what is called a "women's brigade," made up of five women and five men.[8]

As if to show it was serious about the "woman question," the SED held a national women's conference on 5 and 6 January 1962 to follow up the Politburo's communiqué. There it was stressed that women needed to be able to reach their full potential if they were to fulfill their task of achieving peace and building socialism. *Neues Deutschland*, with no apparent sense of irony, reported on 7 January that the "high point" of the women's conference was the closing speech by Walter Ulbricht, which was "time and again interrupted by thunderous acclamation."

In 1963, the SED's Sixth Party Congress included in its program a commitment to build on the "good work" that had followed the Politburo's communiqué of December 1961. Women were to be better trained and encouraged to move into leadership positions, and given advice and help so that they could bring up their children better. Schools would gradually shift to being open all day, so that women with children could stay at work and manage their time better. The economy would, it was said, grow stronger, allowing more nurseries and kindergartens to be set up. More girls at school were to be encouraged to enter the scientific and technical branches of higher education and industry.

Throughout the 1960s, life did become easier for many women in the GDR, not because their triple burden of household, children, and employment was shifted on to men, but because childcare and other services made it easier for them to manage this burden. The historian Sandrine Kott argues that the socialization of domestic tasks in the workplace, providing not just childcare but also hot meals and places to shop and do laundry, was the policy and practice of the GDR authorities in the 1960s. They declared that providing such services outside the home meant there was less need to shift production toward more consumer goods. Such provision also resulted from a certain hostility to the traditional family, with the state arguing that it freed children from the suffocating nature of the family and gave them a high-quality education carried out by professional workers.[9]

The emphasis on improving conditions for women in the workplace was beneficial for women and was often led by the women's committees. Kott confirms, from looking at these committees in the early 1960s, what Harsch says about the later period in the GDR, that the position of women gave them a certain power in relation to the state. In the 1960s, they started to demand that the services be provided near where they lived, not at work, and so challenged the idea of the centrality of work in the GDR. Kott says that women sought, with some success, to bend the productionist society to meet their demands.[10]

However, because of economic shortfalls and political shifts, the women's committees in the workplaces were put under the control of the SED-controlled union, the DFGB, in the mid-1960s. Men continued to dominate in the workplace and treated women patronizingly. Women were seen as having specific qualities relating to being mothers, and lacking technical expertise, even when qualified. Women's brigades were often led by men. At the higher political level, the majority of SED leaders continued to see the married couple and subsequent family as the foundation of society, with no questioning of traditional roles.

Not surprisingly, the Family Law of 1965 saw managing the dual role of mother and worker as a problem only for the woman, even if it recognized in principle that men and women were jointly responsible for their children.[11] Similarly, in the updating of the GDR constitution in 1968—initiated and controlled by the men at the top of the SED—the position of women was again presented from within a male-oriented framework, as if fathers were not directly involved in families: "Marriage, family, motherhood are under the special protection of the state."[12]

The Significance of the Weather

Extremes of weather, particularly some very cold winters and floods, were very damaging in Germany in the 1940s and 1950s. The impact was always greater in the East, which did not have the spare capacity to deal with additional pressures and crises. Even by the end of the 1960s, the GDR had to admit that bad weather caused serious problems, from which it took several years to recover.[13]

In the East, one of the SED's major public events, the Sixth Party Congress in January 1963, was overshadowed by the terrible winter of 1962/63. This congress, like all such SED events, was a spectacle, choreographed to portray the GDR as successful, forward-looking, and at the center (with the Soviet Union) of the world communist movement and efforts to ensure world peace. The program of the congress proclaimed the need for the comprehensive building of socialism and a conclusive break with the past. GDR socialism would be forward-looking, with a modern economy based on science and technology and supported by a socialist national culture. There would be more consumer goods; they would be of better quality; and there would be a gradual reduction of the gap between lower and higher incomes.[14] The GDR press's comprehensive coverage of the congress asserted that things were working well in the present and would be even better in the future. Ironically, at this moment, the winter of 1962/1963 took hold of much of Europe, with huge amounts of snow and extremely low temperatures. For the GDR, this was disastrous.

Eventually, a short report in *Neues Deutschland* on 18 January confirmed what ordinary people knew, that conditions were appalling and that there were desperate shortages of fuel and energy. Homes, factories, and power stations were dependent on the GDR's plentiful supplies of brown coal from surface mines. However, with the earth frozen solid to a depth of three quarters of a meter, it was almost impossible to extract the coal. When coal was produced, the trains were unable to deliver it because the tracks were blocked or because the coal had frozen solid in the wagons. The authorities tried blowing up the frozen coal, but with little success. A graphic report comes from the experimental but valuable iron works in Calbe, which was also the third-largest supplier of electricity in the Magdeburg region: "With their heroic action, the whole collective of the Calbe NOW [the iron works] are battling day and night against the frost. With pneumatic drills and crowbars, they have to break up every ton of ore in the wagons and watch it slither across the shovel into the furnace."[15]

Over the following days, the temperature dropped to minus 33 degrees. Water supplies to the power stations were cut off, and riverside power plants were threatened by huge waves of ice forming natural dams across the Elbe. The ports were likewise blocked by ice barriers. In Wismar, where Lisa Liebmann and her husband lived, the inner harbor froze over and the outer harbor was full of pack ice. The only way to reach the island of Hiddensee was by horses pulling sledges across the ice from Rügen. Nothing but the efforts of the workers and the army—described as tireless, self-sacrificing, and heroic—appeared to stand between survival and catastrophe.

In the West the previous year, there had also been a catastrophe: a storm surge that drove a huge wall of water up the river Elbe from the sea until it met the already full rivers, flooding large areas of Hamburg and causing over three hundred deaths. This catastrophe served as a warning, demonstrating that for all its newfound wealth, the FRG was still living with the consequences of the war: the failure to fully upgrade its infrastructure, such as flood defenses, even after the disastrous North Sea flooding of 1953.

The 1962 Hamburg catastrophe also demonstrated that the FRG could generate the resources needed to transform conditions for the future. In contrast, the winter of 1962/63 showed that the GDR was still, in relative terms, living from hand to mouth and could not make up for lost production, despite its claims that it would catch up with the FRG in the early 1960s.[16]

Changing Times? 1968 and Its Consequences

1968 was the year of a succession of extraordinary events: student rebellions from Paris to Berlin to Mexico and across the United States; the "TET Offensive" in Vietnam; the election of Richard Nixon as president of the United States; the assassination of Robert Kennedy and Martin Luther King in the United States and the attempted assassination of far-left leader Rudi Dutschke in Berlin; the flourishing of the "Prague Spring" in Czechoslovakia and its crushing by Soviet and other Warsaw Pact troops, with the involvement of the GDR; the Biafran war; a new communist insurgency in Malaysia; and the intensification of the "Cultural Revolution" in China. It was a time of sudden turmoil and unexpected change, a time when "alternative" ideas became the basis for a new lifestyle for many young people, a time of rapid economic growth and the expansion of consumerism in Western societies in particular.

In the FRG, the protest movement, initiated by university students, was both linked in spirit to the protests across many parts of the world and a response to specific concerns in West Germany itself: unsatisfactory conditions in the universities; rejection of the preceding generations because of their involvement in or with the Nazi party; hostility to "bourgeois society" and its moral strictures; the perceived failure of those in power to reform and modernize society and political processes; and anti-American feeling because of hostility to capitalism and "American imperialism," epitomized by the Vietnam war.[17] Although the Schönebeck women in the West said almost nothing about how this affected them, there are occasional hints in the letters that their children were thinking differently and perhaps in opposition to them.

By 1968, the GDR was far more developed industrially than it had been in 1961 when the Berlin Wall was built. Many more consumer goods and cars were being produced, though still far fewer than in the Federal Republic. Walter Ulbricht had overseen a change in economic policy that distanced the GDR from the Soviet Union, at least partially, and which antagonized the Soviet leadership. Ulbricht's New Economic System of Planning and Managing (NÖSPL), later modified and known as the New Economic System (NÖS), sought to use some of the same "economic levers" as the West—costs, prices, profits, credits, wages, bonuses—and to get them to work together consistently. The material interests of individual workers were emphasized, along with the need for profit.

The new approach did lead to higher living standards through increased productivity. However, although rents were lower in the GDR, household costs were higher and wages significantly lower than in the FRG.[18] There was still a chronic housing shortage in the GDR. When asked in 1965 why they were not building more houses, the construction minister Wolfgang Junker said they were doing what was possible but that investment had to be concentrated "in the leading sectors of our economy." This meant that they would "above all" build new housing in the areas where the most economically important new industrial complexes were being built.[19]

While experimenting economically, Ulbricht sought to demonstrate his commitment to Soviet policies by not allowing social, cultural, or political modernization. At the end of 1965, the Eleventh Plenum of the SED's central committee condemned prominent writers and banned films by some of the foremost directors because of supposed hostility to the state or for giving a false picture of conditions in the GDR.[20]

Following Lenin's writings on how to prepare for a revolution, the GDR leadership was fearful of things happening spontaneously.[21] Such an attitude, and the associated fear of losing control, made it easy for the GDR to condemn the apparent anarchy of the "Prague Spring" and the Czechoslovak search for a more humane version of communism, and to join with the Soviet Union in suppressing it. For the Soviet Union, the possible loss of Czechoslovakia from its sphere of control was equated with a victory for the world-historical enemy, the United States.

The SED leaders not infrequently attempted to hold contradictory positions at the same time. Since they were happy to point to supposed chaos in the development of capitalism in the West, and to oppose American imperialism, it made sense for them to support and attempt to influence those participating in the protests in the FRG, despite the spontaneous nature of many of the actions. However, the nature of the groups involved, including anarchists, radical leftists opposed to Soviet-style communism, and Maoists, along with their tendency to demonstrate their independence and opposition through the way they dressed and their long hair and beards, caused great concern. The SED leaders were fearful of the contaminating effects on their own young people of contact with those in the West, and of supposed Maoist influences on their own population, and severely repressed any perceived ultra-left groups in the GDR.[22]

When the invasion of Czechoslovakia took place, young people who handwrote protests and put them in people's letter boxes or showed their opposition in other ways were arrested by the Stasi.[23] The party-controlled newspapers asserted that the population supported the decision to intervene in Czechoslovakia, and party members were required to speak out publicly in favor of it. In the Dieselmotorenwerk in Schönebeck, the SED's district secretary told six hundred SED activists that "just in the last few days, forty citizens of the district, most of them young, declared that they wanted to join the party at once, as an expression of their support for the decision of the fraternal countries to provide help to the Czechoslovak Socialist Republic."[24] The director of the principal theater and leader of the Cultural Association in the Schönebeck area, Karl-Albert Ebel, said that he agreed with what was being said in the newspapers and that "it goes without saying that we could not stand by, looking on silently, as the counter-revolution started to spread across the Czechoslovak Socialist Republic with the help of the West German imperialists. . . . Our standpoint has to be that we give not one inch of ground to imperialism, in whatever form it may disguise itself."[25]

The consequences of the invasion and of the societal changes in the GDR and the FRG were far-reaching, however. According to the historian Stefan Wolle, the invasion put an end to the hopes of young people in both the East and West for a form of "socialism with a human face," contributed to the splitting and radicalizing of the protest movements in the West, and ended illusions that still remained about the emancipatory role of the Soviet Union.[26] Just as there are hints in the Schönebeck letters of some involvement in the social changes and protest movements in the West, so there are allusions to the invasion of Czechoslovakia, and these do not simply follow the SED line.

In 1968, even the GDR was not immune to the spirit of protest coming from outside. The SED proposed a new constitution for the GDR and allowed a vote on whether it should be accepted. Under the new constitution, the GDR would have the status of "a socialist state of the German nation." It would be based on "the political organization of the working people in the towns and in the countryside who, together under the leadership of the working class and its Marxist-Leninist party, are committed to making a reality of socialism."[27] In the run-up to the vote, there was a huge campaign urging a "yes" vote. Although the result was a foregone conclusion, only 94.5 percent voted yes. Across the GDR, 409,329 people voted no, 27,685 of them in Magdeburg Bezirk, 1,735 in Schönebeck, and 1,892 in Staßfurt.[28] The numbers may look small but were significant in a country where elections were usually won with around 99 percent of the vote.

The GDR and External Relations

For Walter Ulbricht, one lesson of the invasion of Czechoslovakia and his own attempts to reshape the GDR should have been that it was dangerous to oppose the Soviet Union, even with modest economic reforms or experiments. After the events of June 1953, Ulbricht was only saved by changes at the top in the Soviet Union. By the late 1960s, he was no longer all-powerful. Though it could not be publicly acknowledged, there was a power struggle taking place in the SED, with the Soviet Union supporting Erich Honecker, Ulbricht's eventual successor.

By 1969, the GDR wanted to be recognized in accordance with international law by the Federal Republic, while the Soviet Union wanted a wider settlement of the outstanding postwar issues. The Federal Republic, with its first Social Democratic chancellor, Willy Brandt, and the GDR under Ulbricht, took tentative steps toward seeing if relations between them could be normalized. Two important meetings took place between Willy Brandt and Willi Stoph, formally the head of government in the GDR. At the first meeting, in Erfurt in the GDR in April, Brandt was greeted rapturously by local people, who pushed their way through the police lines in their thousands to shout his name and indicate their support. The GDR leadership, shocked by this response, hardened their position at the follow-up meeting in Kassel and sought to undermine Brandt's standing in the FRG.

Brandt attempted to get agreement on a peace policy based on equality between the two states, the inviolability of boundaries, and the maintenance of the concept of the single German nation. Stoph insisted that there could in future be no question of "inner-German relations" between the two independent states.[29] Erika Krämer mentions this process in her letter from Kassel on 12 April 1970: "Let us hope that when our two Willys meet in Kassel, it will not just be our *Rundbrief* that can travel unhindered from East to West!" Her hopes, it transpired in May, were in vain.

In 1970, however, both Poland and the Soviet Union carried out successful treaty negotiations with the Federal Republic, leaving the GDR isolated. Since the GDR was also having economic problems, with a significant drop in production in 1969 and 1970, Ulbricht was increasingly vulnerable. With Soviet backing, Erich Honecker persuaded the SED leadership to appoint him as its First Secretary on 3 May 1971. Ulbricht was allowed to resign, supposedly on health grounds, while nominally retaining prestigious positions in the state and the party.

The Principal Stories

The long 1950s had been both hard and rewarding for some of the most prominent Schönebeck women. In the 1960s, they felt they were moving toward middle age. Those with children, who were sometimes amusing and sometimes perplexing but always rewarding, watched them growing up and developing lives of their own. Those without children developed their own careers, with Else Hermann changing direction and entering full-time education, and Anna Siebert climbing further and further up the professional ladder. All of them continued to enjoy the embrace of the wider group that held them together across the divided Germany. Outwardly, none of them paid particular attention to the structures around them; on both sides of the inner-German border, they were mostly positive about what they were doing and did not feel particularly inhibited until it came, once again, to being able to travel. However, Else Hermann's life was directly affected in the 1960s by the SED's clampdown on cultural expression. She felt unable to refer directly to this in the *Rundbrief*, but it was a central preoccupation in her interviews.

Hertha Pieper

Writing on 28 August 1964 from Calbe, Hertha Pieper is amusing and surprisingly cheerful: "Once again there's something to wail about and something to apologize for! On 9 August the *Rundbrief* turned up at my place. I put off reading it until the evening. But then I was in such a rush to be finished with the pigs that I put the pitchfork through my foot!" She apologizes for being late sending the *Rundbrief* on, since she was in the hospital. Otherwise, life goes on the same, except it is not the same, since she has had a surprise late addition to her family: "We are all so happy at how well our little Kerstin is doing. On 7 August she was one year old. Käthchen," she says, addressing Käthe Sommer, another to have had a late, unexpected baby, "I'm sure you'll agree, having a late arrival like this has everything to commend it!"

As for the rest of her family, her husband is happier now, training apprentices in agriculture, while the children love sport: Elka has been riding, the boys playing football, and they were all lucky enough to be able to go to Berlin in June to see the competition for places in the combined German team for the Tokyo Olympics in 1964. "It was a wonderful day," she says, paying no attention to the highly political nature of such events, before the two German states finally had their own Olympic teams in 1968. Writing again on 16 February 1966, Hertha says that sport still plays a major part in their lives, particularly for her children: "Since I myself was always so enthusiastic about sport, I don't put anything in the way of the children, even though that can sometimes be difficult." Participating in their mother's interview in 2013, all of Hertha's now-adult children said how good it had been for them growing up in the GDR, with all the sports and so many other activities for them to take part in.

In her letter of 12 March 1967, Hertha stresses how important the group is for her: "Hopefully we'll be able to be at the next class reunion. After all, it is always *the* high point of the year." Otherwise, she again concentrates on news of her family, commenting, "Our littlest is great fun for all of us." The others, however, are all growing up: "Elka will be doing her *Abitur* next year; Wilfried is greatly enjoying his job as a lathe operator; Klaus is being confirmed next Sunday."

Although Hertha no longer says anything directly about the GDR authorities, there is nevertheless a political point in her comment about Klaus: he will be confirmed in the church. This is despite the considerable pressure to undergo the socialist and nonreligious equivalent, the *Jugendweihe*, instead. The *Jugendweihe* had its origins in the secular movements of the nineteenth century but was suppressed by the Nazis. The SED reintroduced it and promoted it as their preferred option for a public coming-of-age ceremony. Accounts suggest that many young people enjoyed it as a significant rite of passage. They liked the celebration among family and friends, with cakes and presents, even if they were required to pledge themselves publicly to work for the good of the socialist society. Some young people went through both confirmation and the *Jugendweihe*, but it is not clear if this was the case for Hertha Pieper's family. Nevertheless, her letter makes clear to the others that they still have a link to the church, despite pressure from the atheist state.

By the time of her next letter (23 April 1968), Hertha remains in a surprisingly good mood, given the problems she lists for them: she is far too busy and her mother is too old now to help with anything; the house is so large; the family is so large; they have so many animals that need to be attended to; her husband was ill for seven weeks with phlebitis and has been in the hospital; and her younger son Klaus has also been in the hospital with a hip injury from playing handball. Despite this, they all enjoy having sports at the center of their lives, and Elka is a keen horse rider, out every spare minute she can find. She will also be starting her studies in September to become a Russian-German teacher. Wilfried, who has finished his apprenticeship as a lathe operator, has to go into the army shortly. He is, she says, "a fantastic footballer." The youngest child, Kerstin, will be five in August. During the summer, she will start at kindergarten.

Again, in this letter, the state is a background presence, not commented on directly. For a start, it has provided the sporting opportunities that they all so love. Wilfried has been trained thanks to the state and now has to demonstrate his commitment to it by serving in the army. Finally, although Hertha and her mother have been looking after Kerstin in her early years, the state has now set up enough kindergartens for her to be able to attend one. What is striking in Hertha's letters during this period is that she says little about her work in the LPG. In the 1950s, she always talked of the endless work she had to do to keep the farm going and meet the demands of the state.

In her next letter (23 August 1969), Hertha expresses her surprise at how the Schönebeck women are all growing older and what this entails. Her daughter Elka, now twenty-one years old, was married in May, and she and her husband are living with Hertha and her husband as there is nowhere else for them at the moment. Hertha's own status is changing: "When I show up at the next reunion, it will probably be as the first grandmother among us. Sometimes I can't really take it in myself, but we are just not getting any younger." Meanwhile, having a much younger daughter keeps her active. She has rejoined the sports club, she says, and goes swimming with Kerstin (now six years old) every Thursday in the new heated pool in Calbe. She finds it particularly satisfying to discover she can still keep up with the young people there. She also tells them other family news: "Wilfried has been in the army since May. Since he is so keen on sport, it is not too hard for him.... Klaus finished school this year, while Kerstin doesn't start until 1970."

Hertha's letters give a picture of everyday life in the GDR in the 1960s revolving around the family and its opportunity for local pleasures. The family does not appear to go away for holidays or to travel anywhere else, except for the one visit to Berlin. A very different picture comes from Else Hermann, for whom everyday life in this period is centered on work.

Else Hermann

The 1960s saw Else Hermann's life change dramatically, several times over. It all started, ironically, with the building of the Berlin Wall, which was greatly to her benefit: "Thanks to the Wall, I got a job offer from Berlin, complete with housing, since the West Berliners working in the East could not come across any more, unless they settled there."[30] Anything else she wrote about this move from Erfurt to the Deutsche Staatsoper (German state opera) in Berlin disappeared with the lost book.

In Else's *Rundbrief* letter of 26 September 1964, it becomes clear that the accommodation provided in Berlin was not ideal. Once again there was an elderly widow to contend with:

> The most wonderful event for me in recent times is that I now have an apartment—small, but my own, something that in Berlin is normally pretty difficult. For two years I lived as a subtenant in a room in the apartment of an elderly widow (aged 81). In her last year she was so frail and in such disarray that I had to do all sorts of things for her. When she died, I fought to get the apartment, since it was a lovely place. But according to the housing office, the one and a half rooms were just too much for me, so they offered me a one-room apartment in Weissensee in one of the blocks built after the war. I was tired of the struggle, so I took it, and am now very satisfied with it.... Whoever comes to Berlin, you are warmly welcome to come here. I can offer space for three to sleep! Just the small kitchen is worth seeing. I'm happy that I never need to depend on the moods of a widow any more.

Else finds her work "totally fulfilling," but there is one major drawback, her boss:

> At the beginning I didn't get on at all with the woman who is my boss and I intended to look for something else. In the meantime, I have managed to battle for a certain level of autonomy and feel much better. For the past three years I have been the costume designer and creator at the Deutsche Staatsoper and I'll stay on for a fourth year. I'm also responsible here for getting all the costumes ready for the Deutsches Theater and the Berliner Ensemble, and particularly have a lot to do with the Deutsches Theater. If masks are needed for an opera, I'm the one who has to make them and then I'm completely in my element. At the moment, I'm making the masks for the witches in the opera *Macbeth*.

Talking in 2013 about this period in her life, Else declared that it was one of the hardest and yet ultimately most satisfying times for her in the GDR. There was tremendous pressure in the theater in Berlin, and her boss was both demanding and disparaging, believing Else would not be able to achieve the quality she expected of her, and patronizing her for being from the provinces. It was not only Else who was treated this way; others too, even from cities such as Dresden, could not work with her and had to leave.

Else had one particular challenge, to dress the characters of Lenin and a number of people from the army in a Soviet play. She could not afford to fail; mismanaging Lenin or putting him in the wrong clothes could be seen as evidence of hostility to the Soviet Union and the GDR. She worked really hard—"I had to make it work, and I did make it work!" she said—and received praise for doing so from people further up the hierarchy, something her boss could not ignore. It was then that she knew she would be able to leave and move on to something else on her own terms.

In her 1964 letter, it is clear that Else still feels emotionally very close to Schönebeck. She stayed at her parents' home there in the summer and greatly benefited from it, despite her concern at her father's decline: "Thanks to the abundance of fruit in the garden and to Bad Salzelmen's salt baths, it was easy to get to feel a whole lot better. . . . My father will be 79 in November. He can hardly see any more and is often unhappy as a result." Her mother, on the other hand, is only 70 and is "astonishingly lively." As for the rest of her family, her sister managed to come from West Berlin to see her in East Berlin, bringing her two children (already thirteen and eighteen years old). This was a high point of her year, a short but stimulating visit that they are all looking forward to repeating soon.

Else, like some of the others by this time, has discovered the benefits of holidays further east:

> In my next holidays, I'll certainly go to Poland again. Last year I had a few days in Warsaw and was thrilled by it. (My brother-in-law says, "Poland is the Austria of the East.") I think I talked once before about my enthusiasm for Poland, but my report on what has been going on in my life would not be complete if I didn't mention it.

Her interest came initially from the "outstanding journal" called *Poland*, by whose courageous graphics she is captivated (in contrast to those in the GDR, it is implied). She has been learning Polish every Tuesday for the past three years. She finds it difficult, but every step is an achievement. She took it up at the beginning to balance the problems she was having at work: "Throwing yourself into such extreme things really is a good way to overcome all sorts of crises."

In her next letter (7 April 1966, one day after her thirty-ninth birthday), Else discusses the family's celebrations for her father's eightieth birthday. However, her real news is that she has said farewell to the theater. She had too many problems with her legs, she says. She wonders how they will react when she tells them that she is now a student of German studies and arts education, with one year completed and three to go: "Maybe you are all shaking your heads? I am amazed myself sometimes." Since she started, her pains have gone and she is happy at the end of every day. As if she knows they will be asking how she is financing her studies, she says she has a student grant of three hundred Marks a month and, thanks to her parents, an apartment to live in and a fur coat for the winter.

Before she left the Staatsoper, Else went on an excellent *Kur* in a *Kneippbad* (where the treatment often involves partial or total immersion of the warm body in cold water, then exercise immediately afterward to warm the body again). She has become an enthusiast for the method, she says, and has hot and cold baths now that she is back home.

With an unnoticed echo of her earlier experience during the war, Else says that before she and her fellow students could start their course, they had to go out and help with the potato harvest (see figure 3.1). Although, given her age and her phlebitis, she might have been excused from this, she wanted to do it in order to get to know her fellow students and not be seen as an outsider: "It all worked out really well. The summer and autumn were ideal and the work was good for my circulation. I could take part in everything, dancing and hiking and so on. In our group of fourteen, there was only one man. Five of us (including me) had already had jobs, the others had just finished their *Abitur*."

Getting the students to work on the land was a way to test their commitment to socialism, and to give them a taste of what the workers had to go through, the workers whose taxes would be paying for their time at university. Sometimes the students learned more than the authorities had intended. Else recounted in an interview that after two weeks they were moved from one LPG to another, both run by the new breed of professionally qualified agriculturalists. One was sloppy and poorly managed, the other extremely Prussian, she said. The party kept control, however, since the former leaders of the cooperatives, both party functionaries, remained as deputy leaders, looking over the shoulder of the nominal bosses.

Figure 3.1. Else (*back left*) with her fellow potato harvesters. Photo courtesy of Akademie der Künste, Berlin.

Else Hermann was not a member of the SED but was not hostile to the state and its wider ambitions. In her *Rundbrief* letters and in her interviews, she praised the GDR for its approach to the theater, declaring that its training of people for the theater and the quality of its productions were widely admired in the West. She felt that everyone in the theater had learned a lot from Soviet producers and benefited from the quality of Russian literature. She also appreciated the chance to go to university. Her attitudes are reflected in her plans for travel and work: in the summer break, she writes, she will be going to Prague for a world congress of educators of children, and then on to Warsaw where she might like to work.

Censorship, Self-Censorship, Humiliation

There were times in Else's career in the theater where the state was shown in a less favorable light. In Erfurt, the theater company wanted to put on Brecht's *Die heilige Johanna der Schlachthöfe* but felt they should ask the SED regional leadership first if they could, since it depicted the working class rather negatively. The answer: "If you yourselves have doubts, then you would be better to choose something else." Fearful of the consequences if they went ahead with the Brecht, they put on *Richard III* instead.[31]

An autobiographical account from another woman heavily involved in the theater recounts a similar story. Anneliese Priewe, born in 1936, was more directly a product of socialization in the SBZ and the GDR. Her difficulties came from a production of *Das Schwitzbad* by the Soviet poet and playwright Mayakovsky, a satire on the growth of bureaucracy in postrevolutionary Moscow. The play was written in 1929, produced in April 1930, and met with increasing hostility before Mayakovsky's suicide in 1930. As the play was almost ready for its premiere in Weimar, it was performed before some local workers, leading the SED to object that "our people are not like that" and that it was not a socialist realist play. At the party meeting, the director was forced to make a groveling apology and go through the Communist ritual of self-criticism. By the next day, the party authorities had discovered that Mayakovsky was indeed "one of us," but still blocked the production. Following that, if Priewe anticipated difficulties, she made sure politically suitable groups could see the play early and give it their blessing, thus accepting both censorship and self-censorship. She says she saw later that what had happened was to do with the run-up to the Sixth Party Congress and the squeeze on artists. She refers particularly to the problems faced in Berlin by the production of Peter Hacks's *Die Sorgen und die Macht*.[32]

It was this production of *Die Sorgen und die Macht* at the Deutsches Theater that caused terrible problems for those involved with it, including Else Hermann as the costume designer and creator, and humiliation for the director,

Wolfgang Langhoff. Langhoff, a Communist since 1928, had been in a concentration camp under the Nazis before escaping to Switzerland. In 1946, he came to the Soviet zone and was appointed artistic director of the Deutsches Theater. He was a good actor and an even better director and was devoted to developing the theater in the new GDR.

The party organization within the Deutsches Theater, where Peter Hacks was the resident playwright, was happy with the work on the production. Early sample performances were well-received in the party-controlled press. The premiere was attended by top SED members who "warmly applauded" the performance; among them was Alfred Kurella, a candidate member of the Politburo and head of its cultural commission. Shortly afterward, the mood changed and official comments became highly critical.[33]

The theater company was given hope by a favorable article in *Neues Deutschland* on 9 December 1962 by Anna Seghers, head of the Writers' Union and one of the party's heroes. However, the play and those responsible for it became the scapegoat at a time when the party leadership wanted to hold out against Khrushchev's thaw and reassert its control over its artistic and literary community. The most vicious attack came at the Sixth Party Congress in January 1963, when Kurella summarized the SED's view that too many artists, writers, and film-makers, particularly in Berlin, believed they could take a line that was independent of the party. Even worse, some of them were party members.

Kurella saw Hacks's play as the prime example of this tendency. He criticized the representation of the greyness of socialism, and the suggestion that the party's policies were a "chain of mistakes" and the party itself just an ethical discussion group. Such views, he declared, led to a general sense of unease, and from there it was just a step or two to the demand for "freedom," freedom for artists to pursue their own creative ideas, freedom from the demands of the state, freedom to break the necessary connection between the party and cultural life.[34]

The attacks on the play and on the theater company at the Sixth Party Congress were the culmination of a long period of increasing pressure, which led eventually to the party group at the Deutsches Theater conceding they had been wrong and discontinuing the play's performances. The theater collective, including Else Hermann, were required to confirm that they had realized their mistakes and had canceled the play themselves. Else said it all felt very sordid and a terrible loss. She was very affected by what was done to the director Wolfgang Langhoff. He was required to appear in front of the Politburo and engage in "self-criticism." After initially disagreeing with the party authorities, he was forced to grovel in front of them, publicly admitting how he had failed the party, betrayed the trust of the people, not adhered to the important and necessary demands of socialist realism, and practiced—against his best intentions— "ideological co-existence," and was grateful to the party for helping him to see his mistakes.³⁵ This demonstration of power was a classic example of humiliation. It was compounded by the SED's subsequent actions: despite everything, they still stripped him of his role at the Deutsches Theater and expelled him from the party. He was already suffering from the cancer that would kill him in 1966.

As noted earlier in relation to the arrest of Erika Krämer, humiliation can have long-term consequences. Else Hermann said nothing in the *Rundbrief* about *Die Sorgen und die Macht* or about what was done to Wolfgang Langhoff. However, the affair was still close to her heart when she talked about it in an interview in 2015. She produced from her desk drawer a collection of press cuttings from the 1980s to the early 1990s, when archival research gave a clearer idea of what had been done. The cuttings were clearly important to her. Along the side of one of them, from 1991, she had written for my benefit: "*Mein Stück!*" (My play!). Her ongoing concern, her clearly expressed bitterness, and the fact that she had collected these cuttings and knew exactly where they were demonstrate the long-term impact of the affair.

Else and Her Father

A year later, Else has a particular preoccupation: the death of her father in 1966, which was noted by one of the other women in Book 10. In her letter of 9 April 1967, Else talks warmly about her father and regrets that he did not live to see her finish her studies, which she is still enjoying enormously, with her second year already behind her.

She discusses his work as a philologist and his research into Plattdeutsch—Low German. The house in Schönebeck is full of his books and writings about Plattdeutsch, along with unpublished poems. She arranged for people from the Science Academy in Berlin to come and take away a carload of his works and things he had collected. A book could result from that, she says, and she would be part of the editorial group for it.

Else was also very proud of her father's work on environmental conservation and was keen to talk about its significance in the Schönebeck area. By the late 1960s, heavy and light industry were both central to Schönebeck. Because of the lack of enforcement of environmental laws, Schönebeck suffered from high levels of pollution and its overall environment was drab and unattractive. Meanwhile, across the river, around Grünewalde and Elbenau—"über Elbe," as local people say in Schönebeck—there was another world, which was partly the creation of Else's father.

After he retired in 1955, his second passion became the natural world in all its variety and complexity. He worked with great enthusiasm and energy as an honorary nature conservation officer for the Schönebeck council.³⁶ He loved the "über Elbe" area, its river meadows bedraggled in the winter after frost and snow, green and sunny in the summer, the woods—river woods, local people call them—so flat you notice every slight shift in the ground as the path rises half a meter and drops back down again, soft underfoot from season after season of fallen leaves slowly decomposing. Everywhere there is new growth, and the woods are dense at ground level, unlike the beech forests elsewhere. In the thickets and high in the trees there are always birds—robins, wrens, chaffinches, and many others—while animals scamper almost unseen across the path, and all around there is the warm, heavy smell of dark, damp, fertile earth. Most of it is below the level of the river and its dikes. When the floods come, the meadows disappear, the trees sit in a meter of water, and the ponds that are dry in the summer are suddenly full of life: fish and birds, insects skimming across the water, even beavers making their dams. After a real flood, once or twice in a generation, these same ponds are a refuge for fallen trees that wash down into them, a refuge that becomes a graveyard when the water drains away and the summer sun cracks the dry earth before the next storm comes. The old trees lie there, trapped, slowly breaking down again, disappearing back into the soil. Sometimes, there is a clearing, bright and sunny, stretching out to become a field full of grain waiting to be harvested. This strange and beautiful world extends north and south for many miles, and all of it now, thanks largely to Else's father, is saved from destruction. That, she said, was a worthy monument to his life.

Nevertheless, her father's achievements also contributed to Else's ambivalence about her *Heimat*. Else was a modernizer, keen to learn and understand and to grow with the times. The Schönebeck *Heimat* was increasingly industrialized, with vast factories and thousands of workers. This was modernity, as far as the SED leaders were concerned, and the basis of a new socialist-realist culture. The population's traditional attachment to Germany's forests and natural landscapes was backward-looking and nostalgic; it was not to be encouraged. Nevertheless, over the decades it became clear to ordinary people just how much environmental damage was being done by the ever-expanding industry. This was seen in the loss of forests, the swallowing up of villages by open-cast coal mines, and the contamination of the rivers and lakes. It was experienced in everyday life through the polluted air and the illness and death resulting from it.[37]

Apparently anachronistic attempts to maintain and protect the physical environment and the physical beauty of the countryside were, paradoxically, more forward-looking than the policy of industrialization. Else herself was pulled both ways: toward the dynamism of the cities on the one hand and the tranquil beauty of the rural areas on the other. However, she knew the cities were also ugly and overpowering, the smaller towns and villages narrow and provincial, and areas such as Über-Elbe rare and under threat. Her father remained a model for her: someone who had both fully used his intellectual and creative talents and pursued his passion for the environment, and had managed to do this in provincial Schönebeck.

A Different Picture of the GDR

In her next letter (25 February 1968), Else says she is in the hospital in Bad Salzelmen because of recurrent digestion problems, in a ward with eighteen beds. Heidi Kempf, who lives nearby, comes in to help look after her. Despite her health problems, her studies are still going well: she has completed five semesters and only has three left.

When Else writes her next letter on 8 November 1969, things have moved on a long way. She has qualified as a teacher and been posted to Berlin-Malchow, an isolated part of Berlin on the northeastern border of the city, to teach German and art. This is a shock, as relations between students and teachers are poor: "Thanks to constant changes of teachers over the years, the level of achievement is indescribably low, and the young people are particularly clever in the tricks they get up to. The police are constantly in attendance." After two years there, she can apply to go somewhere else, a prospect she looks forward to: "After Berlin-Malchow, nothing can surprise me anymore."

This is not how the GDR authorities would like to see their young people and their education system portrayed. In the nearly twenty years of the *Rundbrief*, this is the most political description that Else has written. She appears to have no concern about it being read by the rest of the group or by anyone who might intercept it. It is as if she has forgotten the lesson of the missing book at the beginning of the 1960s, or has come to believe that the GDR at the end of the decade is a more modern, less brutal, and generally safer place for its citizens.

In an interview, I asked Else Hermann how familiar she was with the GDR's history, since many of the things that preoccupy historians and political scientists—the death of Stalin, the events of 17 June 1953, the Hungarian uprising, and the Prague Spring—seemed largely to have passed her by. She had not been particularly interested in such things, she said. Only in the late sixties did she come to learn more about what had gone on. She watched Western television, she said, even though this was an offense, so as not to look foolish by knowing less than her students.

Anna Siebert

Anna Siebert's story takes us back to the early 1960s in the West. One of the most dramatic events in the FRG was the flood catastrophe in Hamburg in February 1962, and one of the people who played a major part in the rescue and recovery operations was Anna Siebert. In an interview, she explained that the flooding occurred on a Friday evening when everyone had gone home. When she heard what was happening, she went to see how she could help and, as the only senior harbor authority person present, was suddenly given all sorts of responsibilities she had never expected. Helmut Schmidt (later the German chancellor) was the senator in Hamburg responsible for the police. He called in the army and got cooperation from the British Army as well. Suddenly Anna found herself advising the army on important details about the harbor and its structures, and being expected to tell them what to do and how to go about organizing the rescue activities. She was so astonished by what was happening and what was being asked of her that she simply got on and did it.

In 1964, the GDR made changes to its policy on travel that would have an impact on a number of the Schönebeck women. Anna Siebert was an immediate beneficiary. From 2 November 1964, GDR citizens who had reached pension age would have the right to visit relatives in the FRG and West Berlin once a year for four weeks. The Council of Ministers said it would have liked to extend the process of normalizing relations between East and West, but its experience was that its citizens were badly treated when they visited the FRG. The Council of Ministers added that it assumed that older people would be spared this treatment.[38] In her letter of 2 January 1965, Anna says that her parents, still living in Staßfurt, are now happily retired and were able at long last to come and see her in December.

Underlying frustrations come out in Anna's letter of 18 May 1966. Initially she says that all is going well for her in Hamburg and that her job with the harbor authority is her greatest interest. After twelve years as a woman in a man's world, she felt she had broken through, only to discover this was not so:

> When a post as Chief Engineer became vacant, the fact that I am of the female sex caused me great problems once again. Since they couldn't claim their decision was based on my lack of professional expertise, they then declared the vacant post was to work out in the harbor, often using boats, and that as a woman I wouldn't be suited to all the climbing up and down ladders that would be involved. And in any case, I would be getting older.

With great determination, Anna argued that she had the ability to do the work as well as any man, and managed to get the job. She is now responsible for the whole of the harbor infrastructure on the water side—docks, piers, floating docks, and harbor walls, for instance—and manages three hundred employees. She has the rank of Chief Engineer and is the only woman in the FRG in such a position.

Another story about Anna Siebert concerns a state visit to Germany by Britain's head of state, Queen Elizabeth. This involved a trip to Hamburg in the royal yacht, with a smaller boat to bring her ashore. Anna's position meant she had full responsibility for all the structures in and adjoining the harbor. However, she was not included in the official welcoming party, quite possibly (judging from her previous treatment) because she was a woman. Since she was often out on the river, she decided to do her rounds in her boat and check that everything was in order. At one point she approached the dock where the royal couple would be disembarking. As she came close, everyone stood to attention, saluted, and lined up to welcome her ashore, thinking she was the Queen. Anna told this story with great delight, aware of its significance: her action undermined the authority of the men around her. By laughing at them she showed they could not humiliate her.

In the 1960s, many of the parents of the Schönebeck women were getting ill and dying. Anna, writing on 27 May 1967, says she is about to go to Staßfurt for her father's funeral: he had lung cancer and death was a release for him. She was there three weeks previously and helped look after him: "They were painful days, particularly leaving him, knowing that we would never see each other again." She says she is sorry she did not get to visit the others nearby, but she had to spend time with her parents and suddenly it was too late.

There are more-mundane reports in her letter as well. Earlier in the year she went for her annual skiing holiday in Switzerland with Brigitte Hansen. Safely back in Hamburg playing tennis, which she loves, she tore her meniscus and had to have her knee operated on.

Over all these years, Anna had not been able to attend the class reunion in the GDR, despite saying in almost every letter that she hoped to do so. With it taking place in Wismar, she writes on 6 August 1968, she could make it at last:

> Well, the reunion was just great. For me it was the first time in over twenty years to be able to meet up again with all of you from Schönebeck still living over the border, and I was completely bowled over by it. It was as if we had never been apart. The old closeness was immediately there. And added to that was the lovely, comforting atmosphere in Lisa's new house. Lisa had set out everything so attractively and served us so royally that it will be really hard to repeat. That I should have the experience for the first time of everyone being so hospitable made such an impression on me, though from the way the reunions have been described over recent years, it seems it is always like that over there.
>
> After we had all opened our hearts to one another during the afternoon while the men were out visiting Wismar, the fun of the evening began with an excellent cold buffet that left us wanting for nothing. Finally, we danced and laughed late into the night.

Three of the women from the West were there, plus Irma Kindler's husband. To the others, Anna says, "It is definitely worth it to go over there and take part in the next class reunion."

On 7 March 1970, Anna says there is little to report, but what she does tell them is significant: she has been appointed to be the first civil engineering director (*Oberbaurätin*) in Germany (meaning the FRG). She was reluctant to leave her old position at first, and the move has been hard on her health, but she realizes that the promotion was worth it. For once, she had to struggle with herself rather than with the prejudices of men: at first, she turned the job down, thinking she lacked the skills for it, but her bosses thought differently, so finally she said yes. Anna is in charge of a directorate and is responsible for all the bridges, docks, and industrial buildings in the whole huge area of the Hamburg harbor authority.

Irma Kindler

Irma Kindler's life in Hamburg in the 1960s is very different from Anna Siebert's, being much more focused on her family and the activities of her husband and children, as well as their travels. Her involvement in the group of Schönebeck women remains an important part of her life. Only late in the decade does she go back to work outside the home again.

Writing on 26 October 1964, Irma says that she and her family have moved into a new house in Hamburg that they are very happy with. On 10 May 1967, Irma says that an underground rail system is being built in Hanover, and, since they are short of expertise to do this, Franz is working there for a year and only returning to Hamburg on weekends.

A year later (30 May 1968), Irma has taken a part-time job. This is only up to the holidays, she says; then she will see how she feels, since it is time-consuming and involves journeys to work. On the other hand, "it boosts my self-confidence inordinately to be able to keep my end up in a job. After thirteen years out, I was a bit dubious about that at first." Like some of the women in the GDR who came to this conclusion much earlier, she realizes there are real personal benefits to working outside the home, and these are not just financial.

Irma's son Joachim is learning Russian as his foreign language at school, she writes. He is enjoying it and making astonishingly rapid progress. This is the first mention of any children of the women in the West learning Russian, whereas in the GDR Russian was the foreign language all the children learned at school. From a later letter, it seems that Joachim had made a political choice and was caught up in the 1968 enthusiasm for breaking with convention and exploring alternative ideas.

As a family, they had their 1967 summer holiday on the Black Sea in Romania and took an unforgettable trip by ship to Istanbul. In May they went skiing in the Tirol and in the coming summer will be going to Yugoslavia. Franz is still building the underground rail service in Hanover, though she hopes this will be over by the autumn.

By the time of her letter of 28 November 1969, Irma is permanently employed half-time in the student services section of the university (the Studentenwerk) and is very happy with her work. Franz, back from Hanover, is working on the new Elbe tunnel in Hamburg. A photo, not noteworthy then but striking now, shows Irma and Franz smoking in the house, in the presence of the children.

Travel continues to be important to them. The family have had a number of holidays, one in the Dolomites in winter, where their son broke his leg on the first day, another in northern Spain in the summer, and yet another in summer, in Montenegro, part of Yugoslavia, which had a particularly interesting moment: "I went with my son, an admirer of Mao, on a trip into Albania, somewhere that's just about impossible to go to from here. They stuffed us full of slogans, but what was most interesting in all of that was what was *not* able to be said and what was *not* able to be photographed." This is a long way from anything any of the women, East or West, would be prepared to say about the GDR. It seems on one level a safe enough comment to include in the *Rundbrief*, since Albania had sided politically with China against the Soviet Union and its allies, including the GDR, and therefore could be openly criticized. More problematic is the reference to her son as an admirer of Mao. The GDR authorities were deeply hostile to Maoists, and the Stasi would certainly have been interested in Irma, a frequent visitor to the GDR, if they had come across this reference in the *Rundbrief*.

Families

In the FRG, there was not so much a "woman question" as a family question, which effectively defined women as subject to men, despite formal equality. In the 1950s, for instance, more-liberal divorce laws imposed by the Western Allies were interpreted restrictively, in accordance with the governing Christian Democrats' commitment to a religious view of marriage. This approach was formalized in 1961, supposedly to protect women but leaving them bound to men they wished to divorce. It was only in the late 1960s that the government and the courts started to reconsider this approach.[39]

For the Schönebeck women in the East, the "woman question" was also mostly a "family question"; they appear to have paid no attention to the SED's constant urgings to prove themselves as women by committing themselves actively to building socialism. Their children were important to them; so was being employed. Frieda Möller (8 March 1966) says she makes a point of going out to work, leaving her mother to look after the three children when they are not at school. She likes her work, because she is "out there fully involved in life, not just a housewife." And they can do with the extra money, she adds.

In the 1960s, the women in the GDR realized that their children were growing up differently from them, with a different outlook on life. They were a new generation, born and educated in the GDR and starting to respond, favorably or not, to its approach—a generation not directly affected by the Nazi period or the chaos at the end of the war.

This change in outlook was not confined to the GDR. In the FRG, too, the children were growing away from their parents, a process that culminated in 1968 in the outbursts of revolt and rejection of traditional attitudes and values and the authoritarianism of the state. The extent of rebellion or even divergence was limited among the children of the Schönebeck women, and there is considerable acceptance of the benefits offered by the new societies in both the East and the West. Nevertheless, some of the letters convey a sense of restlessness among the children, and a wish to break away from what is imposed on them by their parents or by the state.

Highlighting the differences between the generations, Marianne Schneider (20 February 1964) says that she and Johannes sometimes speak in English so that their children do not know what they are saying. Now their two older children are starting to do the same to them by speaking in Russian. She makes clear her own position on this, with an overtly political statement: "We just stand there impotently, since it would all be in vain for us to attempt to get to grips with this language. And by the way, we certainly *don't want to*."

Similarly, Barbara Meier, also in the GDR, has some thoughts about the younger generation and their unwillingness to get involved in things or strive to do their best. Her son is nearly fifteen and, she says on 19 March 1966, like many of the other women's children, particularly keen on winter sports. He would like to become an electrician, not to study medicine, which she would prefer: "In a way he has things in common with some of your children. He just lets everything come to him and does only what is strictly necessary or else only what interests him."

Many of the children reflect well on the GDR and its education system, despite Else Hermann's experiences in Berlin. Lisa Liebmann in Wismar (GDR) responds to Barbara's point on 29 March 1966, saying that their son Paul is not ambitious, but still would like to study medicine. In her letter of 28 January 1968, she says that Paul was accepted to study medicine but was required to work in the hospital in Berlin before starting his studies. Then it turned out that he had to go into the army first, in November 1967, which had its advantages: "Now he is an upright member of the army in the medical service, which means he will no longer need to do his work experience before he begins his studies." By 1969, their son is engaged to a young woman studying to be an engineer at the Technical University in Dresden. The parents think it is too soon and are skeptical about the chances of a successful marriage; he points out that they too got engaged when they were very young.

Keeping the Peace in the Family is Hard Work!

The Schönebeck women are rarely emotional in their letters. A striking exception is Gisela Riedel's entry of 8 July 1964. She now has two daughters, aged three and a half, and one and three-quarters. Looking after them is hard enough, but her position is made worse by an intractable battle between her mother and her husband, and by the impossibility of living anywhere else: "Yes, now I am nothing but a housewife and mother, having chucked in my job for the moment. That would all be fine, if it wasn't for the perpetual squabbling between my husband and my mother, with whom we are still living." Since it is impossible to separate the two households, she is left with trying to get them to make up, and trying to keep the children away from their battles. She is the lightning conductor, she says. Her only peace comes when her husband is away or when the two of them have a holiday together with the children. It is clear that she is beside herself with frustration and overwork and the constant tension, and is barely coping with having to do everything expected of her.

By the time of her next letter (24 January 1966), Gisela has three children. She describes in detail the interminable work involved from the beginning of the day to the end. If she sounds pessimistic, she says, "that is because [she is] always so terribly tired and worn out." Nevertheless, life is basically okay; it is just that she is trying to see herself as "a good mother and a tolerably decent wife." On 1 March 1968, she says again how exhausting everything is and that things are even harder now as her mother is too old to help any more. She herself is wasting away, getting ever thinner, she says: "Soon you will only recognize me if you look through a magnifying glass." The photos she includes show this to be a matter of self-image; she is not particularly thin. Her letter of 19 August 1969, however, indicates that her weight loss is due to a hyperactive thyroid.

Martha Jäger in the 1960s

Martha Jäger continues to stand out in the 1960s with her accounts of the life of a well-off woman in the GDR with a house to run, children, and a part-time job in the family business.

In her letter of 15 June 1964, she talks of their latest run of bad luck: illness, rain causing damage to their house, and not being allocated enough accommodation to have a skiing holiday, with prospects little better for their summer holiday. Writing on 30 January 1967, Martha discusses the long process of having building work done to their house to create a self-contained apartment for her mother. (Her father had died in 1965.) It seemed interminable, she says, but was eventually finished in July 1966. The whole experience was terrible, and she has little positive to say about the builders. Such comments would not have upset the authorities, however, who were hostile to the continued independence of craft workers:

> It was a horrible year for me, with mess everywhere, since everything had to be brought through the hallway. You had to stand there keeping an eye on every tradesman or they wouldn't have built a nice apartment but a shanty. Sometimes I just had to shake my head over the level of stupidity: they would smear so much stuff over the switches and sockets that you couldn't find where they were—and other such absurdities.

After all that, her mother died on 1 September 1966, leaving Martha and her husband to run the business on their own. Once again, in her letter of 19 March 1968, Martha's preoccupations are not to do with building socialism:

> Finally I can come up for air, only to see to my horror that it's time to send the *Rundbrief* on its way. So I shall be brief, and maybe later I'll stick a few photos in. I have had to cope with painters and decorators working in four rooms. On top of that, my cleaner is ill and in the meantime, I have to get along to the business. When it's like that, you often don't know what you should do first, and I really wanted to have the apartment back in order before Angelika's birthday.

On 16 July 1969, Martha says that their son has finished his *Abitur* and is doing work experience before studying to be an engineer. Earlier in the year he had to have an emergency appendectomy; it was discovered that a cyst had formed as well, so he was in hospital for four weeks, a terrible time for them all. Better news is that their motorbike has been replaced by a car, a Wartburg, after a wait of eight years. Talking of her daughter learning to dance and having her school ball, Martha is transported back in time:

> The ball was really nice, but in no way comparable to ours!!! Much better though was her class party that was organized recently, with the parents attending too. There we got to show off our skills on the dance floor as well. Still, the evening also made me feel a little melancholy, since the years have gone by so fast. The party took place in the ballroom of the former "Preußischer Hof," exactly there where we had our school ball. Suddenly there you are back in those days once more, just a young girl again.

Breaking with Traditional Attitudes: Anni Lange

Like Martha Jäger in the East, the opera singer Anni Lange is an exception in the West. Based at the Hamburg Opera, she also tours a lot. Since her husband is now teaching at a university in Ankara, he lives there with their son. Anni visits them when she can, often for only ten days at a time. She writes of her travels in her undated letter in 1967:

I was a guest in Edinburgh with the Stuttgart Opera. That was a lovely time! From 21 February to 3 March I visited Ankara. I went on the Europabus via Zagreb and Sofia to Istanbul, had a look at Istanbul (wonderful city), then flew to meet my family in Ankara. Ankara is 900 meters above sea level, so has a wonderful climate with dry air. But you are really out in the steppes already, so at times it's a bit depressing. On 10 June we set off to Montreal for the World Expo, and after that the Metropolitan Opera in New York. A fabulous year.

Among the Schönebeck women, this is the most unusual way to manage family life, and it matches none of the official expectations or those of the group, in the West or the East. What is clear is that Anni Lange is not burdened by these expectations and will run her life—and enjoy it—the way she wants to. Because the other women see her as one of their models, it is hard for them to criticize her or to try to influence what she does.

Family and Work

In the 1960s, the idea that going out to work would make a significant contribution to the prosperity of the nation was a clear theme in the GDR for men and women, and in the FRG specifically for men. In both, this was a decade where it looked as though one's individual effort might make a difference. Both states developed rapidly, but as the FRG's economic miracle continued (despite a brief slowdown late in the decade), it moved still further ahead of the GDR.

Curiously, in this decade it is the women in the West who talk with more interest about their work outside the home. Anna Siebert stands out, but Irma Kindler too has rediscovered the pleasures of being employed after years at home with the children. Elsewhere, in 1965, Leni Baumann is enjoying her teaching and writing in Braunschweig. Her entry called "Family, Household" features in the *Enzyklopädisches Handbuch der Sonderpädagogik* (Encyclopedia of special needs education), and a copy is tied into the *Rundbrief* for them all to see. Hilde Brenner works for an institution in Sonnenberg in the Harz that organizes international conferences aimed at promoting understanding between peoples. While she was attending her first reunion in 1965 (in the West), Leni Baumann was participating in one of the conferences in Sonnenberg. In 1966, Elfriede Berger says she has played with the idea of going back to study law but has not managed to get enough energy to pursue it. In any case, her husband says she already has enough to do, since he cannot be without her at his offices, where she has worked since his heart attack in 1960.

In the 1960s, the GDR became a relatively modern, technologically advanced, industrial state, but when the women there talk about their work during this decade, it is usually with little enthusiasm. Work is primarily seen as something they like to do as it takes them out of the house and allows them to feel involved in the society around them. Few of them—Else Hermann is a notable exception—see their work as personally fulfilling. No one talks, except ironically, about it meeting the state's key demand, to contribute to building socialism.

Interaction with the State

In their letters, the Schönebeck women in the West and the East often seem oblivious to the state. Nevertheless, their everyday lives continued to be shaped by decisions made by political and administrative bodies. Matters to do with jobs, housing, benefits for having children, taxes, health, travel, social policy, and the environment all involved interaction between the state and its citizens.

In the context of the Cold War, each side was assertively hostile to the fundamental principles of the other and each declared that its approach was fairer and more democratic than the other's. However, the contrast between the attempt to build an effective democracy with a capitalist social market economy in the FRG, and the pursuit of communism under a dictatorship in the GDR, was too great to be ignored.

Marianne Schneider

In the Schönebeck letters, there is a general reluctance to talk about state power. What is striking in the 1960s, however, is that Marianne Schneider, the organizer of the *Rundbrief*, emerges as someone prepared to draw the women in both the East and the West into thinking about the political context of their lives. In her second letter in Book 9, concluding the volume on 22 November 1965, the day of their latest reunion, Marianne declares that for her, the closeness of the group cannot be undermined by the political divisions in Germany. At the reunion, she says, were two of the women "from the golden West" and nine women and five husbands "from the even more golden East." This proves not only the indomitable spirit of their class, but also the friendship "between socialism and capitalism!!"

In January 1966, Marianne introduces Book 10 by addressing the women (in the feminine form) as

> Dear so-called citizens of the GDR!
> Dear citizens of the Federal Republic!
> (in the *two free parts* of Germany!)

While this might look like innocent wordplay, it is an indication that she is prepared to be increasingly bold and assertive in her writing, and that she is seeking to shape the debate, or at least set the tone for the letters. She knows they live in politically complicated times and insists on this being acknowledged. Her form of address is full of irony, echoing the strident, hectoring approach of GDR politicians, and specifically the 1966 New Year address to the nation and to West Germany by Walter Ulbricht, head of the SED and GDR head of state: "Dear fellow citizens, comrades and friends! ... Dear citizens of the West German Federal Republic!" What can Marianne mean by "so-called" when talking about GDR citizens? Is this the language of the West, denying the fact of the GDR's existence? More provocative, however, is Marianne's insistence that both the German states are "free," since each claimed the other was far from free. For Ulbricht, the GDR was the only entity that could legitimately speak on behalf of the freedom-loving, democratic forces in Germany, while the Bonn Government was nothing but the dictatorship of state monopoly capitalism, doing the bidding of its American masters and planning for the repression of its own people in the interests of West German millionaire arms dealers. "We, on the other hand," his message continues, "base our approach on the power of the people, on the ruling principles of human dignity and freedom from need and exploitation, on the participation and shared responsibility of all who are doing something or have accomplished something for the society."[40] In the FRG, the *Frankfurter Allgemeine Zeitung* (*FAZ*) referred briefly to this speech, pointing out that Ulbricht was too ill to deliver it himself. The *FAZ* quoted from the New Year speech by the FRG's president, Heinrich Lübke, who stressed the terrible injustice being done to some of the German population—that is, in the GDR—and the need to keep pressing for reunification through exercising the right to self-determination, as guaranteed by the United Nations. The *FAZ*, in this and other reports, avoided giving even indirect recognition to the GDR, referring to the "Soviet zone" and the "Zone army," while putting all references to the GDR in quotation marks.[41]

In her New Year letter, Marianne addresses Brigitte Hansen in Switzerland. Again, her political observations are wrapped in irony: "Zürich, dear Brigitte, sounds as though it is almost as beautiful as Schönebeck!! If it was more beautiful there, we would all certainly be on our way!! But our government thinks nowhere could be more beautiful than here, so that is what we think too."

At the start of Book 11 (26 December 1966), Marianne writes a heartfelt passage in which there is a deep and very politically conscious yearning for them all to be able to live without their lives being determined by the political differences between East and West:

> I am thinking here particularly of the political situation in our oh so shrunken "Greater Germany." How much we have we lost and how humble and unassuming we have become! How happy and grateful we would be if we could just be allowed to take a trip along the Rhine or to the Black Forest, or above all else, be

able to visit our loved ones over there. But enough of such musings! Two birds in the bush are no use to us; we'll have to see what we can make of the bird in the hand.

Once again, in Book 12 (3 January1968), Marianne's letter is overtly and more subtly political in some of its comments. She again uses irony to satirize the SED's obsession with planning. However, there is also an assumption that after almost twenty years of the GDR, the women there have a shared vocabulary and set of aspirations that they have all accepted as part of their daily lives: "Thank you all for your lovely letters and nice photos. Carry on being loyal correspondents, meeting the requirements of the plan. Doing so is the only way we can hope to make it to the fiftieth anniversary of the *Rundbrief*." Reporting on how 1967 was for her family, she says, "We have no cause for complaint or dissatisfaction. As we both anticipated and wished, everything ran according to plan." With her mother and the children, the whole family went to Karlsbad (Czechoslovakia) at Whitsun, where they met up with her stepfather from the West.

In the following passage from Marianne's letter, some of the consequences of World War II are spelled out unusually explicitly, making clear the sense of loss in relation to the territories to the east. She identifies the Soviet Union as being responsible for the expulsion of Polish people from land that was once theirs and, by implication, of the western movement of the German population from the land subsequently occupied by the Poles. The Oder-Neiße-Peace-Border (Oder-Neiße-Friedensgrenze) refers to the postwar border with Poland, which was disputed still by many Germans, particularly in the West. For people in the GDR, there was a mixture of regret and acceptance about this border, though also some cynicism. After all, the SED leaders had expressed outrage at the prospect of losing the Saarland in the West to France but, in order to comply with the demands of the Soviet Union, accepted (though apparently with some reluctance) the loss of the territories to the east.[42] Marianne's view fits into the narrative heard in East and West that the new Polish residents were unable to look after their land in the way the Germans had:[43]

> The other six of us drove first (ever forward-looking!) to the Oder-Neiße-Peace-Border! My husband still had close relatives on the German side of Forst, a town divided by the Neiße. We dropped our daughter off there. Then the five of us carried on further into the Riesengebirge [the high range straddling the Polish-Czech border] toward Krummhübel, at the foot of the Schneekoppe. We were able to enjoy the natural beauty of the area there to the full, since our permits to travel abroad were valid for both the Czech and the Polish sides. Each day we did some lovely walks and trips. (Dear Lisa and Charlotte, do you still remember the night walk we did to the Schneegruben Hut in 1943? I couldn't find the Hotel Belvue in Harrachsdorf again, by the way.) Unfortunately, many of the mountain huts have been destroyed or are in a desperate condition. My husband,

who often used to have his holidays in the Riesengebirge, was an excellent guide, but the things we saw as we passed through there (things that were not really meant for the tourists) were very sad and depressing. The beautiful old Silesia with its neat houses and well-tended streets was no longer to be found. Still, for the sake of politeness I should keep silent about that. While you can get by well on the Czech side speaking German, it is very much harder to make yourself understood on the Polish side. The people who live there now all originate from the territories that used to be Polish and are now occupied by the Soviet Union. So they are also expellees—oh, pardon me: resettlers. In Breslau we saw the beginnings of reconstruction, but you still find lots of ruins.

Marianne is less comfortable dealing with potential conflict over the very political issues of what men and women should be doing and the roles they should play at home and in the society. At home there have been surprising changes in her life, which highlight both the continuing domination by men in a supposedly equal society and the power of earlier traditions of married women not going out to work: she is giving up her job. Up to now she has been doing some teaching and marking for her school and was planning to continue with it. However, she says, her husband would prefer her not to work, and as they have lots of visitors, she wants to be able to get things ready for them and not always be rushing off to do her marking. Despite her gently mocking tone, it is clear she will comply with her husband's wishes: "But the man of the house would prefer it that his slippers be brought for him when he comes home. (You don't have to take this remark totally literally.)"

Even when talking about her family meeting other women from the group, Marianne cannot resist a few jibes at the SED regime, along with references to anti-communism in the West. In November 1967, she and her husband met Charlotte Krüger (from the West) in Berlin. Otto (Charlotte's husband) and Johannes had long been exchanging postage stamps and now had finally met. Marianne says she suggested papering the walls with GDR stamps: "(Not all of them are red, you know!) But the gentlemen won't agree to that." She pastes into the *Rundbrief* a GDR stamp that says "20 years of the SED," and writes in tiny writing along the margin next to it, "not necessarily to be taken as an advertisement!"

From her next letter on 25 May 1969, it is clear that Marianne is still doing some relief teaching and is happy with the flexibility it gives her. On this matter at least, she has prevailed over her husband. Writing from their "holiday paradise," the teachers' bungalows in Allrode in the Harz, which they visit at least twice a year, she says that they spent Whitsun in Karlsbad, as they had the previous year. This prompts her to make the only comment so far on the invasion of Czechoslovakia, something she is aware she is allowed to say little about: "By the look of it, that's the end of such trips into the neighboring Czechoslovakia. But we are not responsible for that, and nor is anyone else attached to our group. I ought not to say anything more on this theme, or I'll get another reprimand from Lisa." Written next to this is a later comment from Lisa Liebmann: "(was only done with the best of intentions! L.)."

Both of these comments are significant. Marianne suggests that she is aware of the seriousness of what has happened and its implications for the GDR, where there will be no "Prague Spring" or political liberalization. More important, perhaps, for the group as a whole is her confirmation that none of their sons was among the GDR troops who camped by the border, ready to join the invasion if needed. For Germans East and West, there were too many echoes of the invasion of Czechoslovakia under the Nazis in 1938. Lisa's response confirms that there has been a discussion, perhaps at one of the reunions, where she suggested to Marianne that she should beware of making politically sensitive comments.

Marianne is not so easily deterred, however. Describing an enjoyable time in Hungary in the summer, on Lake Balaton, she says that on their way back they had another three days in Prague, though this was "all, naturally, before that particular day in August!" She also makes clear the limits placed on them when they are traveling: "If there had been nothing to prevent us, then of course we would have come back via Vienna, since we were not more than twenty-five kilometers away from there. But the barriers at the border reminded us here too that we had to keep our feet on the 'red carpet.'"

Talking of her children, Marianne is worried: their oldest son has been traveling around in the GDR and will shortly be taking his *Abitur*. But what is worse, she says, is what then awaits him. In other words, he has to go into the army, and she is not happy at the prospect. At least Lisa's son has that behind him, she says.

Expulsion: Käthe Sommer's story

Marianne talks in her letters as if it is safe to say mildly critical things, sometimes half concealed by irony. The story of Käthe Sommer and her family at the end of the 1960s shows the state in a less benevolent light.

Käthe's husband was a highly skilled ophthalmologist, and together they ran an eye clinic in Schönebeck. They had been pushed out of their clinic in Magdeburg at short notice in 1953 as the SED intensified the class struggle and put pressure on independent businesses and skilled professionals. By the end of the 1960s, they had four children, aged between six and twenty-three. Käthe's letter of 12 August 1969 shows how settled and happy the family were in the ordinariness of their everyday life in Schönebeck and in the GDR itself:

> After a wonderful three weeks in Heiligendamm [on the Baltic], I have been overwhelmed by work again back here. This year we have had constantly beautiful hot weather, the like of which I guess you only see otherwise down around

the Mediterranean. We were able to sit outside without our jackets on late into the evening. Unfortunately, I was tormented by my second bout of gall bladder problems, so I have just had myself X-rayed to see if I still need to keep the blessed thing.... We have a lovely circle of friends in Heiligendamm, people we have been meeting there for exactly ten years. They have children the same age as ours. This year they—the children—were constantly on a high, falling in love with one another, almost always happy, though between now and the next year everything will no doubt totally change. We adults just looked on, amused and not bothered. No engagements are in sight and Rainer at the moment is keen to remain unattached.

... Since September 1968, I have been working full-time in the surgery and am happy to be able to make my escape from the household early in the day.... Rainer's third year of study is now underway, starting with rehearsals for opera parts. Next year he will have a lead role in his first full performance at the university. Since he is the only bass-baritone in his group of students, he is greatly in demand. Uwe will be qualified as a hospital nurse next year. Peter is still wrestling with puberty and surprises us now with his enormously witty repartee. He's a keen photographer and does very well with a quite cheap camera. Christa starts school on 1 September with the Riedels' Silke. Thanks to the exuberance of our children (and their mother), our family life is constantly pretty tumultuous.

That's it for this year.

Similarly, when she is writing on 31 March 1971, Käthe appears to have no sense that anything unusual is about to happen to her family. Her news is entirely straightforward. She and Herbert celebrated their silver wedding anniversary in September 1970, and, on same day, Rainer was married. Their new daughter-in-law has finished her five years studying music and is now a singer in the theater in Erfurt where Else Hermann once worked. She has a five-year-old daughter whom they like very much. Rainer, the bass-baritone, has his exams next year. As for the marriage, it is "thoroughly tempestuous, loud and wild, since both are very hot-tempered.... There is nothing new to report about the rest of the family."

Suddenly, a few months later, extreme pressure was put on the family, who represented the old class-based society the SED was trying to get rid of. In the eyes of the state, they were a bourgeois relic, undermining the GDR. Erich Honecker was now at the head of the SED and attempting to reorient it, at least in terms of propaganda, toward meeting ordinary people's needs. As part of the process of completing the nationalizing of industry in the early 1970s, craft workers and people in independent businesses and even semi-state industries were singled out for criticism in SED events and in the press. They were invited to see that it was in everyone's interest for them to "find the path to socialism."[44]

160 *Friendship without Borders*

For reasons that are not clear, however, the authorities decided it was time not just to take control of the Sommers' eye clinic but also to be rid of the Sommer family. By this time, the GDR understood that "selling" actual or perceived opponents to the West was a profitable way to dispose of them, since it earned the state much-needed hard currency and saved judicial and prison costs.[45] The Sommer family were apparently given an ultimatum: allow themselves to be "bought out" or face something worse—presumably detention—in the GDR.[46] They agreed to go to the West and had to leave at extremely short notice, taking almost nothing with them. This split the family: three of the children went with the parents, but Rainer stayed in the GDR (with his tempestuous wife), with no prospect of seeing his parents again. Else Hermann suggested later that this incident, which shocked the whole group, made those in the East feel more vulnerable, and all of them on both sides of the border less willing to speak their mind at the reunions or in the *Rundbrief*.

Travel, Holidays, Leisure

Although the gap between West and East in economic terms continued to widen, for the Schönebeck women in the 1960s it was still housing and the freedom to travel that distinguished the West from the East. Traveling from East to West or West to East was a revelation, making the differences in housing very clear.

Sabine Kleber

Sabine Kleber, a keen traveler whose most significant journey was her escape from the GDR, says on 10 February 1965 that a three-room apartment still strikes her as wonderful and totally different from what she knew before. She compares her position with that of Else Hermann, who is so happy about her one-room flat in Berlin. Sabine is also pleased to have a good job and the freedom to travel around and to think what she likes without having to consider it in advance.

At the same time, Sabine remains dissatisfied. She misses what she has left behind in the GDR, particularly her friends and her family, which is something that they who have stayed over there with their families will never properly grasp, she says. Although she has good friends, she writes, "I have also lost many good friends. Lost: the word is actually too strong, since I remain in touch with them through letters. But when we don't see one another for so long, it's hard to feel we are properly connected." Last year, she tells them, she did manage to go to Schönebeck, but only for eight days and was not allowed an extension to her travel permit by the GDR authorities. She visited Marianne, and her sister from Bitterfeld came over as well. Schönebeck seemed just the same, only smaller.

On 20 July 1967, Sabine says she is going to Greece for a holiday. Others in the West report on holidays in Norway, Sweden, Paris, Salzburg, and in ski resorts. On 14 October 1968, Sabine says that for almost a year now she has had a car and at last can get out and explore properly. She finds herself "really taken by the Pfalz, which has," she says, "become home to me now." She has traveled elsewhere in Germany too, as well as to Alicante and Morocco in the past year. She has only one regret: "Oh how I wish that all of you, too, who have stayed back in our old *Heimat*, could also undertake such journeys."

Others in the West continued to travel extensively. Erika Krämer and her family spend three weeks every year in Locarno. They have also been in Vienna, and to Sweden to see friends from her student days in Rostock. On 25 January 1965, she says, they went walking for three weeks in the Harz and whenever they saw the border, which was often, she thought of them "over there."

For those of them "over there" in the 1960s, now that the West has been definitively cut off, there is the start of holidays in the "Eastern Bloc": Heidi Kempf (1 July 1964) says she has been skiing in Czechoslovakia; Else Hermann recommends Poland, partly for its relatively more liberal communism. Marianne and her family often go to Bulgaria and enjoy being on the Black Sea. Marianne (January 1966) says that they get around now in their car, a red Skoda from Czechoslovakia. Since it takes years to buy a car in the GDR, it is probable this came through Johannes's father in the West.

Barbara Meier (29 March 1967) says that they followed Else's advice and had an excellent trip through Poland, where "every high point was followed by the next" and they met so many particularly interesting people. For her and her husband, who have a constant longing to hear classical music, various trips and events have brightened up their lives. She highlights a recital by a noted violinist from Cologne and a chamber music concert by candlelight in Quedlinburg. With a striking image, she sums up her feelings about their lives in the GDR: "So we seek to pick out the best of the cherries from the large cake that is everyday life."

Although Martha Jäger (30 January 1967) thinks only of "the trials and tribulations of everyday life," others are also keen to pick out the cherries. Sports are popular, Hertha Pieper makes clear, and she is echoed by Barbara Meier and Gisela Riedel. Sometimes the cherries are beyond their reach, however. Frieda Möller (8 June 1969) says that her daughter applied to take up gliding but instead finished up sailing. Gliding was politically problematic, since it could be a way to leave the GDR. Those allowed to join the gliding club in Schönebeck were tied into training to prepare them to join the army.[47] There was also pressure on them to join the SED. It is likely that Frieda's family was not politically reliable enough to be allowed to take up gliding.

Health, Illness, Death

In the 1960s, the Schönebeck women felt themselves getting older and watched their parents grow old and frail. There were also serious illnesses among their children. The end of the decade brought the shocking first death among the women themselves. Suddenly they realized that they, too, were vulnerable.

After the loss of Book 8, there is some catching up to do. Marianne Schneider tells them (20 February 1964) that her father died over Christmas 1962. She herself is on a *Kur* for nineteen days. Her doctor wants her to recover, and she believes she will, though from what, we are not told. In Berlin, Else Hermann has problems with her feet and knees from constantly being on hard floors and from working long days without any real breaks. She has to wear special shoes and is hoping to be sent on a *Kur*. Martha Jäger reports that her father has died. Lisa Liebmann says her mother is sliding into dementia, so is no help anymore; in fact, Lisa has to do an increasing amount for her and is permanently tired. Sometime later, Lisa says her mother is in a psychiatric care home, twenty-five kilometers from their home in Wismar.

On 29 March 1967, Barbara Meier says that all her family had health problems over the past year. She herself needed an abdominal operation. Her husband had problems with his gall bladder and his circulation. Then their son Manfred became ill with what was thought to be meningitis. He could not be admitted to the hospital in either Schönebeck or Magdeburg because of a shortage of beds—the first critical comment about the GDR's health service. In the hospital in Bernburg, no one could say exactly what was wrong, so he was admitted to the specialist hospital for psychiatry and neurology. He is back home but continues to have headaches.

Hilde Brenner's Story

During the 1950s and 1960s, Hilde Brenner lived with her widowed mother in Uhry, a village in Lower Saxony near the GDR border. In the early 1950s, while her father was still alive, she spent eight months in England perfecting her English and getting to see the world differently. She comments (18 December 1955) on how interesting she found London, where "one can see people of every race and skin color." From her letters, she comes across as thoughtful and warm, with a strong commitment to the group, although her isolation with her mother means she sees little of the others. She too would have liked to find a husband and have a baby but did not manage to do so. Perhaps if they are successful in finding a man for Elly, they can turn their attention to her, she suggests.[48]

On 20 May 1965, Hilde says she attended her first reunion (in the West) in 1965 and saw some of them for the first time in twenty years. It was a wonderful occasion:

> And somehow it was really as if the many years had suddenly been expunged; in any case, I had the feeling that we had in no way become unfamiliar to one another. Ilse had prepared everything so nicely, we all had so many things to relate, to remember and to laugh about, and we could all only regret that we still have to have separate reunions in East and West.

On 15 October 1967, Hilde quotes the non-communist Marxist philosopher Ernst Bloch. Bloch stayed in the West when the Wall went up, rather than return to his university in Leipzig where the SED had put increasing pressure on him. On 12 February 1969, she says that the *Rundbrief* has come between her and Carl Jung: "On Christmas Eve, what a lovely surprise it was to receive the twelfth book. And so my program for the evening—to read C. G. Jung's *Memories, Dreams, Reflections*—was completely forgotten, and instead of that I plunged deep into your interesting reports."

The next mention of Hilde comes from Sabine Kleber in her letter of 3 June 1970, from Kaiserslautern. She says first that she has been in hospital for an operation on her heart and is still off work while she recovers, then continues, "And now, to add some sad news: the first of our group has departed from our circle. Hilde Brenner died in May." The death notice, pasted into the book later, says that she died on 13 May 1970 at the age of 43, after a "short, serious illness."

The dismay, shock, and sorrow felt by the others is expressed in subsequent letters in this book.[49] It is as if the whole group, brought together in shared anguish, feels torn open and exposed by Hilde's death. Early memories come back to them: writing on 20 February 1971, Lisa Liebmann says that "the sad news about Hilde Brenner affected me deeply. It was Hilde, after all, that I first got to sit next to when I came to Schönebeck in 1940. Her friendly, helpful nature greatly eased my settling in to my new school situation." In 1973, there is a photo that Marianne has put into the *Rundbrief* of Hilde's grave. This now also includes Hilde's widowed mother, who died in 1972.

Conclusion: No Longer Young

In the 1960s, the group became even more important to most of the Schönebeck women. There was by this stage a sense of solidarity across the group, going beyond their early postwar enthusiasm and their delight in their shared past at school. This can be seen in actions such as Heidi Kempf taking time to visit and look after Else Hermann in hospital, Hertha Pieper putting the pitchfork through her foot in her excitement at the *Rundbrief*'s arrival, or Hilde Brenner putting aside Carl Jung for a different set of memories, dreams, and reflections in the *Rundbrief*. It is there in Hertha Pieper's heartfelt assertion that the reunion is *the* event of the year, in the accounts and photos of the reunions in both East and West, and in the responses to Hilde Brenner's death.

The sense of the group and the cross-German commitment to it appears in the way connections are made across the letters, with Sabine Kleber, for instance, almost lamenting her good fortune in having a large apartment, while empathizing—rather than sympathizing—with Else Hermann in her one-room flat in Berlin, and recognizing Else's happiness there. Connections are also made through references to their shared German history. On 26 March 1964, Lisa Liebmann tells them about what she laughingly calls their "new" house in Wismar. "Yes, we do have a large apartment, but it is also seriously old. (Napoleon, the historians say, once stayed overnight in our bedroom!) It is a former patrician house (see Buddenbrooks)," she says, referring to Thomas Mann's novel *Buddenbrooks*, set in Lübeck, across the border in the West.

The commitment, the letters and photos suggest, comes from a combination of genuine affection, admiration for one another's achievements, and a shared history going back thirty years. It also arises from the women's newfound sense of vulnerability as they enter their forties. Additionally, it appears to have come from their need to convince themselves that physical barriers, such as the Wall, could not keep them apart.

Were they as united as they claimed?

Several of the women played a particular part in constructing both the myth and the reality of unity across the group. Irma Kindler contributed by attending the reunions in both the GDR and the FRG and by inserting her color photos of them in the *Rundbrief*. Some of the women in the West sent money to support the reunions in the East when they could not be there. This might have appeared condescending but was accepted as generosity.

The shared admiration for the role models such as Else Hermann and Anna Siebert was also helpful, while Marianne Schneider's position was crucial. Her encouragement, gentle persuasion, and even her ironic comments on the political scene all contributed to the mood and tone the women adopted in their letters. Marianne could also be self-mocking. In one of her letters she says how wonderful the reunion was and describes it in verse that is clearly not meant to be taken too seriously yet contains the points she wants them to hear. She mentions the cakes (as ever), and pineapples brought from the West, a rare delicacy in the GDR, like all "southern fruits," as they were called there. She evokes idealistically their shared sense of togetherness, which is not just nostalgic but also forward-looking:

They told tales of the past,
Spoke of what was to come,
Each shared the burdens of the other.
That's how it was,
That's how it will be.
We'll all keep on meeting, we'll all keep on writing.

Marianne was charismatic in an understated, self-deprecating way. This allowed her to say such things (in schoolgirl verse) and get away with it. Her presence at the center of the group drew them all toward her, and she had a kind of power that radiated outward. She was like a good psychotherapist: she kept them all in mind, individually and collectively, and they were aware of it and appreciated it and felt held in place in the group by her.

Curiously, they were also brought together by their parents. Many of them on both sides of the border were looking after elderly parents. Additionally, when people of retirement age were allowed to travel from the GDR to the FRG, several of the parents visited their children in the West, giving the whole group a sense that important emotional links existed and were being strengthened, if only vicariously.

There were times that were not so serene. Some complained that others were too slow in sending the book on. Some felt defensive about coming from the West and not making the time to visit the others around them; those not visited felt slighted. There is at least one complaint (with which I sympathize) about Leni Baumann's almost indecipherable handwriting. Overall, however, there are fewer grumbles than in the 1950s, when the separation appeared to cause more anxiety and when there were concerns about the women in the West not organizing their own reunion but becoming individualistic and careless about the group.

In the 1960s, the women felt they had much in common wherever they happened to be living. They say similar things about their children, their husbands, their health, and even their desire to travel. With rare exceptions, they appear equally unconcerned about their interactions with the state or the way it might be shaping their lives. Again, with rare exceptions, they treat the role of women as given, not even something to be thought about. There are surprising hints of convergence, such as children on both sides of the border learning Russian, or families from both the GDR and the FRG enjoying holidays in the Communist countries to the east.

The 1960s were a time of relative comfort for the Schönebeck women. Even though prosperity and the opportunities it opened up in the FRG were much greater, the women in the GDR also enjoyed a sense that life was becoming materially better, and that the long-promised golden future might be within their grasp as well. Two things, however, suddenly shocked the women at the end of this period: the death of Hilde Brenner at the age of forty-three, and the expulsion of Käthe Sommer from the GDR. Although both strengthened the group and helped to make it more aware of its importance, these events also revealed how little power the women really had.

Notes

1. Wilhelm Lohoff and Waldi Schäfer, *Betriebsgeschichte. VEB Traktoren- und Dieselmotorenwerk Schönebeck. Betrieb des Kombinat Fortschritt Landmaschinen Neustadt in Sachsen. Teil 3: 1961–1967* (Schönebeck, 1989), 4–6.
2. *Volksstimme Magdeburg*, 14 August 1961.
3. Frevert, *Women in German History*, 267.
4. Frevert, *Women in German History*, 269.
5. Frevert, *Women in German History*, 333.
6. Rita Bake, *Die Ersten und das erste Mal . . . : Zum 50. Geburtstag des Gleichberechtigungsartikels im Grundgesetz: Was hat er Hamburgs Frauen gebracht?* (Hamburg, 1999), 30.
7. Bake, *Die Ersten*, 31–32; Ute Gerhard, "Frauenbewegung," in Roland Roth and Dieter Rucht, eds., *Die sozialen Bewegungen in Deutschland seit 1945* (Frankfurt/Main, 2008), 199–203;
8. Lohoff, *Betriebsgeschichte III*, 43.
9. Sandrine Kott, "L'égalité par le travail? Les femmes en RDA (1949–1989)," in Corinne Bouillot and Paul Pasteur, *Femmes, féminismes et socialismes dans l'espace germanophone après 1945* (Paris, 2005), 121; Heike Trappe, *Emanzipation oder Zwang? Frauen in der DDR zwischen Beruf, Familie und Sozialpolitik* (Berlin, 1995), 122.
10. Kott, "L'égalité," 128, 131.
11. Kott, "L'égalité," 122–26; Schröter, "Die DDR-Frauenorganisation," 27.
12. 1968 Constitution of the GDR, Article 38, *Volksstimme Magdeburg*, 27 March 1968.
13. "Gute wirtschaftliche Ergebnisse im Jahr 1971," *Berliner Zeitung*, 14 January 1972.
14. "PROGRAMM der Sozialistischen Einheitspartei Deutschlands," *Neues Deutschland*, 25 January 1963.
15. "Kumpel in Calbe bezwingen den Frost," *Volksstimme Magdeburg*, 21 January 1963.
16. "Sieg des Sozialismus in der DDR Garantie der Wiedervereinigung," speech by Otto Grotewohl to SED Fifth Party Congress, 1958, in *Neues Deutschland*, 14 July 1958.
17. Gerrit Dworok, "Einleitung," in Gerrit Dworok and Christoph Weißmann, eds., *1968 und die 68er: Ereignisse, Wirkungen und Kontroversen in der Bundesrepublik* (Wien, 2013), 9–11; Philipp Gassert, "Antiamerikanismus," in Dworok, *1968*, 161–66; Kristina Schulz, "Studentische Bewegungen und Protestkampagnen," in Roth and Rucht, *Die sozialen Bewegungen*.
18. Weber, *Die DDR*, 64–65.
19. "Neues Leben in einer alten Stadt," *Neues Deutschland*, 23 September 1965, repeated in *Volksstimme Magdeburg*, 23 September 1965.
20. Günter Agde, ed., *Kahlschlag. Das 11. Plenum des ZK der SED. 1965. Studien und Dokumente* (Berlin, 2000), 23–28.
21. V. I. Lenin, "What Is to Be Done?" in *Selected Works*, vol. 1 (Moscow, 1970), 150–51, 161.

22. Stefan Wolle, *Der Traum von der Revolte: die DDR 1968* (Berlin, 2008), 93–97, 108, 114–18; *Neues Deutschland*, 2 May 1968, particularly 4.
23. Wolle, *Der Traum*, 12.
24. "TASS-Mitteilung," *Neues Deutschland*, 22 August 1968; *Volksstimme Magdeburg*, 18 August 1968.
25. Karl-Albert Ebel, letter, *Volksstimme Magdeburg*, 4 September 1968.
26. Wolle, *Der Traum*, 13–14, 19, 87–92.
27. Article 1, GDR 1968 Constitution, in *Volksstimme Magdeburg*, 27 March 1968.
28. *Volksstimme Magdeburg*, 7 April 1968.
29. Weber, *Die DDR*, 78–79.
30. Written summary of her life by Else Hermann, given to the author in 2014.
31. Letter to the author, 2 May 2014.
32. Anneliese Priewe, *"War das mein Leben?"—ein Versuch. 1945–2004*, DTA, 1647.
33. "Festtagspremiere im Deutschen Theater," *Neues Deutschland*, 3 October 1962, was favorable. Subsequent reviews were mixed. "Die Sorge um den Schriftsteller," a long review by Willi Köfret in *Neues Deutschland*, 16 October 1962, criticized Hacks (formerly from the FRG) for his lack of understanding of Marxist dialectics and the role of the party. This review criticized Langhoff, withdrew the favorable comments of 3 October, and asked for readers' opinions. Unsurprisingly, the response was increasingly critical of Hacks and Langhoff: e.g., *Neues Deutschland*, 10 November 1962. By 20 November, *Neues Deutschland*, with an article by Hermann Kant, was setting the scene for the play's condemnation at the Sixth Party Congress.
34. Alfred Kurella, "Die Verpflichtung des sozialistischen Künstlers," *Neues Deutschland*, 21 January 1963.
35. "Vertrauen des Volkes nicht enttäuschen: Aus dem Diskussionsbeitrag des Genossen Wolfgang Langhoff," *Neues Deutschland*, 17 April 1963. On Langhoff's initial resistance, see "Die Sorgen und die Macht: DT-Matinee zur politischen Demontage Wolfgang Langhoffs," *Berliner Zeitung*, 5 November 1991.
36. *Magdeburger Biographisches Lexikon. 19. und 20 Jahrhundert* (Magdeburg, 2002), 284–85.
37. The SED occasionally acknowledged the problems of air pollution and allowed the punishment of firms not taking it seriously. These were token efforts with no follow-up, as the resources were not there to make a real difference. A major article in the *Magdeburg Volksstimme* on 22 August 1968, "Staßfurter Luft und die Verfassung," was overshadowed by news of the Warsaw Pact countries' invasion of Czechoslovakia. Concerned by the rise of an environmental movement, the SED kept the official figures about pollution secret in the 1980s: Axel Goodbody, "Literature on the Environment in the GDR: Ecological Activism and the Aesthetics of Literary Protest," in Robert Atkins and Martin Kane, eds., *Retrospect and Review: Aspects of the Literature of the GDR 1976–1990* (Amsterdam: 1992), 238–60. For the impact on health and the government's awareness of it, see Fulbrook, *The People's State*, 108–11.
38. "Mitteilung des Presseamtes zu Besüchsreisen," *Neues Deutschland*, 10 September 1964.
39. Frevert, *Women in German History*, 285–86.
40. "Optimistisch ins neue Jahr!" *Neues Deutschland*, 1 January 1966.
41. *Frankfurter Allgemeine Zeitung*, 3 January 1966.

42. Nothnagle, *Building the East German Myth*, 175; Sheldon Anderson, "The German Question and Polish-East German Relations, 1945–1962," in Hochscherf, Laucht, and Plowman, *Divided*, 91–92.
43. Anderson, "The German Question," 91–93.
44. "Ausschöpfung aller Reserven erstrangige Aufgabe," *Neue Zeit*, 22 February 1972; Steiner, *The Plans*, 149–50.
45. Gieseke, *Mielke-Konzern*, 179.
46. In an interview, Else Hermann said this was what the Schönebeck women understood had happened.
47. *Volksstimme Magdeburg*, 16 September 1968.
48. "Schönebeck Letters," 4 March 1957.
49. "Schönebeck Letters," 14 July, 15 August 1970.

CHAPTER 4

Turning Fifty
The 1970s

Introduction

Political and Economic Development

The 1970s was the decade of the oil price shocks, "stagflation" (inflation and stagnation going hand in hand), and unemployment in many developed countries. The FRG was less affected than others, such as the United Kingdom, but suffered later in the decade through its dependence on exports of goods and imports of oil. Social and economic inequalities became greater and were more evident, making it clear that the economic miracle was over and that it had not spread wealth evenly. Women were disproportionately affected, along with so-called "guest workers" from Turkey and elsewhere.[1] Among the Schönebeck women in the FRG, Ilse Klein had long periods of unemployment between 1976 and 1978, eventually settling for an administrative position that did not reflect her qualifications and experience.

In the GDR, a new leader meant new policies. Erich Honecker promoted "consumer socialism" to provide more consumer goods and better housing. However, the economic historian André Steiner suggests, this was a policy of "social appeasement" that contributed to the long-term problems of indebtedness to the West.[2] Honecker also declared that whoever accepted the SED's version of socialism in the GDR could speak and write freely. While pursuing supposedly normal relations with the West, he actively sought to distinguish the GDR from the FRG and to shift its economic and political orientation toward the Soviet Union and the other Warsaw Pact countries. Another new constitution in 1974 declared in Article 6 that the GDR was bound to the Soviet Union forever and irrevocably, and that it was an integral part of the socialist community of nations.[3]

The GDR at the start of the 1970s was a major and growing industrial society but had underlying economic problems that threatened this status. It soon reached the position of promising more than it could provide, so that, as Harsch says, "the present began to gobble up the future. From 1970 to 1978, social consumption increased by sixty to seventy percent, individual consumption rose by forty to fifty percent, and productive investment declined by ninety to ninety-five percent."[4] This was in part the consequence of not facing up to the long-standing problems of low productivity: the SED leaders could never ensure there was the surplus available to fund the GDR's social initiatives as well as to invest in modernizing its industry. Problems were also caused by the Western embargo on exports of new technologies to the GDR.

The GDR was hit hard by the sudden oil price rises of 1973/74 and 1978, even though the Soviet Union provided it with cheap oil—some of which it refined and sold on to other countries to increase its supply of hard currency.[5] By the end of the 1970s, it could no longer gain significant help from the Soviet Union, which was itself suffering economically and could not go beyond heavily subsidizing Cuba and Nicaragua. The GDR reverted to investing in coal mining and producing chemicals based on coal rather than oil, but this was expensive, damaging to the environment, and diverted resources from other important industrial sectors.[6] By this time, the GDR was increasingly dependent on credits from the FRG, on payments for maintaining the transport links from the FRG to West Berlin, and on the hundreds of millions of Deutschmarks it received for "selling" its undesirable citizens to the FRG.[7] Honecker's "unity of economic and social policy" was based on a model of expanding production and increased productivity, so that future growth of exports would allow the repayment of debts. Increasingly, however, the debts were incurred without any prospect of repaying them.

One of the most significant developments in the early 1970s was the recognition by the FRG of the GDR as a separate (though not foreign) state, with provisions designed to normalize relations between the two states. The agreement covering transport and travel meant that relatives and acquaintances from the FRG could travel to the GDR several times a year, while GDR citizens could travel to the FRG for urgent family matters, not just when they were pensioners.

In August 1975, the Helsinki Conference on Security and Cooperation in Europe brought together the Western nations, including the United States and the Western European states, and the Soviet Union and the communist countries of Eastern Europe. Its aim was to reduce Cold War tensions by agreeing to principles of nonintervention and recognizing existing boundaries. The Eastern countries saw the final agreement as a triumph for them. However, they soon found themselves on the defensive over their commitments under the agreement to human rights and a number of fundamental freedoms, since these commitments raised legitimate expectations in their own countries.[8] The

Schönebeck women, for instance, hoped that they would not have to wait until they were sixty to visit their friends and family in the West.

The SED softened some of its attitudes during the early 1970s and attempted to mollify its population by accepting some aspects of Western culture they had previously condemned, including jeans and rock music. The party spoke less of its heroic past and its utopian visions and concentrated more on simply consolidating its hold on power. It accepted that not everything was working well, and certain levels of criticism were tolerated or even encouraged.[9]

In Magdeburg, Schönebeck's metropolis, for instance, an open meeting in May 1971 of the city's elected representatives, attended by local people and schools' representatives, gives an indication of attitudes at the time. The teachers were criticized for not overcoming young people's lack of interest in joining the army, and their lack of involvement in the official youth organization, the FDJ, and the GST (Gesellschaft für Sport und Technik), the umbrella mass organization for active sports that contributed to premilitary training. Local people were also indignant at the levels of workplace crime and absenteeism. Overall, there was a sense of frustration, exasperation, and a feeling that things were not as they should be, and there were demands to enforce the laws more rigorously.[10]

Although people felt they were allowed to speak out more openly, they soon saw that an underlying illiberalism remained, which could rapidly turn into repression. The Stasi grew significantly during the 1970s and acted against any perceived opposition, whether rock bands singing supposedly anti-socialist songs, or people seeking to leave for the West.

The most public demonstration of a shift by the regime away from tolerating criticism came with the cancellation of the GDR citizenship of the singer and poet, Wolf Biermann, after he appeared at a concert in the West in November 1976. Although the fate of one artist did not usually catch the imagination of much of the population or cause widespread dismay, this example was perceived to have wider significance. For all his promises of consumer socialism, Honecker stood exposed as autocratic and out of touch. Prominent artists and writers who protested were badly treated, prevented from performing or publishing, and defamed in the press. Ordinary people who objected—such as a young man, a waiter in a restaurant who handwrote placards saying "solidarity with Biermann" and who had not previously been actively political—were arrested and imprisoned.[11] It was clear that the supposed relaxation of the Ulbricht approach to repression went hand in hand with a significant expansion of the security services under Honecker. The role of the Stasi became to preserve the SED and its hold on power in the GDR, and to instill a fear of what might happen to anyone speaking out of turn.

Yet Again: The Weather

In her introduction to Book 18 (15 January 1979), Marianne Schneider comments that the winter of 1978/79 was particularly cold. She is happy they did not go to the Harz over New Year, she says, since they would have been stuck there in the snow.

The winter of 1978/79 was catastrophic in much of northern Europe, with huge snowfalls and storm-force winds from the north. Once again, the consequences for the GDR were particularly serious. For the older generations, this winter evoked memories of the winter of 1962/63 and the even harder times after the war, particularly in 1946/47 when shortages of food and fuel meant there was a real prospect of starving or freezing to death.

During the first storm around the end of December, power supplies and telephone connections were cut, roads became impassable, and the wind and snow made it impossible to deliver anything by air to huge areas that were cut off. The GDR army and the Soviet troops based in the GDR were used to get through to stranded vehicles and trains, but the islands in the Baltic remained inaccessible for several days. Supplies of brown coal could not reach the power stations, which soon were running short, leading to further power cuts. The huge machines used to extract the coal in the open-cast mines could not operate, since the ground had been a morass before the cold front, thanks to large amounts of rain, and then froze solid. When efforts were made to excavate nonetheless, serious damage was done to the expensive equipment.

Brown coal is an inefficient fuel with a high moisture content. Thus even coal that was already in rail wagons ready to be delivered froze and could not be unloaded. Despite long newspaper reports of the heroic efforts of the state organizations, the army, the police, the workers' militias, and volunteers—at the initiative, it is stressed, of the SED—it was clear even by 3 January that there were serious problems, with potentially long-term consequences, for many industries: transport as a whole, gas and electricity, steel production, electrical goods production, agriculture, and house building. Many industrial complexes were idle or on standby.

In agriculture, the concern was to keep the number of animals dying to a minimum. Reports of successful efforts to get to the animals in their stalls were highlighted as a great success but served only to show that many remained inaccessible after days in freezing temperatures and deep snow. Similarly, as transport links were restored, trains bringing supplies for industry and food for the population had priority, leaving large numbers of people unable to get to work, even if their workplace was open.[12]

Huge snowdrifts were still in place when the second storm arrived, and the rivers remained frozen. The official response to this storm was to play it down: although between thirty and ninety centimeters of fresh snow had fallen, *Neues*

Deutschland's report on 15 January concentrated on the opportunity to enjoy winter sports in the mountains. It did, however, mention that icebreakers were operating on the Oder and Elbe, dealing with ice a meter and a half deep on rivers that were vital routes for exports and for supplies within the GDR. The cold weather persisted, with serious snowfalls extending into March, followed by flooding during the thaw.

In a richer country with reserves to draw on, such a spell of terrible weather would be imprinted on the minds of those who endured it but would otherwise have limited long-term consequences. This was not the case for the GDR, which was and remained a scarcity-based economy. The winter of 1978/79 highlighted the vulnerability of the GDR and set back its capacity to pay its way and to provide the promised goods and services at a critical time in its history.

It was the workers who were expected to bear the cost of the crisis. The *Volkstimme Magdeburg* on 8 January 1979, for instance, highlighted the determination of the workers in the Dieselmotorenwerk in Schönebeck to make up for lost production by working ever harder, despite the exceptional conditions. Comparing what is said here with other reports on the same day, it is clear that this would have been difficult, since the factories often had no electricity. The SED was unwilling, however, to admit to either the limits of voluntarism or the reality of the GDR's economic fragility.

The "Woman Question" in the 1970s

By the 1970s in the FRG, the short school day still made it hard to resist the pressure on women to stay home and look after their children. Those who were in employment outside the home often had low-status, low-paid jobs, and disproportionately few women gained higher-level qualifications or reached the upper levels of employment.[13] Ute Gerhard suggests that the government in the 1960s, faced with a shortage of labor, explicitly chose to invite in "guest workers" rather than change their family policy and encourage women into the labor force.[14]

In the 1970s, a significant change was the development of a new feminist or (in the West) "women's liberation" movement, with close links in theory and practice particularly to women in France and the United States. In the FRG, the women's movement grew out of opposition to male domination of the student protest movement, and out of the widely supported campaign to legalize abortion. It had as its target individual men and the "patriarchal" organization of the society and its power structures. It set out to be autonomous, based on solidarity among women, with women organizing themselves collectively outside male structures and organizations, and declaring that the personal was political, whether in their relationships, in their interaction with the state, or in work inside and outside the home.[15] A particular concern was violence against women, in whatever form and wherever it took place. Over time, separate currents in the movement developed in different directions, some with their own autonomous organizations, such as those for lesbians, while issues such as class or the particular position of women with children caused tensions and disputes that often remained unresolved.[16] Gerhard says that prominent women writers in the GDR, such as Maxie Wander, Christa Wolf, and Irmtraud Morgner, were widely read in the FRG and played a significant role in strengthening West German women's self-awareness as women.[17]

In the GDR, it was clear that women's roles had radically changed since the end of the war: it was now the expectation of individual women, not just of the GDR state, that they would be well educated or trained, would go out to work, and could enter professions formerly closed to them. Being "just a housewife" was generally looked down on.[18] However, few women reached the higher positions in their field, and many remained in what were still seen as women's jobs, which tended to be paid less.

As in the FRG, women still had the double burden of family and employment, but in the GDR there were more facilities available to reduce the burden of childcare in the home and make it easier for women to be in full-time employment. By 1977, the aspirations of the SED leaders in the early 1960s had become a reality: there were places in nurseries for 58 percent of children under three (compared with 1.5 percent in the FRG), and 88 percent of those aged three to six (75 percent in the FRG, where many places were only part time). Maternity leave was for six months, with the option to take a year unpaid and the right to return to the same job at the end of it. By 1978, 87 percent of all women of working age were employed (52 percent in the FRG), and half the labor force was female (38 percent in the FRG).[19] Such policies in the Honecker era, as Fulbrook points out, continued both the emancipatory strand of policy and the policies designed to stabilize the population after the losses through emigration up to 1961 and the falling birthrate in the 1960s.[20]

What remained, however, were the one-sided expectations about women's roles. A study in 1970 showed that work in the home or caring for the family in the GDR took as many hours as women spent at work outside the home, averaging 47.1 hours a week, of which men did only 6.1 hours.[21] In February 1979, the Central Committee of the SED organized an international conference on the role of women to coincide with the hundredth anniversary of the publication of August Bebel's *Die Frau und der Sozialismus* (Women and Socialism). This was attended by eighty-four parties and organizations. As usual, it was opened by a man (Kurt Hager). The keynote speaker was Inge Lange, one of only two women who were candidate members of the Politburo—all of the full members of the Politburo were men. She recognized that things were not always as she would like to see them in the family in terms of equality or developing a new relationship between men and women. Nevertheless, she said, the GDR's education system had been the key to transforming the lives of women, and facilities provided by the state had made life easier for them. As well as the high figures for nurseries and kindergartens, she noted that 77 percent of children were having a hot meal at school, thus taking the burden off the mothers—apparently not noticing that she had implied this should also be the responsibility of fathers.[22] Lange declared that socialism does not destroy marriage and the family but, on the contrary, provides the material basis and social context that strengthens them by freeing them from material concerns. Her speech ended with a call to women to help make further advances toward socialism and communism, peace and democracy.

Two days later, on 26 February 1979, *Neues Deutschland* published a long exposition of the comments by many of the delegates. Significantly, only the delegate from the Eurocommunist-leaning Italian Communist Party suggested that the issues raised at the conference involved both changes in the law and a battle to put them into practice against the wishes of men. For the rest, the woman question was simply a class issue, which could be resolved by winning the class struggle.

Against this background, any attempts to build a women's movement in the GDR separate from the SED-approved and state-established structures were likely to come to very little. In any case, there were clear differences between the expectations and demands of women in the GDR and those in the FRG. In the GDR, women did feel they had the right to go out to work, to leave their children to be looked after, and to participate in society's structures.

One of the distinctive features of the 1970s was the emergence in the GDR of diary-style or autobiographical accounts by women of their own lives. The most prominent of the early ones was Sarah Kirsch's *Die Pantherfrau*, which told the stories of five women in the GDR, based on tape-recorded interviews.[23] Similarly, Maxie Wander was influential, thanks to her own diary and letters as well as her accounts of women's lives, also based on tape recordings.[24] The significance of these writers, and of other prominent writers such as Brigitte Reimann, Christa Wolf, and Irmtraud Morgner, was that they contributed to and reflected a shift in mood, among women readers in particular, away from the portrayal of heroic men in earlier socialist-realist GDR literature toward representations of the value and importance of women's everyday lives, their contribution to the development of the society, and different ways of moving toward emancipation.

Although their work was significant and their personal prominence important in providing role models, the writers did not constitute a women's movement or give rise to one in the GDR. Still, as Harsch points out, women strongly influenced the policies implemented during the Honecker years. Although these policies stressed the importance of mothers, marriage, and the wife and mother as the one responsible for domestic labor,

> women . . . ignored, resisted, and/or complained about every social or economic measure that affected them. They took stances that one could label as feminist or antifeminist, modern or antimodern, but not as passive. Women could only follow atomized individual strategies, but their negotiations with the state had, nonetheless, a cumulative impact on its policies.[25]

Similarly, Fulbrook points to the determination of women in the GDR to have their say by bombarding the authorities with letters and formal *Eingaben* or petitions.[26]

The Group and Their Letters

For the Schönebeck women, the 1960s started with the loss of Book 8 of the *Rundbrief* through carelessness or interception by the Stasi. As they move into the 1970s, it is clear that this time the Stasi or the border guards have in fact intercepted Book 13 and its accompanying Book 12. In a note at the front of Book 14, Marianne Schneider says with great exasperation that the parcel with the two books had clearly been opened at the border as it crossed into the GDR: "As they poked their noses into our two books at the border control, . . . the authorities no doubt thought they were full of secret writings. . . . They should really spare themselves such pointless work, but of course they don't listen to me—unfortunately." Even in her exasperation, Marianne cannot miss the chance to make the most of a tempting metaphor, using the word *durchschnüffeln*, to sniff or snuffle, pry, or snoop, with *schnüffeln* on its own often used for animals snuffling around after something. The package was sent on to her by Charlotte Krüger, famous in the group (and a little beyond it) as an orchid grower, and so should have smelled of orchids. The word *durchschnüffeln* links the border guards' actions to the smell of the package, and its derogatory sense conveys Marianne's contempt for those so low as to open it. What they have done stinks—and not of orchids, she implies.

Throughout this decade, a time of rapid and often unexpected change, the women frequently reasserted the importance of the group and the reunions. Barbara Meier says on 13 November 1973, "We sustain ourselves by continuing to draw on the wonderful hours we spent with one another, the lively and serious discussions—and even the atmosphere, always so entrancing, so once more my heart-felt thanks to all who yet again helped to make a success of it [the reunion]."

There were occasional signs of disharmony, however, and of the power of the group to punish those who went astray. Book 14 appeared to have been lost, with no sign of it after 4 April 1972. Marianne had previously made a special plea to Inge Fischer in West Berlin not to keep the book for too long. Others asked the same of her. The book suddenly reappeared in May 1973: Inge, apologizing cheerfully for the huge delay, explained that she put the *Rundbrief* among the books on her shelves, forgot about it completely, and only found it again by chance as she was doing a clear-out of her house. The others were not impressed. Marianne decided to exclude Inge from the group, and this was regretfully accepted by the rest of the women.

The group provided many benefits for its members throughout the 1970s. As well as the formal reunions, there were informal gatherings and mini-reunions in both East and West. When Käthe Sommer was forced to leave the GDR, Elfriede Berger, Astrid Greiswald, and Charlotte Krüger were close enough to her for them all to meet up and to help her become part of a new community.

Likewise, it was not unusual for someone in need of warmth or reassurance to confide in the group, confident that what she said would be sympathetically received. Erna Walter reminds them on 28 May 1978 that she has been living in the far north of the FRG with her husband and children for many years: a good life in an idyllic location. Now, however, things are very different:

> A lot has changed for us in the last two years. I can't and don't want to write about that. Only this: we have sold our little paradise in Kronsgaard. Our marriage came close to falling to pieces. But you can't wipe away thirty years of living together quite so easily. It was a horrible, hideous time, one that I wouldn't wish on any of you. Now with a lot of love we are trying to put the pieces together again. For ourselves and for the sake of our children, we hope that this will work.

Erna is comforted by the group, as is Brigitte Hansen in a different way. With her mother, Brigitte left the GDR in the 1950s, moved to the FRG, and then to Switzerland. When her mother died, she was alone, and the group provided a substitute family for her. She took part in reunions and mini-reunions in the FRG, and particularly enjoyed her annual skiing holiday with Anna Siebert. There was great concern when Brigitte became ill in the late 1970s, and real sorrow when she died in 1979. The *Rundbrief* and the reunions gave the rest of the women the chance to mourn collectively, and to confirm, once again, their importance to one another.

This ability to be comforting and compassionate represents a shift in the group over time. Some of the narrowness and the desire to control and rein in the members of the group that was apparent in the early 1950s has gone. They can all be more generous and expansive, having dealt with so many small and large crises of their own, inside and outside their families, over so many years.

The Schönebeck women, however, appeared to have no interest in looking outward and influencing state policies. Only rarely are there hints in their letters that a change in attitude to the "woman question" might be welcome. Gisela Riedel, whose father was the pharmacist in Schönebeck, stopped working after having children. In her letter of 6 October 1973 from Schönebeck, she says she has been back at work for the past eighteen months. This has consequences, one of them being that she has been holding on to the *Rundbrief* for too long: "Oh horror of horrors, now I'm back to being one of the slowcoaches. Please don't be cross with me! Maybe you can make allowances for a working mother who is already about to drop by the time the evening comes."

Gisela is now working for six hours a day in the central laboratory at the hospital in Bad Salzelmen, where Heidi Kempf is her boss—and a very good boss too, she says. But working so hard and having to run the household are not easy for her: "There is so much to do and I get home each day absolutely shattered. Well, then of course there's housework to be done and all the demands the family claim they have a right to make on me. Somehow, it's all just too much, but what's to be done?" It does not apparently occur to Gisela that her husband should take equal responsibility for the household and the children. Her only choice, she suggests, is not to work, but she says they cannot live on a just one salary.

Social Problems and Attitudes in a Time of Great Change

In the 1960s the Schönebeck women left behind their postwar concerns and the economic and social constraints of the 1950s. The 1970s drew them into a world of greater complexity, opportunity, doubt, and anxiety. Already the new certainties were being challenged, particularly by their children. In the letters, there is a clear sense of the next generations moving on and away from them. There are also concerns from both sides of the border about social chaos and the loss of wider social solidarity.

Some letters from the FRG reflect the disarray following the protests of the late 1960s and the shift of some activists into the terrorism of the Rote Armee Fraktion (RAF). There are no direct references to the RAF itself. For the women in the GDR, there are already signs that they are losing confidence in the future, despite the GDR's new position on the world stage. They make clear that, while some things are improving, conditions are sometimes worse than in the 1960s.

In earlier letters, the Schönebeck women tended not to write explicitly about changes in social attitudes and practices. Some of the letters in the 1970s are more forthcoming. Charlotte Krüger's letter of 17 October 1971 is confident and optimistic. She reflects on the way attitudes have changed over time:

> From our silver wedding anniversaries and the weddings of your children, we can see how time elapses. It makes me think of my own wedding twenty-six

years ago. In the meantime, at least some things have changed for the better. One of the girls in the class my husband teaches, the final year class, got married. There was no uproar or moralistic indignation, just friendly congratulations and, from the school staff, the usual presents and flowers. When I think back to that time for myself, how many ugly taunts I had to endure—particularly from the school—and that for a simple engagement.

Charlotte is also surprised to find herself saying positive things about the education provided in the FRG, compared with that in the United States, following six weeks her husband spent in Tulsa, Oklahoma:

> He was able to look around very thoroughly at the high schools and the two universities and talk with various colleagues. He found the whole business, not to put too fine a point on it, frightful. In Tulsa they have a whole squad of police standing by to ensure classes go on peacefully, and to keep order—and that only works through the use of force. He did envy the Americans the huge amount of money available for teaching materials and equipment. Many schools are a dream—on the outside! So let's keep sending our children to our German schools, consoled by the thought that they are by no means the worst. In fact, here in Dierdorf the schools are particularly nice and comfortable.

Reading this, and noting Else Hermann's comments on problems in her school in East Berlin, Sabine Kleber (8 November 1971) reports on the difficulties facing schools and young people in her part of the West:

> I don't have anything very interesting to tell you. Certainly my work is becoming less and less enjoyable, but that has less to do with my increasing age and more to do with the developments of our time. When you have to live through things like a tenth-grade girl throwing herself out the window (the funeral took place just ten days ago), then you have to ask yourself who is to blame and where to find a solution to such things, some of which are the result of the flood of drugs that threatens to sweep away our young people.

Two years later, Frieda Möller (19 November 1973, Barby) recounts a tragic incident at her daughter's school in the GDR which echoes Sabine's report from the FRG: "At the moment the class is consumed by the most terrible sorrow, since one of their classmates—for entirely unknown reasons—hanged herself."

Despite her sharp eye for the pointless and the absurd, Marianne Schneider is not always comfortable about things changing around her. In her letter of October 1974, she puts a number of photos in the book, but none of Jürgen, the older son, explaining there would be none "as long as he goes around with a beard." Similarly, she comments on the photos that show Rolf, the youngest son, with long curly hair: "Unfortunately (!!) he is not wearing a wig!" Her disapproval suggests that the older generation—as they now are—are finding it hard to come to terms with their children shrugging off the old traditions and styles, along with the expectations of their parents, exactly as is happening in the West. Her descriptions of her sons also demonstrate that the SED, while not happy about Western styles and customs affecting the GDR's young people, was having to give ground on the small things, even if she herself was not so accommodating.

The Principal Stories

In the 1970s, as the Schönebeck women turned fifty, many had elderly parents who were ill. This was a particular theme for the women whose stories are told here. What was happening to their parents imposed more work on them and affected them emotionally. The group played a part in sustaining and comforting its members, but its underlying conservatism meant that some things remained unsaid and unknown. For Else Hermann, in particular, there was a fault line between her and the group, one she herself was only half aware of. Its existence is exposed by looking at her letters in conjunction with her later actions and interviews.

Else Hermann

Over this decade, the principal force for change in Else Hermann's life was a power struggle with her mother. However, such was the power of the group, with its unstated but clear endorsement of conservative social values, that Else could not admit in her letters the fact of this struggle, or its unexpected consequences. Once again, her letters were in part a smokescreen designed to protect her from criticism and rejection.

Else's letter of 4 April 1971 is short, lacks her usual enthusiasm, and hints at things she will not say. She has had constant problems with her eyes and has been on a *Kur* in Bad Heiligendamm on the Baltic coast. Her eyes improved, but she started to suffer again when she returned to teaching. She has other problems, she says enigmatically, which she will tell them about at the class reunion. (There was, it transpired in a later letter to me, no mystery here, but something of a surprise: she had been in the hospital to have a hysterectomy at the age of forty-three.[27]) Meanwhile, although she has finished her probationary period, things are no better in the school. She thinks she might take six months off and then start work again. She adds, as if to tantalize them: "Where and how, I would prefer not to say just yet."

It is over two years before we hear something else, and it comes as a shock. Marianne reveals on 12 September 1973 that Else has made a great leap and got married. She tells Else forthrightly that she has done the right thing. Else says in her letter of 1 January 1974:

Since my last entry in May 1971 there has been a change in my life.... I got married on 29 October 1971. My husband was an actor who also started, like me, in Brandenburg in 1954, though not until 1966 did we really became friends. Over the years, the friendship has been tried and tested and not found wanting, for instance when changes of jobs put a particular strain on us.... After seventeen years in the theater, he is now moving into the field of gastronomy, which is particularly well developed in Berlin. He has a position where he has full responsibility himself and where he can demonstrate his artistry.

To make the most of this, he has to undertake some additional training and study. Previously he helped Else with her studies; now she can help him in return.

This is apparently straightforward and conventional. If we are looking for something beneath it, the description of their relationship as "friendship" could be the first clue. Else moves on to say she has changed jobs. After two years of teaching in Berlin, she says, she had to stop because her mother, now eighty, was ill and Else needed to spend more time with her in Schönebeck. This could be the second clue. The third clue comes when she says she then organized things so that she could keep on working in Berlin. She successfully applied for a job as the head of a division in the ZBN (Zentraler Bühnennachweis), an agency under the jurisdiction of the culture ministry. The ZBN, she says, is responsible for identifying and cultivating new talent and acts as an agency for people working in the theater. She herself is responsible for stage, costume, and mask designers, and painters for theatrical productions. She has to make links with the training colleges for artists in Berlin and Dresden in order to recommend people to specific theaters, and organizes conferences and professional development seminars. She is greatly enjoying it and is happy to be back in the theater world.

Apart from that, she had a holiday in Budapest with her husband and enjoyed the hot springs and the beautiful city. Back in Berlin, her one-bedroom flat was too small for them, but they finally managed to get an exchange with an elderly woman. They are now living in Prenzlauer Berg, in a bright, airy apartment on the fourth floor of an old, unmodernized building (figure 4.1). They are happy to have a lot of space, including a room each and a darkroom for her husband to pursue his interest in photography. Else makes a point of telling them that she has kept her own name, though he has hyphenated her name with his. This is perhaps the fourth clue.

The clue to what? Essentially, to the reason for Else's marriage, the nature of this marriage, and the complex attitudes in the GDR that are displayed by the marriage.

Else chose to get married, she told me, so that she would not have to stay in Schönebeck and look after her mother. They had a difficult relationship, with her mother prepared to hit her daughters, and with Else clearly more attached to her father. She also felt her mother had retained a sense of superiority, aris-

Figure 4.1. Else's apartment in Prenzlauer Berg. Photo courtesy of Akademie der Künste, Berlin.

ing from her father (Else's grandfather) being a wealthy factory owner. By the end of the 1960s, Else was making the trip to Schönebeck once a fortnight to be with her mother, who was finding it more and more difficult to cope on her own. When Else visited over Christmas in 1970, her mother could no longer get the coal upstairs for the central heating boiler. The temperature in the house was minus one. Her mother, suffering from pleurisy, was in her fur coat trying to keep warm. As the house was uninhabitable, Else managed to get temporary accommodation in a holiday home in Thuringia. The Schönebeck authorities effectively took over the house and its management so that a large family could move in, with Else's mother moving upstairs.

Else felt weighed down by social pressure, by genuine concern, and by her mother's expectation that she would move back to Schönebeck and look after her. Else went as far as applying for a teaching job in Schönebeck, but there was nothing available. She was then offered the job in the ZBN in Berlin. This alone was not enough to placate her mother, or to satisfy her own conscience. She decided that if she and Bruno were to get married—which would make her mother happy—then the job and the marriage together would make it impossible for her mother to demand that she leave Berlin.

This was a marriage of convenience, though buttressed by genuine affection and at least initially by a certain sexual attraction. In later years, there would be some distance between them, disputes over Bruno's drinking, and too many male visitors for Else's liking. Many of these things become clear from the letters when they are looked at together, but would not have been obvious when they appeared one at a time. When I probed further about the marriage in 2015, Else said casually, as if it went without saying: "Of course, he was homosexual." This was not something she could ever have said to the group. Nor could she have confessed to them her ambivalence about her own sexual orientation. She chose to live like this, in a relationship where each of them was by inclination bisexual, whether they openly admitted it or not, for her sake as well as for Bruno's, and because at least at the beginning she loved him, or believed she did. The arrangement worked well for him too. His acting career had faltered because he had become partially deaf. He was able to move to Berlin, have the marriage as a helpful front and a source of support, and rebuild his own life there.

Else's letter of 18 April 1975 says simply that her mother died in February. A separate account describes Else's long, hard, and eventually successful wrangling with the authorities to be able to get hold of the family furniture and other belongings and send them to her sister in Cologne.

Else herself is enjoying her work but suffers from getting tired too quickly. She has started writing articles about plays written by children, and some of these are now appearing in the magazine on children's literature, *Beiträge zu Kinderliteratur*. Her husband has been working hard and successfully as a chef in the prestigious club for workers in film and theater, Die Möwe (The Seagull, from Chekhov's play of the same name). Unfortunately, an electrical fire destroyed a lot of the fittings and caused extensive damage. It will take a long time to refurbish, she says, as it is a heritage-listed building.

Else's letter of 6 February 1977 contains her account of preparations for hosting the class reunion on 3 September. She has booked rooms in a nearby Christian center for those coming from within the GDR. She reminds those from the West that they said they would arrange their own accommodation in West Berlin. The reunion—which in Schönebeck and elsewhere tends to go on into the early hours of the morning—will have to start and finish earlier in Berlin, since those from the West have to be at the Friedrichstrasse border crossing shortly before midnight, in order to be out of the GDR before their permits expire. She warns them that her apartment is on the fourth floor: "Get on with getting fit!"

Her other news is that after the fire in his previous workplace, Bruno is now in his second year as the restaurant manager in a clubhouse in Pankow. Last year Else went on another *Kur* (without Bruno), this time in Bulgaria. She enjoyed it, and it helped with her spondylosis. She is also enjoying her work. She has several conferences to organize before the summer holidays, and is away a lot, at least twice month.

As the seventies approach their end, all is apparently calm and enjoyable for Else. In her letter of 9 June 1979, she says that Bruno is at last back working at the Möwe, which took five years to rebuild after the fire. She herself has been a guest at the world festival for stage design in Prague.[28]

Hertha Pieper

Hertha Pieper's life in the seventies revolves around the family, work, and illnesses. On 16 April 1971, she says that life has been even busier since she became a grandmother. On top of that, earlier in the year she had to have an operation that she had long been putting off, so spent four weeks in the hospital. She has recovered well and is looking forward to getting back into training in May. Other than that, she has to take care of "my many animals," though it is not clear if these are hers or belong to the cooperative. She does have her own half a hectare of land, however, and gets a lot of pleasure out of working on this.

Hertha is a regular and reliable contributor to the *Rundbrief* and is not happy with it being held up or mislaid. On 30 August 1973, she makes a plea to them all: "Don't store our precious *Rundbrief* in old or overflowing bookcases! That way it could mean we never again have to wait so long for it." She has serious news too: "My husband suddenly had to have a stomach operation and now I'm doing everything I can to look after him and just to be there for him. Last week my mother broke her femur. The children support me, of course, but still I sometimes think that I just can't cope with it all." Despite all her cares, she will still be at the next reunion, "since pleasure is a good healer!"

In her introductory letter to Book 16 in October 1975, Marianne Schneider tells them that Hertha's husband has died. Hertha, on 14 February 1975, offers her heartfelt thanks for their thoughts. Every kind word helps, she says, to manage what is almost unbearable. Her garden is her consolation and a significant enterprise in itself. Telling them about it in detail helps her to put her grief to one side. On the six hundred square meters she has for herself, she grows ornamental grasses, which are then dried and sold in bunches. This is a huge amount of work but is going well, she says. She has had a contract to supply over 150,000 everlasting daisies. However, since the death of her husband, she has more responsibilities: "In order to keep hold of my garden, I have to start working in the LPG again in April! I'll be in the cowshed for four hours a day, running the milking machines."

By the time of her next letter (8 April 1977), it is family news that dominates (see figure 4.2). Her younger son Klaus was married the previous year

Figure 4.2. Hertha's family: Klaus with his wife; Hertha; Kerstin; Wilfried's wife. Photo courtesy of Akademie der Künste, Berlin.

and now has her fourth grandchild. At home she only has Kerstin, thirteen years old, and her mother-in-law, aged eighty. She is also happy with a change in her work. She no longer has to do physical work but is responsible for looking after the animal breeding records at the LPG. She is on duty with the vet two days a week and gives him a hand in the animal enclosures, which she enjoys. She always has the weekend off: "I spend my free time in my large garden. Last year, because of the long drought a lot of things failed to grow. The worst thing was that I got no seeds from our grasses and flowers, so that this year I have had to start again from scratch."

Hertha is pleased to have got her driving license. She was lucky, she says, since in their area people sometimes have to wait up to four years for one. Now she is not dependent on anyone else and can drive herself around in her Trabant. The 1970s have given her mobility and more time for herself, but there is still a gap in her life since the death of her husband.

Anna Siebert

In the 1970s, Anna Siebert was at the top of her profession and featured again in the press. Barbara Meier (27 January 1971) pasted in a press cutting, headed "Built in Record Time," with a photo of Anna: "[Anna Siebert], chief engineer at Strom- und Hafenbau, was responsible for the construction of the Hapag-Lloyd Terminal, now ready for occupation after being built in a record time of just seven months." Anna herself is more modest about her achievements.

She has to work very hard, she says, but she particularly admires those of them who go out to work and also have children and the household to look after. She could not do it "without the household help I have every day," by which she does not mean from her husband.

By 1974, Anna has been promoted again. She notes (on 31 October 1975) that as a female civil engineer she is still an exception in the FRG. In this respect, she says, the GDR is way ahead. She is happy to hear that Astrid Greiswald's daughter-in-law (in the West) is on her way to becoming an engineer and therefore a colleague of hers. This book contains yet another press cutting about Anna's achievements.

In her letter of 23 May 1977, Anna says that the other women in the group are astonished by what she and Leni Baumann have achieved, while in her view, what is certain is that "bringing up children, and all the things that go with that, are far more difficult than our work!!!"

The seventies were also a time when Anna reconnected with her *Heimat*. She attended the reunion in Schönebeck on 1 September 1973, and over the years managed to make a number of visits to her mother, who by 1977 was eighty and still living in Staßfurt. Anna says Barbara Meier and her husband look in on her mother quite often, "which is something she is very happy about and I am very grateful for."

Anna (20 August 1979) says she enjoyed the 1978 reunion at Hertha Pieper's in Calbe. She says it is a pity that those of them in the West do not see one another as much as those in the East manage, "but here we lack a Marianne, who looks out for everyone and holds everything together." Meanwhile, Anna's mother was with them in Hamburg for four months for an operation. For many of them, it had indeed been made simpler to travel from the West to the East, and for their elderly parents to travel from the East to the West. It is also clear that they cling to their belief that Germany is still united, so that it is taken for granted that Anna's mother could go from the GDR to Hamburg for an operation.

Throughout the seventies, Anna remained active, playing tennis as well as continuing to have holidays with Brigitte Hansen. Brigitte had a weekend with her in Hamburg in July 1979, and they greatly enjoyed being with each other. For the first time, they had not met for their skiing holiday, since Brigitte's illness, polyarthritis, made this impossible: "That's why our joy at being together again was even greater, and she was slowly getting better again." Unfortunately, back in Switzerland, Brigitte suddenly relapsed. Anna urges them to "cross your fingers and pray that she gets through it, since things are not looking good."

Irma Kindler

At the start of the seventies, Irma Kindler (writing on 26 May) is still working half time at the student support services organization. While the family was on holiday in Turkey last year, she says, they had an unexpected but very welcome visit from Ankara: Anni Lange, the opera singer, and her husband. She attaches photos of them all and points out the extremely long hair of her son, almost sixteen at the time but at least "no longer a devotee of Mao." There was bad news as well: shortly after she had sent on the last *Rundbrief*, her father died suddenly of a heart attack, two days after turning seventy-four. It was totally unexpected and a great shock to them all.

In her letter of 11 May 1975, Irma describes their holidays in Corsica and Austria, but also says that since her mother has had a slight stroke, Irma now has to visit her every day. Two years later (11 May 1977), Irma says her mother died last summer and now her daughter has left home; suddenly she is having to get to grips with the third stage of her life. With all of them turning fifty, losing their parents, and seeing their children move on, there is a hint of melancholy here that is present in many of the letters at this point.

Irma is cheerful again in her next letter (17 July 1979). Her son has a position as a trainee in a pharmacy, while her daughter has finished her third semester in sociology. Once more she and Franz have been skiing in Austria, and they will be holidaying again in Greece later in the year. She says she has met up with Anni Lange, who had been to Schönebeck to wind up her mother's affairs there. This is a common enough theme in the letters: being gathered back into the *Heimat* through family celebrations, illnesses, and deaths.

Interaction with the State

Between Speaking Out and Self-Censorship

In the early 1970s, the most dramatic event for the group was the sudden expulsion of Käthe Sommer to the West. When Elfriede Berger writes on 4 October 1971 from Cologne, news of the move has already got around. She says: "It was a great joy for me and my family that Käthe and Herbert have come to live so near to us." Marianne Schneider (12 August 1973) would like to hear more about this great "leap," and uses with deliberate irony the SED's jargon: "We await with bated breath your first capitalist-imperialist report in this Book.... Dear Käthe, please give us a full account!"

Marianne cannot resist another indirectly political comment in the same letter. She says that their daughter Silvia went with the school choir to Berlin "and sang cheerful songs, since at the beginning of August there was good reason to be cheerful! (I am deliberately overlooking Lisa's admonishing finger here.)" Among the "cheerful" events in August 1973 were the Tenth World Youth Games in Berlin, where Silvia was singing. Marianne's readers in the West would have seen the Games as a Communist propaganda exercise; those in the GDR would have had the SED's wooden language echoing in their ears. The Communist leaders (including Brezhnev from the Soviet Union and Honecker from the GDR) sent a special greeting to the young people participating in the Games:

> We extend our heartiest greetings to the delegates from every continent who have gathered here in Berlin, capital of the German Democratic Republic, for the Tenth World Youth and Student Games. The Tenth World Games are an eloquent expression of the tireless striving of the broadest strata of youth for peace, security and cooperation between the peoples of the world. May this powerful manifestation of the youth of the world have an impact well into the future and give a new impetus to the just struggle of youth for anti-imperialist solidarity, peace and friendship.[29]

While the talk of Lisa's imagined admonishing finger might be taken as light-hearted banter, there is a serious point here. Lisa's finger is Marianne's internal censor, warning her to be careful of what she says about such pronouncements, which Marianne clearly sees as nonsense. Lisa is also warning the whole group. But how should Lisa's warning be seen? Does she mean that they all know there are things to criticize but should avoid mentioning them, for their own safety, as somebody might be reporting on them? Or could she mean that she herself does not share their critical views and does not want to see them in the letters? This seems unlikely, yet so much in the GDR that seemed unlikely turned out to be true.

Closer to home, Marianne inserts a press cutting with a photo of Schönebeck's 750-year celebrations. More than thirty thousand people attended the formal opening of the historic market in June, while the anniversary events themselves carried on until August, principally in the *Kurpark* in Bad Salzelmen. Marianne is both pleased and skeptical: "Thanks to this noteworthy anniversary, some of our buildings, squares and streets have been made to look reasonably presentable. Hopefully this program of improvements will be carried on at least before the 1,000-year celebrations."[30]

Echoing this comment in her letter of October 1974, Marianne reports one local achievement: the S-Bahn is now in place between Bad Salzelmen, Schönebeck, and Magdeburg. However, she is skeptical about the events being organized for the GDR's twenty-fifth anniversary on 7 October, and about the plans for transforming Schönebeck by 1980. Highlighting increasing difficulties, she asks where the capacity is to undertake such work, and where the materials and the money might be. The energy will not come from ordinary people: "The GDR's citizens don't have a lot of enthusiasm any more for big projects; they are all too tired, since by now it's been uphill all the way for the past twenty-five years!"

A little over two years later (15 January 1977), Marianne's letter has the most overt example of political frustration, and of self-censorship of the expression of this frustration, in the whole of the Schönebeck letters. Her husband Johannes plays a part in this, attempting to protect her from herself, or from what the Stasi will do to her if they read what she really thinks. It is clear that at the very least the women suspect that the letters might be being read by Stasi agents. A worse possibility is the suspicion in the group that someone in their own circle—one of the husbands, for instance, or even one of the women—might be passing information to the Stasi. On the second-to-last page of her letter, after telling them she is now a grandmother, Marianne says,

> We are all well, so there is reason enough to be grateful. But right now, my dearest wish, just for once, soon (if at all possible before reaching the well-known hurdle of turning sixty), is to visit my father-in-law. It would not even occur to me to stay over there, since I have so many Schneiders and little Schneiders over here. But how can you make that clear to Herr Honecker and his comrades? Luckily the now great-grandfather can still regularly come over here.

Immediately following this, there are seven lines over which brown paper has been pasted (see figure 4.3). The first word underneath it is "But," and this is the only word that can still be deciphered; the rest is too well covered. On the brown paper, Marianne writes: "My lord and master would not give his permission for what appears under this. Please be understanding; it was in fact really meant *only for our circle*" (emphasis in the original).

Barbara Meier (13 November 1973) says that she and her husband are still living and working in Neugattersleben, not far from Schönebeck. Taking up the issue of censorship, she tries to be careful in her criticism of the authorities: "Despite a number of not so pleasant things to do with work, which I won't go into in writing for reasons you understand, we are still living in our 'romantic' castle. (I could write a whole novel about our life in our accommodation at the Institute, but it would certainly fall victim to the censors—so I'll give that a miss.)" She is more explicit about their visit to Poland in 1972, where they appreciated the "clean, free air" and could "move around and travel unhindered, as used to be possible when we were young." Although she does not mention that their time of unhindered movement was also the Nazi period, she makes one of the rare mentions of that period. She includes a photo of the ruins of Hitler's bunker (the "Wolf's Lair") in what was Rastenburg, with their son Manfred standing on top of it. The caption says "Manfred 'gets to grips with our history'—blown-up bunker in Rastenburg / now Poland." Below the photo she has written "Quartiera Hitlera."

In Barbara's letter of 27 March 1977, there is more that she cannot spell out about the repressive nature of the GDR state. She and her husband are unhappy because their son Manfred, "despite unbelievable difficulties and even more formalities," has married a Polish woman. Their first grandchild lives in

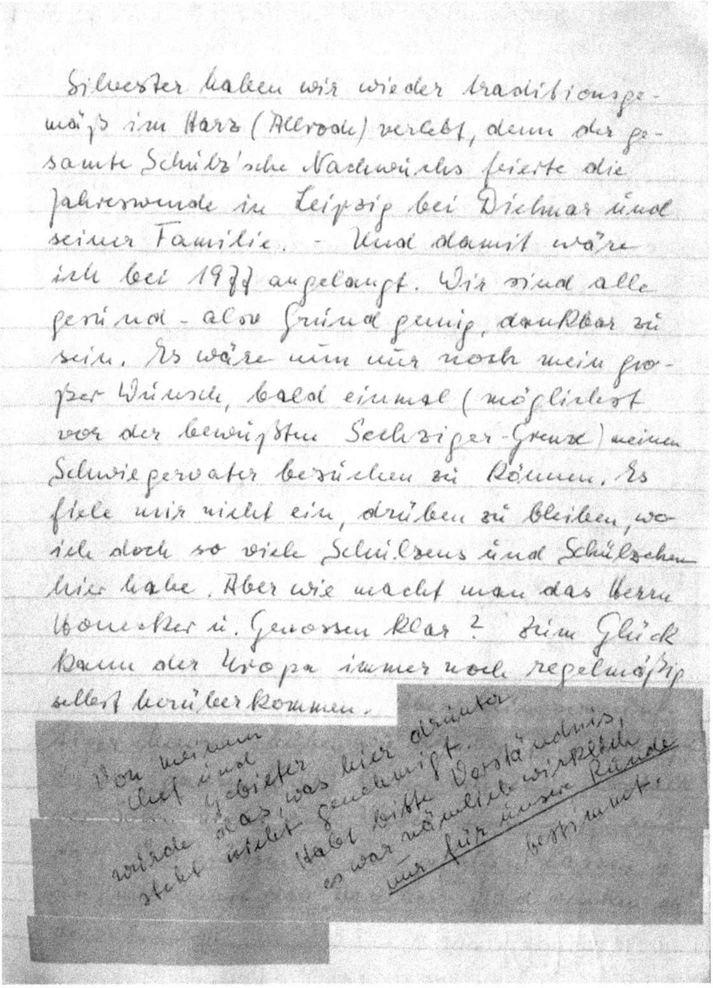

Silvester haben wir wieder traditionsgemäß im Harz (Allrode) verlebt, denn der gesamte Schulz'sche Nachwuchs feierte die Jahreswende in Leipzig bei Dietmar und seiner Familie. – Und damit wäre ich bei 1977 angelangt. Wir sind alle gesund – also Grund genug, dankbar zu sein. Es wäre nun nur noch mein großer Wunsch, bald einmal (möglichst vor der bewußten Sechziger-Grenze) meinen Schwiegervater besuchen zu können. Es fiele mir nicht ein, drüben zu bleiben, wo ich doch so viele Schulzens und Schulzchen hier habe. Aber wie macht man das Herrn Honecker u. Genossen klar? Zum Glück kann der Uropa immer noch regelmäßig selbst herüber kommen.

Von meinem Chef und Gebieter würde das, was hier darunter steht, nicht genehmigt. Habt bitte Verständnis, es war nämlich wirklich nur für unsere Runde bestimmt.

Figure 4.3. The self-censored letter, Book 17, 1977. Photo courtesy of Akademie der Künste, Berlin.

Poland, and they have not yet seen him. Manfred wants his wife to be allowed to live in the GDR, but has had no success so far:

> As a result, the young family remain separated, since he didn't want to resettle over there. So, you see, there are always parallels with the problems between East and West (as in the case of Käthe Sommer's family); only the likely outcome is different. . . . In any case, we are not *yet* very happy parents-in-law, but hope to become happy grandparents. I guess there is too much that is serious and depressing and is weighing us down, what with our elderly mothers and the daily

business of our jobs—about which I neither want nor am able to write—for us to be able to look to the future with optimism.

Everyday Oppression, Resistance, and Its Consequences

Unsurprisingly, given the circulation of news around the whole group, much that is said in the letters from or about the GDR at this time is gloomy and pessimistic, with a certain wariness in the writing. Käthe Sommer (1 April 1974, Bad Münstereifel), resisting Marianne's urgings, is sparing in her comments about the family's expulsion and about the material benefits of the West, as if not wanting to jeopardize the position of those still in the GDR:

> At the beginning here, two and a half years ago, when we had to start absolutely all over again and with practically nothing, I thought my world had come to an end. In the meantime, I have settled in really well and I love this area of Münstereifel in a way I initially never thought would be possible. Our practice got going well and now we can hardly manage the avalanche of patients. We have to be very efficient with our work, but it is all going very positively. You quickly get used to the capitalist world, although so much was previously unfamiliar. And with all the latest technology, even just running the household is so much less tiring.

Curiously, in her letter of 28 February 1976, Käthe says that she and her family were allowed to return to the GDR for the wedding in Schönebeck of their son who had remained behind. She does not explain why the GDR authorities, previously so hostile, were suddenly so accommodating, or why she and the rest of her family felt comfortable returning, if only briefly, to Schönebeck.

"Life Gets Us in Its Clutches": Elly Haase

Elly Haase (6 November 1973) responds to the difficulties facing them in the East with a clear sense of where the power lies between the ordinary citizen and the GDR state: "Studying our beloved *Rundbrief*—a joy to me every time—it's possible to make out that on *our* side pretty much everyone has a cross to bear. Enjoying life doesn't come into it, quite the opposite: some of the time, life gets *us* in its clutches and determines what we do. Nevertheless, you have to try to keep your chin up."

Returning to this theme on 12 February 1975, Elly tells them that her mother has died, and says how pleased she is that she was able to look after her at home. Their sympathy and their letters will give her the strength to bear her fate. Elly says she has had to live through a lot of hard times over the years, but it is these that have shaped her and given her experience of life: "I have learned to live *with* my neighbors in a neighborly manner and to get along with people in every way. I must say, it has involved many years of learning in the school of life, but these are years I would not have missed."

Two years later (18 March 1977), it is clear that this has not been so easy, since her "neighbors" include the authorities who determine so much of their lives. Elly says how much she enjoyed the class reunion in Wismar and how much she is looking forward to the one in Berlin, but she is not particularly happy:

> Life's joys really are somewhat thin on the ground, they've made sure of that. So for us last autumn there was just a lot of strife and confusion and my nerves came apart at the seams. Well, that's my weak point and the difficult years before this have not gone by without leaving their mark on me too. I should have been able to take everything less seriously, but I'd have needed a hide like a rhinoceros. My friends and people around me were most concerned and stood by me, which gave me strength.

This account is as opaque as the censored section in Marianne's letter, but the implication is that the authorities have been making life difficult for her over a long period, right from their early refusal after the war to allow her to study because of her "bourgeois" background.

Finally, in 1978, Elly finds a husband. Ironically, he is an electrician, a real "worker" with a factory job, and with a son who comes to live with them. Their honeymoon is typical of Elly: a long road trip—1,800 kilometers—in their "Oldtimer BMW."

Martha Jäger

Martha Jäger's letters in the 1970s are full of interesting contradictions: her family benefits from the support of the state but also suffers at its hands. Often she appears blind to the impact of her own actions and words. Her letters are direct and uninhibited in their expression. The mundane and the politically significant intertwine, without her being aware of it. What seems clear to the reader almost at once does not occur to Martha until later: that the state is making difficulties for the family for ideological reasons.

In the first of her 1970s letters (20 March 1971), Martha says that their son Holger is studying medicine. Doctors were highly valued in the GDR, but because of the possibility that they might try to go to the West, medical students had to be politically reliable. Holger must have passed this test. Things are different for Martha's daughter Angelika. She is now in the eleventh class at the high school in Schönebeck, but cannot plan for her future:

> Things look really grim when it comes to getting a place to study. Somebody somewhere must have planned this badly! Angelika wanted to study pharmacy: "oversubscribed!"; biology: "oversubscribed!"; dentistry: "oversubscribed!" There

was really something going on at the parents' evening. Now it means she has to decide on something else. What will be the right thing?

Martha does not seem to think that the authorities might be deliberately obstructing Angelika. After the experience of her son, she would not expect her daughter to be treated differently for ideological reasons or to be discriminated against as a woman.

Martha's next letter (23 October 1973) is full of bitterness and frustration. Her first complaint is to do with housing. She thinks back to the time and energy they spent rebuilding their house so that her mother could move from her large apartment and be in a separate apartment in the house with the whole family. Since her mother's death, the housing office has claimed the right to put tenants in this apartment. Now, as Martha's family grows again, she would like to have these tenants out:

> The time since the last *Rundbrief* has again been a tumultuous one for us, with many things to stir us up. . . . In June this year we had our twenty-fifth wedding anniversary. In the meantime, Holger got married and now has a son . . . . We really wanted the young family to be able to move into our house, so suitable for two families. Eight years ago, when my parents wanted to move in with us, our tenants would not even consider an exchange of accommodation. So we turned our loft into an apartment, and this time we hoped it could all work out, especially as the authorities got back the large flat my parents were in, entirely as a result of our initiative. (Just imagine!) For a whole year I have been trekking around from one office to another, I've even written to the Council of State, but all for nothing! The end result: the young people still don't have their own apartment.

Martha's next grievance has to do with problems traveling to the West:

> Seven weeks ago, my sister had a major stomach operation. As she was already in a serious condition when she went into hospital, her life hung by a thread. (She is getting better now.) So I asked for a travel pass since, according to the new law, you can travel to the West if your sister in the Federal Republic is dangerously ill. When I asked if my papers were ready, I was fobbed off for a whole week. It is just impossible to describe what I experienced in that week. I was continually packing and unpacking my case. After a week, they told me that my application had been declined, "on security grounds!" This came like a bolt from the blue, it was something I just couldn't make sense of!!! But I didn't give up so easily. I went to the highest authority in Schönebeck, without success. Finally, I went to Magdeburg, where I also achieved nothing. I almost had a nervous breakdown!!

Martha's third complaint concerns the efforts of her daughter to get into university, after being told a year previously that many areas of study that interested her were oversubscribed.

Our Angelika did well in her *Abitur* a year ago. Her heart's desire, to become a dentist, unfortunately came to nothing. If she had been the child of a worker or someone in agriculture, it would still have been possible to slot her in there. On her own initiative, she applied to every university, but the best they could do was to fob her off with the idea of applying some time later or recommend she become a teacher. She decided to do engineering and now has two semesters behind her. Hopefully as time goes by she will enjoy this even more. Angelika would certainly have made a good dentist. For us as parents it is truly a bit saddening, when you find you can do absolutely nothing to help your child.

Martha assumes that Angelika is being punished for Martha's class background, and her distress is understandable. After all, there is no consistency in the authorities' actions that would allow her to make sense of what is happening. If her son was allowed to study medicine, why is Angelika still being blocked, and why is she herself not allowed to visit her sister? It could be that the authorities' attitude has hardened since they allowed Holger to study medicine. The fuss Martha made about the housing problem and about the refusal to allow her to travel no doubt caught the attention of the authorities higher up, who might well have thought that she wanted to go to the West and remain there. It is also likely that they have become aware of her personal connection to Käthe Sommer, another reason to see Martha as unreliable. In their eyes, it would have been reasonable, rather than cruel and arbitrary, to refuse her permission to visit her ill sister.

Another clue to the way the family is seen comes from their attempt to book a summer holiday: "Unfortunately we couldn't have our holiday on the Baltic Sea, since there were just no holiday places available, even though we had been trying since January."

From her letter of 31 January 1975, it is clear that the family's struggles with the authorities have left Martha feeling ground down and defeated. The tenants upstairs, she says, have at last moved out, but still Holger and his family have not been able to get the apartment. They have been on the housing list for so many years, so why are they not allowed to move in? she wonders.

Naturally the new tenants were just forced upon us. So much for our "rights." . . . Now we have a family with two very lively children on top of us. The children, a boy and a girl, are five and six years old. So on Saturdays and Sundays, it is these two children who determine whether we get to sleep in or not. Most times our night is over between six and seven o'clock. I'm sure you can understand that after so many disappointments we are gradually becoming too tired even to do anything about the house. It's much the same with holidays. Last year we had arranged through the travel agency to have a lovely holiday right by the water in Schwerin. Then, days before we were due to leave, it was suddenly canceled and somewhere in the Spreewald offered as an alternative. We assumed it was of comparable quality and set off there, only to be extremely disappointed! The accommodation was terrible! If they hadn't offered us somewhere better in a quieter area the next day, we would have come straight back home. Now the battle has started up again to get somewhere for our summer holiday.

Two years on (9 March 1977), life is still no easier for Martha. She had hoped that, now they were all turning fifty, they might be allowed to travel to the West. She particularly wanted to see her sister and her family after eighteen years apart. "But sadly we had to bury this hope too," she writes, "like so many others before it!!" As well as this, her husband at the age of sixty is now on a disability pension. Because of that, they have had to give up the business. This is especially hard for her, as she feels that she and the business grew up together. In the meantime, their tenants have changed again, but again Holger and his family have not been allowed to move in. Holger's child, an active five-year-old, still has to sleep in the same room as his parents. Her better news is that Angelika is working as an engineer for the water authority in Halle.

Another two years on, Martha reports on 9 March 1979 that Angelika has married a stomatologist from Erfurt and has a baby. Things are no better for Martha at home, however:

> We are still having bother with our house, just as before. Again the tenants have moved out, but even for us as landlords it was a real tussle just to get the key in our hands!!!! I'd better stop there, otherwise I'll be working myself up to no point. I have already had to swallow many a sleeping tablet, thanks to the damned house. How lucky you are, those of you who own a small single-family house and have no one you have to defer to. *Unfortunately*, the hope that we *might* be allowed to travel to the West at the age of fifty has also come to nothing, and so I guess I shall have to wait a good seven more years until I can visit my sister again.

Things Fall Apart

In the 1970s, the women sense something new: the GDR is no longer moving ahead economically. Marianne Schneider's skepticism about attempts to improve Schönebeck is one example. On a more immediate level, Frieda Möller says on 19 November 1973 that in the hospital where she works the heating broke down in September and needs to be totally replaced. The patients have been moved elsewhere or discharged, and the staff have been scattered around hospitals in Calbe, Schönebeck, and Bad Salzelmen. Winter is coming on, and nothing is planned for the heating until January.

There are problems in the West with buildings too. Leni Baumann says she has been promoted again and is now a professor. However, their building is a disaster. Sabine Kleber (5 June 1974) says that the school buildings where she teaches in Kaiserslautern are also a disaster: although they are new and architect-designed, they are airless, overcrowded, and falling apart. The difference, Charlotte Krüger reminds them, is that in the West there is the possibility of improvement and of things working well.

In the East, the problems were only likely to get worse, and official accounts could not disguise this. An article on the "planned raising of living standards" in the *Volksstimme Magdeburg* in the early stages of "consumer socialism" spoke of great gains as well as pointing to continuing shortages and the problems of quality, with many goods returned under guarantee.[31] There are sudden surprises in the press: on the same day as the triumphalist accounts of the GDR's twenty-second anniversary, there is a large, framed advertisement with the key words in very large print, calling on everyone to gather apples and pears that have fallen from the trees in the streets and out in the countryside, and deliver them to the fruit processing organizations for a payment of seventeen Marks per hundred kilograms.[32] While this is a laudable attempt to avoid waste, it is also a reminder of the persistent shortage of fruit and vegetables. There were also reports on water courses being polluted, and on air pollution. The factories in Staßfurt and Schönebeck were identified as some of the culprits, even if in principle they were trying to do something about the problems they were causing.[33] In July 1973, a report indicated that not as many kindergarten places or sports halls as planned had been provided. Similarly, while many of the larger manufacturing firms were exceeding their targets, significant ones were behind, and it was difficult to produce enough building materials.[34] Such problems appeared intractable throughout the 1970s, with the winter of 1978/79 confirming that they had not been overcome.

Other Concerns: From Holidays to Health

Travel, Leisure, Holidays

Sometimes in the letters the discussion of travel, leisure, and holidays highlights the lack of power of ordinary people in the GDR. An example of this is Martha Jäger's account of her holiday difficulties and of not being allowed to travel to the West to see her sister. In contrast, however, a sense of personal power is clear in the accounts of the women in the FRG. This can come from almost incidental remarks: Anna Siebert says how much she loves playing tennis, while her skiing holidays are something she just takes for granted. Irma Kindler talks of what has happened on their holidays, rather than seeing it as some kind of miracle to be allowed to travel across the whole of Europe, and to be able to afford it. Similarly, Elfriede Berger writes (25 March 1974) that she had two weeks in Florence and two in Rome, and adds, casually, that she was particularly impressed by an audience with the Pope. Sabine Kleber (5 May 1974) has gone even further afield: to Iceland, Greenland, Thailand, and Japan.

Sometimes the accounts of travel show the difficulties the women face when trying to meet up. Ilse Klein (18 September 1974) offers one way around this. She proposes that they hold their reunions in the East between 1 and 9 September. That is when the Leipziger Messe takes place and it is easier, she says, for Westerners like her to be allowed into the GDR.

Erika Krämer (21 January 1978) is upset by a tightening of restrictions by the GDR. She had grown used to coming from Kassel to visit her sister most years (though still without visiting the others nearby): "For two years now, we have had no more permits to come and visit Calbe. It's clearly not to do with us, since we are allowed to go everywhere else in the GDR, so it must be to do with my sister not being allowed to have or to seek any contact with the West."

Barbara Meier's letters in the 1970s complicate the picture of the GDR. Over the years, Barbara has shown how unhappy she is with some aspects of life in the East, and how frustrating it can be to live with constant shortages and stubborn political leaders. However, for her and her husband, attending musical recitals has been some compensation, along with their work. Travel has also been important to them. In 1974 they had an extraordinary trip that they are sure will stay in their minds forever. Barbara reports on it at great length in her letter of 28 February 1975:

> After long preparations, we were allowed to make a trip on our own by car, driving over 8,000 kilometers. Have you ever had the experience of not learning until midday that your trip has been approved, when by the morning after next you are meant to have crossed two national boundaries? Still, we made it and were right on time when we reached the border crossing into the vast Soviet Union.
>
> We used 825 liters of fuel, wore out five new tires on the Soviet roads, crossed rivers that we once learned about at school or that our soldiers in their day had to get over . . . , went through five Soviet Republics (Ukraine, Belarus, Azerbaijan, Georgia and Armenia), went up to a height of 3,000 meters in our car, were able to enjoy heat, storms, fog, sleet, and hail and, when it was forty-six degrees inside the car, understood what subtropical temperatures are like. We traveled through three time zones. Manfred, by the way, was both our translator and our driver, and without him our safari would certainly not have been such a success. We had to revise many of our preconceptions. Above all, we quickly learned to think in terms of different dimensions.

The scale of everything astonished them: the distances, the amount of water everywhere, the long highways through high mountain ranges, and the superabundance of things worth seeing. They were impressed by the hospitality, the quality of the hotels, and the opportunity as independent travelers to have some choice over when and what they ate. They appreciated the specialist interpreters at key sites with such broad knowledge of botany, geology, and archeology. They loved the opera and music in Tbilissi and Sochi, and swimming in lakes high in the mountains in Armenia, or in the Black Sea, surrounded by palm trees. As if to excuse her enthusiasm for the Soviet Union, Barbara sums up the trip by saying, "Well, since a large part of the world is closed off to us, then our only choice is to follow the route to the east to be able to see the key sites of early Christianity."

To give a better idea of their trip, Barbara includes many photos: their car in the Soviet Union with its GDR sticker on the back; wild, high, snowy mountains; towns, buildings, and markets; ancient ruins in Armenia; and the Stalin Museum in Georgia.

Barbara and her family are not the only ones to have traveled to the Soviet Union: Lisa Liebmann describes a trip to Leningrad and Moscow, while Heidi Kempf was in the Caucasus a year earlier. Although it is mostly those from the GDR who travel further east, Irma Kindler and her family have been happy to go to Yugoslavia and Albania.

Health, Illness, Death

Two more of the group died in the 1970s, along with some of the women's parents. Others had serious illnesses. Lisa Liebmann (29 November 1973) tells them she had to have an operation for breast cancer. She is recovering and getting physically stronger. Lisa, until now one of the liveliest and most energetic of the women, hopes that "perhaps as time goes by I shall also be able to put the psychological consequences behind me."

One unexpected benefit has come from the illness: she is now classed as an invalid and, as a pensioner (at the age of forty-six), was allowed to visit her father in the West. She also managed a brief visit to Irma Kindler. At the end of her letter, Lisa responds to Marianne: "By the way, my dear Marianne, I won't be wagging my warning finger any more—I am off duty!"

Two years later, in 1975, Lisa appears to have put her illness behind her. She and her husband have an enjoyable trip to Leningrad and Moscow. A further two years on, in 1977, Lisa still seems perfectly well. There is no mention of her invalid status. Instead, she wonders what they are to do with a ramshackle old hotel on the lakes south of Rostock, which they have inherited from an aunt; it is a millstone around their necks. Among the photos of the most recent class reunion, there is a photo of Lisa and her husband. His dazzling smile prompts Marianne Schneider to comment (15 January 1979): "Such is the smile of a hotel owner."

Ilse Klein (18 September 1974) says she has heard from Marianne that Agnes Braun has died, the second one of their group. There is no news of the cause of her death. She says that Anna Siebert's mother died suddenly as well, just after Anna's entry in the last book. In 1974, Marianne reports that both Hertha Pieper's husband and her mother have died. Marianne also asks if anyone knows anything more about the death of Agnes Braun; the package with the two volumes of the *Rundbrief* was sent back, marked "Addressee deceased." Curiously, no one seems to know anything.

Later in the seventies, after Anna Siebert's ominous report, Erika Krämer tells them that Brigitte Hansen died on 1 September 1979, the third of their group. At this stage, none of the Schönebeck women who remained in the GDR has died.

Conclusion: Turning Fifty

In the 1970s, it became more difficult for the Schönebeck women to assert that Germany remained essentially undivided. Political efforts to reduce tension between the FRG and the GDR were successful, but also made it easier for the GDR to proclaim its separation from any traditional concept of Germany, and to turn—politically, economically, and culturally—toward the Soviet Union and the other Warsaw Pact countries. The actions of the GDR state at many levels, from reshaping the constitution to interfering with the Schönebeck letters as they crossed the border between the FRG and the GDR, had a significant effect on the whole group: influencing what they wrote, determining where they could travel and meet, and imposing on all of them a sense of being under attack.

Nevertheless, the group, through the *Rundbrief* and the reunions, continued to provide comfort and reassurance, along with the opportunity for a process of collective mourning. Increasingly, they found they were mourning the loss not just of their parents, but also of their partners and the women themselves. At the same time, the group retained its social conservatism and its power over the lives of the individual women. Else Hermann felt this when choosing to give only a partial view of her life and her marriage, one she knew would be acceptable to them.

Additionally, the group's power was shown by the development of a realistically cautious, collective view of what should be said in the *Rundbrief*. When it comes to censorship and self-censorship, however, it is the husbands who appear to be the power behind the letters. The husbands' involvement in the reunions was accepted and welcomed by the women, but the men were kept at arm's length and remained marginal figures while the serious business took place: the discussion among the women themselves. At the same time, at least some of the women accepted that their husbands would read the letters in the *Rundbrief*, and the most overt example of self-censorship was in fact censorship by Marianne's husband of what she wanted to write.

In the 1970s, the women rarely commented on political events such as the major changes in relations between the FRG and the GDR. A few of them from the GDR did make clear their frustration with the way their lives were being controlled or interfered with by the state, and there were echoes of this from the women in the FRG who wanted to visit their old *Heimat* more often and more easily. Some of the women also gave the first indications that things might not be continuing to get better in the GDR, even materially.

While some of the concerns expressed are specific to the GDR, what also emerges is an overall sense that social attitudes and conditions in both countries were becoming more complex and more unsettling. There are expressions of frustration and disappointment at the way society is developing on both sides of the inner-German border. It is here that the reported deaths of school students are significant, along with the comments about long hair and beards. Ironically, however, their children appear to be doing well, to be happy with their lot, and to be taking advantage of the opportunities offered to them, both in the East and in the West.

What is also clear is that the opportunities available across the generations are far greater and more diverse in the FRG than in the GDR, reflecting the gap that continued to widen, even though both sides were affected by economic uncertainties in the 1970s. The Sommer family, after their expulsion from the GDR, were able to adjust rapidly to life in the FRG. This was partly because of the support from the Schönebeck women living around them. It was also because of the economic opportunities the West offered.

The women's contrasting descriptions of their travels also highlight the broader opportunities available in the West. However, the women in the East, accepting the limitations imposed on them by the GDR state, found a new and fascinating world opening up to them when they traveled further east. Vast excursions through the Soviet Union were something they could see as normal holiday trips in a way that was not so easy for the women in the FRG, or that made no sense to them because of the strongly anti-communist culture in the West.

Finally, although the women could be assertive in relation to their power to shape aspects of their everyday life, it is clear that the bulk of the power in both societies was exercised by men, who continued to put in place and maintain the framework within which the women's decisions were made and their attitudes shaped. This applied in the home as much as outside it. Any challenges to this framework were not echoed in the letters of the women and featured only rarely and implicitly in some of their actions. The rise of the feminist movement and the efforts to achieve women's liberation in the West are not mentioned anywhere. The parallel but distinctly different assertions of strength by women in the GDR also appear to go unnoticed.

The Schönebeck women in the GDR had other concerns: their families, finding ways to make the best of things, and looking after elderly parents with too little support from the state. At the same time, the women from both the FRG and the GDR appear, in a number of the letters, puzzled and perhaps subdued by the thought of turning fifty; they were growing old, and they were not sure they liked it. The 1980s would bring further changes in politics and society that the Schönebeck women could not fail to notice and be affected by, even as they saw themselves approaching retirement and looking forward to a quieter, less-demanding life.

Notes

1. Bake, *Die Ersten*, 41.
2. Steiner, *The Plans*, 141–43.
3. Weber, *Dokumente*, 345.
4. Harsch, *Revenge*, 314–15.
5. Steiner, *The Plans*, 163.
6. Steiner, *The Plans*, 173.
7. Gehler, *Deutschland*, 295–96.
8. Gehler, *Deutschland*, 225–26.
9. See "Citizens' Communications (*Eingaben*)," in Fulbrook, *The People's State*, 271–77; Siegfried Suckut, ed., *Volkes Stimmen: "ehrlich, aber deutlich": Privatbriefe an die DDR-Regierung* (Munich, 2016.)
10. "Mehr Ordnung und Sicherheit in unserer Elbestadt," *Volksstimme Magdeburg*, 13 May 1971.
11. *Stasi Files and Related Procedural Files*, AdK Kempowski-BIO 6232. See Leask, Sewell, and Tóth, "Families."
12. "Zehntausende im Einsatz gegen die Wetterunbilden," "Komplizierte Lage in den Kohle- und Energiebetrieben," "Erneute Verwehungen auf Verkehrswegen im Norden," "Auf Rügen Meter um Meter voran," *Neues Deutschland*, 2 January 1979.
13. Bake, *Die Ersten*, 41.
14. Gerhard, "Frauenbewegung," 200.
15. Frevert, *Women in German History*, 292–98.
16. Bake, *Die Ersten*, 43–44; Gerhard, "Frauenbewegung," 204–7.
17. Gerhard, "Frauenbewegung," 208.
18. Trappe, *Emanzipation*, 215.
19. Frevert, *Women in German History*, 283.
20. Fulbrook, *The People's State*, 149–54.
21. Fulbrook, *The People's State*, 159.
22. "Internationale Konferenz des ZK der SED zur Rolle der Frau," *Neues Deutschland*, 24 February 1979; *Volksstimme Magdeburg*, 24 February 1979.
23. Sarah Kirsch, *Die Pantherfrau: fünf Frauen in der DDR* (Reinbek bei Hamburg, 1979; first published in Berlin, 1973); Dodds and Allen-Thompson, *The Wall in My Backyard*, 3.

24. Maxie Wander, *Guten Morgen, du Schöne. Protokolle nach Tonband* (Darmstadt, 1980); Maxie Wander, *Leben wär' eine prima Alternativa. Tagebücher und Briefe*, herausgegeben von Fred Wander (Munich, 2004; first published in Berlin, 1979).
25. Harsch, *Revenge*, 313.
26. Fulbrook, *The People's State*, 170–71.
27. Letter of 25 April 2014.
28. *Neue Zeit*, 2 June 1979, has a long account of this festival. The United Kingdom and the Soviet Union shared the top prize.
29. "Gruß an die X. Weltfestspiele in Berlin," *Neues Deutschland*, 1 August 1973.
30. "Schönebecker und ihre Gäste feiern den 750. Geburtstag," *Volksstimme Magdeburg*, 29 June 1973, where the contributions of local factories are particularly stressed.
31. "Planmäßige Erhöhung des Lebensniveaus," *Volksstimme Magdeburg*, 18 March 1971.
32. "Achtung! Achtung! FALLOBST," *Volksstimme Magdeburg*, 7 October 1971; see 11 April 1974 for a report on shortages of vegetables in the shops.
33. "Für reine Luft an den Arbeitsplätzen,""Weniger Flugasche aus Schornsteinen," *Volksstimme Magdeburg*, 25 August 1971; "Der Schutz der Natur ist Sache aller Bürger," *Volksstimme Magdeburg*, 30 August 1971.
34. "Die Halbjahr-Bilanz unseres Bezirkes," *Volksstimme Magdeburg*, 20 July 1973.

CHAPTER 5

Toward Retirement
The 1980s

Introduction

In the 1980s, both parts of Germany operated as if they were independent entities with control over their destiny. Curiously, the Schönebeck women can be seen to act in much the same way, whether in the East or the West. Much of their energy was directed toward tying up loose ends and preparing for life after sixty, when they would have time to themselves and could all meet up again in the West. It was as if growing old (and many of them did feel old at sixty) meant starting a new life, where the border had less meaning and they could experience the reality of what they had always proclaimed: the unity of the group and the unity of Germany. They remained aware of the differences between the two sides of Germany, but were prepared to live with them, and to move toward a relatively comfortable retirement together. They were aware of political developments and shared the anxiety arising from them, but these affected all of them equally. They seem from their letters to have been much less aware of the economic problems of the GDR and their implications.

Political and Economic Context

The logic of the Cold War meant that both parts of Germany were battlefields for the struggle between the United States and the Soviet Union. This struggle threatened the existence of both the GDR and the FRG. The Soviet invasion of Afghanistan, the Reagan government's denunciation of the Soviet Union as the "evil empire," the expansion of the nuclear arsenals of both the USSR and the United States, and the determination of the superpowers to confront each other meant that these powers would locate their missiles in their respective parts of Germany. The two German governments gave their approval, but there was significant opposition among ordinary people in the GDR as well as in the FRG. This opposition helped to shape political and social developments for the rest of the decade.

Another significant development was the formation in Poland of the independent trade union, Solidarność (Solidarity). With its clear challenge to the communist government, this was the first substantial sign of organized opposition in the Warsaw Pact countries since the Prague Spring in 1968.

In the FRG in the 1980s, political control shifted to the right under Chancellor Helmut Kohl. Economically, the FRG survived the oil price shocks and the widespread downturn in the early 1980s, and subsequent higher inflation and unemployment, better than many of its Western competitors.[1] However, the continuing or renewed political activities of "anti-imperialist" groups, and of the violent RAF in particular, caused substantial political turmoil. Other social movements, such as the environmental movement and the peace movement, developed a much wider base and had a far greater social and political impact.[2]

In the East it is easy to see, looking back, many different events and actions that were undermining the apparently stable GDR. Despite the SED's assertions that conditions were consistently improving, there were continuing economic difficulties. Once again, difficult winters, such as those of 1981/82 and 1986/87, caused serious problems.[3]

The communist societies of Eastern Europe (not including the Soviet Union) increasingly promoted a kind of everyday socialism and based their definition of social need on what they understood to be the perspective of women. The result was that they were spending more than 20 percent of their GDP on social programs and subsidies keeping their childcare provision going, guaranteeing jobs, and building more housing. For the GDR, this meant that by the early 1980s they were spending more than they were bringing in. The SED leadership, Harsch says, "recognized that social security and consumption were undermining, rather than promoting, economic efficiency, but the Politburo felt it dare not change course."[4]

Denial was a feature of the SED leadership's behavior during this period. For them, the missile crisis was provoked by the West and had nothing to do with actions by the Soviet Union. It supported the autonomous peace movement in the West while only allowing a state-sponsored peace movement in the GDR. It used the Stasi against unofficial groups who suggested that both sides were culpable. Similarly, it would not admit that the crisis in Poland had anything to do with mismanagement or misrule by the communist party there, that Solidarność might have legitimate grievances, or that it was reasonable in a workers' state for the workers to set up their own trade unions, independent of the state, and call a strike if necessary. In the local press available to the women in and around Schönebeck, the emphasis was on interference by the Western powers, who risked starting a nuclear war, while ordinary people were shown raising money for the suffering women and children in Poland, the alleged victims of Solidarność.[5] Following the military takeover in Poland by the communist general Jaruzelski, the press emphasized the need for "normalization": the elimination of "elements hostile to the state" and "'Solidarność' counterrevolutionaries."[6]

As the decade progressed, the SED became more and more cut off from its own population and from some of its international allies. Internally it persecuted, at times brutally, the increasingly daring and confident small opposition groups—often backed covertly or openly by the churches—who were active around issues of peace, the environment, and eventually questions of democracy, freedom of assembly, and freedom to form independent groups. While the party continued to ensure that its own views were the only ones available through the state-controlled media, word-of-mouth communication and access to Western television for much of the GDR meant that people were better informed than before and could see the dishonesty of their own government.

Internationally, the GDR initially supported Mikhail Gorbachev's attempts to reduce tension between the Soviet Union and the United States, and to work toward the reduction of nuclear weapons. However, the SED distanced itself from Gorbachev's moves to open up the society and the economy and to be more truthful about both the present and the past. It sought to deflect attention from Gorbachev's internal reforms and found ways to avoid implementing similar reforms in the GDR. In 1988, it even banned the circulation in the GDR of the popular Soviet journal *Sputnik* for giving a supposedly distorted view of history.[7]

1989 saw the start of huge changes. In May, the clearly fraudulent communal elections generated a wave of anger. The SED responded by making clear it was prepared to resort to force to keep hold of power in the GDR. It openly supported the Chinese leadership in the crushing of the pro-democracy movement in China[8] and continued to justify the Warsaw Pact invasion of Czechoslovakia in 1968.[9]

As the year progressed, large numbers of people from the GDR found ways to escape as refugees to the West, while others stayed and participated in the growing demonstrations against the regime. The SED denounced even its supposed allies, such as Hungary, for opening their border to Austria and allowing GDR citizens through. The final isolation of the SED came when Gorbachev made clear at the GDR's fortieth anniversary celebrations in October that the Soviet Union would not help them to keep control and that the GDR leaders should think again about was happening. Huge demonstrations, the collapse of SED membership, and the loss of Soviet support led to the most dramatic event, the opening of the Berlin Wall in November.

The "Woman Question"

After the prominence of women's struggles, and the gains made in the 1970s, the 1980s were more difficult years. In the face of an economic slowdown and the election of a conservative government in the FRG in 1982, there was what Frevert calls "a palpable restoration of old-style government policies in respect of women and the family," and attempts to "restore the appeal of the domestic role for women."[10] In parallel, the autonomous, highly diverse women's movement largely retreated from making demands on the male-dominated state, political parties, and trade unions, since it expected to get nothing from such "patriarchal" institutions. Despite this, initiatives at the state level, and the implementation of laws to do with, for instance, part-time work and paid parental leave, left many women better off and kept the arguments about equal responsibilities for men and women alive.[11]

In the GDR at the start of the 1980s, it appeared that little had changed in terms of the balance of power between men and women. An announcement about the new governing council for the Magdeburg district listed the fifteen members, all of them men.[12] Similarly, the SED's Central Committee reception for International Women's Day in 1981 still had Erich Honecker as its main speaker, with the top table dominated by men, and, according to news reports, his speech was given a "rapturous reception."[13] The official women's organization, the DFD, concentrated on SED-approved activities, speaking out in favor of the party's approach to achieving peace, and stressing the role of women in building socialism.[14] The same words were still being used for International Women's Day in 1989.[15]

In the workplace, where equality was said to have been achieved, women were still paid less than men and blocked from higher positions. Eva Kolinsky, using a document written after 1989 by the former head of the GDR statistical services, demonstrates the open and hidden discrimination against women in the GDR. The presumption was that if a woman had to be put into a leadership position to meet prescribed targets, she had to be over forty, living alone, and have no children. She also shows that there was no possibility of career advancement for anyone working part time, as huge numbers of women were.[16]

When it came to childcare provision, the GDR was totally different from the FRG. In the 1980s in the GDR, 80 percent of children under three had nursery places, compared with 4 percent in the FRG; 94 percent had all-day kindergarten places, compared with around 68 percent (mostly morning or afternoon) in the FRG; and 81 percent of children aged six to ten had after-school provision, compared with 3.6 percent in the FRG. Nevertheless, when the children came back from school or childcare, it was still the women in the GDR who mostly looked after them. Even when men were entitled to take time off because of their children, they almost never did.[17] As for housework, the amount done by women was still astonishingly high. In 1989, women in the first year of marriage did nearly 70 percent of cleaning the house, 82 percent of clothes washing, 66 percent of cooking and preparing meals, and 50 percent of food shopping. Men did much more than women only in the traditionally male areas of household repairs and heating the house.[18]

Nevertheless, it became clear late in the decade that women working outside the official structures could be articulate, strong, and organized, despite the security services' attempts to suppress their new groups.[19] In late 1989, an independent women's union, the Unabhängiger Frauenverband (UFV), emerged, with a program very different from that of the DFD. The first article of its draft constitution declared, "The women in the UFV consider themselves part of a world-wide women's movement which fights to abolish oppressive power structures and ways of thinking, and which will establish a non-violent, democratic, ecologically stable, socially just, multicultural world."[20] Such women demonstrate, as Fulbrook says, "that by the 1980s, women had not only found a voice—something that was not always easy for individuals brought up in a system in which there were only rewards for conformity—but also acquired the capacity for highly effective organization, strategic and tactical skills."[21] These women were principally from generations younger than the Schönebeck women, however.

The Group: Coping with Tensions and Losses

Strengthening the Group

The Schönebeck group evolved significantly during the 1980s. Illness and death reduced their numbers, but the group responded by tracking down and reclaiming some of the women who had been involved in the *Rundbrief* but had lost touch for various reasons. Additionally, several of the men were incorporated into the group. Although they were treated as honorary women, their entries are strikingly different and give a different perspective on the "woman question."

In this decade, the Schönebeck women in both the East and the West were looking forward to the freedom turning sixty would bring them. In 1987, they held their first joint reunion (see figure 5.1). This took place in Hamburg and was organized by Irma Kindler and Anna Siebert. The letters describe it as a wonderful event, with many of the women not having seen one another for decades. The reunion was made possible by the women in the West pairing with ones from the East, whose travel and accommodation they paid for. A curious side effect was that these pairings led to the deepening of friendships between some of the partners, and to the formation of what can be seen as mini-groups within the larger group. Else Hermann became close friends with Irma Kindler, and they wrote to one another frequently over the next twenty-nine years, sometimes gently mocking the other women.

Figure 5.1. Arriving in Hamburg in 1987 for the first joint reunion. Photo courtesy of Akademie der Künste, Berlin.

Noticing the Political

In the 1970s, nothing suggested that the Schönebeck women could ever imagine the end of the world they now accepted as normal, a world where their myth of a united Germany seemed no more than a dream. Surprisingly, however, some of their letters in the early years of the 1980s show their anxiety about political developments and the impact of these on their children. There is a sense of threat hanging over them, for all their familiar talk of families, illness, travel, and jobs.

In March 1980, Marianne Schneider, affirming the division of Germany as well as asserting its continued existence as one country, addresses the other women happily and perhaps defiantly: "All of you in both parts of our Fatherland!" In January 1982 she comments, less happily, "What is happening in Poland is unsettling to all of us. Who will finally do away with conflict in the world? Why is there still no possibility of making wars impossible?" Elly Haase (30 March 1982) also refers to the events in Poland: "In 1981 there were already difficulties in traveling to Poland, so we just went for the day to Karlovy Vary and a day to Prague." As with Czechoslovakia in 1968, one of the GDR's important allies and fraternal socialist states was out of bounds for people from the GDR.

The lesson from Barbara Meier (10 April 1982) is that the politically difficult period they are going through makes the *Rundbrief* and the class reunions doubly important. They bring, she implies, a sense of common identity across the group. She is particularly grateful, she says, "for the way we have all stuck together, for the sense of involvement and empathy that comes from you all." Sometimes, she says, she thinks about the time

> when the serious situation in Poland cast such dark shadows, and about our children who still are not allowed to visit Agnieszka's parents and brothers [in Poland]. And when in our daily lives such things happen as Anna S. describes them in Staßfurt, then you'll understand what I mean—that we are happy and grateful that out of our school class, such a connection emerged as the one we have! And so let us all meet up together as often as we possibly can, whether in words or in deeds. Who knows how much longer it will remain possible! And wasn't the time that Martha and Kurt arranged for us all to be together again, something that we can draw on for a long time to come?

Nevertheless, in the late 1980s came the threat of the first real rupture in the group. The response to this threat is a good example of how the group kept itself together over such a long period through quite subtle and yet powerful ways of reducing tension and avoiding damaging confrontation.

Erika Krämer: The Long-Term Consequences of Humiliation?

Erika Krämer had always been a member of the Schönebeck group, writing in the *Rundbrief* when she was still in the GDR and again when she was settled in Kassel, in the FRG. She met up with some of the women in the West in the early years, but did not attend the reunions in the GDR, even though she often traveled there. After her shocking accounts from the early 1950s, her letters from the West were cheerful enough, commenting on her family or her visits to her sister in Calbe. She was often effusive about the *Rundbrief* and the accounts in it. Even her children loved it when the *Rundbrief* arrived and they could all sit together and read it.

At the same time, there was always a sense that Erika's commitment to the group was only superficial, going no further than words on the page, and that many of the women found this frustrating. Marianne Schneider, normally so patient, tells Erika with unexpected sharpness on 12 August 1973 that she should get a camera, so that at least they can see pictures of the family, since she does not have time for them on her visits to the GDR. Erika responds in a friendly manner on 14 March 1973, talking again of the family's excitement about the arrival of the *Rundbrief* and their commitment to speeding it on its way. She includes a number of photos: the whole family with a group of friends and relatives; her and her husband and the two children having dinner at home; and herself in a bikini on the Baltic coast.

On 13 February 1976, Erika looks back over her past, saying how much she suffered in the early years with her imprisonment, the death of her parents, illness, and the time in the sanatorium, and how happy and untroubled the last twenty years have been. Again she includes a selection of family photos. Although she still does not attend the class reunions or visit the women in the East, her letters over the next decade are similarly warm, friendly, and accompanied by family photos as the children grow up. Over this period, she is visited briefly by Lisa Liebmann and her husband and by Hertha Pieper (though it is notable that it is not Erika who mentions these visits). Even in her letter of 27 March 1984, telling them that she has had a setback—breast cancer, which has been operated on—she remains cheerful and friendly. On 7 October 1986, she says that their annual trip to the GDR is not long enough for them to catch up with everyone, but wishes them all the best for the class reunion.

Suddenly, in a letter dated Whitsun, 1988, Erika attacks the group she has apparently participated in happily for over thirty-five years. She complains that the rest of them in their "so tightly knit community" see and treat her as an outsider, and that it was like that at school as well. The five of them from Staßfurt, two from Calbe (including her), and Carla Brunner from Glinde, came later than the others to the school in Schönebeck, were seen as outsiders, and were treated as such during the years before their *Reichsarbeitsdienst*.

Many of the other women are stung by the rejection and hostility in this letter. Elly Haase (9 November 1988) is indignant. She takes issue with Erika for suggesting that the girls from Staßfurt and Calbe were treated as outsiders. She does not think this is right and quotes examples from then and later, such as her close connection with one of them, Agnes Braun. Elly regrets that Erika has kept herself apart, pointing out that on all her visits to Calbe, she has never even had time for a coffee with Hertha Pieper, also in Calbe, to which Elly and others would happily have come. Nor did she attend most of the mini-reunions in the West.

In mentioning the reunions, however, Elly attempts to defuse the situation by taking attention away from Erika's complaint and offering her the group's forgiving embrace. She urges Erika to look into her heart and take the plunge, since they are reaching out to her. In an elegant sideways move, Elly says that Erika is not alone in not attending: perhaps she could bring or come with Leni Baumann, since the two of them coming would make it easier for both of them. This diversion of any blame allows Elly to change her tone and almost make light of the whole problem, as she addresses Leni personally: "Dear Leni, since our first reunion in 1950, I have seen nothing more of you, and I have such a deep longing to. . . . And here I am sending out invitations even though I am not the host, and as well as that I belong to those who can't even pay for their overnight stay! Oh dear!"

Maria Stein (11 February 1989) confirms the shift of attention away from Erika and her complaint. As someone who had been out of touch, she says how wonderful the reunions were for her in Hamburg and Sinzig. She adds that she was terrified when the opportunity first came up to meet them all again after so long, "and would sooner have gone to the dentist than to the class reunion. But right from the very first moment, I felt comfortable among you all and there was not the slightest feeling that we had been apart from one another for all those years. Dear Erika, do give it a try, you will certainly never regret it."

Barbara Meier's response (18 April 1989) is to acknowledge the complaint while finding a way to say it is not significant. There were groups within the overall group, she acknowledges, but that is always how things work, and the fact that the larger group has held together for fifty years proves its strength. Taking up Elly's point about the reunions, she urges both Erika and Leni to take a chance and come back to them.

The longest, most considered response comes from Anna Siebert's letter of 19 June 1989 and needs to be looked at here, rather than in the account of Anna's life in the 1980s.

Anna says that Erika was right: the girls who had to travel to school in Schönebeck were outsiders. The ones from Schönebeck were naturally closer because they were together more after school and had their free time together over many years, "going to dancing lessons, getting to know young men," and so on. And naturally this continued later, when she, Erika, Brigitte, and Leni went off to other schools, and to jobs in other towns, in some cases beyond what would be the GDR:

> Here we had to start again completely from scratch, even just to get a foothold, and for a long time we hardly had the opportunity to come home very often and be in our *Heimat*. On top of that, in our adopted homes things developed very differently, thanks to our jobs, to getting married and to the need to fit in with the careers of our husbands. With that, there was just not the time any more for keeping up our old connections, and these decayed so far that there was no chance of reviving them again. Even for Erika and me, who were so close because of the time we spent together during our *Arbeitsdienst* and while studying in Berlin, a certain distance has crept in, which is something I *deeply* regret but also something I don't know how to account for.
>
> Here in the West, I guess, everyone has so many outside distractions and so many family things to do that we don't look back with a sense of loss at the past. As for Leni, we should probably excuse her, since she is still really caught up in the stress of her professorial duties. I know myself how hard it is as a woman to occupy such a position. There may be equality on paper, but it looks different in practice; women still have to accomplish more than men.

Erika herself (9 July 1989) sees this as the end of the matter. Anna has so well clarified the issues about their early years, she says, that there is no need for her to comment further. Although she has a daughter in Ulm and a son in Aachen, she has kept in touch with many people in the GDR since, she adds, "my whole tribe" lives there.

What has frustrated many in the Schönebeck area, however, is just that: Erika has visited her family often, but not them, despite all the opportunities to do so and the number of times they have said they would like to see her. It is clear to them that she has positively avoided them, and they feel perplexed and frustrated by this.

Why Erika Krämer acted in this way remains an open question. It is helpful to consider to what extent her behavior arose out of her early experiences in the GDR. What happened to Erika and the permanently missing Karl was the most shocking incident mentioned in all the years of the letters. These experiences were humiliating and extremely traumatic. A common response to humiliation is for the victim to assume that she herself is to blame for it, and to feel an entirely unjustified sense of shame for her actions or the position she is in. Shifting the blame in this way allows her to deny the reality of her own powerlessness.[22]

In the early 1950s, Erika confided in them, telling them what had happened and how she felt. However, there was also a critical, bitter, and carping edge to her letters. They could not really know what it was like to suffer what she was suffering, she told them, and implied that their responses were superficial and their feelings shallow. After her recovery from tuberculosis in 1956, it was as if she had consciously disposed of her past: her terrible experiences, the responses from the other women, and her willingness to confide in them, all seemed to have disappeared. From then on, she distanced herself from the group, writing letters that were warm and enthusiastic as well as strangely impersonal, visiting the *Heimat* without ever visiting them, never attending the class reunions, and finally turning on them in her 1988 letter.

Erika's letters and her behavior suggest that she is still battling to deny what happened to her in the 1950s and overcome her sense of shame for it. This denial shuts her off from her past as well as from the other women in the present. Perhaps, in their expressions of warmth and closeness, they cannot help but remind her of the past she wants to believe did not really happen. She becomes angry with them for having witnessed her humiliation, for still asserting that there is continuity with the past, and for knowing the reality: her hurt and suffering, her impotence, and her terrible sense of injustice. They know her too well and the only way she can deal with this knowledge, as well as her self-knowledge and her recurring memories of the humiliating events, is to attack them, denying that they were ever the close, warm group they claim to be.

In doing so, she displays some of the predictable consequences of humiliation: impotent rage at an injustice about which she can do nothing, and the sense of exclusion and loneliness such experiences bring. Although the feelings associated with humiliation can be buried and denied for decades, they are always still there, waiting for some event, comment, thought, or dream to haul them back up to the surface, mostly when the victim is least expecting it.[23]

Health, Illness, and Death

Marianne Schneider: The End of an Era?

At the start of the decade, Marianne Schneider was her normal cheerful self, keeping an overview of what was going on for everyone, managing the *Rundbrief* and making sure the reunions took place. Marianne embodied the myth of the unity of the women, centered on their Schönebeck *Heimat*. She also kept her eye on what was happening around her politically and socially.

In her letter of 10 February 1982, Marianne shows that family life can turn out to be sad and painful. It all started with a holiday romance. Rolf, their youngest son, became involved in a relationship that was not particularly serious—until the young woman became pregnant. Rolf decided to stand by her and to be a good father to the new baby:

> We smoothed the way for them as they prepared to become a new family, and when Stefan was born on 16 May, everything seemed to be fine. The tiny new grandson was welcomed into our house, and before long utterly into our hearts. The young mother was happy staying with us, gratefully accepted bits of advice and was happy for us to help her. We could no longer see any problems in this unanticipated—one might say premature—birth. The date for the wedding was fixed for 4 January 1982 and the necessary preparations were made.

It was not to be so straightforward, however:

> Then at the end of November another man (married) popped up in Nina's life, and everything fell apart. Suddenly she declared that without this man she could no longer keep on living, and stayed away from the house for night after night. That was terrible, not just for Rolf but also for us. Rolf forgave her many times. She came back, full of remorse, and then the next betrayal followed. It went on like this until sixteen days before the date of the wedding. And then everything finally disintegrated.

The consequences were distressing for all of them and were made worse by the GDR's laws (which were similar to laws in many other societies at the time). Neither their son nor Marianne and Johannes would be able to keep in contact with the child:

So now we have to get used to realizing that over the space of a year we both acquired and then lost our sixth grandchild. We are very unhappy, since we would finally have been able to watch a grandchild growing up close to us. Rolf is deeply disappointed. He wanted so much to be a good father. Now he can't even see his son any more, since the mother doesn't want him to and that's the way the law works. Only after a divorce—which is not technically what happened in this case—is the father permitted to play a part in bringing up his child. It is almost as bad as if there had been a death in the family. It will be a long time before we've grasped that there is really nothing we can do to change anything.

In her next letter, in 1983, Marianne has to apologize for the first time for being late sending the *Rundbrief* out. Her mother was confined to her bed for a year, for the last six months did not even recognize them anymore, then died a long, terrible death. Marianne thanks Johannes for doing such a huge amount for her mother and says how grateful she is that they have lived together so harmoniously, first when both her parents were living there and then over the last two decades when it was just her mother. "Now the two of us are alone," she says, "since all the children have flown the nest." However, there is good news too: Rolf and his girlfriend have been reconciled. Stefan, the former lost grandchild, is two years old and often stays with Marianne and Johannes.

Book 22 starts with a shock for the women: Frieda Möller, introducing it on 18 February 1985, explains that Marianne has had an operation and needs more time to get her strength back and make a full recovery. When it comes to her turn to write (1 June 1985), Marianne is full of warmth toward them all:

> What true friendship means is what I have so powerfully felt over the past few months. Thank you for that from the bottom of my heart. It has helped me so much to know how close together we have grown over all the years, and when my spirits sink, to sense that I am not being forgotten about.
>
> But things are already going better for me again. After my long stay in hospital (December, January, February, March), I have now recovered and can do the housework on my own, even if more slowly. Johannes encourages me and helps me when he is at home, and keeps a good eye out to be sure that I don't carry anything too heavy.

At this point, health and the family are closely intertwined for Marianne, and it is notable that she has never lost the sense that the housework is her responsibility, with the man's role to watch and encourage her. She says how happy she is to have had a seventh grandchild since she last wrote in the *Rundbrief*. This is the second child of Rolf and his wife, a brother to Stefan, the grandchild they thought they had lost. The family has a newly built flat in Schönebeck, and Marianne and Johannes see them almost every day. This is particularly nice for them, she says, as they are the only grandchildren living nearby.

Marianne's other two sons have recently been required to do three months of reservist duty in the army. She is not happy about this and still has the strength to make a political comment in the context of the ongoing arms race: "Freedom is what we all want, and we don't have to be armed to the teeth!!"

With everyone having left home, Marianne would like to move to somewhere smaller, but Johannes cannot be separated from the house they are in. Her only other news is that they had a good holiday last year in the Caucasus. She then talks about being constantly checked at the hospital in Magdeburg and concludes in a way that sounds ominously like a farewell:

> But I won't lose hope. It is like this for so many people, and some of you had to get to know illnesses like this much sooner. Whatever happens, I shall come to terms with it. I am grateful for everything that I have been able to have and for every joyful moment that will still be granted to us. I have had so many visits and letters. They give me strength and confidence.
>
> Finally let me wish you all the very best! There is simply nothing better than being healthy!

The first part of the next book (Book 23) is dominated by the news of Marianne's death. The death notices from the newspapers have been inserted by Frieda Möller; these are simple, somber, and not religious. There is then a letter inside an envelope, with a full account from a distraught Johannes Schneider. He wanted to write much sooner, he says, but just could not manage it. Now he needs to tell them what happened.

It all began (Johannes's report starts) in the summer of 1984. Marianne started to get severe pain for around twenty minutes at a time in the region around the base of her spine. Only in mid-December, after long and systematic investigations, did a gynecologist discover a grapefruit-sized cyst. She was operated on in Schönebeck on 19 December 1984 and got through that all right, but analysis showed on 14 January 1985 that it was cancerous. She was transferred to the medical academy in Magdeburg and there had radiotherapy. After her release, she was regularly monitored throughout 1985. On 12 December she was operated on again. By 6 January 1986, it was clear that the cancer had spread to her bowel, which needed removing at once. He, Johannes, consulted four cancer specialists privately; the conclusion was that the cancer had spread so far that there was no point in further intervention.

> Only a few months left!! Marianne did not realize how serious things had become for her. On 14 December we were in Ilmenau for Jürgen to defend his doctoral thesis. After that things went downhill fast. She could no longer sit down but kept on writing standing up! . . . She ate almost nothing anymore and drank only very little. On 16 February she was due for surgery here again but was already too weak for that. In the end her kidneys failed. On 2 March (one

day after my birthday!) she was *finally* released from her suffering. She weighed no more than 30 kilos! I myself lost fifteen kilos but am slowly getting physically better. In February and March I was never left on my own, although three of my children live 240 kilometers away. I am particularly proud of my children now!

It is difficult for Frieda Möller (21 April 1986) to keep on with a normal *Rundbrief* after this. Nevertheless, after long expressions of shock and grief, she says Johannes has told her that on her death bed Marianne made him promise that he would organize the next class reunion. As the first of the men to make it on to the *Rundbrief* list, Johannes, writing on 21 July 1986, invites them all to the next class reunion in October: "Believe me, this is ABSOLUTELY what Marianne wanted, and I promised her I would see to it."

The death of Marianne could easily have led the group to fragment. She had been central to the *Rundbrief* and the reunions for thirty-five years. Her way of writing and her skill in accommodating differences within the group were powerful forces that helped hold the group together. She was always trying to make life better for others around her and believed that together they could make a difference, to one another and to the society they lived in. She was, in many ways, conservative in her actions and attitudes, and therefore contributed to maintaining socially conservative attitudes in the group and preempting discussion of other ways of living.

However, Marianne's strong moral sense meant that she also took chances with what she wrote about the state she lived in. She gave the group a slight sense of daring, a feeling that they were more than just a group of women growing older and chatting to one another. At least partly through Marianne, they became a group with opinions and strong positions and a wish for things to be better, on both sides of the inner-German border, even if they were wary of expressing these views explicitly.

Above all, what Marianne did was to feed back to them constantly the importance of the myth they had constructed for themselves, that the unity of the group, centered on their Schönebeck *Heimat*, was powerful enough to maintain the unity of Germany, no matter how strongly the structures and forces of their different societies seemed to contradict this myth.

Marianne's Other Letters

There is a curious postscript to this assessment of Marianne Schneider. It comes from one of those almost accidental discoveries so beloved of historians.

In the German Diary Archive (DTA), there is a large collection of diaries and letters from a young woman, "Sybille," who in 1984 was in love with a somewhat older protestant theologian.[24] He was a prominent participant in the peace movement in the GDR, a musician, and an unofficial social worker among young people in Berlin. In early 1984, he applied for permission to leave the GDR. He then visited the FRG's permanent representative office in Berlin—the equivalent of an embassy, established in accordance with agreements between the GDR and the FRG—to inform them of his wish to live in the West. After his second visit, he was arrested and charged with giving information to the West that could be damaging to the GDR. He was sentenced to fourteen months' imprisonment. After his release from prison, both he and Sybille went to the West and settled in the Freiburg area; it appears that he was bought out, while she was simply allowed to go.

The archive contains some four hundred and fifty letters from friends, acquaintances, and relatives in the GDR to Sybille in the West. They are often in response to letters from her, but her letters are not in the collection. In the collection are three letters and a card from Marianne Schneider (also signed by Johannes) to Sybille, who, it turns out, is her niece. These were all written late in 1985, after Marianne's last *Rundbrief* entry.

Marianne and Johannes were very close to Sybille. This was potentially a problem for them, since Western contacts, particularly with prominent people, could lead to persecution in the East. It would have been safer to cut off contact with her. This is the last thing Marianne was prepared to do. Her responsibility, as she saw it, was to reassure, encourage, and calm her niece so that she could make the most of her new life after their *Umsiedlung*, their "resettlement," without being overwhelmed by anger at how they had been treated in the GDR. Marianne had to do this without criticizing the GDR, and at a time when she herself was ill and getting steadily worse. She is very personal in her letters, asking Sybille in July 1985 what they would like as a belated wedding present—a nice casserole dish perhaps, or might they prefer a table cloth? ("If so, please tell me what size.") Marianne is realistic about the differences between East and West, but being able to give them something is important to her: "We know that over there everything you can get is certainly much better, but nevertheless you should have a small memento for your wedding from us." Marianne senses that life is in fact "complicated and confusing" for Sybille in the West and urges her to take care of her health above everything else: "It is the precondition for everything that awaits you in the coming years." She plays down her illness much as she did to the Schönebeck women: "Thank you for asking about how I am and for your good wishes. I'm not going to complain; even though things don't always go so smoothly, I still remain happy that I can do all the housework that needs to be done myself. Uncle Johannes of course supports me in everything and keeps my spirits up."

Sybille sends special stamps to "Uncle Johannes" for his collection, though it is left to Marianne to thank her for this. In all these letters with news about family and short holidays, and even about renovating their house, Marianne's last concern is for herself and her first for everyone else. The last thing she writes to Sybille is a card for Christmas, dated 18 December 1985, when Marianne knew how ill she was. If Johannes's account is correct, she wrote this letter standing up as she could no longer sit down. All she gives away to Sybille about her condition is this: "Unfortunately, I'm still not as well as I would like to be. Last week they got me into Magdeburg for five days again and went over me once more and pounded me from pillar to post! What is next year likely to bring for me?"

Marianne knew, but would not say.

The Deaths of Others

It was not just political events, past and present, or Marianne's death that shook the group in the 1980s. These were the years of accidents, illnesses, and death. An awareness of mortality suddenly hung over the Schönebeck women and became central to the way the group started to think of itself. This happened when the women were still in their fifties, which we would no longer consider to be old, when they were looking forward to all the new things they could do when they retired.

Reading their letters, we see several of the women develop cancer. Some sense they will not recover. Mostly their tone remains optimistic, but this comes across as an understandable denial of how serious things are. Lisa Liebmann's letter of 25 September 1983 from Wismar is a difficult one to read, being full of suffering that she tries to make light of. She slipped and fell against one of the sharp corners of their Art Nouveau piano, she tells them, and broke some ribs on the side where she had had the breast operation. Meanwhile, her husband Helmut has not been well because the injury from his wartime plane crash has flared up. He now has diabetes, too, and it was thought he would have to retire early on health grounds. Still, she says, he has been treated well and is now okay again and back teaching his students chemistry. She goes on to tell them that her daughter-in-law's only brother hanged himself, aged thirty-six. Fortunately, thinking of the *Rundbrief* and the way their group has held together for so long comforts her and gives her strength, she says.

Anni Lange, the opera singer, was based in Hamburg for many years. She traveled the world while her husband and child lived in Ankara, where he worked in the university. Eventually she spent less time performing and more time in Ankara. In her letter of 9 July 1982, she says that she is living there permanently with them and has a job that has nothing to do with the opera. Now, ironically, it is her husband who gets to travel back to Germany:

> Since January I have managed to have a permanent job as an assistant in the library of the German cultural institute. It is interesting and satisfying, I feel fulfilled and so life is a lot more fun. Thanks to the hours I work, I can combine

being there with managing the household and doing the shopping. Being in a job again is definitely not so easy, particularly at our age. My long holiday begins on 9 July and ends on 31 August, absolutely in the crazily hot period. We have a beautiful penthouse flat with a fantastic view over Ankara, but with the temperature already up to 30 degrees by seven in the morning, the heat just spoils everything—though I can also easily picture myself back in Germany, desperate for every ray of sunshine.

Wolfgang will be traveling with his choir to Berlin from 3 to 13 September. Seven concerts have been organized for them, one in the Philharmonia.

On 1 February 1984, it is Wolfgang who writes in the *Rundbrief* from Izmir in Turkey, where they are now living: he tells them that Anni is in the hospital and asked him to reply for her.

Susanne Becker (11 May 1984) has spent a lot of time in hospital. She has cancer that has spread widely. She has had operations, radiotherapy, and chemotherapy. Now they suspect it has got into her bones, but after more treatment she is feeling all right again, she assures them.

Things come to a head in Sabine Kleber's letter of 20 May 1984 (still well before Marianne's death). Despite her natural optimism, she feels that this volume of the *Rundbrief* conveys the sense of a stricken generation, one that is unlikely to grow old. The *Rundbrief* speaks of lovely times, she writes, but also of many a painful hour. She adds,

> It falls to me now to pass on to you another shocking piece of news: Marianne wrote to tell me that Anni Lange died of her illness on 6 April in Izmir.
>
> And so now we have lost four of our group, something that makes me feel apprehensive. I wonder whether many of us will be lucky enough to grow old in good health; I fear our generation won't manage it.

Erna Walter (6 June 1984, Kappeln, on the Baltic coast between Flensburg and Kiel) has also been suffering from breast cancer. She has been operated on and had radiotherapy, but is not confident about the future. She is trying to lead an ordinary life with gardening and tennis and running the household, and is, she writes, "grateful for every beautiful day and for so much that I previously just took for granted. I live with greater intensity and greater perceptiveness."

The death of Anni Lange has shocked and saddened Frieda Möller. Anni had visited them in Barby a couple of times and always looked astonishingly young. "It is good," she says, "that we don't know when our end is nigh." She also says that Lisa Liebmann is ill again, so they are canceling the class reunion that was to have taken place in Wismar in August 1985.

Lisa herself writes on 23 February 1985 from Wismar that her cancer has returned after twelve years and that she feels "so despairing." Despite this, she says how pleased she is that Susanne Becker seems to have the worst behind her. For herself she says, "I am not quite giving up hope that once more the sun will shine on me too." Lisa's letter is concluded by her husband, Helmut:

> I can tell you that Lisa got through her first dose of chemotherapy, but at the moment is very weak. She doesn't want to walk and it takes a lot to persuade her to come out for a short stroll. But still, she is in relatively good shape and has even put on a bit of weight again. I'm not giving up hope that we'll be given a few more years of happiness together.

In 1984, Susanne Becker was concerned about the spread of her cancer but felt she was getting better. Writing on 19 October 1985, she is just trying to hold on as long as possible, since there are still demands on her:

> At the moment I am relatively well, after another round of radiotherapy sessions. When I had my checkup on 8 May, they found another growth on my spine. The radiotherapy totally drained me, but things are better now. I certainly don't have the time to *surrender*, since I first have to be there for my son's wedding. He has finally found the right woman and is getting married at the end of the month. And then of course I want to become a grandmother, which is due to happen in April. Someone I know said to me recently: "Next year we'll be sixty—awful, isn't it?" My answer to her: "I'll be happy *if* I reach sixty!" It's all a matter of perspective.

She concludes by saying to Lisa Liebmann that she really understands how she feels at the moment.

In the meantime, however, Lisa has died. Her husband Helmut (11 August 1986) says he has been on an invalid's pension since 1 March. He is keen to thank them all, but most particularly Irma Kindler and Astrid Greiswald (both in the West) for all their help and sympathy over Lisa's death. He has been traveling around a lot, including as far as Rumania, partly to help him forget how he feels: "But all such distractions just don't help. I still haven't got over the awareness of being alone."

Shortly after, Anna Siebert says that she has heard that Susanne Becker died on 25 September 1986.

Barbara Meier's reaction to the various deaths is to say on 8 July 1986 that the terrible things afflicting them must make them think about how much they have and all they should be grateful for: "One part of that is our group, our friendship, and the way we keep together."

Sabine Kleber writes a long, thoughtful letter on 10 January 1987 in response to all the deaths and illnesses. She says it is important for them all to keep going, despite their sadness, and in memory of the thirty-six years of effort Marianne put into keeping their group together. She reminds them how they all promised they would meet up again in 1950 and of what became of that promise:

> It turned into reality! For the first time after leaving school, we met up together in the Domplatz in Magdeburg. How young we still were then, how brimming with life, how full of energy! Our carefree years are behind us now, but still life has a purpose and holds out many more joyous moments for us. In any case, this is what I wish for all of us for 1987.

Life Goes on

Charlotte Krüger, quietly breeding orchids in her small town near Koblenz, is caught unawares by the sudden death of her husband Otto in July 1980. He was sixty-five; she was fifty-three. A photo in 1966 shows Charlotte looking young and fit, and Otto clearly much older. Everything about Charlotte appears neat, tidy, and controlled. In 1974, she includes seventeen photos of orchids, each of them named. There are others of her in the garden, with her husband mowing the lawn.

Otto's death shocked her terribly. She found herself going through the motions, trying to live in some way normally, but never quite managing, seeking distractions, but finding them never enough. Loneliness overwhelmed her. Even the strength of the group could not help her much. By 1983, she was able to stay with friends in England. Some of her photos show her on her travels; others, back in her garden at home.

In 1984, Charlotte decided she needed a change of direction in her life. A friend of hers in Linz am Rhein had a boutique, and Charlotte started to design clothes and pullovers for it. She worked in a studio at the back of the shop. As if disasters cannot come singly, however, in May 1984 a Dutch jet crashed on to the building, destroying it. One person in the hotel next door was killed. Her friend was in the doorway talking to the postman. She rushed out of the way but was injured and hospitalized. If Charlotte had been in her workshop, she would have been killed, she says in her letter of 16 September 1985, but by chance she was out. The one good thing to come of it was that her friend stayed with her for six months while looking for an apartment and somewhere new for the boutique. They started the business again in May 1985, and Astrid Greiswald and her husband came along for the opening. Charlotte is pleased to be working, she says, since she feels miserable alone in the house. Once again, the photo she includes is of her in the garden.

Writing on 4 July 1988, Charlotte says she is well again after being ill. However, she adds, she will never get used to being alone, and to the evenings sitting in silence, fighting against the sadness that creeps over her. She keeps herself busy, and being so busy has had an interesting effect on her. She is able to laugh at herself now, saying that since "eco-gardens" have become fashionable, the wilderness that has emerged in her garden does not stand out: "So now it is full of creatures that previously used to avoid the orderliness." She has a toad and a hedgehog, rabbits and hares hopping around on the lawn, and birds nesting in the hedge, and knows she will have to wait to cut the hedge until the fledglings have gone: "I just sit back and let it all do whatever it wants to do."

The men, too, suffered when their wives died. For Helmut Liebmann, writing on 14 March 1988, life has been difficult since Lisa's death: "I have just come back from Lisa's grave, since the *Rundbrief* carries memories almost too hard to bear." However, after two years, things have changed significantly:

> In the meantime, I have also found a new partner, who has greatly helped me to get over the difficult times. I have already introduced her to some of you in the group.... We travel a lot and are enjoying the time left to us while we are in good health....
>
> When I kept hearing people telling me that life goes on, I used to think to myself: "That's all very well for you to say," and now I have come to understand that it is so.

Similarly, Irma Kindler tells them (12 September 1986) that Anni Lange's husband has been in touch with her. His work was helping him to cope with his loss, he said. But Irma also had surprising news, to which she reacts generously: "And then in April a wedding notice came through the door—without further comment. I wished him happiness from the bottom of my heart; why should he go around with a long face for all the few years left to him!"

Finally, in an undated letter apparently from March 1988, Johannes Schneider says that he has "shacked up" with a woman called Irmgard. The problem is that she has her own house which, if they formalize their marriage, will be taken away from her, so now they live in two houses.

The deaths of the women had significant consequences for the nature of the group as a whole. In principle, it was and remained a group of women who had been girls at school together. Gradually, the husbands found their way into it, reading the *Rundbrief*, influencing or controlling what their wives were writing, and writing in it themselves when their wives were otherwise engaged. On the death of their wives, the men became full members of the group with a right to have a letter in the *Rundbrief* and to attend the reunions. When the men remarried, they introduced their new wives to the other women. The new wives then had the right to attend the reunions. In this way, the makeup of the group started to change fundamentally in the second half of the 1980s. Seeking out some of the women who had been previously involved, such as Gerda Höpfner, was a successful way to keep the men and their new wives at bay by shifting power back to the original group, the Schönebeck women themselves.

The Principal Stories

What is true for most of the women in the group is also true for Else, Hertha, Anna, and Irma: this is a decade where getting older and what it does to them is a central concern. They all have loose ends to tie up, although in Else's case the others were unaware how loose some of her ties had always been.

Else Hermann

In her letter of 9 August 1980 from Berlin, Else says that she cannot help thinking about her sister in the West: "I feel a great yearning for her and can hardly wait until finally I'm allowed to travel to Cologne to see her." She speaks warmly of her nephews, whom she sees occasionally in Berlin and who provide a sense of family for her. The letter includes a photo of the party they held for Bruno's fiftieth birthday; Bruno looks strikingly handsome with a beard and wearing a tuxedo.

In May 1982, Else says how grateful she is to the group for their closeness and cohesion. She has little news of her own, except that she slipped on a step in the park in Schönebeck, fell and tore ligaments and had her leg in plaster. Her work is still enjoyable, and this year's conference will be in Karl-Marx-Stadt (Chemnitz). From there she and her colleagues will go up into the Erzgebirge and see the restored theater in Annaberg. There is a change of tone in this letter. Else makes no mention of Bruno, and when she talks about holidays, it is clear that he does not go with her. This might not have surprised the rest of the women, as she always had her own, independent way of doing things.

Else reports in October 1983 on another successful conference of costume and stage designers and says she is already arranging more. She is now doing some teaching arising from her work and has been offered extra sessions at the arts university in Berlin. She enjoyed the visit to Annaberg and writes of the changes there: "I had a look around the places where I had slogged away in the fields in 1945. I had mixed feelings, firstly because of all the trees from Oberwiesenthal upwards, and then because of all the smart Datschas that have emerged out of what were farm buildings."

Having scarcely mentioned Bruno in her previous letter, Else says that he is back in Berlin after two and a half years in Stendal (north of Schönebeck and Magdeburg). He came back "because he was sick of provincial life," but now he has no holidays (which may be her way of justifying having holidays without him). In the next letter she will tell them more about the gastronomic scene in Berlin, she promises.

From her letter of 17 June 1985, it is clear that Else is starting to feel her age and thinking about retirement: "I still have a year and three-quarters until I am sixty. I feel ambivalent about it, since I love my work and there are things where I can have an impact." However, it is now too time-consuming and too tiring. She will not be organizing any more conferences, since she was promised assistance but none has been forthcoming. She will continue with her teaching until she retires; it is satisfying and keeps her connected to young people. Meanwhile, Bruno is running a restaurant in Pankow, which is flourishing.

Else was pleased that Lisa and Helmut Liebmann visited her in Berlin shortly after the class reunion in Neugattersleben at the end of August 1984. She herself was able to visit Cologne for the first time to see her sister for her sixty-fifth birthday, a brief visit on a six-day permit. Apart from that, her only holiday will be to Yugoslavia in September with a woman friend; Bruno will be in Sochi.

Else's letter of 20 August 1986 is another confirmation of the importance of the group, to her and to all of them, and of the need to keep it going after Marianne's death. Even her work feels less significant, now that she is coming to the end of it.

> Dear Everyone!
>
> A few days ago, I ran into Elly in Salze [Bad Salzelmen] as I was on my way to the cemetery. She recognized me and jumped off her bike. We talked about the things that are most important in any of the *Rundbriefe*—our sorrows, our memories, our desire to stay connected to one another. So I heard from her and have now read in Johannes's letter that we'll be meeting up again and that he has invited us on Marianne's behalf. I am really pleased about that, as are you all, so thank you to him and also to Frieda for keeping things going for us! I shall keep the day free and not plan any work trips for it. In my last six months of work, I am certainly not going to try to move mountains. I finish at the end of March, and in the meantime, somebody has already been found to take over my responsibilities.... I shall keep on with my teaching at the arts university for as long as they will have me.

When she does finish work, she knows she will have to get to grips with everything she has just put to one side and get some order in her life. Then she will travel:

> First to Cologne, where I'll give you all a ring, any of you who are around.... And then maybe I'll also come to Hamburg! But first my bag is getting packed for Gernrode in the Harz, where I last was thirty years ago. There was an FDGB (trade union) holiday place for me. We'll see... In July, Bruno was in Wernigerode for the first time. As someone from East Prussia, he didn't know the Harz

at all and was captivated by it. However, for reasons to do with our work, we can't go traveling together.

Bruno's restaurant is being renovated, so he has been transferred to somewhere with a huge number of meals to cook. This is painful for him, "since he puts his heart into his cooking."

The real news comes in Else's letter of 27 March 1988, though she had already let a number of them know at the "fantastic" class reunion in Hamburg. From a close reading of her previous letters, this is not entirely unexpected:

> I was divorced on 18 December 1986. There were many reasons for that, one of them being alcohol, not unusual for someone working in the restaurant business. But when I had to suffer too from the consequences of this, as reason no longer prevailed and I was afraid for myself and my belongings, then the fun was over. The trouble is, Bruno is still living here. Only through a petition to the government have I been able to overcome the accommodation problem. I am now due to get an apartment in a new block in the second quarter of the year.

In her interviews, Else made clear that, as far as she was concerned, it was not any problem over their different sexuality that caused her to call an end to the marriage. Her frustration with the larger number of men visiting at unpredictable times might be seen to conflict with this assertion, however. She was more concerned by Bruno's drinking and his consequent unpleasantness toward her, which became intolerable—though it is not clear if Bruno's attitude to their different sexuality might have contributed to this. The incident that brought everything to a head (which she described to me in an interview, not in her letters) involved men breaking into the apartment, tying her to a chair, and demanding the Western currency that they believed Bruno had hidden away. Eventually they left, having been convinced that Bruno had nothing but small change from tips at the restaurant where he was working. Understandably, this was all too much for Else. Later she felt personally offended when she heard from the police that these men were from Magdeburg, her *Heimat*.

Else writes that she finished working in April 1987 but says she is still doing some teaching on a contract basis. Additionally, she is teaching at the school run by DEFA, the GDR's film production company. She is flattered, since this arose out of a special request from them.

By the time of her letter of 18 May 1989, Else is happy to have left Prenzlauer Berg. Much of it is being pulled down, she says; where she lived almost everyone has moved out, and it is now looking very shabby. (When we talked about this, she could scarcely comprehend that thirty years later the Ryke Strasse, in the Kollwitz Kiez, had become one of the most sought-after streets in the whole of Berlin, with its designer shops, bars, specialist bakeries, restaurants, beauty salons, and so on, and its apartments expensively refurbished and equally in demand.) She has made many trips to the West in the past year, twice to Cologne, and to Hanover, Bremen, Braunschweig to visit Leni Baumann, and Sinzig to visit Astrid Greiswald. At last she is getting around Germany as she has long wanted to do.

Hertha Pieper

Hertha Pieper (27 June 1980) starts the decade happy with her work, particularly her dried grasses and flowers. However, she has a sense of imminent loneliness in the large house as her younger daughter Kerstin will be going away to upper school in September. By 1982, Hertha has made some changes:

> I have given the house over to my son Wilfried. I'm going to be moving upstairs, hopefully soon. We actually just wanted to change a few things and do some renovations, but when you start on such a large house (built in 1921), you soon become aware of so many shortcomings that renovation turns into rebuilding. But though there's plenty of enthusiasm and goodwill, there's a chronic shortage of materials, so that the pleasure of doing the work gradually slips away.

Hertha expects the work to be finished by the time of the class reunion and offers to put up two people; they are all doing this to take pressure off Marianne. With Kerstin away, Hertha feels acutely lonely, as she feared, but she is still enjoying working in the LPG. Her free time, she says, belongs "to my gardens and fields with their flowers and grasses, and at the moment to the building works!"

Many years earlier, Barbara Meier suggested that enjoyment meant picking out "the best of the cherries from the large cake that is everyday life." There is an ironic echo of this when Elly Haase, in her letter of 21 August 1983, tells them that Hertha is in the hospital with a broken vertebra, after a fall while picking cherries. Hertha herself writes from the hospital. She is getting better, she says, is walking again, and hopes to be out in three weeks. She jokes that she has been warned to stop climbing trees at her age.

By the time of her next letter (22 May 1985), Hertha is full of life and energy again "as if by a miracle," and is out and about in her "Trabi," visiting the others in the Schönebeck area. She, too, is upset by "the sad news about dear Marianne and Lisa." She is now particularly looking forward to finishing work: "Just seventy-eight more working days until I reach retirement age!" She still has her loneliness to contend with: "My youngest, Kerstin, got married last October. They are still living with me but will get their own apartment in the autumn. Then everything around me will be so quiet. But I still have my large garden and am always out there with my family."

From her letter of 12 May 1986, it is clear that the group and her family are central to Hertha's sense of herself. She was pleased that Barbara and Heinz

Meier brought the book to her in person and stayed around for a chat: "And that was so good for us! Especially farewelling our dear Lisa and Marianne, we just want to see one another more and chat together more often." She also went to the West to visit relatives and friends there, including Erika Krämer and her family in Kassel.

Hertha is still happy working in her large garden with its grasses and flowers, although that is also getting to be too much for her. The children and grandchildren are a great joy. Now that she has her sixth grandchild, Kerstin's son, and Kerstin is very often at her house, she is particularly pleased, since he is "actually the first grandchild that I can really enjoy to the full." Despite all this, Hertha does feel despondent at times: "Those of you who get to grow old together with your partner, be grateful. I've been alone now for almost thirteen years. Despite the children and grandchildren, who are all so loving and warm—what you are, still, is alone."

In all of this discussion of family and work and travel, the state is never far away. In her letter of 3 March 1988, Hertha says that since becoming a pensioner, she no longer travels eastward—that is, to the other communist countries. She adds enigmatically: "I haven't had good experiences there. You never know who you might have to share a room with."

Anna Siebert

Anna Siebert (13 October 1980) starts the decade grieving both for her close friend Brigitte Hansen, whom she saw in one last visit in Zürich, and for her mother, who died in March 1980 in the GDR. Her mother suffered a stroke, and Anna, summoned by telegram, was able to be with her while she was still conscious, and to stay by her bedside while she died in her home in Staßfurt. The consequences are profound:

> Sadly, I have now lost not just my mother but also my *Heimat*. Never before had the barrier between "over there" and "over here" been so clear to me as it became in those days in Staßfurt. There were so many difficulties that in my grief I just could not comprehend. When it came down to it, they were tiny things, but just so hard to cope with. Our address in Hamburg was not allowed to appear in the notice of her death, we couldn't say that the urn with the ashes would be brought over here, and many other things too.

> It was a great joy for me that Heinz Meier came to the funeral service, since the young people with whom my mother had such close contact felt able to come and convey their condolences but not to attend the funeral service. No doubt you will find the grounds for this obvious!

> Because of time pressures, I had to clear out the house in a rush. I took only a little away with me. Several pictures and pieces of furniture have now finally

reached me, after checks to be sure they were not heritage items. I'll have to have everything restored, since arranging for the packing of the bedcovers, rugs and cushions and so on would have been extra, and so the pieces of furniture were all just piled up on top of one another and significantly damaged. How fortunate it was that we took the crockery with us in the car.

Once again the GDR authorities have carried out a number of small but significant acts of humiliation. Anna's reasonable expectation was that in relation to the death of a relative, they would behave with compassion and a sense of shared humanity, in line with their socialist ideals. However, at every step, Anna came up against their inhumanity and cruelty, which was imposed on her simply because she was from the West. Even the damage to the furniture was not a matter of chance, but rather a way of teaching Anna a lesson.[25] Her rage is clear in her letters, along with a sense of impotence and injustice. Fortunately, the presence of Heinz Meier, representing the Schönebeck group, provided some comfort.

In July 1982, Anna announces that she is planning to retire from her beloved job in October, when she will be fifty-five. She says she just does not have the strength any more to do what is needed, and does not want others remarking on that, "since unfortunately it is still the case in my job, even today, that as a woman you constantly have to prove yourself over and over again. Any weaknesses or mistakes are immediately seen as the result of being a woman, while for a man they are just accepted or excused." Nevertheless, she still gets on well with all her colleagues and is quietly satisfied that they have not been able to find a suitable successor. Only now do they recognize how much she did, and that what she did was equal to what a man could do.

Health concerns made her decision to leave work easier. Two years earlier, she found a lump in her breast. She decided to have radiotherapy rather than a mastectomy. She was able to keep on working but it drained her strength. She is looking forward to a new future and will come more consistently to the reunions. Two years later, having put her breast cancer behind her, Anna says self-mockingly that she is far too busy now that she has retired, and is playing a lot of bridge and tennis.

In 1986, Anna sends out the invitation to the next reunion, the first one in the West for the women from the GDR. She says she was sorry she could not make it to the reunion in Schönebeck, but she did not have the four weeks' notice needed to get an entry permit. After talking of deaths and illnesses among her relatives, she fervently offers the rest of the women "many good wishes, but above all for health, harmony and peace!" This is a gentle reminder to them of what is going on in the wider world, despite so much personal suffering and loss.

Irma Kindler

As well as commenting on holidays in Greece, Austria, and Italy, Irma puts at the center of her letter on 2 September 1980 a comment that anticipates the suffering of the coming decade: "Well then, the most important: we are still healthy and happy and things are going well for us. When I was younger, that seemed just something we would take for granted, but when I see what is happening around me, in our close circle but also further away, I am now infinitely grateful for it."

Her family news is that their son is now a pharmacist with a job in Harburg. She herself has been working full time at the Studentenwerk because of others being ill. At home, after eighteen years they thought it was time to renew things, so they are getting a new kitchen. All in all, it is not a life of luxury, but the sense of choice and of possibilities is far different from the life described in the GDR.

Once again, in November 1985, Irma is concerned to read about so many problems and illnesses: "I wonder whether it is our generation that is hit particularly hard, or whether it's just an overall result of getting old. When you're coming up to sixty like this, you find yourself having all sorts of thoughts, not all of them the cheeriest." However, Irma is enthusiastic about the work Franz is doing, a superb project, she says, which will last two years: they are boring a six-kilometer circular research tunnel. This is for the particle accelerator known as the Deutsches Elektronen Synchrotron—DESY—Hamburg. Such a vast project demonstrates the gap between the FRG and the GDR in terms of having money to develop new technologies; this is not a point Irma makes, however. She pastes into the book a stamp showing the design and location of the Synchrotron. When that is finished, she says, it should be time for Franz to retire. Until then, she will keep working at the Studentenwerk. She has enjoyed being there for nearly sixteen years and hopes she might still be useful to them even after stopping full-time work.

Writing before Christmas in 1988, Irma says that a routine check found that Franz has a heart defect. He is now on a strict cholesterol-free, salt-free diet. Both of them expect to retire next August, she says. In her letter of 18 May 1989, she confirms that she is now retired. Their travels continue: they have been on a number of trips and have been skiing in the Dolomites, as well as doing a lot of cycling outside Hamburg. Even at what will turn out to be this late stage, there is no mention of the mounting problems across the border in the GDR.

Interaction with the State

In the 1980s, there are numerous references to the state, but few are explicitly critical. The comments on Poland express a general anxiety—admittedly, an existential anxiety—spreading across East and West, while unemployment in the West is taken as a fact of life, not as the result of the government's policies.

Frieda Möller's letter of 9 July 1980 highlights the division of Germany. Despite not being retired, she says, she was lucky enough to be given a pass to travel to the West for her younger brother's silver wedding. Being used to a land of shortages, she could hardly believe what she discovered: "I felt I was in a fairytale land, finally to go into a shop and be able to say, 'I would like,' rather than 'Do you have?' In seven years, many of the rest of you will be able to try it out too."

In her 1982 letter, Marianne Schneider reports at length on the class reunion that Martha Jäger arranged for them in 1981, the first of their reunions to take place in a hotel rather than at home. This was a large event, with twenty-one of them there, including several husbands. There were "unanticipated complications" about getting permission for those from the West to visit. The event nearly went awry, as the visas only arrived at the last minute, despite being applied for nearly seven weeks earlier. Marianne mentions that a recent change means that all of these are now sent from Berlin, rather than being processed locally.

There are, as ever, many of Irma Kindler's reunion photos in the book. As was normal for a public venue, there is a photo of Erich Honecker on the wall, and the portrait appears in several of Irma's photos, though only the bottom half of his face, up to his glasses, is visible. (Such photos of Honecker or Ulbricht before him never appear in any of the photos from the reunions held in the women's homes.) In one photo, the eight men in the group are sitting around their own table, which is arranged, consciously or not, so that Honecker is looking away from them and they cannot catch his eye. In her note on who the men in the photo are, Marianne refers to Gisela Riedel's husband as being "under the half-Honecker." Her comment could be interpreted as making fun of the General Secretary; it certainly shows Marianne's awareness that he is there, and perhaps her unease at having him "participating" in their reunion. The women's table is placed so that Honecker is looking sideways across at them, keeping his eye on them in the paternalistic way that was common for the male leadership of the SED.

In her 1983 letter, Marianne explains that she is now organizing the circulation of the *Rundbrief* so that it covers those in the GDR first, then is passed over "to our 'better half' personally . . . In this way we get around the checks on post at the border." This comment shows her lack of confidence in the GDR authorities, and her realistic perception of the level of control over their lives by these authorities. It is surprising, however, that she is prepared to refer to those in the West as the group's "better half."

At this stage, there are still references to housing problems in the GDR. Heidi Kempf, who is in charge of the hospital laboratory in Bad Salzelmen, has been living alone with her mother since her husband died in 1959. Now (5 August 1983) she says she has found a new man, but finding suitable accommodation is an insurmountable problem for them:

> We are together now, and yet kept apart: he lives in a family house in Weimar, I live here with my mother. Those of you in the GDR know that getting an exchange is a huge problem here. We just have to make the best of it. Every three weeks we have a weekend marriage, which is also quite delightful though not an ideal solution.

Heidi is reluctant to move because she wants to do her last three working years in Bad Salzelmen, and because her mother is now in a wheelchair.

Even building or rebuilding a house remains a problem. Elly Haase (21 August 1983) expresses some of the now familiar frustrations with life in the GDR. They have been doing a fair bit of work on their house, she says, but it is very wearing just trying to get hold of the building material; she adds, "that's something at least a few of you can well understand." As well as that, they want to visit her mother-in-law in Poland, but the GDR will still not allow it, because of the continuing uncertainties in Poland.

One of the early victims of repression in the GDR in the 1950s was Gerda Höpfner. Gerda was the only one of them working in one of the large and politically important manufacturing plants in Schönebeck, the Gummiwerke, where millions of shoe soles were made over many decades. In 1953, while she was pregnant, Gerda's husband was arrested for "agitation against the state" and imprisoned for eighteen months. Now (21 July 1986) she is writing her first letter since being invited back into the group.

Gerda says how pleased she is to be part of the group again, and that it was Johannes, Marianne's husband, who gave her the last *Rundbrief* to read. She is looking forward to being at the next class reunion. She herself has now been a widow for two and a half years. She is still working as the secretary to the directorate and has been in that post for the past twenty-one years (which suggests that she is seen as politically reliable). Although she, too, is now approaching retirement age, being at home and out of work is not what she wants: "Provided I remain healthy, I really would like to continue to work, since it is very lonely at home and in the factory I have a very nice, entertaining set of colleagues."

Families and the State

Families are often the place where the apparently private and personal meets the hard reality of the public domain, since the family operates within a set of rules determined by the state, often buttressed by long-established practices and customs. Marianne's account of the way the law did not recognize the father's or grandparents' rights when the parents of a child were not married highlights the power of the state. A more deliberately cruel approach from the GDR authorities was to imprison parents who were caught seeking to go to the West without permission, and to put their children into homes or foster care.[26] However, as Käthe Sommer shows (24 August 1982), families can also be reunited through action by the state: "As most of you know, just over a year ago our children in Leipzig were allowed to emigrate to us over here, under the category of family reunification." Even in the West, they faced problems, however, "since nobody makes any concessions because of the unemployment we have here. But now things are going better for them, slowly but surely."

Concern about unemployment was widespread in the FRG in the early 1980s. Ilse Klein was unemployed again in 1981 and could see no chance of finding a job. In 1982, she started making a bit of money by doing home visits for massages and foot treatments. Other women in the FRG were concerned about members of their family being unemployed. In 1985, Ilse Klein's husband was unemployed, while Irma Kindler reported that her daughter, looking for a job as a sociologist, sent in two hundred applications and had to settle for an administrative job in her father's firm. Erika Krämer was able to take early retirement at fifty-eight on 70 percent salary so that her position could be filled by someone younger.

The women in the GDR had no such problems. This was partly because it was obligatory to have a job and because there was a constant labor shortage as a result of the earlier loss of so many people to the West. However, full employment in the GDR was also partly the result of many enterprises—like the tractor and diesel engine works in Schönebeck—having far more workers than they needed, because of the state's commitment to everyone having a job. Many families would have suffered if the state had taken a more capitalist approach to productivity and only employed the numbers genuinely needed. To do so was politically unacceptable; not to do so was economically unsustainable.[27]

Later in the 1980s, the increasing economic, social, and political problems in the GDR, and the attractiveness of life in the West to young people from the East, caused problems for some of the families. In March 1988, Johannes Schneider says that his son Dieter keeps trying to get permission to take his family to the West; Johannes keeps hoping he will be definitively refused.

Martha Jäger and Her Family

"How quickly time goes by," Martha Jäger laments on 12 February 1982. She has little but family news. Her daughter Angelika, who wanted to be a dentist, became an engineer and married a dentist who works in Calbe, running one of the state dentistry centers. The family lives in Schönebeck, and Angelika is expecting her second child in April.

The following year (19 July 1983), Martha was finding life trying again. They could not have a holiday because they were looking after her seventy-five-year-old mother-in-law who was plagued by sciatica and could hardly walk. Angelika would have taken over but was away at the same time with her family. Despite this, Martha says, "We absolutely can't complain of being bored. On the contrary, we often no longer manage to do what we had planned to do. We are just getting older!" With her choice of photos of her grandchildren for the *Rundbrief*, Martha appears to be illustrating the contrasting sides of her life in the GDR: one photo shows a classically angelic boy, four and a half years old, looking thoughtful; in the other, her granddaughter, thirteen months old, is standing deeply distressed, tears running down her cheeks.

In her next letter (18 March 1985), Martha has good news: despite not being a pensioner, she was finally, after twenty-five years, allowed to visit her sister in the West. However, because she was not yet a pensioner, her husband—himself a pensioner who had been "over there" many times—was not allowed to go with her, apparently to ensure she came back. Despite this, she had a great time with her sister and her sister's husband and children, and enjoyed a visit from Käthe and Herbert Sommer.

Martha, too, was shaken by Anni Lange's death. It makes her see, she says, that "we have no need to complain about everyday tedium." She then complains that Ernst has problems with his knee; she has rheumatism, circulation and heart rhythm problems; the cellar gets flooded; the roof has suffered storm damage and needs immediate repair; there are problems with martens; and the kitchen is repeatedly turned into a mess by people working on the chimney. The roof is a particular frustration, thanks to the chronic shortage of both labor and materials in the GDR: "We have been waiting for the roofers for three years. They have already come and taken a look four or five times! But then there's always a problem over the shortage of stones for the chimney, as well as of new guttering."

On 10 May 1986, Martha tells the only grandparenting joke in all the years of the *Rundbrief*. Here, the politicization of everyday life in the GDR reaches right down to the uncomprehending children. She overheard her grandson, around six years old, say to his younger sister: "All right then, if you won't play with me, you won't be allowed to travel to the West when you're a pensioner!"

Writing on 19 January 1988, Martha is more cheerful because she herself is now a pensioner and can travel to the West. She had a wonderful week on Nordeney with Gisela Riedel and another friend from their Weimar days. In September, she had eight days with her sister in the Allgäu, and on the way back they visited Astrid and her husband: "In Sinzig we were made welcome and looked after with so much love and warmth! They were lovely moments, in complete harmony, that we were able to spend with Astrid and Walter in their cozy home." Following that, she had two days with Gisela in Kassel in October, then went with her husband to West Berlin to visit to an old friend of his who was ill.

Still, their housing problems continue to torment her. In her letter of 20 January 1989, Martha tells them, "From us there's nothing special to report. We are being driven mad again by our impossible tenants. They are so brazen that last year we had to go as far as taking them to court." Despite her troubles, Martha still has confidence in the state's legal structures, at least on matters that are not overtly political (since "political" cases were determined by the SED rather than by the judges).[28]

Travel, Leisure, Holidays

For the women in the GDR, turning sixty made a reality of their desire to move freely throughout the whole of Germany, as if it was indeed a single country. The gap between East and West remained, however, and the women in the FRG continued to travel even further afield, enjoying Greece, Italy, Tenerife, and Israel, as well as branching out to America. Sabine Kleber (16 October 1982) is pleased to read in the *Rundbrief* that a lot of them in the GDR have been traveling, because it relieves her guilt: "Sometimes I have a bad conscience, as everything is going so well for me and I can plan my trips entirely according to what interests me." Three years later, Sabine announces that she retired from teaching on 1 August 1985. Now, she says, she is really going to travel! Already she has been to Ecuador and Peru.

The women in the GDR, as Sabine Kleber suggests, often found themselves clashing with the power of the state when they wanted to find somewhere to go on holiday. This was a long-standing problem for them, since the less they engaged with the state and participated in its mass organizations and events, the less likely they were to get a holiday place.[29] One report, however, is bound to have provoked the question: how close to the authorities does one have to be to get such an opportunity?[30] This comes from a letter written on 17 May 1982 by Lisa Liebmann's husband, as Lisa had suddenly been allowed to visit Hamburg. He says that in 1981 they went by ship on a five-week trip to Cuba. There were 550 passengers and 220 crew, and they saw the Azores, Haiti, and the Bahamas from the ship. They were not allowed to land there, as the purpose was to visit another communist country, not the capitalist West. They were in Cuba for five days, with excursions from Santiago and Havana.

Frieda Möller on the other hand, writing on 7 July 1983 from Barby, says that they will be spending their holidays at home this year and that "the GDR-ers know how hard it is to get a reasonable place for a holiday." This is a much bleaker view of the GDR than they had in the late 1950s and 1960s, when most of them wrote happily about their holidays on the Baltic coast, in the Harz, or in Thuringia.

Frieda's frustrations continued. In her letter of 18 February 1985, she says she is furious because the family was offered the chance of a cruise to Leningrad. However, the school authorities would not allow it as it meant taking four days away from school. Later, things did not seem so bad: "We had a great thing happen over Christmas. After waiting for eleven and a half years (no, you haven't misread that!), we got our new little car, a 'Trabant de luxe,' and are now *happy* [in English]."[31] In her 1986 letter, Frieda says that her husband flew to Canada in 1985 to visit his ninety-year-old mother. They were amazed that he was given permission. He seems not to have seen his mother since 1954, a year and a half after his parents were driven off their farm in late 1952 and fled to the West; a plan to visit them in 1958 came to nothing when the travel laws were changed by the GDR authorities.

Frieda's letter of 5 March 1988 overflows with enthusiasm about a trip she and Karl-Heinz made to Moscow and Leningrad. So many years after the war and the early problematic times of the Soviet occupation, they, along with others in the group, seem to have forgotten or overcome any early anti-Russian attitudes. Frieda is patronizing in her attitude to the state that is meant to be the model for all of the Warsaw Pact countries: "We were very taken by the Russian people. Our impression was that they were friendly and orderly, although they have to live much more modestly than we do in the GDR."

Writing on 17 September 1989 from Rösrath-Kleineichen on the outskirts of Cologne, Edith Friebe says: "Maybe next year I'll be able to set down a few holiday experiences for you, since on 18 September I'm taking up an invitation from a close friend and flying to Denver, Colorado. This will be my first flight over the 'Big Pond.'" This, it transpired, was to be much more than a normal holiday.

The Denver, Colorado, Connection

The Lübschütz Family

It is time to extract ourselves from the 1980s and the chronological and thematic consideration of the letters; the downfall of the GDR and its consequences will have to wait. There is another side of Schönebeck's history, from the time when the girls were still at school, that has so far only been hinted at in the letters. Underlying the stories, there has been an unasked question: what happened to Schönebeck's Jewish population?

Edith Friebe's 1989 letter mentioned she was about to fly to Denver, Colorado, to visit a close friend. From her subsequent letter (17 September 1990), it becomes clear she did not travel alone, but went with Maria Stein from Schönebeck (see figure 5.2). This could not be mentioned earlier as Maria only

Figure 5.2. Jutta, Maria, and Edith in the United States, 1989. Photo courtesy of Akademie der Künste, Berlin.

had permission to travel from the GDR to the Federal Republic, certainly not to fly to the United States, and only now can Edith tell the full story of the holiday. In this account the name of their friend is not changed, since her story has become widely known in Schönebeck.

> I'd like to make clear at the start that Maria was there too. At the time, we had to be sure that the GDR authorities knew nothing of that, so we had to keep it secret and could only talk about it after the borders had disappeared.
>
> We were invited by our friend, Jutta Lübschütz, to visit her in Denver, Colorado. Jutta is Jewish and was with a lot of you in the school in Schönebeck, up to the time the family moved to Salzelmen and she was in our class there. Do none of you remember her anymore? She was great friends with Anni Lange at the time.
>
> After the class reunion at Anna Siebert's in Hamburg [1987], we had a mini-reunion with our former class teacher, Frau P. (formerly Fräulein B.). Irma arranged it for us, and those of us there were Edith J., Elly, Maria, Irma and I. During that warm and friendly get-together, the question came up, what might have become of Jutta and whether she had even survived the dreadful Hitler years. And yes, she had survived! When Maria got home from the reunion, there she was at her door. What a moving moment that was, seeing each other again. From then on, we have kept up a lively correspondence, which is still going on, interspersed with frequent telephone calls. A year later Jutta returned to Germany again with her husband (originally from Vienna) and had a three-part hol-

iday. After arriving in Amsterdam, they had three days in Cologne. They loved the trip along the Rhine in the hydrofoil to Rüdesheim, and I showed them the sights around Cologne, the Bergisches Land, the Sauerland, Westerwald, the Ahr Valley, the Eifel, and Cologne itself. Four days was pretty tight for that. Then their journey took them on to Goslar, where they met up with Maria. To finish off, they met up again in Hamburg with Frau P. and Irma. Jutta was pleased to hear news of old friends from the former *Heimat*, old friends with whom she now felt reconnected. Fifty years had to go by before that could happen!

I shall describe briefly Jutta's awful experiences after the fearful *Kristallnacht* on 9 November 1938. From then on, she was no longer allowed to attend our school. She went to Jewish schools in Hamburg and Leipzig until she left Germany with her mother in the autumn of 1940. Her father had already emigrated to Shanghai in 1939. With just ten marks and very little luggage, they set off by train on a sixteen-day journey. There were no longer any ships because of the war. The train took them via Russia to China. In Shanghai she was able to throw her arms around her father again. There they lived for six and a half years in a camp for emigrants, her parents with nine other married couples in one room, Jutta with twenty-four girls and women. Can you imagine it! In the meantime, the war broke out there and the Japanese, who had occupied Shanghai and almost the whole of China, made them live in a ghetto where there were 20,000 European emigrants. It was in the ghetto that she met the man who became her husband—they were married in 1947. In 1948 her parents went to America and Jutta and her husband went to Israel. . . . Their daughter Ruth was born in Tel Aviv in 1949, and later two sons in America. They lived for three years in Tel Aviv, then for a year in Vienna before they left Europe for America. There they lived for eight years in Pennsylvania and New Jersey, before they finally settled down in beautiful Colorado, in Denver. Sadly, her sister, seven years older, did not survive the massacre in Auschwitz, along with her husband and three children (the third child having been born shortly before).

Despite all the terrible things they must have been through, these two lovely people show not the tiniest sign of hatred. They are indescribably generous, and so they embraced us warmly too at the airport in Denver on 10 September 1989. Maria and I were able to spend three unimaginably wonderful weeks with them, a time that will remain with us forever in our memories—such days are impossible to forget!

The full story of the Lübschütz family is more complex and tragic than this relatively short but vivid account conveys.[32] To understand it better, it is necessary to look a little more closely at the history of Schönebeck and the coming to power of the Nazis.

By 1932, Schönebeck had a population of 32,258. About a quarter of a percent of this population was Jewish: eighty-seven people, spread across twenty-five families, made up of thirty-three women, thirty-one men, twelve girls, and eleven boys. The Jewish population had always been tiny but was long-established, having spread from a larger grouping in Magdeburg over several centuries in the face of pogroms there. There had been a synagogue in Schönebeck since 1877, with ceremonies and services carried out by a rabbi from Magdeburg. Many of the Jews of Schönebeck were well off; some of them owned the department stores that everybody used in the center of the town.

After the Nazis came to power in January 1933, things changed dramatically. The SA storm troopers led by Walter Karpe ransacked and destroyed the premises and businesses of Social Democrats. They assaulted, shot, and even killed individual members of the Social Democratic Party. They then turned on the Jewish community. Even before the national decision on 1 April 1933 to boycott Jewish businesses, Karpe and the SA tried to close Jewish shops and businesses on 10 March 1933, but were blocked from doing so by the local population. The SA had its revenge on 11 March, demonstrating that it could act with impunity by wrecking the offices of the left-leaning newspaper, the *Volksstimme*, and openly stealing Jewish property. The formal boycott from 1 April was enforced by the SA and supported by the Hitler Youth; an article in the *Schönebecker Zeitung* on 3 April commended them for their disciplined implementation of the boycott.

From then on, the Jewish families were subject to constant vilification in the press and to further harassment by the SA. Many were forced to dispose of their businesses cheaply to non-Jewish Germans. Edith Friebe mentions "the time the family moved to Salzelmen." This understates the brutality of the enforced move—designed to make the street where they lived in the center of Schönebeck "Jew-free" by the end of 1936—and the obstacles put in their way when they tried to find a new place to live. Fortunately, some of the teachers were kind to Jutta at the new school.[33]

The pressure on the Jewish population eased during the 1936 Olympics as Germany sought to portray itself in a favorable light to the outside world, but new measures followed immediately afterward. One of these, in early February 1937, involved the setting up of a detailed register of Jews, a *Judenkartei*, which was implemented by the police and Gestapo in Schönebeck and Bad Salzelmen. Jewish children were no longer able to undertake the *Kur* in Bad Salzelmen and, from 1937, Jews were forbidden to use the facilities of the Solbad Salzelmen (the salt baths); they were excluded from the *Kurpark*, and their children were no longer allowed into the playground.

Everything changed again with the Pogromnacht or Kristallnacht of 9–10 November 1938, a coordinated, nationwide set of attacks on Jewish people, their property, and their synagogues. By this time, the girls at school were all at least eleven years old. In Schönebeck, the attacks were prepared by the Nazis in the Stadtpark, with many of the SA dressed in civilian clothing and equipped with clubs and axes so that they could portray themselves as the indignant people of Schönebeck. (The pretext for the Pogromnacht was the assassination by a Jewish man of a German diplomat in Paris.) They went first to the synagogue, smashed down its doors with their axes, ransacked the building, gathered up and took away anything valuable, and hoisted a dead pig, dressed in a rabbi's robe, high up under the chandelier. Some of the Nazis started a fire high up in the synagogue, but after protests by neighbors whose properties would also have been burnt, they extinguished the fire. Jewish businesses were ransacked and looted, individual buildings listed on the *Judenkartei* were searched, their inhabitants brutally beaten, furnishings destroyed, and property stolen. Jewish graves were desecrated. Many Jewish men were arrested and taken to Buchenwald concentration camp. On 11 November, piles of gravel were dumped outside the synagogue and groups of boys were brought by their teachers to use the stones to smash the windows.

After the Pogromnacht, all remaining Jewish businesses were given over to non-Jewish owners. The Jewish men from Schönebeck imprisoned in Buchenwald were released at the end January 1939, mostly because they had declared their wish to emigrate. By 1941, the remaining few were forced to move either to the upstairs of the synagogue or to the *Judenhaus* (the "Jews' house") in Bad Salzelmen. By the end of 1942, Schönebeck was declared to be "free of Jews." Of the eighty-seven who had lived in the town, forty survived by emigrating: eleven women, fifteen men, seven girls, and seven boys. At least thirty-nine were murdered in the Nazi concentration camps and gas chambers. Two others died of natural causes after 1933, while the fate of three adults and one child remains unclear. One solitary concentration camp survivor—he had been deported to Buchenwald in 1942—returned home to his non-Jewish wife in Schönebeck at the end of the war. He died in 1950.

In common with the other families, the Lübschütz family found their lives transformed by the Pogromnacht. Their house in Bad Salzelmen was invaded by Nazis, the older daughter, Ruth, was badly beaten in front of Jutta and her mother, and the father, Julius, was taken away. The Jewish children were banned from attending school, and there is an account of Ruth and one of the others being deliberately humiliated in front of the whole class. Another later account by an eyewitness, one of the other girls at the school, says, "Fräulein Lübbe, the history teacher, declared that henceforth it was forbidden to greet or even to speak to the Jewish girls if we saw them in the street. And anyone who did so, despite this order, could count on being severely punished by the school and the BDM."[34]

While Jutta Lübschütz was at Jewish schools in Hamburg and Leipzig, her father was released from Buchenwald and emigrated on 29 March 1939, traveling to Shanghai by boat from Genoa. There were already tensions in Shanghai over the number of refugees arriving, though the Japanese accepted anyone with a German passport, even with the "J" for Jew stamped in it. After the outbreak of the war in Europe, the lack of ships available to take refugees to Shanghai, and the problems of obtaining foreign currency for the last trips that were possible, effectively cut off the sea route to Shanghai. However, the land route, through the Soviet Union via Moscow and Vladivostok, remained at least partially open until the German invasion of the Soviet Union in June 1941. This was the route Jutta and her mother took, leaving Schönebeck on 23 October 1940, and taking a Japanese steamer from Vladivostok to Shanghai.

They lived in the extraordinarily overcrowded area that housed most of the Jews, in an area under the control of the Japanese. It was only after the Japanese attack on Pearl Harbor in December 1941 that they were confined in what was effectively a ghetto until the end of the war. Jutta and her husband, Ernest Urman, left for Israel on 30 December 1948, traveling via Capetown, where they met up with two other Jewish families who had managed to emigrate from Schönebeck.

There was no such happy outcome for her older sister Ruth, who was also known to some of the girls in the late 1930s. Ruth was married in Magdeburg in July 1939, then went with her husband Max Nathan to Hamburg to emigrate, but they were delayed, trying to persuade his parents to leave too. Their first child was born in December 1939, by which time they were unable to leave Hamburg because of the war, and their second in March 1940. Apparently with Max's parents, the family was deported to Theresienstadt on 19 July 1942. Their third child was born on 13 Sept 1942 in Theresienstadt. Max was transported to Auschwitz on 27 September 1944, Ruth and children on 6 October 1944, and all were killed in the gas chambers there in early October 1944.

After the American occupation of Schönebeck, the head of U.S. forces in Schönebeck from 18 April 1944 was a Captain Stuart H. Cowen. Previously named Cohen or Cohn, he had emigrated from Hessen to the United States in 1936. He had had relatives in Schönebeck and Magdeburg. By the end of April, he had ensured that the Junkers aircraft parts manufacturing operations based in the synagogue were cleared out, and the synagogue was given back to the Jewish community in Magdeburg. Later in the year, when Schönebeck was under Soviet control, former Nazis from Schönebeck were required to complete the clearing up of the synagogue and to put the Star of David back on the facade. From 1946 to 1983, the building was variously used by the Schönebeck authorities as an employment office, a furniture store, a gym hall, and a museum. In 1983, the Jewish Community of Magdeburg sold it to the Protestant church in Schönebeck. By May 1986, the building had been restored with funds from that community and a contribution from the GDR state, and was renamed the "Schalom-Haus." On the fiftieth anniversary of the Pogromnacht in 1988, a plaque was put on the facade, demanding that no one forget what had happened: *"Gedenke und vergiß nie!"*

Conclusion: Toward Retirement

An Ending, a Rethink?

The approaching end of the GDR made it almost inevitable that the women on both sides of the inner-German border would look again at the lives they had been living over many decades and reconsider their meaning. The Lübschütz family story is significant in this context, emerging as it did in the late 1980s, even if it was not written into the *Rundbrief* until 1990. For later readers of the *Rundbrief*, it prompts many questions. What shaped the Schönebeck women, and how did they respond to the many terrible things that happened around them, and to the power being exercised, both in the Nazi period and in the time of Germany's division? How deep and effective was the Nazi indoctrination of the girls? How much did their attitudes change over the following decades? How much did they think about what had been done to them, by them, or by their parents during the Nazi period? Why do their references to the war tend to be bland, cheerful, or even romantic? Did the emergence of a second German dictatorship, the GDR, divert attention from these issues and provide an excuse for not talking about them? One partial answer could be that the women's immediate suffering as women in the GDR or as pained observers from the FRG was more significant than the suffering of others during the Nazi years. Some of the letters in the next period, during and after the process of reunification, tend to confirm this interpretation.

Failing to Notice the External World

The most striking thing about the women's letters in the 1980s, with the final volume of the decade ending late in August 1989, is that none of them appeared to have any sense of the significance of the changes taking place around them, or of the impending loss of power by the SED.

It is not that the women's minds were elsewhere; they were aware enough of the overall political situation. It is rather that they were so used to the framework within which they were operating that it never occurred to them that it might be crumbling around the edges. The historian Hartmut Zwahr argues that this was a feature of the generation the women were part of. He suggests that those from this generation who were in leadership or state positions were, out of all the GDR generations, most caught by surprise by the Wende and most concerned about the disadvantages it would bring. On the other hand, those not in such positions shifted relatively quickly toward support for it and for reunification.[35]

The women must have had some sense from their children that a crisis was approaching—some were applying to go to the West, after all. However, in their letters, they are preoccupied by other things in their lives: how to manage retirement and life after it; the suffering of many of their group; the deaths in the group, which were devastating to them; and, for those in the East, the joy of being able to travel to the West at last.

As ever, they were concerned not to let anything damage the group itself. The attack by Erika Krämer was a shock. In their letters, they showed real skill in finding ways to prevent this turning into a crisis and destroying their unity. The other threat to the group was the intrusion of men into it, and then of other women these men brought with them. They showed some awareness of the danger by finding ways to enlarge the group, ensuring the power stayed with those who so many years before were at school together in Schönebeck. The extraordinary changes that were underway by the time they next started writing in the *Rundbrief*, and the move toward German unity, would be the greatest challenges to the unity of the group and to their founding myths that they had ever faced.

Notes

1. Werner Plumpe, *German Economic and Business History in the 19th and 20th Centuries* (London, 2016), 273–5.
2. See, for instance, Roland Roth and Dieter Rucht, "Chronologie von Ereignissen," 681–85; Karl-Werner Brand, "Umweltbewegung"; Dieter Rucht, "Anti-Atomkraftbewegung"; Andreas Buro, "Friedensbewegung"; all in Roth and Rucht, *Die sozialen Bewegungen*.
3. For the problems of bringing anthracite from Czechoslovakia to the GDR, or industrial products from Schönebeck to Czechoslovakia, because of the Elbe alternately flooding and freezing over, see *Volksstimme Magdeburg*, 22 December 1981, and 7, 11, and 19 January 1982; *Neues Deutschland*, 12 and 14 January 1987.
4. Harsch, *Revenge*, 315–16.
5. "'Rock für den Frieden' im Palast der Republik," *Volksstimme Magdeburg*, 19 December 1981. "Die Initiative der Schuljugend," *Volksstimme Magdeburg*, 21 December 1981, makes clear that the supposedly spontaneous local initiatives of schoolchildren were part of an organized, official campaign, with all the schools open on the weekend so that parents, teachers, and children could pack up the goods together.
6. "Ausnahmezustand in der VR Polen verkündet," *Neues Deutschland*, 14 December 1981; "Weitere Schritte in Polen auf dem Weg der Normalisierung," 2 January 1982; "VR Polen bereitet Normalisierung vor. Ausschaltung staatsfeindlicher Tendenzen notwendig," *Volksstimme Magdeburg*, 13 January 1982.

7. "Mitteilung der Pressestelle des Ministeriums für Post und Fernmeldewesen," *Neues Deutschland*, 19 November 1988; "Gegen die Entstellung der historischen Wahrheit," *Neues Deutschland*, 25 November 1988.
8. "Erklärung der Volkskammer der DDR zu den aktuellen Ereignissen in der Volksrepublik China," *Neues Deutschland*, 9 June 1989.
9. "Unsere Verbundenheit mit der CSSR und der 21. August 1968," *Neues Deutschland*, 18 August 1989.
10. Frevert, *Women in German History*, 299.
11. Frevert, *Women in German History*, 299–30; Bake, *Die Ersten*, 66–69.
12. "Neuer Rat des Bezirkes Magdeburg," *Volksstimme Magdeburg*, 1 July 1981.
13. "Dank und Anerkennung für die hervorragenden Leistungen der Frauen in unserer Republik," *Neue Zeit*, 7 March 1981.
14. There is no indication in the letters that any of the Schönebeck women from the GDR were involved in the DFD.
15. See, for instance, *Neues Deutschland*, 6, 7, and 8 March 1989; *Berliner Zeitung*, 7 and 8 March 1989.
16. Eva Kolinsky, *Women in 20th-Century Germany: A Reader* (Manchester, 1995), 95–96, 144–45 (Dokument 2.31).
17. Kolinsky, *Women in 20th-Century Germany*, 144–45.
18. Kolinsky, *Women in 20th-Century Germany*, 267–68.
19. On an autonomous women's organization aiming to overcome the patriarchy and achieve true equality, see *Frauen in die Offensive: Texte und Arbeitspapiere der Gruppe "Lila Offensive"* (Berlin, 1990). Also see Samirah Kenawi, *Frauengruppen in der DDR der 80er Jahre: eine Dokumentation* (Berlin, 1995).
20. Cordula Kahlau, ed., *Aufbruch!: Frauenbewegung in der DDR: Dokumentation* (Munich, 1990), 62.
21. Fulbrook, *The People's State*, 170.
22. Leask, *Losing Trust*, 136–37.
23. Leask, *Losing Trust*.
24. SQ, *Briefwechsel und Tagebücher*, DTA 1687/I-9.
25. See the case of the Klaus Renft, founder of the legendary GDR rock group, the Klaus Renft Combo, which was banned in 1975 for "defaming the working class." When Renft was eventually allowed to leave for the West, he and his Greek fiancée packed their belongings with great care, only for them to arrive in West Berlin smashed to pieces. "I could have howled with rage," Renft says; Klaus Renft, *Zwischen Liebe und Zorn. Die Autobiographie. Herausgegeben von Hans-Dieter Schütt* (Berlin, 1997), AdK Kempowski-BIO, 6893UF, 106, 126.
26. For a personal account, see A. B., *Beiträge zur Familiengeschichte der B. im 20. Jahrhundert*, AdK Kempowski-BIO 6894, 169.
27. Matthias Judt, "Aufstieg und Niedergang der 'Trabi-Wirtschaft,'" in Matthias Judt, ed., *DDR-Geschichte in Dokumenten* (Bonn, 1998), 101.
28. Hermann Wentker, "Justiz und Politik in der DDR," in Rainer Eppelmann, Bernd Faulenbach, and Ulrich Mählert, eds., *Bilanz und Perspektiven der DDR-Forschung* (Paderborn, 2003); Heiner Timmermann, ed., *Die DDR—Recht und Justiz als politisches Instrument* (Berlin, Duncker and Humboldt, 2000).
29. Fulbrook, *The People's State*, 238–40.
30. Else Hermann raised this question in an interview.

31. Judt, "Aufstieg," 140, gives figures for waiting times for cars in 1987. In the Magdeburg area, it was eleven and a half years for a Trabant.
32. The account that follows draws upon Günter Kuntze, *Juden in Schönebeck* (Schönebeck, 1991), Stadtarchiv Schönebeck; Hans-Joachim Geffert, *Fragmentarische Nachrichten*; Judy Urman, *From Quiet Hope to Freedom: The Life Story of Ernest and Judy Urman* (self-published, 2012), Stadtarchiv Schönebeck; Günter Kuntze, *Unter aufgehobenen Rechten* (undated), Stadtarchiv Schönebeck, Bl. 955.
33. Kuntze, *Juden in Schönebeck*, 48.
34. Kuntze, *Juden in Schönebeck*, 54.
35. Zwahr, "Die DDR auf dem Höhepunkt der Staatskrise 1989," 450.

CHAPTER 6

Reunited?
The 1990s and Beyond

The Context

The SED's Sudden Loss of Power

Between the end of Book 25 in August 1989 and the start of Book 26 in February 1990, extraordinary things happened in the GDR that changed the nature of Germany as a whole. Following the fraudulent declaration of the local election results in May 1989, pressure grew from the population for the SED to relax its grip, but the SED remained determined to hold on to power. These developments were not happening in a vacuum. In Poland and Hungary in particular, the movement for reform had become unstoppable, with the Soviet Union under Mikhail Gorbachev choosing not to intervene.

One result of popular frustration was that more and more people attempted to leave the GDR. In May 1989, Hungary made it easier to travel into Austria, and in September it opened the border completely. Tens of thousands of GDR citizens used this route to go to the West. The GDR authorities responded indignantly to what they saw as an unfriendly act by one of their socialist allies.[1]

In the GDR, opposition groups—still illegal—explicitly aimed to transform the society and its power structures so that people would want to stay. In and through the church, but also outside it, the opposition movement continued to grow with mass peaceful demonstrations, despite infiltration into the groups and brutal attacks by the Stasi, and threats from the party leaders. Within the SED itself, there was increasing unease and incomprehension about the course being pursued, and hostility toward the leadership. Many members simply deserted the party.[2]

After the huge demonstrations in Leipzig and elsewhere in October and an implied acceptance that it could not crush these by force, the SED finally tried to make changes that would rescue its position as the governing party. On 18 October, Erich Honecker was replaced as leader, and a few weeks later was expelled from the SED. (The party had never been sentimental; sixty years of service to the communist movement, including years in a Nazi prison, counted for nothing at this point.) The new leader, Egon Krenz, promised a "*Wende*," a significant change, but even larger demonstrations, particularly in Leipzig and then in East Berlin on 4 November, included demands for a complete change to democracy. Further changes in the central committee to get rid of key figures from the Honecker period were followed by the sudden decision to allow unhindered travel to the West, and by the opening of the Berlin Wall on 9 November 1989.

Changes in the Schönebeck Heimat

What happened in the Schönebeck area over these few months was astounding. Suddenly, people spoke out and acted against the SED, and the old *Heimat* presented a totally different face to the outside world.

Initially, there was still uncertainty and resistance from the SED. In early September 1989, the *Volksstimme Magdeburg* was publishing articles that demonstrated the SED's anxiety, asserting the need for party members to prove themselves strong and worthy.[3] In describing the determination of the construction workers in Schönebeck to work quickly and to a high standard (12 September 1989), it continued to repeat the language of the past forty years. It praised the success of the Gummiwerke in Schönebeck, where production was maintained with the help of twenty-four Vietnamese workers, a cheaper solution than raising productivity through capital investment.[4] In reporting on the GDR's fortieth anniversary celebrations in the Magdeburg area, the *Volksstimme* said that a tiny group of young people tried to cause a disturbance. Ninety-two of the demonstrators were arrested. This was followed by letters from supposedly ordinary people, saying how indignant they were about the disturbances and how pleased they were that the police did their duty.[5]

Subsequently, the *Volksstimme* reports conveyed an air of panic, with frequent declarations and statements from officials, who were unable to keep up with the pace of change. After Honecker's resignation, the Magdeburg regional authorities declared they fully supported the decisions of the new Central Committee and would involve themselves in widespread discussions about the future "in an atmosphere of openness and realism."[6] On 26 October, there was a report on a peaceful demonstration in Schönebeck of around two hundred people calling for freedom, an event unthinkable a few months previously. In Magdeburg, the cathedral square where the young women had met in 1950 was turned into a huge political forum for debates and demonstrations.

A report on 9 November, before the Berlin Wall was opened, conveys the disarray of the SED itself. Addressing Magdeburg's governing council, the head of the council (*Oberbürgermeister*) Werner Herzig, a senior party official, spelled out the consequences of the party's failure to develop adequate political structures. He noted that of the hundred thousand people, mostly young, who had already left the GDR, two thousand were from the Magdeburg area, and that forty-two young children had been left behind by their parents.[7] This and the huge demonstrations had to happen, he said, before it was clear to the party that there was a deep political crisis. The party had been paralyzed, and the trust that people had shown was being eroded. He was clear that the blame for this lay with the political leadership at the center, who had always insisted on their right to make the decisions and pass them down to the lower levels. Paralysis at the center meant that at his level they had no idea what to do. By default, they had found themselves recognizing and engaging in discussions with the opposition groups. The party had always talked about being close to the people, but that was mere words, not reflected in deeds. As a result, he said, "no one was interested in whether we had taken great strides forward in our city since 1945 and since the founding of the first workers' and peasants' state on German soil. And here we have this awakening of the people, showing us that we can rescue nothing by patching things up with cosmetic changes." He then resigned with immediate effect.

Subsequent issues of the *Volkstimme Magdeburg* contained the outlines of a renewal program for the SED, appeals to doctors to remain in the region, and the recognition of economic failings and the terrible environmental consequences of past policies. The condition of the Harz, it was said (23 November 1989), was desperate but not hopeless, while there were serious long-term problems of air pollution in the Magdeburg region, particularly in Schönebeck and Staßfurt (6 December 1989).

Local reports stressed the gap between the SED's rhetoric and the reality on the ground. A letter on 23 November from the X-Ray department of the hospital in Calbe talked of the awful conditions the workers had to endure, including long periods where they worked endlessly, away from their families, with no time given to make up for it. In addition, they did not even have telephones, and there was no prospect of this changing in the foreseeable future. On 28 December 1989, a report expressed concern about the rise of Nazi activity in the GDR, particularly in Rostock. On 6 January 1990, it was acknowledged that there had been neo-Nazi and far right activity in the Magdeburg district, both recently and over recent years, and that anti-Semitic slogans were being used in Calbe. The same issue carried the official government announcement that the ban on singing the national anthem had been revoked after more than two decades. (The ban had been imposed because the SED no longer wanted to declare that Germany was a "united fatherland.") Early in 1990, the *Volksstimme Magdeburg* ceased being an organ of the SED and presented itself as an independent, non-party newspaper.

At the national level, the SED's power disappeared rapidly in December 1989 and January 1990. The "leading role" of the party was removed from the constitution; its private militia—the armed workers' groups in the large industrial complexes—was disarmed and disbanded; and the Stasi could no longer operate as the "sword and shield" of the party. By February, the party had turned itself into the Partei des Demokratischen Sozialismus (PDS—Party of Democratic Socialism) and declared a break with its Stalinist past. In fact, many of its problems went back to its Leninist structures and ideology. These contributed to the contradiction that faced committed but anti-authoritarian socialists throughout the time of the GDR: without the Marxist-Leninist party to push through revolutionary changes, there was no chance of building a socialist society in Germany, but the Marxist-Leninist principles and practices of the SED made it impossible to develop the economic strength and the social commitment necessary to build socialism.[8]

One of the PDS's new leaders, Hans Modrow, became the head of government. His primary tasks were to transform the GDR into a democracy and to establish a new relationship with the vastly richer Federal Republic in the face of increasing demands from both sides for the reunification of Germany. Modrow's own proposals for reunification were tied to free elections taking place on 18 March 1990. His government also had to deal with the disastrous economic position of the GDR, which was effectively bankrupt and living on credits from the West.

The process of political transformation, referred to as the *Wende*, culminated in the dissolution of the GDR in October 1990 and the reunification of Germany as the Bundesrepublik, the Federal Republic of Germany. The *Wende* was the context for the entries in the *Rundbrief* for 1990, when the women in both the West and the East reacted with delight, amazement, bewilderment, and anxiety to the speed and the nature of the changes, and reflected on the impact on them as older women, and on their children and families in the East.

Responding to the Wende and Reunification

The first two books of the *Rundbrief* written during and after the *Wende* are very different from the earlier and later books. In Book 26 (3 February to 1 December 1990) and Book 27 (8 January 1991 to 22 October 1991), everyday life is suddenly and openly dominated by the political events, for the women in the West as well as for those in the East. The earlier themes of family, travel, and work, and even interactions with the state, are largely put aside by the Schönebeck women. Instead, they try to get to grips with what is happening around them politically, economically, and socially. Apart from that, only illness and death remain a continuing, ever-present concern for them. What is notable is that the women in the West were also consumed by the political events and the *Wende*'s practical consequences. The Schönebeck area, their long-lost *Heimat*, drew them back in, restoring an important physical and emotional connection.

These two books also represent in simple terms a serious lesson for the women. They had spent much of the previous forty years consciously or unconsciously turning away from what was going on around them or being done to them and, in so doing, asserting a certain power of their own over events and their individual lives. The *Wende*, however, demonstrated to them both the overwhelming power of the formal political structures and the unexpected power of the population as a collective when they came to challenge the power of the GDR authorities. It is one of the ironies of the history of this period, that the state which so strongly promoted the importance of the collective should in the end fall victim to the power of collective action.

In these letters, the women recognize their impotence, but there is little sign of them considering what is happening to them as women. This is significant, since one of the immediate consequences of the disappearance of the GDR was the reduction or elimination of services designed to make it easier for women to play a full part in the society, such as childcare provision and access to education, training, and jobs. Women were, in a way, returned to the home and to their household responsibilities, which men had successfully refused to consider as shared responsibilities over the previous forty years. The position was made worse by women being more likely than men to lose their jobs in the early years.

Some studies suggest, however, that many women had gained real strength, self-confidence, and independence as a result of their upbringing in the GDR, and that this benefited them substantially after the *Wende*. It enabled them to aim for and be accepted for jobs where they could show they had the appropriate skills, and to set up or be involved in successful new businesses.[9] Some women asserted strongly that it was time to fight back against their portrayal as victims of the *Wende*, and against the traditional image of women this implied.[10] The Schönebeck women, as they left the labor market, watched both the reality and the debate about it mostly from the sidelines or through the eyes of their children. When they commented on the *Wende*, it was not on the position of women.

In the group, the women were faced increasingly with attempts by the husbands and widowers, who participated as honorary members, to dominate and shift the debate into the supposedly more important areas of the political and economic. The women found ways to let most of these attempts simply pass them by and continued to welcome the men into the group. Nevertheless, the tone of the *Rundbrief* changes when the letters are written by men.

In this chapter, the focus is much less on the earlier themes and more on the individual women and how they reacted to the *Wende* and the collapse of the GDR, and, later in the decade, to the years when reunification was simply a fact of life, a new context in which they sought to live their lives as they grew older. Although the principal stories continue to be told, more attention is paid to the stories of some of the minor characters, who suddenly write differently after the *Wende*. Some of the men's accounts are also included, in order to give a different view of what was happening and to contrast their way of writing with that of the women.

New Feelings, New Attitudes

Book 26 of the *Rundbrief* contains many assertions about the strength and importance of the Schönebeck group, which are matched by accounts of personal disorientation and uncertainty about the future. This book covers the period when attempts to transform the GDR gave way to the move toward reunification and the end of the GDR. By the time Book 27 (8 January 1991–22 October 1991) traveled around the group, the GDR had disappeared. Controversially, much of its industry was disappearing too, closed down as being uncompetitive or too polluting, or sold off for relatively little, mostly to investors or industrialists from the former West. Not surprisingly, there were high levels of unemployment by this time, and the towns of Schönebeck, Staßfurt, Calbe, and Barby, being so dependent on large factories, were particularly affected.

One of the earliest local changes, noted with some irony by the letter writers, involved renaming streets as a way of stripping the old East of its GDR symbols. The names of key communist figures were the first to go. These included streets named after Wilhelm Pieck, the first president of the GDR, one of the old communists who had spent the Nazi years in exile in Moscow. In Schönebeck, the change was to the innocuous "Am Stadtfeld"; in Wismar, it was back to its old name: Bürgermeister-Hauptstrasse. In Frieda Möller's Barby, Clara-Zetkin-Strasse had been named after one of the few women heroes of the socialist and communist movement, and a joint initiator of International Women's Day. After the *Wende*, the street was renamed in honor of the local pastor, Frieda Möller's father. Johannes Schneider, getting ahead of himself, gives his address as "Lenin or Friedrichstrasse" before it reverted formally to Friedrichstrasse.

Many other responses are highly personal. Martha Jäger's letters over the years suggested she was mostly unaware of how or why power was being exercised against her and her family. She says now (21 February 1990) that she is astonished by what is happening politically: "Time is flying by ever more quickly, thanks to the political events—which are going down well with every one of us, and which we all support."

The rest of the women knew that Martha had been seriously ill, but Barbara Meier's letter of 12 June 1990 contains unexpected bad news: Martha has died. Barbara had hoped that in the new circumstances Martha might have been helped by the health service in the West, which Barbara recognized as more advanced than in the GDR, "but the terrible illness, unknown here, was apparently too fast-moving and had already spread too far." Barbara sums up Martha's life and her contribution to the group: "Martha was truly one of the liveliest among us, always smiling in the photos, always concerned for her loved ones, often having to struggle with the challenges of everyday life in the GDR, and despite various little aches and pains always in good spirits, since she was buoyed up by her faith." Here, there is another clue as to why life in the GDR was often made so difficult for Martha and her family. As well as having a "bourgeois" background—owning her own house and being and involved in the family business—she was a confirmed Christian who held to her faith in an atheist state.

Barbara's letter also reveals more about her own family's position in the GDR. First, she describes at length further travels in the Soviet Union in 1989, including a cruise on the Don and the Volga, a retirement present to Heinz from his head office. As with Helmut Liebmann and his trip to Cuba, it is unlikely that Heinz Meier would have been given this present if he were not an SED member or, at the very least, someone who cooperated closely with the party leadership in his college. This implies that he had made his peace with the SED and accepted the way life was organized in the GDR. Barbara's position is less clear, but she certainly took advantage of the benefits he gained from this.

Second, referring back to the war, Barbara attaches a photo, under which she has written, "View out the window of our cabin on to the promenade along the river bank in Volgograd—for us, remembered sadly as 'Stalingrad.'" For the SED leadership, Stalingrad represented a major victory and the first step on the way to the necessary defeat of the German army and the Nazi state; it was never portrayed as something to be sad about, despite the huge numbers of German soldiers who died in the battle there or later as prisoners of war. Regardless of Heinz's closeness to the SED, forty-five years of occupation and communist rule had not been enough to change Barbara Meier's view or (by implication) that of her readers, the other Schönebeck women, that the German defeat at Stalingrad was to be mourned, not celebrated.

Gisela Riedel

Some of the women suddenly come out of themselves after the *Wende* and have much more to say. Gisela Riedel (31 January 1991) gives her address in Schönebeck as "Platz der DSF" (German-Soviet Friendship Square) or "Marktplatz?"—the question mark being hers. It has been more than forty-six years years since she was the lively, lighthearted young girl, inseparable from Martha Jäger during their time in Weimar. Over the years, she has worked in her father's pharmacy, married a younger man and supported him during his training, had children and stayed at home to look after them, gone out to work again, this time at the hospital laboratory in Bad Salzelmen, been ill a lot and spent time in hospital, hosted at least one class reunion, traveled with Martha to the West when she reached retirement age, and generally been a quiet, though constant, presence in the *Rundbrief*. Suddenly, she has become politically outspoken.

In her previous letter (24 February 1990), Gisela said she was wondering what would happen in the run-up to their planned reunion: "I mean, with unification and so on." She said she has never in her life spent so much time reading the newspapers before, so much so that "I can hardly get my housework done." In early 1991, she is decidedly more anxious:

> Well folks, at last there is actually a lot to report, but I really don't know where to start with it. I'm also afraid that you Westerners will think: the Ossis are never satisfied and just go around grumbling.[11] The whole change-around of everything, and above all the uncertainty, just does us in. Every day there's something new in the paper.

One aspect of her uncertainty is to do with jobs. Her husband had spent many years trying to keep the roads in the region in good condition. He now works in the recreation center and hopes to be there until June. After that, she suspects, there will be nothing new for him, since he is in his fifties. He is having to fill in endless questionnaires, so thank goodness he was never in the SED, she says.

Gisela then takes issue with Elfriede Berger, whose letter of 20 August 1990 from Cologne was strikingly insensitive and condescending. Elfriede suggested that if she could cope with the chaos in the West after 1945, they can do the same now in the East: "Now you are free at last, dear friends in the GDR. Still, there will need to be a lot of patience before that desperate land can climb back up again. But that time too will pass. We had to start with forty Deutschmarks, our money lost its value, and we managed it. So just keep your spirits up!" Many years earlier, Elfriede had been equally insensitive, talking in 1955 about the joys of driving around in her Mercedes. Addressing Elfriede, Gisela says,

> You write, by way of consolation for us (and I have already heard this line a lot), that starting out for you was hard too. Nevertheless, it's completely different for us. But I won't go on about that now. Of course, we can fill ourselves full of orange juice and bananas now and travel wherever we want to, if we have the money. Bus journeys are certainly relatively cheap. Perhaps we'll head east again, since we just want to see snow-covered mountains.

And then, after all the years of never commenting on political events or the outside world, Gisela asks, "What will the Gulf War bring us?" She is concerned that so much money is put into armaments while at the same time there are pictures of starving children for whom no money is available. There is an echo here of the constant GDR propaganda, which seems to have left Gisela genuinely concerned about the importance of peace and sensitive to the suffering caused by war.

Finally, to Astrid Greiswald, who is ill but who puts a lot about her Christian faith and belief in God into her introductions and letters, Gisela makes clear where she stands in relation to religion: "Astrid, I envy you your faith. It will help you a lot." She herself will have to make do without it, she implies.

In her next letter (25 January 1992), Gisela is still disturbed by the gulf between the former West and East. Things are getting worse rather than better, she says, but they are so small and insignificant that they can do nothing about it. Their house (with the pharmacy on the ground floor) has been given back to them, but now they have no money to refurbish it. Meanwhile, some of her children and their partners are unemployed and are being retrained for possible new jobs. Gisela then offers one of the rare responses to Edith Friebe's account of meeting up again with Jutta Lübschütz: "Edith, your Jewish friend, like Heidi, was in the parallel class to ours, so she was not someone we knew. I was very affected by hearing of her fate. How her sister and her family must have suffered!!"

Two years later (29 January 1994), Gisela exclaims in frustration that she herself still has no telephone. She adds some family news: her much-younger husband has taken early retirement, while her daughters finally have jobs. On 18 January 1995, Gisela has one important thing to tell them: "A great joy for us is that *finally* we now have a telephone."

There is a hint of Schönebeck's troubles in Gisela's letter of December 1995: "The pharmacy has closed, the rooms are all standing there empty. And they will probably stay empty now." By the end of the decade (28 February 2000), Gisela and her husband have moved out of the former pharmacy into an apartment, which she says she is having trouble getting used to. Schönebeck's decline since the *Wende* is evident and distressing to her: "At night I still dream a lot about the old house. I also still feel a pang whenever we go past it. At this time of the year, the crocuses would be flowering. Instead, you look over at a pile of rubbish and rubble."

Heidi Kempf

Heidi Kempf (9 February 1991) is extremely happy about reunification. She also loved the class reunion that Sabine organized in the Rheinland-Pfalz (see figure 6.1), and stayed on for another week with Sabine after it. She does not try to hide the rift in the group over Elfriede Berger's comments. She says sharply: "Elfriede, you were all forty years younger then—can you not see that might be

254 *Friendship without Borders*

Figure 6.1. Fifty years on: class reunion, Burg Wilenstein, 1 September 1990. Photo courtesy of Akademie der Künste, Berlin.

the difference?!" Still, as she is unfailingly optimistic, she says the good things in life are worth concentrating on; it is just a pity that being older makes it hard to take up the new opportunities on offer. In any case, she notes, being told what to think and feel for forty years cannot fail to have left its mark on them. Like Gisela, Heidi also mentions the Gulf War. Her wish is that everyone should see that peace does not come through war.

Gerda Höpfner

Gerda Höpfner (27 April 1990), after decades at the Gummiwerke in Schönebeck, is missing the collective that was at the heart of her working life.[12] Because of the changes and problems in the factory, she has had to stop working, and is not yet clear how to keep a grip on her life: "It's not so easy, suddenly to be at home on your own all the time, when you are used to always being around other people and having a particular task to carry out. But still, despite that, I am optimistic!"

A year later, reluctantly out of work and retired, Gerda (3 March 1991) wonders what they should all do next. She has joined a voluntary organization from the West that is now needed in the former East. It organizes activities and help for people feeling isolated or vulnerable: "I have got used to being retired. In order not to be completely inactive, I have joined the Deutsches Sozialwerk e.V. (whose head office is in Bonn) and I head our section here in Schönebeck. I have already been to a number of seminars, in Bonn, Münster and Bad Pyrmont."

Gerda is keen to have a class reunion this year and would be happy to travel somewhere (provided it is not too expensive), since "here in Schönebeck the possibilities really are still very limited, though maybe things will look better next year." She, too, is not happy with Elfriede Berger's remarks:

> I must also say, in response to Elfriede's surely well-meant but truly unthought-through words of "consolation" about the forty Deutschmarks, that it really must make a difference whether you are making a new start while still young (and in a market economy), or whether you are sixty-four, a pensioner, suddenly faced with the ruins of the past forty years and what is left in your savings account. At this age we hardly have the possibility of starting again, let alone any way of building up any assets! All we can do is try to get by on what we have left now!
>
> Still, I'll sing no song of woe here; I am an optimist and very happy about the *Wende*. In any case, not everything can be looked at in terms of money: this constant feeling of freedom is something I guess you can only understand if you have lived tied down as we have here for forty years.

Johannes Schneider

Writing in June 1990 from Schönebeck, Johannes Schneider addresses them in the style of Wilhelm Pieck, the GDR's first president: "Dear compatriots in both east and west of our German homeland!" He adds, "As I detest his likeminded comrades (including the PDS!), I prefer to write: 'Dear classmates, both sisters and brothers!'" His news from home is that Dieter and his family, who had applied to emigrate to the West, were allowed to go in June 1989. They were given a flat near Hanover, the children went straight into school, and there was a job ready for Dieter. Then came the "real existing capitalism," Johannes says: since the state was paying half of his salary for a certain period, he lost his job at the end of that period so that the firm could employ another refugee from the GDR, with half the salary again paid by the state. Dieter was then out of work for six weeks before getting a permanent job.

In his next letter (17 April 1991), Johannes says he too disagrees with Elfriede's comments. He is pleased, however, to have had enough money for an excellent, cheap holiday in Greece. His other news is that his children want to refurbish and modernize the house, now they have the chance to, and that, in an echo of the turmoil and lawlessness after the war, they were burgled in May 1990 by Russian soldiers from the local garrison.

Elly Haase: The Group, the GDR, and Differing Attitudes

Elly Haase's letter of 29 March 1990 follows the first free elections in the GDR. These showed a clear majority for rapid reunification, effectively on the Federal Republic's terms. Elly says what a joy it is to read the *Rundbrief* and to be reminded of the many lovely memories of the last class reunion and the "unforgettably beautiful days" they spent together. She goes on to refer to events in the GDR:

> In the meantime, there is really so much that is happening, things that none of us would have dreamed of. We have the freedom to travel, and the first free elections have now taken place. Otherwise, however, many questions that are very disturbing to us remain open. We piggy-bank savers are also worried; are we to be lucky or not, that is the question.
>
> Well, our generation has already been through so much and we haven't let it get us down, so we'll get through this time too....
>
> We can look back with pride at our many cross-German meetings, but I think the class reunion of 1990 will be especially significant.
>
> There is not a lot to report about us. We are counting the days. We are a bit squeezed here and there but can still feel satisfied.

Before the *Wende*, Elly Haase spent her whole working life as a carpenter in the GDR, when she would have gone to university if she had been allowed. She uses her letter of 20 February 1991 to sum up the experiences and circumstances that have made their lives different, depending on where they lived. It is clear she has been provoked by some of the comments from the West, particularly those of Elfriede Berger.

The past year, Elly says, has brought great things: freedom, the Deutschmark, and the first all-German elections, but at the same time "growing together has turned out to be harder than expected, and now the Gulf War has broken out." Looking at their group, she notes that there are only two of them whom she calls "real" Wessis, who were there a few years before 1945 and the division of the country. Another nine from the East gradually disappeared over the border and rediscovered one another as "elective" Wessis. She describes their different fates:

> The original two, and some of the other nine, started over again after the currency reform [in 1948] with their forty Deutschmarks in a free market economy: it was tough, but "each step was a step forward." The rest of the nine didn't leave the *Heimat* until after the currency reform, left some or all of what they owned behind and were bold enough to start anew: it was tough, but that too meant that almost every step was a step forward, and apparently none of them regretted it since not one came back. We eight "genuine" Ossis remained in the *Heimat*

right up to this day. (*Der dusselige Rest D.D.R.* [The dimwitted remainder].) We too started with forty Ostmarks after the currency reform. That meant 13.33 Deutschmarks, since the exchange rate was precisely 3:1, and we were forced to buy with that what we needed just to survive. For us, however, what passed for an economy, our free market, meant a market free of goods. We had ration cards for groceries until 1958 and cards to get an allocation of briquettes and coal until April 1991. Like muzzled dogs on a leash, kept behind barbed wire, we took one step forward and two steps back.

Elly is clearly referring here to a key Communist text, Lenin's *One Step Forward, Two Steps Back*.[13] She was one of the few who had been willing to use such irony during the life of the GDR, when it could be dangerous to do so. Here there is more than irony; there is real anger. She continues her account:

So we stayed down at rock bottom with absolutely no way out. Then the *Wende* came and with it the Deutschmark for us too, up to 6,000 DM at 1:1, the rest at half that value, and in the meantime we've all become pensioners. Now they're saying we have to battle our way up from the bottom of the valley and climb up over the peaks ahead of us, and once again we are just marking time, still roped together with the same old team, but even they can't seem to get moving.

As ever, Elly is playing with her metaphors here. She uses the word *Seilschaft* to convey the sense of a team of climbers roped together as they climb the mountains, but the word also has the sense of a clique or coterie or old boys' network: the SED and their collaborators still clinging on and forcing their fellow citizens to do their bidding. She continues, scornfully:

And all around us, bad luck, breakdowns, bankruptcies, and on top of that the state coffers are empty!

But we won't give up even now. Keep your chin up, even if you're in a mess from the neck down (as Harald says to console me if ever I'm a bit low). I think that the eight of us will adopt that as our watchword, since we really are stuck in the muck right up to our necks.

Still, we can look back with pride at our class reunions. We have spared neither expense nor effort and through all the hard years have managed to arrange [in the East] thirty large reunions as well as various smaller ones.

Contrast that with the four large and a few smaller reunions over on the other side!

And yet these four really did mean a lot to us and provided solace for our sore and suffering souls. Each one in its own way was an experience, the most recent one too since it brought us all together under one roof and we no longer had to look like the poor relations. Yes, we know: you did it willingly, so let me say here, many thanks yet again, as indeed for everything that you have done for us over all the years.

But how do we go on from here? We really would be a pitiful all-German community of old school friends, were we to collapse now. Let's just hope we can get another reunion set up for this year.

A year later (19 February 1992), Elly says they are all lucky to be alive at this time, but she believes that the collapse of the once so powerful "Ostblock" brings with it problems that will affect them all, some more, some less. Seeking to draw an end to the Elfriede Berger controversy, she says that "the forty-five years we have stuck together should bind us so firmly that neither a thoughtless word nor an oversensitive reaction can pull us apart." Like many of the others, she is keen to have a reunion in the Harz, with its symbolic importance: "For forty years, each side was only half of the Harz."

Criticizing the GDR: Frieda Möller

For the first time, Frieda Möller (24 June 1990) makes clear her thoughts about the GDR itself and the Stasi, which, as she sees it, buttressed the rule of the SED:

> At the moment things are really going crazy in our land. We are overjoyed to be free at last, after all these years living behind walls and barbed wire, and on top of that, with our mouths sealed shut. *Free* at last: an indescribably wonderful feeling. Many, many tears of joy have already been shed and, believe me, we are still gripped by a certain fear that everything could be clamped down on again. So we are awaiting unification with deep longing, something that would be good for you Westerners to better understand. It is incomprehensible to me that some citizens of the Federal Republic are not prepared for unification to take place so rapidly. But *we* are the ones who sacrificed more than enough over so many years and had to give up hoping for so many things. And now so many of us in the GDR are once again losing thousands of Marks through the currency changes.
>
> We are overjoyed to be rid of the huge apparatus of power, the Stasi. At a time when nothing worked, these rogues worked perfectly, down to the tiniest detail. We could never write or talk about that, our post was photocopied, our telephone conversations listened in to and recorded. The new currency is just around the corner and our inferior *Ostmark* is disappearing from our purses. But at last in West Germany we no longer have to look like the penniless sisters and brothers from the East, and no longer need to be given handouts...
>
> In memory of the peaceful revolution, the church choirs of Calbe and Barby performed in the Calbe and Barby churches on 16 and 17 June. It was a beautiful concert to give thanks, and we went and were overjoyed to be there.

The letter is signed by both Frieda and her husband, Karl-Heinz. Karl-Heinz adds comments of his own, however, complaining that nothing has properly changed yet and that the Ministry of the Interior still has six thousand "comrades." Addressing those in the West, he says, "So despite a lot of progress, we still feel very much alone. Cross your fingers for us."

Frieda and Karl-Heinz soon encountered problems arising from the collectivization of agriculture in the GDR. One curious feature of this collectivization was that formal ownership of the land used by the cooperatives remained with the original owners. This only became a problem when the regime collapsed and some people sought to extract themselves from the LPGs. In 1952, the authorities had put pressure on Karl-Heinz's parents to bring their farm into the local LPG. In the face of this, his parents left for the West. Now, Frieda writes (3 May 1991), the property is about to be back in the ownership of his mother. It is, however, in a terrible state, requiring "millions" to be invested in it to reestablish some semblance of order out of "this socialist dilapidation."

Frieda also highlights the contrasts arising from the *Wende*. She says that they have been to Canada to visit Karl-Heinz's family. She includes a postcard of lakes and wooded islands in northwestern Ontario, beside photos of buildings going to rack and ruin along the "once so beautiful banks of the Elbe."

In her next letter (26 June 1992), Frieda makes clear her view that what took place politically, economically, and environmentally should not be seen as water under the bridge. The water in the Elbe and the Saale is already a lot clearer, she says, but "we are waiting to see what still lies concealed within it!" She has her own way of interpreting what happened in the East: "You could say we lost the last war twice over. For forty years we alone had to bear the burden of reparations, and in return for that we were given the lowest possible wages!!"

How Genuine Are the Criticisms?

The critical accounts in letters such as Frieda Möller's need to be considered carefully, not simply taken at face value. When the communist leaders returned to Germany from the Soviet Union at the end of the war, they commented bitterly that almost everyone they talked to turned out to have secretly opposed the Nazis. There is a similar chance that people who were happy to go along with the regime in the GDR suddenly found that it was better to portray themselves as always having opposed the SED. In the case of the Möller family, however, there are indications in earlier letters of problems they faced, and of their frustrations.

Frieda's father was a pastor in the Protestant church. He received an award from the state in the early years for his activities in favor of peace—that is, for being part of the state-managed peace movement when there were still hopes of Germany being united under a peace treaty favorable to the Soviet Union. Nevertheless, we can see from Frieda's comments that his movements and his ability to speak out were severely circumscribed. As early as July 1952, Frieda criticizes the GDR for not allowing her sister from the West to attend her wedding. In 1954, she recounts having their house searched and their furniture seized after her parents-in-law went to the West, and the letter conveys her fear and uncertainty. In 1958, she portrays herself as a victim of the new travel restrictions, which made it impossible to visit her parents-in-law in the West, even though she and her husband had gone—and come back—in December 1954. In 1973 she criticizes the failure to maintain the infrastructure of the hospital where she works. When in 1980 she is pleased and surprised to get a permit to travel to the West for her brother's silver wedding anniversary, her comment about the goods in the shops contains a clear criticism of conditions in the GDR. In 1983, she says how difficult it is to find a decent place to go on holiday in the GDR. In 1985, she says how pleased they are to get a car at last, after eleven and a half years.

The criticisms are there, then, if mostly fairly mild. At the same time, there are many positive things in her letters, about education for her children and her husband, about holidays in the Soviet Union, and about the health service and the opportunity to go on a *Kur*, along with many cheerful entries about everyday life and friendships with people locally. The subsequent expressions of indignation and relief might well be entirely heartfelt and sincere, but it does not necessarily mean that they are. The comments of the others about the end of the GDR need to be considered in a similar way.

In discussions with Else Hermann, Anna Siebert, and Irma Kindler in 2012 and 2013, it became clear that there was in fact deep anxiety about saying how they all really felt during the time of the GDR, not just in the letters but also in the class reunions. At one of the reunions, Helmut Liebmann had apparently had too much to drink and started telling political jokes. There was consternation, and he was rapidly silenced; they were afraid that someone would hear, even though there was no one there except those in the group itself. In other words, even in this intimate gathering of women and their husbands, no one could be sure there was not a Stasi informer ready to report back on what was being discussed. Else, Anna, and Irma (at least) guessed, perhaps wrongly, that Helmut Liebmann was an SED member who could have been trying to provoke them into anti-party or anti-state comments. In an interview in 2015, without being prompted, Else Hermann named one of the women as having been a Stasi informer. Whether this assertion was true or not, the group's knowledge of how the Stasi worked meant that they really did feel safe only when, as Frieda Möller says, their mouths were sealed shut.

Views from the West

Leni Baumann says on 13 August 1990 that she has been to see for herself how things are back in the GDR, before its disappearance:

Visiting my relatives in the GDR, I wanted to see how the currency union was working out on the ground. May the deep misery that the still-existing GDR is plunging into not carry on for too long! May the gap between the two Germanys soon perceptibly narrow! I am skeptical but optimistic, despite the problems that are clear to see.

And now Martha has left us as well. It is painful to see our group getting smaller.

I wish you all good health and the strength to bear the suffering that is inflicted upon us. So far, things are fine with me. At the beginning of 1992, at the latest, I'll reach retirement, but I'll still be working hard until then.

On 25 July 1991, Leni tells them she has now retired from her position as professor. She wanted to attend the class reunion after all these years, but was suddenly ill and unable to go.

Erika Krämer (16 August 1990) seems unreservedly happy about the end of the GDR: "Who could have imagined that our generation would experience a united Germany again!" On 4 August 1991, she says she is appreciating the chance to travel widely in the former GDR, which was largely closed to her before the *Wende*. Braving snow and fog, she climbed the Brocken, the highest point in the Harz, and walked in the Thüringer Wald, as well as visiting Weimar, Meißen, Dresden, the Baltic coast, and Rostock, where she was a student after the war. "What a beautiful fatherland we have!" she declares.

Sabine Kleber (11 August 1991) says how sad she feels about the loss of some of their group, as well as about the critical comments on differences within the united Germany. Her concern is to maintain the integrity of the group:

> But we aren't to allow such differences to bring about discord in our circle. In two to three years, the differences will all have been swept away.

> Aren't we lucky to have been able to live through the *Wende*! Who wants to be piling up riches at our age? Isn't our health and that of your children and grandchildren the thing we value most?!

> I also hope that the dreadful expressions, "Ossis" and "Wessis," will disappear from our vocabulary as quickly as possible.

On 17 September 1990, Edith Friebe also says how wonderful it is to see German unification, which none of them believed they would experience. She hopes the hard times in the former GDR will not last long. How wonderful it was, she says, to be able to go back to her—and their—*Heimat*, after twenty-seven years. She spent time there with Maria, Heidi, Elly, Gisela, and Martha, who rode off afterward on her bike, just a few weeks before her death. But, she adds, what a desperate state the previously attractive Bad Salzelmen was in!

Edith's feelings are echoed by Charlotte Krüger (12 October 1990), who was in Nordhausen for the funeral of her aunt before the end of the GDR. Nordhausen is, or was, a beautiful town, she says, but with so much that needs to be done there just to restore it to order. "The streets! The houses!" she exclaims.

Edith, writing again on 16 August 1991, is a peacemaker and a unifier. For her, the unity of the group is an expression of the unity of the nation, and a demonstration that life can be normal, banal perhaps, but even in its everyday qualities full of things to be valued and shared:

Dear All,

The washing flaps on the line, the sun smiles down at me, the doorbell rings and the postman hands over the *Rundbrief*. At such a moment, nothing better could happen. So I enjoy the summer weather out on the terrace and plunge into your letters at once, letters that talk of joy, troubles and suffering. It is depressing to read of the deaths of Martha, Barbara, and Erna. How lovely our last reunion was in Kaiserslautern, where Barbara was such a lively presence. It seemed to me that she had got over her serious illness and was heading toward recovery. With what joy she told us all about her trip to Mexico! No one could suspect that there wouldn't be another reunion with her at it. In a couple of weeks, we will be having our next reunion at Ilse Klein's, and it will certainly be overshadowed by the deaths of our three dear friends.

In many of the letters there is the sound of dissatisfaction over the way things are at the moment in the new federal states. Hopefully that won't bring a discordant note into our circle! We personally are not responsible for the way things are. Let's stick together, let there be no estrangement! Who should we blame for things having followed a path they should not have taken? Everything is clearer with hindsight! We were all really so happy about unification, something none of us had ever thought would happen. Are there not already small signs to be seen of an upturn? Everyone knew that such an economically devastated land would not blossom again in the short term but would take years!

It really would be nice if expressions such as "Ossis," "Wessis," "over here and over there," "the former GDR," and so on could disappear forthwith! And that the gap we have seen opening up should become no wider, and that we should truly and as rapidly as possible grow together. Arrogance on the one side, but also hypersensitivity on the other, are things we need to be rid of, since only that way can the whole people become united. I hope that, as ever, we will enjoy the brief time we spend together and that no barriers will be set up between us.

It is in this spirit that I send you all my warmest greetings. I look forward to seeing you all in Bad Oeynhausen.

Käthe Sommer (2 October 1991) also finds herself thinking about what happened to the GDR and the society it was trying to construct. At least into the

1960s the GDR seemed to be advancing, she says, "leaving aside the psychological pressures if you didn't go along with things." Then, expelled from the GDR, they had the experience of starting again in the West:

> We came with nothing into a society that had been completely renewed and were seen at first as spies or agents. I must say for myself (from me personally) that even in the fifties we could have left, but at that time I was afraid of leaping into the unknown. Nobody here had any idea that in the seventies everything would go downhill so fast in the GDR, to the point of absolute devastation.

If the Wall had stayed up, she says, conditions in the GDR would have been like those in the Soviet Union, Rumania, and Bulgaria: "empty shops (!) and no doubt unemployment as well." Nevertheless, she too remains optimistic, declaring that "in a few years our children will hardly notice any difference."

The Principal Stories

Hertha Pieper

By June 1990, things had moved on fast in the GDR in ways that directly affected Hertha Pieper and her family. State-owned facilities, including the agricultural cooperatives, were to be transformed into capitalist legal entities operating in market conditions. This made the future of their LPG uncertain and undermined the production and distribution of food. Writing on 20 June 1990, Hertha says that although the family are all well, it has been a difficult time:

> The upheavals of the last year certainly haven't let us settle. And every day we are rocked by something further, there are always new things being revealed.
>
> Now we are just hoping that there are people who are clever and skilled enough to move things in the right direction. Sometimes I'm a little afraid that too much is expected of us.
>
> Healthwise, I am fine, and so is the wider family.... Unfortunately, we couldn't dispose of any of our production this year.

Economic problems continued for Hertha's family over the following year. On 21 April 1991, she says that her older son Wilfried is busy getting a roofing business underway and retraining at the age of forty-one to acquire the necessary skills. His wife is unemployed. Hertha herself is not so surprised at how things have turned out. With her mix of metaphors, she evokes the situation vividly:

> People have said at times that I was being a Jeremiah because I was still anxious, while everything looked rosy to them. Things were—well, yes, they still are—in

a state of utter devastation. It is like with a ruin, you pull one stone out and the rest collapses in on itself. And that's what we are confronted with, that's what we look back on. Then what happens is that the branch with the little people on it gets lopped off and thrown away, while those who are still dangerous are at ease in their armchairs. How much money has flowed into illegal channels! But you've read all that in the previous letters, so enough about that.

There were particular problems for the LPG. As industries were being closed down or restructured for the market economy, so the LPGs were under pressure to be broken up or bought out. The LPG Hertha's family were involved in fought for the right to continue. Hertha writes, "Our LPG is one of the few that will keep going. It was dissolved and many members left, but then it was reestablished as a company with thirty-six members, four of them from our family. Starting up again is naturally difficult and they will be working without being paid all the time up to the harvest!!"

By the time of her next letter (21 June 1992), Hertha is able to say that she is enjoying a quiet life with friends and family, and that she traveled to Kaiserslautern with Heidi Kempf to see Sabine Kleber there. She is looking forward to the reunion in the Harz. It seems that the economic crisis for the LPG and her family is over, and in her letter of 16 June 1993, Hertha suggests that her financial and economic worries are now largely a thing of the past.

Holding to her vow not to travel in the former socialist countries, Hertha says she has been on a coach trip with a friend to Austria: "My dream of seeing the Alps was fulfilled! And it was even more beautiful than I had dreamed!" She also comments on progress since the *Wende*: "This trip and getting a telephone have been the greatest joys of this year." However, she is starting to feel her age:

> As you know, I am very much involved with my family and still try to help where I can. I only take care of half my garden now. My hand and elbow joints are giving me a lot of trouble. As ever, I also get a lot of pleasure out of my children and grandchildren. Isn't that a blessing, something that comes out of having such a large family?

Over this period, Hertha becomes close to Leni Baumann. Leni says on 19 October 1993 how much she enjoyed the reunion in Alexisbad in the Harz. When she heard that the following year's reunion was canceled, she and Hertha had the idea of having a mini-reunion there in October, with Heidi Kempf and Elly Haase. She followed this with a tour of Saxony-Anhalt and Schönebeck with Hertha. After the next reunion, Hertha drove her around the area, to Staßfurt, Neugattersleben, and Calbe, so she could see all the old haunts. Significantly, this reunion in 1994 was hosted by Hertha in what Elly Haase (27 February 1994) told them would be the old style, with homemade cakes and everyone sitting around together in the evening, plus an outing the next day. Hertha says (10 May 1994) how much she enjoyed it and how pleased she was to have done it in this way, with help from her daughters, after it had become more and more lavish over previous years.

From her 1994 letter, it is clear that Hertha is still active and enjoying life. Every afternoon, she has Kerstin's two children, aged eight and four, as Kerstin is doing further training in Schönebeck. She loves having them, and describes sitting up in the tree house with them, watching the storks and other birds in the fields. She draws a sketch in the *Rundbrief* of three hedgehogs that visit them every day.

In 1996, Hertha finds herself yearning for spring after a long winter that has made her joints suffer terribly. By the start of 1997, she says she can hardly write, her arthritis has got so bad: "On some days it's unbearable, particularly when there's a sudden flare-up. I was able to go on a *Kur*, but that didn't help." Later she is well enough to be getting a lot of pleasure out of her large extended family and the choir she now belongs to. She finds time rushing by ever more quickly, she says, just as she gets around ever more slowly. In her letter of 2 May 2000, Hertha says she is looking forward to the class reunion but effectively signs off from the *Rundbrief*: "I keep putting off writing in the *Rundbrief*. With my handwriting, it doesn't make sense anymore, my hand just won't stay on the page. Anyway, not much worth mentioning has happened to me. I'm happy that I have my children around me."

Anna Siebert

Like others writing from the West soon after the *Wende*, Anna Siebert (13 July 1990) also has much to say about the changes in the GDR, as well as about the nature of the group. Her view (expressed somewhat didactically) is that there are several kinds of identity within the Schönebeck group of women: one for those who live in and identify fully with the Federal Republic and have effectively lost touch with their former *Heimat*; one for those who live in the GDR and identify with it and see themselves as always having been part of Germany as a whole; and one for those living in the West but with close enough and strong enough connections with the GDR to have a different sense of a single Germany and to empathize with the people of the GDR. For Anna, who is in this last category, there is a mix of joy and indignation, even if there remains a sense of "over here" and "over there":

Dear All!

How truly happy we are, along with all of you, that the borders have finally disappeared. We hope now that everything over there will take a turn for the better and that you will all get to enjoy the prosperity that has been predicted. I am often deeply disturbed when I hear the views of West Germans who have no connections with your area and are not prepared to do anything at all to help you with reconstruction over there. Sadly, they can only see their own interests and are looking to making more money even out of the unification of the country. Just how everything is going to be paid for if everyone from here or over there wants to get their former property back, I simply don't know....

And now I wish you all good health, positive thinking and only just as much suffering as can be borne.

In her next letter (8 July 1991), Anna agrees wholeheartedly with what Elly Haase has to say about the different ways the West and East developed. She is respectful of the efforts those in the East made despite the difficulties that faced them. There, she says, individual hard work could never be enough:

We here in the West who were able to begin again with very little while we were still young had it much easier than you over there and, with hard work and initiative, could achieve things and get set up, which wasn't possible in the GDR in the conditions there, for all the hard work, effort and commitment. And that is something we in the West should not forget, particularly since even now in the eastern part of the country there is no improvement to be seen in material conditions. Sadly!

Anna thinks they should have the next class reunion in the western part of the country and that the "sponsors" there should take responsibility for ensuring those from the East can come. That is, they should continue to subsidize them. Meanwhile, life has been comfortable and interesting for her, in ways which only serve to emphasize the difference between West and East: she has been to New York, and in the winter is planning to go to Singapore, Bali, the Philippines, and Taiwan.

A year later (12 August 1992), Anna says how much she regrets that many people she knows in the West who have no connection with the East just see it as a drain on their purse, and that it is hard to convince them otherwise. As for herself, she greatly enjoyed her trip to the Far East.

On 3 October 1993, Anna says how sorry she is that the class reunion was canceled, as she had arranged to visit many of them in the Schönebeck area. She is still playing a lot of tennis as well as bridge, and they have a bridge holiday planned for Morocco. By the time of her letter of 14 July 1995, faced with more illnesses and deaths in the group, Anna says she realizes that she and her husband are also no longer so young. She will not go skiing anymore, she says, for fear of falling and breaking something. Instead they are off to Morocco again to enjoy their tennis and bridge.

On 27 April 1996, Anna says she will be brief as she will take the book to the reunion and will talk to them there (see figure 6.2). Her husband, at the age of 75, is still working. Both of them are active and happy: "We are

Figure 6.2. Class reunion, Schönebeck, 4 May 1996. Photo courtesy of Akademie der Künste, Berlin.

well, we are content, we have no financial worries, and we are lucky enough still to have each other, something we give thanks for every morning." The following year (23 February 1997), Anna is distraught over the death of her much younger brother at the age of sixty. He was like a substitute child for her, she says.

A further death returns Anna to the subject of the GDR. She tells them (4 January 1998) that her father's second wife died in Staßfurt. Anna inherited the house she had grown up in, but this brought with it all sorts of problems: "Truly, in Staßfurt it is exactly the way Johannes describes Salzelmen—25 percent unemployment, empty apartments, so that a splendid house finishes up being sold, if at all, for a price far below that in the West, and generates nothing but difficulties and frustrations." (A visit to the house in 2013 showed that it had been converted into six apartments, all of which were occupied.) Talking of a trip they made around the Baltic after sorting out these difficulties, she says she was shocked by the poverty they saw in Russia.

In May 2000, Irma Kindler inserted in the *Rundbrief* a cutting from the *Hamburger Abendblatt*, 23 July 1999, headed "Women in Men's Occupations—a Long Struggle." Anna Siebert, because of her work as a harbor engineer, was one of the women featured. In her letter of 29 May 2000, Anna comments on the cutting (reluctantly, she says) and gives an account of the press conference associated with the report:

So, I was invited by our second woman mayor (Green Party) to a press conference at the town hall, which of course I went to. There was a room full of people from the press and four women in men's occupations who had to give an account of how it had been for them. The presentations by the three women—fire service, police, ferry captain—went according to the alphabet, so that I was the last—which has its advantages. . . . The other women all started with "My name is . . . and I am 32 (or 35, or 33) years old." They looked very attractive, since they were young, and outfits like the fire service's smart uniform do make an impression. . . . But fortunately, I was able to give a much livelier and more interesting account, so that straight afterward I had the radio and television people around me. So I spoke on the radio, Hamburg 90.3, but declined to appear on television.

As well as this, Anna has been playing tennis, which is still very important for her. She and her husband have been to Tunisia for a bridge, tennis, and cultural holiday, and they will shortly be going to Sylt. They have been to Berlin to see all the work going on there: very interesting for them both, she says. She makes life sound easy and straightforward, but it is not always so. In her previous letter she mentioned a recurrence of her breast cancer and the need to have it operated on this time. She says she has been lucky again, hopes the next checkup will confirm that, and looks forward to seeing them all healthy and happy in Bad Salzelmen in September 2000.

Irma Kindler

Writing on 11 December 1990 from Hamburg, Irma also says that it is wonderful to see Germany unified, something they had never dreamed would happen. "We are together again," she says, "which is how it should be." She says they have to hope that things will improve in the future, and yet, looking at the unexpected deaths, the future is not something they can depend on: "There is only one thing to conclude: don't look too far into the future . . . just get the best from the present."

Irma and Franz were in Egypt when the Berlin Wall came down. There they only had fragments of information, so on the plane home they grabbed every newspaper they could get hold of. They felt a kind of delirious euphoria that was both disturbing and moving. Irma then resumes her more familiar, everyday tone: she is happy to report that Anna Siebert was in the winning tennis team for the Hamburg Seniors championship.

From her letter of 10 July 1991, it is clear that Irma is another who has been thinking seriously about their common history and the different fate of those who lived in the GDR compared with those who went to the West. It is significant that she sees the way of life in the West as "normal" and as the model for all of them to aspire to:

On the one hand, at our age we live our lives with more self-awareness and prefer to emphasize the nicest of our experiences. On the other hand, we really wish that this business with being at "rock bottom" could be got out of rather more quickly, so that those of us who remained in our *Heimat* can start to get some pleasure out of the reunification. There is a feeling around of "uneasiness" [in English] that we all grew up in comparable conditions and with a comparable level of expectations and yet our standards of living have diverged so markedly from one another. Still, that is no reason to turn back the wheel of history. It is and remains a miracle and a great gift that we can at least experience the beginning of the process of normalization.

Thinking back to their shared past and concerned to stress what they have always meant to one another, Irma includes a program from a musical evening held at their Schönebeck school, dated Sunday, 17 November 1940, where she, Else Hermann, Barbara Meier, and Maria Stein were among the performers. Remembering Anni Lange as well, Irma includes opera programs from events in Hamburg in the 1950s and 1960s where Anni performed and which Irma is happy to have attended. Her letter confirms a trend in this book, a shift away from the facts of the *Wende* to a concern to make a reality of their own founding myth, that they were all equal and equally valued in a Germany that remained fundamentally united.

Bringing them back to present delights, Irma rhapsodizes about a rare event: ice spreading across the Elbe, and the Alster (the lake in the center of Hamburg) freezing over. They loved the festival on the Alster, with the stalls for sausages and mulled wine, the skating and skiing, and the thousands of people out enjoying themselves.

On 18 August 1992, Irma says how much she is enjoying life and repeats her mantra from earlier entries:

> [Franz and I] are pleased about every day that we can enjoy together without health or other limitations—the fact that it can suddenly or gradually become so different from that is something we are very aware of, even just from reading your entries. If one is able to, one should in fact just live in the present and not look so much toward the future (which in any case turns out quite differently).

Accordingly, she says how heavily committed she is: "tennis, cycling, still a lot of classes, keep-fit, French, bridge (something new), choir, and along with all of that, the house and garden still have to be looked after." They have been to Prague for a long weekend with their tennis friends and to Vienna, and had a wonderful holiday in Kenya, camping at the foot of Kilimanjaro. Recently, however, she says, as if it was just an incidental matter, she was out of action for a few weeks, having broken her ankle during a keep-fit class.

Irma assertively takes up the theme of what has happened since the *Wende*: "In case anyone notices that I haven't said anything about East-West problems, these have been adequately covered already. On the personal level, there has never been a distinction between us, and that's something we should hang on to." She subsequently says (29 September 1993) that, like others, she regrets the cancellation of the planned reunion but is pleased to read all the reports in the *Rundbrief*. She says she and Franz have nothing to complain about but, "on the contrary, are thankful for everything that our good health allows us to enjoy." She mentions that they attended a reunion of Franz's wartime comrades in Odenwald; this is one of the rare references in the *Rundbrief* to the war.

On 13 July 1994, Irma again expresses her gratitude that they can enjoy their retirement with so much sport and other activities. She and Franz went skiing in Austria (see figure 6.3)—she is slightly losing her taste for that, she says, though Franz is as keen as ever—then to Berlin for a few days. In May, they had what she says is now the annual reunion of Franz's comrades from the Luftwaffe, this year in the Harz.

Year after year, Irma has said how grateful she and Franz are for all they are still able to do and for the good health that makes this possible. In her next letter (7 July 1995), after she has set out the photos from the class reunion, there is a shock for the reader:

> The reunion would be the last wonderful experience in life for my beloved Franz. Just a few days later, I lost him forever. No one could have guessed, there were no warning signs, no symptoms: full of life, in his best, most cheerful mood, doing one of the things he most loved, playing tennis, he collapsed. His tennis partner is a doctor and attended to him at once—in vain. For me the world that was so beautiful, so secure, has suddenly been shattered and it will be a long time—I can't tell how long—until it's no longer so terribly painful.
>
> I know there are many reasons to be grateful for a long and happy life together with nothing to ever seriously threaten or overshadow it. We were aware of that and were always content (which for me is the same as happy), and we fully enjoyed the past almost seven years of our retirement with many lovely trips and experiences—and then this quick, merciful death, in fact just the way one would want it....
>
> How things will go from here remains to be seen. For the past three weeks I have been working again, helping out in the Studentenwerk. It demands a lot of concentration, since office technology has not stood still in the meantime, so that by the evening I'm really shattered, and although there are other things that still need to be done, this is the way I like it.

In her letter of 21 April 1996, Irma says that a year has gone by since Franz's death. Intellectually, she says, she can come to terms with the change in her life, but emotionally it is not so easy. In the meantime, she has a second grandchild on the way. The following year (19 February 1997), Irma says she is gaining solace from being a grandmother for the second time, and from other social

Figure 6.3. Irma and Franz in Austria, winter 1994. Photo courtesy Akademie der Künste, Berlin.

activities. She took part recently in the annual reunion of Franz's "Luftwaffencrew" who, in a reversal of what has happened in the Schönebeck group, "have fully integrated me into their group without Franz; a very warm friendship has developed without being forced, since we all come, so to speak, out of the same stable." These reunions differ from the Schönebeck ones because there is always a cultural aspect: "This time we had a tour of the north Eifel area and visited the pretty town of Monschau, and of course we looked in on the old imperial city of Aachen. . . . Oh, and the next reunion will be in Weimar." Irma has also been at another reunion of her old friends from Halberstadt, where she was at boarding school during the war. Otherwise, she keeps busy:

My days are filled with keep-fit, tennis, singing in two choirs (which also means taking part in concerts and concert tours from time to time), and being called on to help with the grandchildren. One afternoon a week is devoted to our dear old primary school teacher from Bad Salzelmen, Frau P. As Johannes has mentioned, she turned ninety-five last autumn and is still mentally very sharp. We had a lovely birthday celebration for her with relatives and friends.

In her final letter (20 May 2000), Irma says she has been traveling a lot, twice to Greece and once to England. There she visited Coventry, with its new cathedral, along with the ruins of the old, destroyed cathedral. Toward the end of the year, she got pneumonia, and this made her think, she says, about herself and about the others in the group: "It seems irrefutable that people of our age get something. The news from Bad Münstereifel is very disturbing. Käthchen, I'm sending you my very warmest wishes! See you all in September (my room is already booked)."

Else Hermann

Else Hermann, writing on 29 November 1990, almost two months after reunification, has curiously little to say about the end of the GDR. November can be a gloomy time in Berlin, and this seems to have affected Else's mood. All around her there is chaos and disorder, and they are not yet out of the woods: Else uses the expression "über den Berg"—literally, "over the mountain." This foreshadows the many references in other letters to economic conditions in the East, where metaphors abound of valleys and mountains. She tells them of the recent death of Barbara Meier and of her own sorrow about so many deaths in the group. She puts her faith in the return of hope, "when it becomes brighter in the spring." As if she is happier looking back to earlier times or wants to stress how long they have been together and how much it means, Else includes a photo of herself on her tenth birthday, with some of the others also present.

Seven months later (21 June 1991), Else says she is delighted to have done some traveling. The high point was Paris. There she discovered what she assumes many of them have now discovered, how wonderful it is to see the reality of what up to then has only been seen in pictures. She is keen to travel more, "as long as the bones hold up, and the finances too." As part of the Paris trip, she stopped at her sister's in Cologne, where they organized a mini-reunion.

Else's other news is that she is moving again. When she left Prenzlauer Berg after her divorce, she moved to one of the new developments in Hellersdorf. There the physical condition and size of the apartment appealed to her—and she has a telephone! she exclaims—but over time she has felt less comfortable with it. Now she is moving to Buch, also a long way out but a long-established and more urban settlement with, as she says approvingly, "a more substantial, grown-up feel to it."

On 26 April 1992, Else says she is much happier in Buch. She was pleased to be able to visit Frieda Möller's husband in the hospital there after he had a heart attack in June 1991. Frieda says in response, "A thousand thanks again, dear Else!" Else's other news is that, since she is no longer working, she is considering leaving Berlin altogether in a couple of years and moving back to the Magdeburg area, where she feels at home.

In 1993, Else took over introducing and dispatching the *Rundbrief*. She thanks them all for this vote of confidence in her. Later in the year, she says, she will be seeing her sister in Cologne, and will visit Walter Greiswald, Astrid's husband, to pick up all the *Rundbrief* volumes.

On 10 September 1993, Else says she has moved again and is now in Weissensee, since, although she liked Buch, she felt too far out. She is in a small apartment on the ninth floor of an eleven-story block and enjoys the view and the changing light from her balcony, where she has plants growing. She knows a few people in the block but otherwise appreciates its anonymity. She would have preferred to move to Magdeburg but could not get an exchange of apartments there.

In April, Else visited Edith Friebe, of whom she says, "We were not in fact at school together, but both learned tailoring with the same master-tailor and became master-tailors ourselves!"

Else introduces Book 30 on 15 January 1994. She says she has made space for the earlier books on her shelves, where she will guard them with her life. She lists the contributors—there are now twenty-one of them—and urges them to keep involved and keep the reunions going. She is still in Berlin but is traveling a lot, in Germany and also to Florence: "Yes, traveling, there we have some catching up to do, those of us from the East, though admittedly we are limited by our health and our finances."

Since moving away from the theater, Else has a new interest in local social and cultural studies. She is surprised that objects from the former GDR are now sought after in the West, and implores them, "Please don't throw anything away. It could be valuable to collectors, even the old familiar grey carrier bags from the Konsum and the HO [the state-owned shops]!"

Introducing Book 31 (7 January 1995), Else says she tore ligaments in her shoulder, falling in the snow as she was getting off the S-Bahn in Berlin-Ostkreuz, and the injury has been slow to heal. Despite that, she has been to Vienna and then to Cologne, where she visited Elfriede Berger and went to the opera. In Book 32, the second volume of 1995 (since the *Rundbrief* is circulating ever more quickly), Else writes on 26 November of her sadness over yet another death, that of Charlotte Krüger, the orchid grower, after a number of painful years, and fondly recalls her first visit to the opera with Charlotte when they were twelve years old.

Else says in her letter of 14 September 1996 that, after a period of indecision, she is definitely leaving Berlin. By the time of her following letter (27 July 1997), she is living in a village near Schönebeck. She has enjoyed visits from many of them there, including for her seventieth birthday in April, and has almost forgotten Berlin. A further year on (11 November 1998), she seems to be at home in her village, where there is a strong, nondoctrinaire religious community that has welcomed her.

Talking in 2013 about her move back to the Schönebeck area, Else said that in Buch and even in Weissensee she was too far from the center of Berlin. This distance, and losing her professional connection to the theater, left her feeling isolated. For many years she had loved all that Berlin had to offer culturally and intellectually but had been less and less able to be involved in it. She had felt herself retreating, for better or worse, into a more modest way of being, where she would live like other people, like the rest of the Schönebeck women, concerned about the more mundane aspects of everyday life.

However, Else remained ambivalent about her *Heimat*. For her, Schönebeck had always been a center of creativity for artists and designers and writers. When she returned, this was what she was imagining, the kind of intellectually active life her father had led. What she discovered was that it was too late: creativity had largely gone from Schönebeck as the artists had died or moved away or, in the case of Hans Oldenburger, been arrested by the Stasi and "sold" to the West. Even the novelist Erik Neutsch had shifted his Schönebeck narrative out into the wider world, conjuring up a new and highly politicized *Heimat* that encompassed the GDR as a whole. In 2013, fifteen years after her move from Berlin, Else was feeling frustrated by her distance from the world of the theater and serious intellectual pursuits. She knew that very few of the women had ever really shared her interest in these.

Else introduces the next and, as it turns out, last volume of the *Rundbrief* on 18 February 2000. She is pleased to be in her permanent apartment: "Everything is new and solidly built, not so makeshift and cheap as I was used to in the prefab block in Hellersdorf." She remains active in the local community, and much of her attention is focused on it. In one of the rooms above the hall that is the church, she has set up a permanent exhibition of traditional women's bonnets from 1750 to 2000, as well as displaying samples of the special marbled paper the community is known for. She has also been helping out in the administrative office of the old people's home. At the same time, she continues to look outward toward the group, many of whom are now much nearer to her. She tells them there is great excitement about meeting on 1 September in Bad Salzelmen. She urges them all to attend, since this will be their celebration of fifty years of the *Rundbrief* and the class reunions.

Figure 6.4. Else reading from Book 1 at the 1998 reunion. Photo courtesy of Akademie der Künste, Berlin.

Decline

The Changing Nature of the Group

Book 28 of the *Rundbrief* was introduced by Astrid Greiswald, who mentioned that once again she had serious bowel problems. This was to be her last entry: the book concludes with a letter (17 March 1993) from her husband, Walter, telling them of her death in 1992. He encloses a copy of the deeply religious funeral service. Walter Greiswald says he has had the *Rundbrief* there for several months and now should send it on at last, even though he finds it hard to take up where Astrid left off. He says how close he feels to their group. Can they include him in it too, like the other widowers who have become his friends through all the reunions they have attended?

Over the first half of the decade, the group became smaller as more of them died: Erna Walter, Martha Jäger, Barbara Meier, Astrid Greiswald, and Charlotte Krüger. Others asked to be taken off the list, including Gerda Höpfner in the East and Erika Krämer in the West. Gerda remained close to those of them living in Schönebeck. Since Erika had long been semidetached from the group, at times a controversial contributor to the *Rundbrief* and a complete nonattender of the reunions, resisting all attempts to welcome her back, her departure passed without comment. On the other hand, Leni Baumann, another prolific nonattender but one who was always a warm presence in the *Rundbrief*, was welcomed back with great joy and enthusiasm when she attended the reunion at Alexisbad in the Harz. During this period, the balance tipped back toward the East, where some of the women who had dropped out of the group returned to it.

As the focus of attention shifted away from the *Wende*, the women returned to writing about their travels, their children, grandchildren and great-grandchildren, their health, and being satisfied with what they had. Part of what they had was their continuing involvement in the group with the other women, and increasingly with the husbands of the women who had died.

The widowed husbands, treated as honorary members, are a strange presence in the group. They long to be part of it, and some go out of their way to show their commitment. Barbara Meier's husband Heinz, for instance, organized the successful reunion in 1992. However, their commitment is not based on the familiarity that has come from over fifty years of growing up and growing old together and constantly feeling part of an enclosed, intimate group. The women consistently refer to their annual reunions as "class reunions," something the men can never legitimately do. In an almost stereotypical way, the men's voices tend to be different, too, once they have got over their initial emotional turmoil: bluff and hearty, louder and more dominant; this can be felt even from reading their letters. For them, what is important is the outside world of politics. They are keen to impose their views through the *Rundbrief* and are less concerned with the domestic and family matters that the women talk about and whose political significance the men do not acknowledge.

Despite this, there is a desire among the women to be inclusive and to welcome the men, as if they can at least represent emotionally the women who are no longer there. Elly Haase (1 June 1993) says that "the fact that the husbands of those of our classmates who have died remain so close to us, indicates how strongly our group has grown together." The men complicate matters, however, by getting together with new partners and edging them into the group, risking its dilution. Heinz Meier (11 May 1995) is full of enthusiasm about the reunion at Heidi Kempf's new apartment in Bad Salzelmen, and pleased that they all visited his new house by the river in Schönebeck. However, his letter conveys the awkwardness caused by the presence at the reunion of two of the men—Heinz Meier himself, and Ernst Jäger, Martha's husband—with their new partners. The tension is eased when Anna Siebert suggests that the two new women should be addressed, like all the others, with the familiar "du" form, and so be seen as full members of the group.

As the decade progresses, many of the women have less and less to say. Travel, families, and health are their main preoccupations, and there are different views of growing old. There are occasional reminders of the wider issues and some attempts to sum up what they have achieved as a group, but overall there is a sense of slowing down and bringing things to their natural conclusion.

Elfriede Berger and Käthe Sommer find their stories intertwine at this point. Elfriede (1 September 1994) has had a hard time with a complicated fracture of the wrist, while her husband is recovering from an operation that stopped them coming to the reunion. Nevertheless, they have been traveling a lot and going to concerts and the opera in Cologne. Käthe (3 September 1994) adopts as her theme the saying "Man proposes, God disposes." Her husband, who has run an eye clinic for decades, in Magdeburg, in Schönebeck, and finally in Bad Münstereifel after their expulsion from GDR, now has eye problems himself, with only 10 percent vision left.

In 1997, Elfriede's husband died. She had to wind up his legal practice and get used to doing things without him: traveling, trips to the theater, concerts, and the opera and so on. Some of these she does with Käthe Sommer, who otherwise is tied up looking after her very frail mother. Elfriede tells them on 27 May 1999 that she is still traveling a lot. She was on a study tour to Italy and will shortly be going to America with a friend. She recommends meditation and yoga as ways to overcome one's troubles. She also recommends that they have a class reunion on 1 September 2000 to celebrate their fifty years together. After that, taking up a suggestion from Leni Baumann, she suggests they meet every two years.

On 26 June 2000, Elfriede tells them of an excellent study tour to Andalucia and a year of concerts, theater, museums, a visit to Berlin, and Christmas with Käthe Sommer and her husband, commenting that "good friends don't leave you on your own." Then, as so often happens, she has to bring them bad news: Käthe sends her greetings to them all but does not want to have the *Rundbrief* as she is very ill. She has been in various hospitals since February, being treated initially for heart problems until finally it was discovered that she had a tumor pressing on her spine. She was operated on and could sit in a wheelchair for a while, but now is back in bed, where Elfriede spends several hours a day with her. Elfriede says she herself will probably not come to the class reunion now. A typed letter tucked into the last book announces that Käthe Sommer died in November 2000.

Heidi Kempf (writing on 1 February 1995) says that 1994 was a good year. As well as moving house, she went on a *Kur* in Bad Wiessee in Bavaria, somewhere quite out of reach when the GDR still existed. She also had a twelve-day cruise to Norway, where she found the landscape "enchanting." In February 1999, she tells them she has been to Ireland with Maria Stein and that they will soon be going to Cornwall and London together. She is also attending classes for "English for Seniors" and is actively and consciously enjoying her retirement.

Elly Haase (1 March 1995, Schönebeck) is amazed at how the years have gone by: they are all approaching seventy, and it is five years since the *Wende*. Looking back, she is happy with her life, but with a significant reservation: "Actually it's been an eventful life, rich in experiences and events that I would not have wanted to miss. But still, I would like to have experienced all of that ideally as a hedgehog, able to hide away all one's vulnerable parts and only display one's spines to the outside world!"

Despite the end of the GDR, housing and property problems continue to exist, but Elly has to think differently about them in the capitalist world, since they lease space to other businesses:

> Of the three people living with us, two are in need of constant care. That is both sad and hard on the nerves. On top of that, our leaseholders are suffering problems with their wallets! They are not shy of making demands, but paying us is a different matter. And if no money comes in, then we are close to going broke. Up to now, "competition" and "going broke" were just words, but now we are learning from experience just what they mean.

On a happier note, she is now singing in one of the local women's choirs and finds that even the old folk tunes are "balm for the soul."

In her letter of 14 March 2000, Elly says she is pleased to have made it to the year 2000. She has talked with Hertha Pieper on the phone about this and about the first meeting in 1950. She says it is a shame that only eight of the fourteen who appear in the photo of that meeting are still alive to see this anniversary. She seeks once again to sum up their lives: "We certainly have a full, eventful life behind us, and still have not started to get bored. At least, that's how it is for us. We are satisfied with things and just hope that we can remain relatively healthy and get by from day to day without needing outside help."

Sabine Kleber (12 March 1997) is sorry to see how short the entries are in the *Rundbrief* and how little there is to read in it. Once there was interesting news about the children, and then the grandchildren, but, she asks, have they too grown beyond their sweet, endearing age? And what about the desire to travel that everyone once had? "Well, I admit, the old bones are getting weak (and I mean that literally). So maybe we just prefer to enjoy the view out the window and indulge ourselves. I myself have a lovely view from my balcony on to part of the Pfälzer Wald, the woods that are so magnificent whatever the season." She says she has been to Ireland and Andalucia with her older sister but is pleased that the long trips are now behind her. On 8 May 1999, she is packing to go to St. Petersburg with her sister: "This is likely to be the last study trip of this sort, since the effort required is becoming too much for me now. But I really have seen enough of the world and am quite content with that."

Sabine has never had children of her own, but central to her life are a friend's three children, aged thirteen, eleven, and five. Having been very close to them all since they were born, she sees them as virtual grandchildren, and they all go on holiday together. On 12 June 2000, Sabine says she is typing now because she has trouble writing. She is the first of them to use what she still refers to as a "word processor." She finds it difficult but sees it can be useful. Her substitute grandchildren, who cope so easily with new technologies, laugh at her problems. They are happy to be able to teach her what to do and are a great joy to her, she says: "They bring a lot of fun and variety into my life. This is something I think all of you who have grandchildren will confirm."

Edith Friebe (18 July 2000) says that her aunt, for whom she had long been caring, has died. She misses her terribly and needs to reorganize her life to avoid sinking into depression. Her brother, known to a lot of them, died too, in November. Like many of the others, she is increasingly aware of the passing of the years and says that it is important "to enjoy to the full the time that is left to us." She is looking forward to a visit from Maria Stein, and to traveling with her to Alsace, her first holiday since the trip in 1989 to Denver, Colorado. She hopes to make it to the class reunion in September.

The Shadow of the GDR

The changes taking place in the outside world still impinge on the group, though it is mostly the men who comment on such matters. Helmut Liebmann (29 August 1993) is enthusiastic about one benefit of reunification: "Here is the good news: after twenty-five years of applying for one, at last I have a telephone.... And just now the telephone rang and it was Elfriede on the line. What a lovely surprise! With a telephone, life just feels different. Can those of you in the West understand that?"

Meanwhile, Johannes Schneider is now mostly living in Coswig, near Dresden, with his new partner, Andrea. He is back in Schönebeck from time to time and keen to describe it in his report of 1 April 1996 for the benefit of those not living there:

> There are just a few buildings left of our former coconut matting factory. If only my father-in-law had known that! The old tractor works (Weltrad) has also been torn down, except for its facade. All the large works have effectively long ceased to exist. This is reflected in the condition of the job market. Saxony-Anhalt has the highest rate of unemployment and Schönebeck the highest number of people unemployed....
>
> A row of new houses has sprung up on the river bank. That is where Heinz Meier is now living. On the way out of town in the direction of Welsleben, the "garden city" (detached houses) has been built. The Russian compound adjoining it is still just as our purveyors of culture left it.

... In the spring we had a celebratory trip; that is, to where I was at the end of the war: Husum [on the North Sea coast, near the Danish border]. It was near Husum that I got a lucky shot from a Spitfire on the last day of the war—it saved me having to go into a POW camp. . . . In autumn we were on Ischia. At the beginning of November we were swimming in the hotel pool that was fed from a hot spring (42 degrees Celsius).

In his next letter (3 December 1997, Coswig), Johannes tells them yet again that economic conditions in Schönebeck are disastrous: "All the large factories have closed down (exports from the East), unemployment has reached 26 percent! And the trend is upward. Not the slightest prospect of things getting better!!"

Helmut Liebmann (14 December 1997) says that there are lots of new residential areas springing up around Wismar and these are "selling like hot cakes." On the other hand, the old GDR prefabricated blocks are continuing to empty out.[14] He is happy that all his children and grandchildren have jobs and go on trips "that we in our youth never even dreamed of."

Elly Haase (18 August 1997) has not yet forgotten the GDR. They have had their house and the attached buildings painted. During the time of the GDR, she says, the paint would never stick properly, but they are hoping they will be lucky this time.

Walter Greiswald (6 June 1999, Sinzig) wants them not to forget their recent history and points out that things really have improved since the *Wende*:

> It's almost a decade now since Germany was reunited. There were so many tears of joy, "madness" was the word used to describe our relief. The barriers came down, people were in one another's arms, the Trabis came rolling into the West.
>
> It also could have been different if the man with the power to the east of us had said "Njet." Our politicians forget that and act as if it was their achievement.
>
> In September I had a few days on the island of Rügen. It was a long journey there by coach through West and East, and you could see that in the new states in the East a lot of work had been carried out. New windows, doors, roofs, people had been painting both inside and out. There was fruit, vegetables, good coffee, flowers and so on.

An Echo from the Nazi Period?

Late in this decade, there is a curious incident that throws a new light on one of the prominent women, Frieda Möller. It starts with an account by Sabine Kleber in February 1998.

Sabine says how much she enjoyed the class reunion in Gommern. However, when she got to Magdeburg to go home, her train was canceled, and as she rushed on to another, she was ambushed in the corridor by two men who stole her purse. It is not just this that upsets her: "What really annoys me about it is that it happened in our *Heimat*. When I'm traveling abroad in places where pickpocketing is the order of the day, I'm prepared for it and behave accordingly, most of the time." She warns them to look out at the station in Magdeburg for "these foreign bands," although until then there was no indication that the thieves were anything but local.

Frieda Möller's letter (10 February 1999, Barby) responds to Sabine's report. It contains an astonishing section that seems entirely out of character, after what she has written for nearly fifty years:

> Hasn't it become an awful time? The lax courts mean that criminals have no fear of punishment. If things don't start to get a bit stricter, conditions will become like those during the war. My recommendation: single cells with no radio, television or newspapers, and no time outside! Then some of them would think more carefully about whether better behavior and loving your neighbor might be more appropriate. Rapists should be operated on and turned into women. Tough, but without that there's no peace in this land.

The brutal phrasing in this section of the letter appears even stranger when compared with the ordinariness of the account following it, talking of the lovely time they had visiting Else, and the improvements being made in their street, the upgrading of the water, sewerage, and telephone infrastructure.

Leni Baumann (25 April 1999) also comments on Sabine's account, since something similar, but with a very different outcome, happened to her, too, after the class reunion:

> Hertha and I had driven to Bernburg to see the castle. We climbed up the hill and just before the top we sat down on a bench for a rest. And when we set off again, I forgot to pick up my handbag! Everything was in there: documents, money and so on. I had nothing but the keys in my trouser pocket—including the car key. So I drove back to Braunschweig that same day. And then, a miracle: two or three days later I heard from the police that my bag had been handed in at a police station in Bernburg, with everything listed, money and documents, not a penny missing. And I had around 700 Deutschmarks in my bag! The honest finder was from Halle, had found my bag while she was out walking in the grounds of the castle, and taken it to the police station. It goes without saying that she got a good reward from me. So it can turn out that way too.

Here, as so often over the lifetime of the group, no one is allowed to swamp the *Rundbrief* with gloom and pessimism; something negative is always followed by something positive. Equally, however, no one confronts Frieda over the outburst in her letter, with its distant echo of statements in the Nazi period.

The Slow Death of the Group

Back in February 1990 when she introduced Book 26 of the *Rundbrief* from Sinzig in the West, Astrid Greiswald linked the political events with their experience as a group, declaring, "Oh, what fast-moving times we live in! . . . How thankful we can be that we have been able to really and truly enjoy this wonderful bond between us all for forty years now." Similarly, there was a special entry in Book 26, dated 1 September 1990, celebrating the fiftieth anniversary of their decision as young girls to meet again ten years later in Magdeburg, and the fortieth anniversary of that meeting. This entry presented them as a happy, united group at the reunion Sabine Kleber hosted in the woods near Kaiserslautern. There were short notes from many of them, all saying how wonderful it was to be together again for this special reunion, the first without borders dividing them.

But there were divisions in the group too, and no longer a central theme holding them together. The need for their founding myth about the underlying unity of Germany no longer existed, since Germany was in fact united again. It is curious to look back at the letters from the 1990s and see that for many years, the former border that had meant so much to them for so long still seemed to be there, a shadowy fault line that continued to separate the two sides of the group, making them see the world differently and struggle to feel that Germany really was a single country again.

Elfriede Berger's comments about starting with forty Marks are one example of this. More subtle are the accounts of travel and holidays, which make clear that it is still the ones in the West who can travel the world without thinking about it, while those from the East mostly travel closer to home, feel that this is a real privilege, and worry about how much things cost.

Another example comes from Anna Siebert's letters. These convey a sense that different subgroups within the group have different perceptions of the East: some are unconcerned about it, settling happily into their own feelings of superiority, while others are deeply concerned about what happens there and its impact on the women in the former GDR. In all her categories, however, there is still a sense of division, with the area of the former GDR seen as a different place with special needs, not yet or not quite part of Germany as a whole.

Still, there are signs of real closeness. Some of the women from the West have made or remade connections—Edith Friebe and Maria Stein; Hertha Pieper and Leni Baumann—which seem to erase the border. From 1995, Gerda Höpfner no longer writes in the *Rundbrief* but continues to meet up regularly with some of the other women in Schönebeck. These small groups and pairings are particularly important for the women concerned, and start to appear more significant than the group itself.

In the end, the class reunions become central to holding the group together and bringing in many of these smaller groupings. However, even the reunions are not straightforward. Too many of the women have died, and around half of those left do not attend because of a lack of interest, distance, illness, or being away. In her letter of 15 January 1994, Else Hermann pleads with them to get more involved; five years later, Heidi Kempf (5 February 1999) complains again that too many are losing interest.

At least three of the planned reunions were canceled, one for reasons not explained, the second because of the cost, the third because it was said to be the wrong time of the year. In any case, the reunions that did take place show how diluted the group became during the 1990s, with husbands, widowers, and new partners threatening to outnumber the core group. At least one reunion (1997) was organized by one of the widowers and his new partner; she had been at school with the Schönebeck women but was five years younger and, according to Else Hermann, was never fully accepted into the group. Meanwhile, as the reunions faced problems, the *Rundbrief* itself started to circulate ever faster and with ever shorter contributions.

Despite the steady decline of the group, there were countercurrents that kept it alive. When the drama of the *Wende* was over, new routines and new patterns of living were emerging, establishing once again something that they as a group could agree to recognize as normal. This returned a certain power to the group: what was "normal" was what they determined to be normal, as if they had created both the new society and the new routines that were their way of being in it. There was considerable self-deception in this, but that is often true of assertions of power. The unspoken purpose of the group's reassertion of its own power was to bring them together and hold them together around a common understanding: their loyalty to the group and to the *Heimat* over the past forty years meant that they had both the right to be proud of themselves and the obligation to stay united.

Edith Friebe (8 September 1995), who had lived so far away for so long, says of Schönebeck: "Yes, no matter how far away one might be from it, it remains our *Heimat*. Where we were born, where we grew up, where we have our friends: that is where our roots lie." Writing about the latest reunion, Käthe Sommer (15 May 1997) says how much she loved being back in the "old *Heimat*." However, some of them have a much wider view of what constitutes the *Heimat*. For Irma Kindler, it has become Berlin, which also appears to stand for the wider area of the former GDR or, because of its combination of the East and the West, for the united Germany she wanted to believe in. Irma says in her letter of 17 July 1994, "In earlier times I was frequently in Berlin since all our relations lived there. Since the war I had only been there twice for a few hours (once being for the class reunion at Else's) and yet always had an immediate sense of being back in my *Heimat*."

Frieda Möller's long letter of 31 August 2000 is the last entry in the *Rundbrief*. It is almost a throwback to the earlier days, focusing on the things that have interested them all for so long: families and travel, fond memories of earlier years, the time when they were still divided, and its passing:

> Recently I was talking with Karl-Heinz about earlier reunions when we were all still so very young. How cheerful we often were, and we happily look back on so much fun. Thank God the Wall is no more. Finally, to be able to get around, as free as a bird. Only as time has gone on has it become clear to us just *how* tightly we were shut in and *how* closely we were spied upon. Unfortunately, some of these villains have once again managed to find a comfortable little niche for themselves.

She concludes with good wishes to everyone and particularly warm greetings to those not able to attend the class reunion the next day. The group, she implies, is strong and will endure. The photos she includes seem to sum up what all of them are involved in: travel, with a visit to the Bodensee and skiing in Thuringia; the family, represented by her grandchildren, enjoying time together on New Year's Day; and, as a central image of *Heimat*, a quiet walk in the woods.

In the end, although nostalgia for, or rediscovery of, the *Heimat* was a strong force, it could not replace the grand vision that had united and energized the group. With an increasing sense of weariness and of their time having passed, the group moved quietly toward its own dissolution. They could remain friends—good friends, some of them—but the need for the group itself had disappeared, and old age did the rest. After fifty years, Book 36 would be the last volume of the *Rundbrief*, and their meeting in September 2001 the last class reunion. There the decision was made to send the books to be archived, with the women hoping that one day they would be discovered by someone who would write about them and make sense of their lives.

Looking Back Later: The Principal Figures

The interviews that took place more than ten years later gave a different view of what had happened over the decades, and a sense of how the principal women had moved on since the end of the *Rundbrief* and the reunions.

Anna Siebert

Sitting in her comfortable ground-floor apartment, looking out into the lush garden, Anna Siebert came across at once as someone who was used to telling her story and was proud of how her life had gone. At the same time, she was still fighting her battles with the men she had worked with, and still trying to prove she had been their equal. What became clear was that the battles had taken place not just at work but also at the formal political level, with Hamburg politicians frequently interfering (as she saw it) with the work of the harbor authority and her work specifically.

Anna was personally warm and generous. She was also sometimes critical of or mocking toward the other women. She was very interested in her own family's story and the inevitable interaction between East and West, but not so sure that the group's overall story was worth telling. One surprising comment was that she had known Erika Krämer's Karl: he had visited them when she and Erika were living in Berlin, and although the story of his imprisonment and disappearance was terrible and tragic—for Erika too—Anna had found him an arrogant, unsympathetic person.

Irma Kindler

Irma Kindler came across as intelligent, straightforward, direct, pleased with how she had coped in the difficult times, and modest about what she had done. She encouraged me to ask more questions by letter and answered them at length.

It was clear to me that Irma was one of the powerful people in the group, and that she exercised her power in a quiet, unassuming way. She felt strongly about the group and about the fate of all the women in it, and they all appreciated her close involvement and her determination to make things work. Her genuine concern for others reassured them and comforted them when comfort was needed. In a way, however, Irma also seemed somewhat emotionally detached when talking about dramatic events in her own life. I asked her how she had felt during the dangerous journey home from her *Reichsarbeitsdienst* camp, or when crossing the border into the Soviet Zone. Her answer was that they did not concern themselves so much with their feelings back then. Much later, in her letter after Franz's death, she says that she and Franz were "always content (which for me is the same as happy)." She was used to having things orderly and under control and was not given to outbursts of strong emotion. She was understandably pleased about Franz's "quick, merciful death," and talks as if being reasonable about things will make them manageable and acceptable. Nevertheless, it is clear to the reader of her letters in the *Rundbrief* that she was beside herself with grief. She goes back to work, and works until she is "shattered," which is how she likes it, she says. It is significant that she attributes feeling shattered to her work, not to her grief, even though she also knows she is using her work to mask or overcome her feelings.

Hertha Pieper

When I met Hertha Pieper, she was frail and suffering, yet also warm and emotionally generous, with a wry, self-deprecating sense of humor. She was straightforward about her involvement in the BDM. She was ready to reflect on her past, suggesting her commitment to the Nazi cause was marginal and her interest had been in singing and playing and getting the youngest girls to enjoy themselves. She talked about her detention in the camp in Paderborn, which she did not feel was unjust. The interview reflected her letters: her children were central to her satisfaction with her life, and here they were, all of them, interested in what she had to say and sometimes astonished by what I reminded her she had said in the *Rundbrief*.

When I asked her about her time in the LPG, she smiled and said it had been wonderful for her. She was surprised and puzzled to hear of her earlier complaints about the pressure from the authorities and the forced collectivization. In the LPG she had a working day that ended at a reasonable time; she had training, holidays, and free time. They had been lucky to have a good person in overall charge, she said, and had managed to keep going with both crops and animals. The children interjected here, saying how good it had made their childhood, and how they had enjoyed so many opportunities in the GDR. What they missed was the sense of the collective, they all said. And they still resented the way people from the West had come over and bought up and stripped out so much of their industry.

Some of these now very grown-up children had stuck with the LPG and had made it profitable. Others had been successful in other work over the years. None of them wanted to see a return to the GDR. None of them had joined "the party," but there had been pressure to do so, even toward the end, if they wanted to progress, and the temptation had been there. Hertha listened and smiled, proud of them and of all they had done, and happy with the life she had led.

Else Hermann

In our first interview in October 2012, Else Hermann was both keen to talk and a little wary. She had so much to say, so much she wanted to get across to me and to explain about what life had been like in the GDR, and about the Schönebeck group as a whole. She went from talking about the church she was involved in to expressions of hostility to much that was going on in the West, with occasional favorable comments about Marx and his thinking. She was keen for me to write about the women and the *Rundbrief*, but most concerned that I should be fair and balanced and not portray those of them who stayed in the GDR as foolish or gullible or as victims of the Stasi. I had to realize, she insisted, that the Stasi was not directly part of everyday life for them.

Else became very enthusiastic about the Schönebeck project, and I was able to visit her many times. Our interviews ranged far and wide. They were always serious. Although we inevitably had *Kaffee und Kuchen*, Else had no time for small talk or concerns about her health. She wanted probing questions, ones that made her think and which she could respond to with challenges to any of my assumptions she disagreed with. She often pointed to or sought out books from her shelves, or objects that were significant to her: her Christof Grüger shawl, for instance, or her gravestone, waiting in the corner, missing only the date of her death.

Else was proud of the whole story of the Schönebeck women, of how they had started out and stuck together, despite everything, and of their *Rundbrief*. One of the many reasons she had for being so involved and for contributing so much before and after the group's dissolution was that she wanted to keep the group alive beyond the death of its members. The group had meant a lot to her, and she had been central to it, even though her personality, her attitudes, and her different way of being in the world had often made her feel that she was only on the edge of it.

Else was also proud of what she had achieved in the theater and in her work developing new talent for the theater. She greatly appreciated the opportunities she had had in the GDR for her own intellectual development, and often harked back to what she had learned from her father. She was open about the nature of her marriage to Bruno and about his homosexuality, but not explicit about her own sexuality.

Else's stubborn, demanding side was often difficult for others to deal with. It was useful in the interviews, however. Although she could move rapidly from one point to another, she was concerned to be rigorous about how she answered my questions and was happy to be brought back to the central point. She always wanted to provide as much information as possible and always had more to say, even though she knew that what she said was just her view of how things had been, or how they were still. Many of her apparently incidental asides were helpful. They can be seen in Freudian terms not as incidental but as her way of rounding out a point she had not consciously intended to make and of ensuring I knew things that she was less keen to say directly: about the Stasi, for instance, or sex and sexuality.

Else said many surprising things in our conversations. At one point, she revealed a hidden sadness that she had not felt able to talk about in the *Rundbrief*. The GDR made a point of providing assistance to "third world" countries, particularly where there was a chance of reducing Western influence. It brought many young people to the GDR to study. Else met and became very close friends with a young man from Ghana who was studying to become a pharmacist. Such students had to return to their home country at the end of their studies in order to apply their skills there. Else was very upset when her friend had to leave, but they agreed to keep in touch. She was puzzled not to hear any more from him, and only learned some time later that he had become ill and died shortly after returning home. This was all too sensitive and painful to reveal in the letters; she felt the other women would not have understood and might even have disapproved of this friendship, although she was careful not to accuse them of underlying racism.

Else benefited from having a committed and patient personal helper who attended to many household affairs as well as taking Else shopping or to medical appointments, or sometimes driving her out to her old haunts. During the time I knew Else, she became less able to walk or to climb stairs, so moved from her upstairs apartment with its view out into the trees and the square to a ground-floor, much smaller apartment. She still furnished and arranged her new apartment to look like the previous one and like her much earlier apartment in Prenzlauer Berg. By this time, she was suffering from the throat cancer that would kill her. She had consciously decided not to be treated or operated on but to let it run its course.

In 2016, Else moved into a hospice in Magdeburg, the city she had always felt was her real *Heimat*. To the extent that it was possible, she laid out her room to look like all of her previous ones. During my visits to her there, she displayed a wistful, softer side, knowing her life was coming to an end and hoping it would not be a long and painful process. Nevertheless, she insisted on hearing more questions and giving more answers. She continued to look outward, too. She was concerned about "Brexit" and annoyed and frustrated at how little Germany and the West understood about Russia. In her view, they had missed an opportunity at the end of the GDR to reduce the chance of conflict between Russia and the West, and could have learned from those of them who had lived with the Russians in the GDR. She knew she had more to say and was keenly anticipating my next visit in November, but died quite suddenly in October 2016.

The Impact of the Interviews

After my first visit to Else, the news of my interest and the interviews created a wave of excitement among those of the group still left. They found themselves contacting one another again after long gaps. Connections that had been lost were revived: suddenly Else had a call from Hertha, whom she had not spoken to for some years. Irma and Anna kept in touch after deciding to arrange my initial interview with them together at Anna's apartment. Else and Irma had kept in touch, but my involvement led them to speak more often on the phone and to write to each other frequently.

Attempts, with Else's help, to track down some of the others mostly led nowhere, and sometimes to the realization that yet another of them had died.

Else only learned of Leni Baumann's death from me. She was upset that Leni's relatives had not thought to let her know. Else's disappointment was personal but also involved a broader realization: when the women died, the connections died with them. The Schönebeck women's children had been interested and often involved in the group but had no long-term commitment to the group as such. Other relatives had no interest at all and, for the outside world, the group might as well never have existed. It was this that Else sought to change. The Schönebeck group was too important for her, confirming as it did that she too, so often alone, isolated, and awkward, had been part of an exceptional community of women who had entertained, comforted, reassured, and stood by one another for over sixty years and, in doing so, had turned their own myth into reality.

Conclusion: Reunited?

Both the FRG and the GDR claimed for many years to be committed to the reunification of Germany. In practice, after the early 1950s, they played down this commitment and failed to use it to energize the population or to create a sense of solidarity across the inner-German border. For each of them, unification would have to be on their own terms, reflecting their own ideological approach and their own founding myths, or not at all. Since this looked so unlikely, neither side was anticipating reunification before the opportunity suddenly arose at the end of the 1980s.

Equally, the Schönebeck women were taken by surprise by the *Wende*, the collapse of the GDR, and reunification. From one *Rundbrief* volume to the next, they were able to shift from being politically wary, self-censoring citizens of their respective states, constantly aware of the power that could be used against the members of the group in the East, to scornful, angry, puzzled, and, above all, outspoken critics of almost everything the GDR authorities had done over the previous forty years. However, the letters for this last decade also reveal how difficult the speed and unexpectedness of the change were for them.

Some of the difficulties were obvious: the economic uncertainty facing many of them and their families, particularly the next generation; the social upheaval that made them feel less secure; the differences in attitudes and perceptions that were revealed between those in the West and those in the East; and having to adjust at a time when they were older and more likely to be ill, frail, or alone.

Another problem, however, was one they did not recognize: neither the society around them nor the group itself allowed the women in the East to acknowledge how much they had lost through the *Wende*. The refusal to allow space to mourn their losses involved an exercise of power by the women in the West, who mostly expected those in the East to be pleased and grateful and in no way ambivalent about the *Wende*. There are hints in the letters of loss and suffering—missing the collective, for example, or worries over the value of their savings—but there is, as ever, an unstated requirement to appreciate the present and be optimistic about the future. The irony is that the group had always been so good at collective mourning for the loss of any of its own members. Faced with something as dramatic as the *Wende* and the end of the GDR, however, they could not see how traumatic these events might be. The requirement to hold together and to adapt to a new version of everyday life made most of them blind to the losses incurred.

The letters written after the *Wende* reveal an underlying problem with the way the group functioned. This was to do with their unspoken agreement to remain optimistic and not raise awkward issues from their earlier years. As a result, they lacked the capacity to stand back and reflect on the past. As if Edith Friebe had broken the group's rules, very few of the women responded to her account of the fate of the Jewish family they had known during their time at school. For most of them, this appears to have been consciously or unconsciously put together with the whole of the Nazi period as something they could not bring themselves to think or talk about. Openly criticizing the GDR regime was something they could unite around; looking further back at the earlier German dictatorship was not something they were inclined to do. Nor could they look at how some of them, disoriented by the changes around them and a new sense of insecurity, found themselves adopting attitudes and using language that harked back to the Nazi propaganda of their much earlier years.

Notes

1. "Note des MfAA der DDR an ungarisches Außenministerium," *Neues Deutschland*, 13 September 1989.
2. Weber, *Die DDR*, 109–10.
3. See, for instance, "In den Kämpfen unserer Zeit muß sich jeder Genosse Tag für Tag neu bewähren," *Volksstimme Magdeburg*, 8 September 1989.
4. Steiner, *The Plans That Failed*, 183. Labor shortages meant that the number of foreign "contract workers" in the GDR increased from twenty-four thousand in 1981 to ninety-four thousand in 1989. Sixty thousand of the contract workers were Vietnamese: Mike Dennis, Eva Kolinsky, Karin Weiss, "Erfolg in der Nische—Die vietnamesischen Vertragsarbeiter in der DDR und in Ostdeutschland," in *Erfolg in der Nische? Die Vietnamesen in der DDR und in Ostdeutschland* (Münster, 2003), 8.
5. *Volksstimme Magdeburg*, 9 October 1989.
6. *Volksstimme Magdeburg*, 20 October 1989.
7. It later became clear that 343,854 people had left the GDR for the FRG in 1989: *Volksstimme Magdeburg*, 6 January 1990.
8. Leask, "Humiliation as a Weapon."

9. Dodds and Allen-Thompson, *The Wall in My Backyard*; Griebner and Kleint, *Starke Frauen*; Rellin, *Klar bin ich eine Ost-Frau!*
10. Ulrike Helwerth and Gislinde Schwarz, *Von Muttis und Emanzen: Feministinnen in Ost- und Westdeutschland* (Frankfurt/Main, 1995), 187–89.
11. Initially, some of the women use the terms "Wessi" and "Ossi" for those in the West and the East respectively. The terms were soon seen as derogatory and effectively banned from the *Rundbrief*.
12. On the sense of loss at the ending of involvement in work, see Barbara Rocksloh-Papendieck, *Verlust der kollektiven Bindung: Frauenalltag in der Wende* (Pfaffenweiler, 1995), 176, 179–87.
13. V. I. Lenin, "One Step Forward, Two Steps Back," in *Selected Works*, vol. 1 (Moscow, 1970).
14. Wismar, a Hanseatic port, benefited after the *Wende* from being close to Hamburg and Lübeck. Unlike Schönebeck, it attracted new investment and new residents. Nevertheless, its population dropped from 58,000 in 1987 to 42,330 by 2014 and has only recently started to increase again.

Conclusion
The Schönebeck Women and Their Group

The Group's Belief in Its Power

The stories of the women in the Schönebeck group give a striking picture of individual lives across many decades. During this time, external events shaped their social and political attitudes and the ways they lived far more than most of them recognized. They preferred to think they were making informed choices and acting in accordance with them. They wanted to believe that they had a substantial amount of control over their lives, not that so much of what they did was determined by others.

The way the Schönebeck women built and maintained their group perpetuated this belief in their power. The group developed its own ways of seeing the world, and its own rules on how to behave. As if they were creating a protective cocoon, the women spun around themselves a web of myths, expectations, and shared beliefs that helped to deflect or repulse attacks from the outside. From this safe space, they could venture out into the world, knowing that the group was there to support, comfort, and reassure them if times became difficult. Through their letters and reunions, they reinforced one another's views that even if there were problems and frustrations, they had managed to ensure that their everyday lives were satisfying and enjoyable. Instead of seeing their lives as broken up by historical and personal ruptures, they created a collective "narrative of continuity,"[1] one that confirmed their power over their own lives and justified their underlying optimism.

At times the optimism on display seems a little forced. Certainly it was tested by food shortages and housing problems, such as those experienced by Irma Kindler when she and Franz had to build a shelter for themselves in a ruined building in Hanover, or by Anna Siebert during the Berlin Blockade. Similarly, it looked misplaced when alarming events were reported, such as the arrest of Erika Krämer and her fiancé, and the imprisonment of Gerda Höpfner's husband in the 1950s. The women's determination, in Barbara Meier's words, to "pick out the best of the cherries from the large cake that is everyday life" caused them to look away from what the reader of their letters can see so clearly, that some of the cherries were riddled with worms.

The Schönebeck women's optimism amounted at times to defensive denial, which served to strengthen the group and hold it together. Their narrative of continuity asserted that everything was going well: their families, their jobs, their homes, their holidays, their imagined Germany, and the group itself. Denial defended them against the threat of collapse and chaos. Denial encouraged them to believe they were in charge of their own lives and not subject to irresistible external forces.

Complying without Noticing

The women's behavior raises a fundamental question: how could they see themselves as acting freely and autonomously? After all, they complied willingly with the requirements of their own group, and shaped their lives to fit in with the demands made, explicitly or implicitly, by those who constructed the political and social framework within which they lived.

One answer is that they resorted to what Fulbrook calls "anticipatory obedience." Speaking of the GDR, she says that the Stasi's real strength was to "produce the effect that millions of people behaved towards one another with anxiety, self-control and suspicion. They ensured that if you told a political joke you automatically lowered your voice. Anticipatory obedience spread through every sinew of society and intimidated a whole nation."[2] There are many examples in the letters and in the comments about the reunions that demonstrate this process. The acts of self-censorship stand out.

There are various ways of considering this tendency to comply with rules both stated and unstated. One is to take Gramsci's analysis of the power of hegemonic beliefs or cultures and apply it to the women's behavior.[3] In both the East and the West there were dominant beliefs that were explicitly promoted as well as reinforced in more subtle ways: through newspaper articles and opinion pieces, films, radio and television programs, and even the way social, community, and political events were organized and framed, regardless of their explicit message. A relevant example is that political parties held their meetings at times and places that were more likely to exclude than to include women. The message was always clear: it is men who take the lead in politics. The power of such an idea was that it was accepted and internalized without even being noticed.

A similar explanation of why the Schönebeck women mostly accepted the power exercised by men, both in the GDR and in the FRG, is offered by the philosopher Martha Nussbaum. Nussbaum says that people "adjust their preferences to what they think they can achieve, and also to what their society tells them a suitable achievement is for someone like them. Women and other deprived people frequently exhibit such 'adaptive preferences,' formed under unjust background conditions. These preferences will typically validate the status quo."[4]

However, the status quo is not fixed over time. For the young women at the end of the war, it was "natural" to defer to men and to take charge of the household and look after the children at home without going out to work. Their views were based on attitudes from the Weimar period (and earlier), which merged with or were overridden by attitudes toward women from the Nazi era. There was a tension here between pressures to live within and for the collective, and the temptations of an individualist approach. The historian Moritz Föllmer argues that within the collectivist practice of the Nazis, individual agency remained important and was promoted by the Nazis. For him, Nazism should be understood "through the prism of a distinct form of modern individuality rather than as a collectivist ideology and regime."[5] Over the decades after the war, the women continued to experience this tension, clinging to their own collective as well as going beyond it to lead distinctly individual lives, which gradually changed their attitudes and those of the group.

Despite the modernizing tendencies of the postwar period, underlying attitudes in both societies about the roles of men and women continued to form a restrictive framework for women in particular. The Schönebeck women generally accepted this framework and adapted their preferences to make the most of life as it was presented to them. They committed themselves to enjoying it and remaining optimistic.

However, just as the status quo is not fixed, so hegemonic power is not absolute, and there were women in the group who challenged it implicitly and explicitly. Many in the group looked with a wary longing at those who had broken out of the framework put in place for them and who gave glimpses of what women could achieve if they dared to try. The tendency to see Anna Siebert, Anni Lange, Leni Baumann, and Else Hermann as role models implied a wish for something better for themselves, for a world where women could be seen as strong and equal, able to do "men's jobs," and able to challenge at least some of the conventions that keep women subservient.

When they looked at these role models, they saw one of their number who did not have children despite trying; one whose husband was their child's primary carer; one who never married and had no children; and one who married late and unconvincingly and also had no children. Such women were not just working differently and achieving more, they were also challenging some of the fundamental assumptions of the group itself. This affected even those who most wished to maintain the group's early, somewhat narrow values and attitudes. They could not fail to notice that, as a result of the role models' achievements and prominence, they themselves were slowly becoming more liberal and flexible than they had anticipated.

Elly Haase and the Limits of Optimism

An interesting example of a woman pulled in both directions, toward compliance on the one hand and toward challenging the exercise of hegemonic power on the other, is Elly Haase. Elly resented from the start the power used to stop her going to university. She was an independent spirit who made extraordinary train journeys around Germany in the early years after the war, when most of the Schönebeck women were happily adapting to the new circumstances and setting out to lead conventional lives in accordance with what was now expected of them.

Having been refused entry to university, Elly did not become a teacher, nurse, or factory worker, as might have been expected, but trained and worked as a carpenter with her father, later running the business herself. She would have been under pressure on many occasions as the SED sought, for class reasons, to reduce the number of independent craft workers in the GDR. In her letters, she sometimes refers directly or indirectly to this pressure, to the way it wears her down, and to finding a way to resist. At the same time, Elly is particularly keen to find a husband, and risks being seen as superficial and even ridiculous when trying to get the others to help her.

What helps Elly throughout is her sense of humor, combined with her clever, often subtle use of language. While many of the women write interesting accounts of what they are doing, Elly steers clear of the easy resort to optimism. Her ability to use words gives her writing a power that is exceptional, a power that marks out her position in the group and in the world more widely. It cannot completely defend her against the power of the GDR state, however.

While others look away from what is happening, having internalized their anticipatory obedience, or, like Marianne, use irony to minimize the impact of what is being done to them, Elly stares power in the face. This takes its toll on her. The many small attempts at humiliation she has been subjected to, and which she has always sought to deflect or resist, leave her committed to making the best of things but still worn down. In 1973, she says that even as they set out just to enjoy life, "life gets *us* in its clutches and determines what we do." In early 1990, she expresses her sorrow at what was done to them in the GDR. A year later, she writes that in the GDR they lived like "muzzled dogs on a leash, kept behind barbed wire." In 1995, she is more open than any of the others about the impact of power on her over the years and about her deepest feelings, with her poignant admission that she would have preferred to live like a hedgehog, "able to hide away all one's vulnerable parts and only display one's spines to the outside world!"

Looking Away from the Past

The Schönebeck women formed a group that was extremely strong and durable. It emerged at school with the promise made in 1940, was formalized in 1950, and came to an end in 2001. Like all groups, it was exclusive, and so defined itself as separate from everyone who was not a member.

It is clear from the letters that the victims of the Nazi regime were excluded from the collective consciousness of the group. The most striking demonstration of this, because it is so personal, was how few of the women responded to the account of the Jewish family they had known in their childhood. The involvement in the war of people close to them was also almost entirely ignored. When the girls were at school during the war, some of their fathers were still young enough to be in the army. The boys or young men who were the girls' dancing partners went off to the war, and a high percentage never returned. When the women got married, many of them had older husbands who had fought in the war. Nevertheless, the closest the women come to talking in the *Rundbrief* about what happened are a few fleeting references to wartime accidents and to time spent in prisoner-of-war camps.

As for the women themselves, some of them took part in the *Kriegshilfsdienst*, the service that directly involved them in the war effort. Others who only did their *Reichsarbeitsdienst* talk of how they enjoyed themselves and of their adventurous journeys back to the *Heimat*. The collective narrative was that the *Reichsarbeitsdienst* was purely a rite of passage that led them into the adult world, a time that was tedious, amusing, enlightening, dangerous for some, and personally beneficial. The women did not see it as directly involving them in the German war effort.

It would be too harsh, and not supported by the evidence, to suggest that the Schönebeck women were imbued with Nazi attitudes and values that persisted throughout their lives. However, there are conflicting strands in the *Rundbrief*. On the one hand, women such as Else Hermann, Leni Baumann, and Marianne Schneider do think about what a decent society would look like and how they can contribute to it, in contrast to the one that they grew up in. Similarly, Irma Kindler raises the question, eventually, of what happened to their Jewish classmate, while Edith Friebe and Maria Stein take the initiative in maintaining contact with Jutta Lübschütz and telling her story. It is clear that some of the women either never really accepted the Nazi approach in the first place or changed significantly over the years, coming to reject Nazi values and attitudes. Hilde Brenner, who died so young, was cosmopolitan in her outlook, consciously and actively anti-racist and, it appears, anti-nationalist. Hertha Pieper, who was a leader in the BDM during the war and was imprisoned because of this, appears to have lived an exemplary life of warmth and generosity toward all those around her, even in the difficult circumstances of everyday life for independent farmers in the early years of the GDR. Sabine Kleber, too, spent decades as an interesting, thoughtful woman, the latter part of it deeply committed to bringing up her substitute grandchildren, who clearly loved her in return.

On the other hand, Sabine Kleber can talk after the *Wende* about "foreign gangs," and Frieda Möller can call for their castration, in tones that echo Nazi propaganda. Even comments that are less emotionally charged, such as Barbara Meier's mention of Stalingrad, suggest that some of the women's attitudes to the war remained in line with those promoted by the Nazis.

Why is there so little evidence of the women looking back at the Nazi period and considering its significance? Their silence about this key part of their lives is the single most striking feature of the collective narrative the women spent so long constructing.

At an individual level, people need to create and hold on to a reasonably coherent set of self-narratives to function well. Such self-narratives constitute a "narrative skin" that holds them together, giving them their sense of continuity of being. However, both self-narratives and continuity of being are threatened by changes or ruptures that are too extreme (such as acts of humiliation or other traumatic events) or too frequent.[6] In response, there is often a tendency to tell and retell stories in their original, unchanging form, as a way of warding off the threat from outside.

Collectively, the Schönebeck women created a narrative where certain things could not be talked or written about. This involved turning their back on the past, except for the happy times of their childhood. They could not discuss openly and honestly what their fathers or older husbands might have done during the war. Even indirect suggestions of Nazi involvement could have led to the group disintegrating. This was a risk they could not afford to take. As a result, they appear to have lived their whole lives silently denying what was so central to them, that their formative years were those of the Nazi period, when they were subject to a conscious, systematic program designed to turn them into Nazi children.

Continuity or Rupture?

The power of myth, friendship, and habit all combined to give the group significant influence over its individual members. The group established the annual *Rundbrief* and the annual class reunions as the key institutions. The familiar rhythm of these helped to keep the women involved and committed and provided a reassuring sense of continuity. It helped them to believe in the necessity of the group and to accept and even welcome its power over them. It allowed them to see their lives as both normal and exceptional.

Any breaks in the rhythm were unwelcome and damaging. There was concern when the *Rundbrief* circulated too slowly or even, in later years when numbers had fallen, too fast; or when class reunions were planned and canceled or failed to materialize. There was always an underlying fear of rupture and consequent disintegration. This can be seen from their very first decision in 1940 to meet again in Magdeburg ten years later. In 1940, the threat of rupture—of being dispersed and therefore losing touch with one another—was very real. After 1945, they preferred not to notice the rupture that involved the division of Germany into two competing states.

Paradoxically, they did experience the reunification of Germany as a moment of rupture, one which threatened their own unity. The letters portray the women in the East in the bottom of a valley, struggling against the odds to climb the peaks to where the women in the West were waiting for them. Some of the women on the peaks shouted encouragement; others were irritated and impatient, blaming the victims. For the first time, solidarity across the group appeared to be lacking. Nevertheless, the women struggled to restore their sense of unity and continuity, through persisting with the *Rundbrief* itself, through further assertions of optimism, and through the reunions on both sides of the former border.

An unintended consequence of the GDR's decision to allow its citizens to travel to the West upon retirement is relevant here: it led to increased East-West solidarity. Many of the women from the East traveled to the West, where they reconnected with others they had not seen for decades. At last, instead of just writing to them, they could meet face to face, rebuilding and deepening their friendships. The strong sense of genuine unity that arose out of this was something to fall back on after the *Wende* and helped to prevent the fragmentation of the group. It was reinforced after 1989 by the return of many of the women from the West to the *Heimat* in the East. Even so, it took some years before the sense of rupture and separation fully disappeared from the *Rundbrief*.

Humiliation as a Moment of Rupture

Historical events are often the cause of major ruptures on a grand scale, with whole populations affected. An act of humiliation is also a moment of personal rupture for the person subjected to it. Suddenly, the world is not the way it was before, and it never will be again. In the stories of the Schönebeck women, this is most obvious for Erika Krämer, but there are other examples too. Gerda Höpfner's life was changed by the humiliation of her husband. Else Hermann was part of a theater group that was forced into a humiliating admission of failings they did not in fact accept. She saw her director, whom she greatly admired, publicly humiliated by the party he had always supported and whose cause was close to his heart. Frieda Möller saw her parents-in-law treated terribly and endured the direct humiliation of having her home invaded and her furniture seized. Käthe Sommer and her husband, happily living in Schönebeck and fully involved in the life of the community around them, were suddenly expelled from the GDR.

These are all examples from the East. In the West, Ilse Klein was twice afraid that she might be shamed or humiliated by the responses or reactions of the others in the group. The first occasion was when she told them she was divorced, an admission that few of them responded to. The second was when she told them of the birth of her daughter. This time there was no response at all, which could have felt like an exercise of power against her, an unspoken rejection. However, by insisting on her rightness *before* they could respond, she called into question their own prejudices and required them to change them. Anticipating humiliation, she prevented it taking place.

Much of Anna Siebert's working life can be seen in the same way. A strong, powerful woman, she reached the top of her profession in what had always been a man's world. However, for many years she had to fight for promotion in the face of prejudice and attempts to belittle her. The seemingly inconsequential episode when she was mistaken for Queen Elizabeth demonstrated that she too could avoid humiliation, on this occasion through the use of laughter.

Agency and the Illusion of Power

It is helpful at this point to return to the concept of "agency," the capacity for individual people to act effectively with power of their own in the context of the structures that surround them, as both Ilse Klein and Anna Siebert did. Individual agency is always constrained not just by the broader social structures but also by practices, customs, habits, and personal links and loyalties.

An example of the problematic nature of agency comes from the general wish of the Schönebeck women to get married and have children. This wish arose out of a number of influences: individual biological needs or desires; a sense that this was what they were expected to do by their parents and the community they lived in; and real pressure from the group, which oversaw and attempted to shape their decisions in line with implicitly agreed values and attitudes. The state, too, played a major part. In the Nazi era and the years of the division of Germany, the different regimes combined propaganda with material incentives and structures to encourage marriage and childbirth, and sought to impose a specific view of the "natural" position and responsibilities of women. Power operated here at many levels. The women were always free not to get married, but this had emotional consequences, most particularly disapproval and a fear of social exclusion, and financial or other material consequences, such as greater difficulty getting access to decent housing. However, in the specific circumstances of this generation of women, all becoming adults at the end of the war, individual agency was also limited because women greatly outnumbered men. It is significant that the Schönebeck women's husbands were often five to ten years older than their wives: the men had so many women to choose from; the women, so few men.

The power of the Schönebeck group was always a threat to individual agency. Women as strong as Else Hermann felt forced to hide from the group who they were and what they really wanted. Equally, individual agency could be a threat to the group. Ilse Klein's bold assertion of individuality is one example. Another is Anni Lange's life as an opera singer, with her husband taking primary responsibility for their son, and with Anni mocking (in her photos and descriptions of her life) the puritanical strain within the group. Even Erika Krämer's apparently strong but in fact paper-thin commitment to them is a maddening challenge to the rest of the group.

The power of the Schönebeck group was also a challenge to the power of the state and a threat to the structures the state had established, cultivated, or tolerated, in both East and West. Turning away from the explicitly political and asserting their power as individuals and as members of a group was, as Georgina Paul suggests when analyzing the literature of GDR women writers, a radical act in itself.[7]

However, in relation to the GDR in particular, their claim to a certain level of power was largely illusory when it came to significant political events. Quite apart from the examples of humiliation carried out by the GDR state, the context established by the SED's decision to press ahead in 1952 with building socialism caused real suffering for a number of the women. They could not ignore such suffering or pretend it had not happened. Similarly, the building of the wall and the tightening of the borders in 1961 confirmed divisions the women wanted to believe did not exist. The letters that tell of seeing one another or family members after more than twenty years are clear reminders of the power of the state. Most significantly, the collapse of the GDR demonstrated both the impotence of the women in the East and the gap that had opened up between those in the East and many of those in the West. In terms of rebuilding lives that were suddenly turned upside down, individual agency counted for little. And yet, despite this demonstration of how little power they had, the women did regroup in the 1990s, and the support from the West and from one another always remained important for them. After so many years, the group itself had built into each of its members the strength to cope with adversity and to reassert themselves in a world reshaped by forces outside their control.

In the end, the story of the Schönebeck women is a story of friendship, power, and impotence. It is a story about the usual concerns of everyday life—desire, pleasure, and pain; love, loss, and sorrow; creativity and artistic expression; self-expression through work; and the sense of life proceeding on through the generations—within a framework largely established by others. It is also, in a way, a story of self-deception, of turning away from things they did not wish to see, and of denying the reality that faced them. Ironically, this self-deception and defensive denial also gave them the strength to push on with lives that, for all their frustrations and disappointments, were full and satisfying and never to be regretted.

Notes

1. Maggie Turp, *Narrative Repair in Psychotherapy* (New York, forthcoming).
2. Fulbrook, *The People's State*, 247, taking the term from Claudia Rusch, *Meine freie deutsche Jugend* (Frankfurt/Main, 2003).
3. Christine Buci-Glucksmann, *Gramsci and the State* (London, 1980), 56–68; Mark McNally, "Gramsci, the United Front Comintern and Democratic Strategy," in Mark McNally, ed., *Antonio Gramsci* (Houndmills, 2015), 21–26.
4. Martha C. Nussbaum, *Frontiers of Justice: Disability, Nationality, Species Membership* (Cambridge, MA, 2006), 73.
5. Föllmer, *Individuality and Modernity*, 8, contrasts his approach with that of historians considering comradeship and collective commitment, including Michael Wildt, *Generation des Unbedingten: Das Führungskorps des Reichsicherheitshauptamtes* (Hamburg, 2003); Catherine Epstein, *The Last Revolutionaries: German Communists and their Century* (Cambridge, MA, 2003); Thomas Kühne, *Kameradschaft: Die Soldaten des nationalsozialistischen Krieges und das 20. Jahrhundert* (Göttingen, 2006).
6. Maggie Turp, *Hidden Self-Harm: Narratives from Psychotherapy* (London, 2003), 62–66.
7. Georgina Paul, "Gender in GDR literature," in Karen Leeder, ed., *Rereading East Germany: The Literature and Film of the GDR* (Cambridge, 2015), 120.

Bibliography

Archive Sources

Akademie der Künste, Kempowski Biographienarchiv, Berlin

6158. *Flugblatt der SED zum 17. Juni 1953.*
6168. *Lebenslauf* (Berlin, 1964).
6232. P. E./K. ("Erdmann"). *Stasi Files and Related Procedural Files.*
6328. *Bericht/Erinnerungen Jahre (Nachkrieg) bis 1972.*
6383. *31 Originalbände Klassenrundbriefe von ehemaligen Schülerinnen einer Oberschule in Schönebeck an der Elbe. Jahre 1950–2001.*
6455. *Sputnik–Digest der sowjetischen Presse,* 1988/1990, Moskau.
6599. J. T. *Aus meiner Zeit. Autobiographie* (1993).
6658. *Tagebuch, 1959–60.*
6779. S. K. *Briefe und Erinnerungen 1939–1946.*
6780. A. K. *Fluchtberichte und Alltagsbriefe, Mai 1961 bis Dezember 1989.*
6893UF. Renft, Klaus. *Zwischen Liebe und Zorn. Die Autobiographie* (Berlin, 1997).
6894. A. B. *Beiträge zur Familiengeschichte.*
6896. A. C. *Zeitzeugungenbericht zum 17. Juni 1953 und Familiengeschichte mit diversen Dokumenten dazu.*
7043. F. K. *Lebenserinnerungen, 1939–1956.*

Deutsches Tagebucharchiv (DTA), Emmendingen

1647. Priewe, Anneliese. *"War das mein Leben?"—ein Versuch. 1945–2004.*
1687/1-9. S. Q. *Briefwechsel und Tagebücher.*
1712. Dollmann, Carolina. *Lebenserinnerung 1945–1960.*
1874. Bentz, Rudolf. *Geschichte an der Havel. 1921–1991.*

Stadtarchiv Schönebeck

Amtliche Bekanntmachungen der Stadt Schönebeck (Elbe), 1946.
Amtliches Mitteilungsblatt, Schönebeck (Elbe), 1945.
Bl.955. Kuntze, Günter. *Unter aufgehobenen Rechten* (undated).
Bl.3786. Cramer, Gerd. *Schönebeck (Elbe), Plakate von 1945–1954.*

Geffert, Hans-Joachim. *Fragmentarische Nachrichten aus dem Leben jüdischer Mitbürger Schönebecks* (2012).
Kuntze, Günter. *Juden in Schönebeck* (Schönebeck, 1991).
PA 23. *Personalakte: Walter Karpe.*
Schönebecker Nachrichten. Mitteilungs-Blatt des Militärbefehlshabers und der Behörden der Stadt Schönebeck, 1945.
Schönebecker Zeitung. Mitteilungs-Blatt des Militärbefehlshabers und der Behörden der Stadt Schönebeck, 1945.
Urman, Judy. *From Quiet Hope to Freedom: The Life Story of Ernest and Judy Urman* (self-published, 2012).

Newspapers

Berliner Zeitung (Berlin).
Daily Express (London).
Frankfurter Allgemeine Zeitung (Frankfurt/Main).
Neue Zeitung (Berlin).
Neues Deutschland (Berlin).
The Times (London).
Volksstimme Magdeburg (Magdeburg).

Published Sources

Agde, Günter, ed. *Kahlschlag. Das 11. Plenum des ZK der SED. 1965. Studien und Dokumente* (Berlin, 2000).
Ahrberg, Edda, and Dorothea Harder. *Abgeholt und verschwunden (1). Von sowjetischen Militärtribunalen Verurteilte aus Sachsen-Anhalt und ihre Angehörigen* (Magdeburg, 2012).
———. *Abgeholt und verschwunden (2). Nichtverurteilte Speziallagerhäftlinge aus Sachsen-Anhalt und ihre Angehörigen* (Magdeburg, 2012).
Alsop, Rachel. *A Reversal of Fortunes? Women, Work, and Change in East Germany* (New York, 2000).
Amicale des Déportés à Neu-Stassfurt (Kommando de Buchenwald), https://sites.google.com/site/kommandodeneustassfurt/home/2-notre-histoire-1/la-vie--neu-stassfurt.
Anderson, Sheldon. "The German Question and Polish-East German Relations, 1945–1962." In Hochscherf, Laucht, and Plowman (2010).
Aretz, Jürgen, and Wolfgang Stock. *Die vergessenen Opfer der DDR. 13 erschüttende Berichte mit Original-Stasi-Akten* (Bergisch Gladbach, 1997).
Arnold, Jörg. *The Allied War and Urban Memory: The Legacy of Strategic Bombing in Germany* (Cambridge, 2011).
Atkins, Robert, and Martin Kane, eds. *Retrospect and Review: Aspects of the Literature of the GDR 1976–1990* (Amsterdam, 1992).
Autorenkollektiv, Institut für Marxismus-Leninismus beim ZK der SED. *Geschichte der Sozialistischen Einheitspartei Deutschlands. Abriß* (Berlin, 1978).

Bahrmann, Hannes, and Christoph Links. *Chronik der Wende* (Berlin, 1995).
Bake, Rita. *Die Ersten und das erste Mal . . . : Zum 50. Geburtstag des Gleichberechtigungsartikels im Grundgesetz: Was hat er Hamburgs Frauen gebracht?* (Hamburg, 1999).
Baumgart, Hildegard, ed. *Briefe aus einem anderen Land: Briefe aus der DDR* (Hamburg, 1971).
Bebel, August. *Die Frau und der Sozialismus* (Berlin, 1922; first published 1879.)
Beevor, Antony. *Berlin: The Downfall. 1945* (London, 2002).
Beleites, Michael. *Dicke Luft: zwischen Ruß und Revolte: die unabhängige Umweltbewegung in der DDR* (Leipzig, 2016).
Bennewitz, Inge. *Zwangsaussiedlungen an der innerdeutschen Grenze* (Berlin, 1994).
Bergerson, Andrew Stuart, and Leonard Schmieding, lead authors for ATG26 Collective. *Ruptures in the Everyday: Views of Modern Germany from the Ground* (New York, 2017).
Berghahn, Sabine, and Andrea Fritzsche, eds. *Frauenrecht in Ost- und Westdeutschland: Bilanz, Ausblick* (Berlin, 1991).
Berghoff, Hartmut, and Uta Andrea Balbier, eds. *The East German Economy, 1945–2010: Falling Behind or Catching Up?* (Cambridge, 2013).
Bessel, Richard. *Germany 1945: From War to Peace* (London, 2009).
Betts, Paul. *Within Walls: Private Life in the German Democratic Republic* (Oxford, 2010).
Beyer, Karl. *Die Geschichte der Apotheken und des Apothekenwesens im Kreis Schönebeck* (Schönebeck, ca. 1980).
Bland, Caroline, Catherine Smale, and Godela Weiss-Sussex. "Women Writing Heimat in Imperial and Weimar Germany: Introduction," *German Life and Letters* 62/1, 2019, 1–13.
Blatman, Daniel. "The Death Marches and the Final Phase of Nazi Genocide." In Jane Caplan and Nikolaus Wachsmann, eds., *Concentration Camps in Nazi German: The New Histories* (London, 2010).
Bouillot, Corinne. "'Mouvement des femmes' ou rejet du 'séparatisme féminin.' De la création des comités féminins antifascistes en zone d'occupation soviétique à la transformation de l'organisation des femmes de RDA en un relais du pouvoir socialiste." In Bouillot and Pasteur (2005).
Bouillot, Corinne, and Paul Pasteur. *Femmes, féminismes et socialismes dans l'espace germanophone après 1945* (Paris, 2005).
Braun, Juliane, ed. *Ein Teil Heimat seid Ihr für mich. Rundbriefe einer Mädchenklasse, 1944–2000.* 2nd edition (Berlin, 2002).
Bridenthal, Renate, Atina Grossmann, and Marion Kaplan, eds. *When Biology Became Destiny: Women in Weimar and Nazi Germany* (New York, 1984).
Bruce, Gary. *Resistance with the People: Repression and Resistance in Eastern Germany, 1945–1955* (Lanham, MD, 2003).
Brunner, José, Doron Avraham, and Marianne Zepp, eds. *Politische Gewalt in Deutschland: Ursprünge—Ausprägungen—Konsequenzen* (Göttingen, 2014).
Buddrus, Michael. "A Generation Twice Betrayed: Youth Policy in the Transition from the Third Reich to the Soviet Zone of Occupation (1945–1946)." In Roseman (1995).
Buci-Glucksmann, Christine. *Gramsci and the State* (London, 1980).
Buck, Hannsjörg F. *Mit hohem Anspruch gescheitert—Die Wohnungspolitik der DDR* (Münster, 2004).
Burdumy, Alexander. *Sozialpolitik und Repression in der DDR. Ost-Berlin, 1971–1989* (Essen, 2013).

Butler, Judith, and Elizabeth Weed, eds. *The Question of Gender: Joan W. Scott's Critical Feminism* (Bloomington, IN, 2011).
Caplan, Jane, and Nikolaus Wachsmann, eds. *Concentration Camps in Nazi Germany: The New Histories* (London, 2010).
Cecilienschule zu Schönebeck/Elbe: Bericht über das Schuljahr 1937/38. https://goobiweb.bbf.dipf.de/viewer/image/101166545X_1938/1/LOG_0003/.
Cecilienschule zu Schönebeck/Elbe: Bericht über das Schuljahr 1939/40. https://goobiweb.bbf.dipf.de/viewer/ppnresolver?id=101166545X_1940.
Clemenger, Michael. *Everybody Knew: A Boy. Two Brothers. A Stolen Childhood* (London, 2012).
Crowley, David, and Susan E. Reid, eds. *Pleasures in Socialism: Leisure and Luxury in the Eastern Bloc* (Evanston, Illinois, 2010).
Dahlke, Birgit. "Tagebuch des Überlebens: Vergewaltigungen 1945 in ost- und westdeutschen Autobiographien." In Davies, Linklater, and Shaw (2000).
Davies, Mererid Puw, Beth Linklater, and Gisela Shaw, eds. *Autobiography by Women in Germany* (Bern, 2000).
Demshuk, Andrew. *The Lost German East: Forced Migration and the Politics of Memory, 1945–1970* (New York, 2012).
Dennis, Mike, Eva Kolinsky, and Karin Weiss. *Erfolg in der Nische? Die Vietnamesen in der DDR und in Ostdeutschland* (Münster, 2003).
Diefendorf, Jeffry M., ed. *Rebuilding Europe's Bombed Cities* (Basingstoke, 1990).
Dodds, Dinah, and Pam Allen-Thompson, eds. *The Wall in My Backyard: East German Women in Transition* (Amherst, 1994).
Dworok, Gerrit. "Einleitung." In Dworok and Weißmann (2013).
Dworok, Gerrit, and Christoph Weißmann, eds. *1968 und die 68er: Ereignisse, Wirkungen und Kontroversen in der Bundesrepublik* (Vienna, 2013).
Eckart, Gabriele. *So sehe ick die Sache: Protokolle aus der DDR; Leben im Havelländischen Obstanbaugebiet* (Cologne, 1984).
Eisert, Wolfgang. *Die Waldheimer Prozesse: der stalinistische Terror 1950* (Esslingen, 1993).
Eley, Geoff. "Foreword." In Lüdtke (1995).
Engelmann, Roger, and Clemens Vollnhals, eds. *Justiz im Dienst der Parteiherrschaft. Rechtspraxis und Staatssicherheit in der DDR* (Berlin, 1999).
Engels, Friedrich. *The Origin of the Family, Private Property and the State* (Chicago, 1902; first published 1884).
Eppelmann, Rainer, Bernd Faulenbach, and Ulrich Mählert, eds. *Bilanz und Perspektiven der DDR-Forschung* (Paderborn, 2003).
Epstein, Catherine. *The Last Revolutionaries: German Communists and Their Century* (Cambridge, MA, 2003).
Evans, Richard J., and W. R. Lee, eds. *The German Family: Essays on the Social History of the Family in Nineteenth- and Twentieth-Century Germany* (London, 1981).
Ferchland, Rainer. "Von der Endzeit- zur Umbruchsituation. Gender-Aspekte 1987/88 und 1990 in der DDR." In Schröter, Ullrich, and Ferchland (2009).
Fischer, Alexander, ed. *Die Deutsche Demokratische Republik. Daten, Fakten, Analysen* (Cologne, 2003).
Föllmer, Moritz. *Individuality and Modernity in Berlin: Self and Society from Weimar to the Wall* (Cambridge, 2013).
Fowkes, Ben. *Communism in Germany under the Weimar Republic* (London, 1984).
Frauen in die Offensive: Texte und Arbeitspapiere der Gruppe "Lila Offensive" (Berlin, 1990).

Frevert, Ute. *Die Politik der Demütigung. Schauplätze von Macht und Ohnmacht* (Frankfurt/Main, 2017).
———. *Frauen-Geschichte. Zwischen Bürgerlicher Verbesserung und Neuer Weiblichkeit* (Frankfurt/Main, 1986).
———. *Women in German History: From Bourgeois Emancipation to Sexual Liberation* (Oxford, 1988).
Fricke, Karl Wilhelm. *Politik und Justiz in der DDR. Zur Geschichte der politischen Verfolgung, 1945–1968. Bericht und Dokumentation* (Cologne, 1979).
———. *Warten auf Gerechtigkeit. Kommunistische Säuberung und Rehabilitierungen. Bericht und Dokumentation* (Cologne, 1971).
Fulbrook, Mary. *Anatomy of a Dictatorship: Inside the GDR 1949–1989* (Oxford, 1995).
———. *Dissonant Lives: Generations and Violence through the German Dictatorships* (Oxford, 2011).
———. *The People's State: East German Society from Hitler to Honecker* (New Haven, CT, 2005).
———, ed. *Power and Society in the GDR, 1961–1979. The "Normalisation of Rule"?* (New York, 2009).
Fulbrook, Mary, and Andrew I. Port, eds. *Becoming East German: Socialist Structures and Sensibilities after Hitler* (New York, 2013).
Gassert, Philipp. "Antiamerikanismus." In Dworok and Weißmann (2013).
Gebhardt, Miriam. *Als die Soldaten Kamen. Die Vergewaltigung deutscher Frauen am Ende des zweiten Weltkriegs* (Munich, 2015).
Gehler, Michael. *Deutschland. Von der Teilung zur Einigung. 1945 bis heute* (Vienna, 2010).
Geipel, Ines. *Zensiert, verschwiegen, vergessen. Autorinnen in Ostdeutschland 1945–1989* (Düsseldorf, 2009).
Genth, Renate, ed. *Frauenpolitik und politisches Wirken von Frauen im Berlin der Nachkriegszeit 1945–1949* (Berlin, 1997).
Gerhard, Ute. "Frauenbewegung." In Roth and Rucht (2008).
Gieseke, Jens. *Mielke-Konzern. Die Geschichte der Stasi 1945–1990* (Stuttgart, 2001).
Ginzburg, Carlo. "Microhistory: Two or Three Things That I Know about It." *Critical Inquiry* 20/1, 1993.
———. *Threads and Traces: True, False, Fictive* (Berkeley, 2012).
Glossner, Christian L. *The Making of the German Post-War Economy: Political Communication and Public Reception of the Social Market Economy after World War II* (London, 2010).
Gombert, Max. *Historiographie du kommando de Neu-Stassfurt* (Paris, 2003).
Goodbody, Axel. "'Es stirbt das Land an seinen Zwecken': Writers, the Environment and the Green Movement in the GDR." *German Life and Letters* 47/3, 1994.
Grafe, Roman. *Die Grenze durch Deutschland. Eine Chronik von 1945 bis 1990* (Berlin, 2002).
Greenberg, Karen J., and Joshua L. Dratel. *The Torture Papers: The Road to Abu Ghraib* (Cambridge, 2005).
Griebner, Angelika, and Scarlett Kleint. *Starke Frauen kommen aus dem Osten: 13 Frauen, über die man spricht, sprechen über sich selbst* (Berlin, 1995).
Grube, Joachim, and Diethard Rost. *Dorferneuerung in Sachsen-Anhalt. Alternative Siedlungsentwicklung* (Schönebeck, 1995).
Grünbacher, Armin. "Cold-War Economics: The Use of Marshall Plan Counterpart Funds in Germany, 1948–1960." *Central European History* 45/4, 2012, 697–716.

Grünbaum, Robert. "Die Biermann-Ausbürgerung und ihre Folgen." In Eppelmann, Faulenbach, and Mählert (2003).
Grunenberg, Antonia. *Antifaschismus—Ein deutscher Mythos* (Reinbek, 1993).
———. *Die Lust an der Schuld. Von der Macht der Vergangenheit über die Gegenwart* (Berlin, 2001).
Harmssen, G. W. *Reparationen. Sozialprodukt. Lebensstandard. Versuch einer Wirtschaftsbilanz.* Vol. 1 (Bremen, 1948).
Harsch, Donna. *Revenge of the Domestic: Women, the Family, and Communism in the German Democratic Republic* (Princeton, NJ, 2007).
Herausgeberkollektiv, eds. *Wörterbuch zur sozialistischen Jugendpolitik* (Berlin, 1975).
Heinritz, Charlotte. *Der Klassenrundbrief. Geschrieben 1953–1989 von den Schülerinnen des Abschlußjahrganges 1925 der Altstädter Höheren Mädchenschule in Dresden* (Opladen, 1991).
Helwerth, Ulrike, and Gislinde Schwarz. *Von Muttis und Emanzen: Feministinnen in Ost- und Westdeutschland* (Frankfurt/Main, 1995).
Helwig, Gisela. "Einleitung." In Helwig and Nickel (1993).
———. "Frauen in der DDR zwischen Familie und Beruf." In Eppelmann, Faulenbach, and Mählert (2003).
Helwig, Gisela, and Hildegard Maria Nickel, eds. *Frauen in Deutschland, 1945–1992* (Berlin, 1993).
Henke, Klaus-Dietmar, Peter Steinbach, and Johannes Tuchel, eds. *Widerstand und Opposition in der DDR* (Cologne, 1999).
Herf, Jeffrey. *Divided Memory: The Nazi Past in the Two Germanys* (Cambridge, MA, 1997).
Hersh, Seymour M. *Chain of Command: The Road from 9/11 to Abu Ghraib* (London, 2004).
Hertle, Hans-Hermann, and Stefan Wolle. *Damals in der DDR. Der Alltag im Arbeiter und Bauernstaat* (Munich, 2006).
Hervé, Florence. *Geschichte der deutschen Frauenbewegung.* 5th edition (Cologne, 1995).
Heym, Stefan. *Die Architekten* (Munich, 2000).
———. *Schwarzenberg* (Munich, 1984).
Hochscherf, Tobias, Christoph Laucht, and Andrew Plowman, eds. *Divided, but Not Disconnected: German Experiences of the Cold War* (Oxford, 2010).
Hoffrogge, Ralf. *Sozialismus und Arbeiterbewegung in Deutschland. Von den Anfängen bis 1914* (Stuttgart, 2011).
Hook, James C. Van. *Rebuilding Germany: The Creation of the Social Market Economy, 1945–1957* (Cambridge, 2004).
Jäker, Vikar. "Über die Einnahme der Stadt Schönebeck (Elbe) durch die amerikanischen Panzertruppen am 11. und 12. April 1945." In Uwe Niedersen, ed., *Soldaten an der Elbe. US-Armee, Wehrmacht, Rote Armee und Zivilisten am Ende des Zweiten Weltkrieges* (Dresden, 2008).
Jansen, H. *Freundschaft über Sieben Jahrzehnte. Rundbriefe deutscher Lehrerinnen, 1899–1968* (Frankfurt/Main, 1991).
Janssen, Wiebke. *Halbstarke in der DDR: Verfolgung und Kriminalisierung einer Jugendkultur* (Berlin, 2010).
Jantzen, Eva, and Merith Niehuss, eds. *Das Klassenbuch. Geschichte einer Frauengeneration* (Reinbek bei Hamburg, 1997).

Jarausch, Konrad, ed. *Dictatorship as Experience: Towards a Socio-cultural History of the GDR* (New York, 1999).
Jesse, Eckhard. *Demokratie in Deutschland. Diagnosen und Analysen* (Cologne, 2008).
———. *Diktaturen in Deutschland. Diagnosen und Analysen* (Baden-Baden, 2008).
Johnson, Jason B. *Divided Village: The Cold War in the German Borderlands* (London, 2017).
Johnson, Jason, Craig Koslofsky, and Josie McLellan. "Taking Place." In Bergerson and Schmieding (2017).
Judt, Matthias. "Aufstieg und Niedergang der 'Trabi-Wirtschaft.'" In Judt (1998).
———, ed. *DDR-Geschichte in Dokumenten* (Bonn, 1998).
Kaelble, Hartmut, Jürgen Kocka, and Hartmut Zwahr, eds. *Sozialgeschichte der DDR* (Stuttgart, 1994).
Kahlau, Cordula, ed. *Aufbruch!: Frauenbewegung in der DDR: Dokumentation* (Munich, 1990).
Karcher, Katharina. *Sisters in Arms: Militant Feminisms in the Federal Republic of Germany since 1968* (New York, 2017).
Karlsch, Rainer. *Allein bezahlt?: die Reparationsleistungen der SBZ/DDR 1945–53* (Berlin, 1993).
Karlsch, Rainer, and Jochen Laufer, eds. *Sowjetische Demontagen in Deutschland 1944–1949* (Berlin, 2002).
Kenawi, Samirah. *Frauengruppen in der DDR der 80er Jahre: eine Dokumentation* (Berlin, 1995).
Kerr-Boyle, Neula. "The Slim Imperative: Discourses and Cultures of Dieting in the German Democratic Republic, 1949–90." In Fulbrook and Port (2013).
Kerski, Basil, Andrzej Kotula, and Kazimierz Wóycicki, eds. *Zwangsverordnete Freundschaft? Die Beziehungen zwischen der DDR und Polen 1949–1990* (Osnabrück, 2003).
Kirsch, Sarah. *Die Pantherfrau: fünf Frauen in der DDR* (Reinbek bei Hamburg, 1979; first published in Berlin, 1973).
Klinksiek, Dorothee. *Die Frau im NS-Staat* (Stuttgart, 1982).
Klose, Joachim. *Heimat in der Diktatur* (Leipzig, 2014).
Kohli, Martin. "Die DDR als Arbeitsgesellschaft?" In Kaelble, Kocka, and Zwahr (1994).
Kokula, Ilse. *"Wir leiden nicht mehr, sondern sind gelitten": lesbisch leben in Deutschland* (Cologne, 1987).
Kolinsky, Eva. *Women in 20th-Century Germany: A Reader* (Manchester, 1995).
Kolinsky, Eva, and Hildegard Maria Nickel, eds. *Reinventing Gender: Women in Eastern Germany since Unification* (London, 2003).
Kott, Sandrine. "L'égalité par le travail? Les femmes en RDA (1949–1989)." In Bouillot and Pasteur (2005).
Kreisleitung der SED Schönebeck, eds. *Zeittafel der Chronik der Kreises Schönebeck (Elbe)*. Vol. 1: *1945–1949* (Schönebeck, 1985).
Kreisleitung der SED Schönebeck, and Rat der Stadt Schönebeck (Elbe), eds. *750 Jahre Schönebeck (Elbe). Bilder zur Geschichte der Stadt. 1223–1973* (Schönebeck, 1973).
Kühne, Thomas. *Kameradschaft: Die Soldaten des nationalsozialistischen Krieges und das 20. Jahrhundert* (Göttingen, 2006).
Lammers, Marie. *Lebenswege in Ost- und Westdeutschland: Frauen aus einer Stettiner Schulklasse erzählen* (Frankfurt/Main, 1996).
Last, George. *After the "Socialist Spring": Collectivisation and Economic Transformation in the GDR* (New York, 2009).

Leask, Phil. "Humiliation as a Weapon within the Party: Fictional and Personal Accounts." In Fulbrook and Port (2013).
———. "Losing Trust in the World: Humiliation and Its Consequences." *Psychodynamic Practice* 19/2, 2013.
———. "Power, the Party and the People: The Significance of Humiliation in Representations of the German Democratic Republic," Ph.D. dissertation, University College London, 2012.
Leask, Phil, Sara Ann Sewell, and Heléna Tóth. "Families." In Bergerson and Schmieding (2017).
Leeder, Karen, ed. *Rereading East Germany: The Literature and Film of the GDR* (Cambridge, 2015).
Lenin, V. I. "One Step Forward, Two Steps Back," and "What Is To Be Done?" In *Selected Works*. Vol. 1 (Moscow, 1970).
Leonhard, Wolfgang. *Die Revolution entlässt ihre Kinder* (Cologne, 1962; first published 1955).
Lindenberger, Thomas. "Divided, but Not Disconnected: Germany as a Border Region of the Cold War." In Hochscherf, Laucht, and Plowman (2010).
Lippmann, Lothar, and Hans Dietrich Moschütz, eds. *Das System der sozialistischen Gesellschafts- und Staatsordnung in der Deutschen Demokratischen Republik. Dokumente* (East Berlin, 1970).
Lohoff, Wilhelm. *Betriebsgeschichte. VEB Traktoren- und Dieselmotorenwerk Schönebeck. Betrieb des Kombinat Fortschritt Landmaschinen Neustadt/Sachsen.* Vol. 2: *1945–1961* (Schönebeck, 1986).
Lohoff, Wilhelm, and Waldi Schäfer. *Betriebsgeschichte. VEB Traktoren- und Dieselmotorenwerk Schönebeck. Betrieb des Kombinat Fortschritt Landmaschinen Neustadt in Sachsen.* Vol. 3: *1961–1967* (Schönebeck, 1989).
Lüdtke, Alf. *Eigen-Sinn. Fabrikalltag, Arbeitererfahrungen und Politik vom Kaiserreich bis in den Faschismus* (Hamburg, 1993).
———, ed. *The History of Everyday Life: Reconstructing Historical Experiences and Ways of Life* (Princeton, NJ, 1995).
Lüdtke, Alf, and Peter Becker, eds. *Akten. Eingaben. Schaufenster. Die DDR und ihre Texte. Erkundungen zu Herrschaft und Alltag* (Berlin, 1997).
Ludz, Peter C. *Die DDR zwischen Ost und West. Von 1961 bis 1976* (Munich, 1977).
Maaß, Anita. *Wohnen in der DDR. Dresden-Prohlis: Wohnungsbaupolitik und Wohnungsbau 1975 bis 1981* (Munich: 2006).
McNally, Mark, ed. *Antonio Gramsci* (Houndmills, 2015).
Madarász, Jeannete Z. *Working in East Germany: Normality in a Socialist Dictatorship, 1961–79* (Basingstoke, 2006).
Magnússon, Sigurður Gylfi, and Davíð Ólafsson. *Minor Knowledge and Microhistory: Manuscript Culture in the Nineteenth Century* (New York, 2017).
Magnússon, Sigurður Gylfi, and István M. Szijártó. *What is Microhistory? Theory and Practice* (London, 2013).
Major, Patrick. *Behind the Berlin Wall: East Germany and the Frontiers of Power* (Oxford, 2010).
Mallinckrodt, Anita M. *The Environmental Dialogue in the GDR: Literature, Church, Party, and Interest Groups in Their Socio-political Context* (Lanham, MD, 1987).
Margalit, Avishai. *The Decent Society* (Cambridge, MA, 1996).
Maron, Monika. *Flugasche* (Frankfurt/Main, 1981).

McLellan, Josie. "Even under Socialism, We Don't Want to Do without Love." In Crowley (2010).
——. *Love in the Time of Communism: Intimacy and Sexuality in the GDR* (Cambridge, 2011).
Magdeburger Biographisches Lexikon. 19. und 20 Jahrhundert (Magdeburg, 2002).
Megargee, Geoffrey P., ed. *The United States Holocaust Memorial Museum Encyclopedia of Camps and Ghettos, 1933–1945.* Vol. 1 (Bloomington, IN, 2009.)
Meinicke, Klaus-Peter. *Industrie- und Umweltgeschichte der Region Sachsen-Anhalt* (Halle/Saale, 2003).
Merkel, Ina. "Die Biographieforscherin und ihr Subjekt." In Zentrum für Interdisziplinäre Frauenforschung der Humboldt-Universität Berlin (1995).
Meyer, Sibylle, and Eva Schulze. *Von Liebe sprach damals keiner: Familienalltag in der Nachkriegszeit* (Munich, 1985).
Miller, Martin A. *Freud and the Bolsheviks: Psychoanalysis in Imperial Russia and the Soviet Union* (New Haven, CT, 1998).
Millington, Richard. *State, Society and Memories of the Uprising of 17 June 1953 in the GDR* (Basingstoke, 2014).
Moranda, Scott. *The People's Own Landscape: Nature, Tourism, and Dictatorship in East Germany* (Ann Arbor, 2014).
Morina, Christina. *Legacies of Stalingrad: Remembering the Eastern Front in Germany since 1945* (Cambridge, 2011).
Mühlen, Armgard zur. "Kein Platz für 'Junker.'" In Baumgart (1971).
Müller, Michael, and Andreas Kanonenberg. *Die RAF-Stasi-Connection* (Berlin, 1992).
Müller-Enbergs, Helmut, Jan Wielgohs, Dieter Hoffmann, and Andreas Herbst, eds. *Wer war wer in der DDR?* (Berlin, 2006).
Münchow, Michael. *Die friedliche Revolution 1989/1990. Eine Analyse der Ereignisse* (Kremkau, 2007).
Murdock, Caitlin E. *Changing Places: Society, Culture, and Territory in the Saxon-Bohemian Borderlands, 1870–1946* (Ann Arbor, 2010).
Naimark, Norman M. *The Russians in Germany: A History of the Soviet Zone of Occupation, 1945–1949* (Cambridge, MA, 1995).
Neutsch, Erik. *Der Friede im Osten.* Vol. 1 (Halle/Saale, 1974).
——. *Spur der Steine* (Halle/Saale, 1966).
Niethammer, Lutz, Alexander von Plato, and Dorothee Wierling. *Die volkseigene Erfahrung. Eine Archäologie des Lebens in der Industrieprovinz der DDR* (Berlin, 1991).
——. "Zeroing in on Change: In Search of Popular Experience in the Industrial Province in the German Democratic Republic." In Lüdtke (1995).
Niven, Bill. "The Sideways Gaze: The Cold War and Memory of the Nazi Past, 1949–1970." In Hochscherf, Laucht, and Plowman (2010).
Nothnagle, Alan L. *Building the East German Myth: Historical Mythology and Youth Propaganda in the German Democratic Republic, 1945–1989* (Ann Arbor, 1999).
Nussbaum, Martha C. *Frontiers of Justice: Disability, Nationality, Species Membership* (Cambridge, MA, 2006).
O'Mara, Shane. *Why Torture Doesn't Work: The Neuroscience of Interrogation* (Cambridge, MA, 2015).
Palmowski, Jan. *Inventing a Socialist Nation: Heimat and the Politics of Everyday Life in the GDR, 1945–1990* (Cambridge, 2009).

Pence, Katherine, and Paul Betts, eds. *Socialist Modern: East German Everyday Culture and Politics* (Ann Arbor, 2008).
Patel, Kiran Klaus. *Soldaten der Arbeit. Arbeitsdienste in Deutschland und den USA, 1933–1945* (Göttingen, 2003).
Paul, Georgina. "Gender in GDR literature." In Leeder (2015).
Peetz, Hilla, ed. *"Wir kennen uns noch viel zu wenig!": Frauen aus Ostdeutschland erzählen von sich* (Cologne, 1992).
Peltonen, Matti. "What is Micro in Microhistory?" In Renders and De Haan (2014).
Pitts-Taylor, Victoria. *The Brain's Body: Neuroscience and Corporeal Politics* (Durham, NC, 2016).
Pohl, Dieter. *Justiz in Brandenburg, 1945–1955. Gleichschaltung und Anpassung* (Munich, 2001).
Port, Andrew I. "The Banalities of East German Historiography." In Fulbrook and Port (2013).
———. *Conflict and Stability in the German Democratic Republic* (Cambridge, 2007).
———. "Love, Lust, and Lies under Communism: Family Values and Adulterous Liaisons in Early East Germany." *Central European History* 44, 2011.
Plato, Alexander von. "The Hitler Youth Generation and Its Role in the Two Post-War German States." In Roseman (1995).
Plumpe, Werner. *German Economic and Business History in the 19th and 20th Centuries* (London, 2016).
Pritchard, Gareth. *Niemandsland: A History of Unoccupied Germany, 1944–1945* (Cambridge, 2012).
Rademacher, Cay. *Der Trümmermörder* (Cologne, 2011).
Reimann, Brigitte. *Alles Schmeckt nach Abschied. Tagebücher 1964–1970* (Berlin, 1998).
Renders, Hans, and Binne de Haan, eds. *Theoretical Discussions of Biography: Approaches from History, Microhistory and Life Writing* (Leiden, 2014).
Reese, Dagmar. "The BDM Generation: a Female Generation in Transition from Dictatorship to Democracy." In Roseman (1995).
———. *Growing Up Female in Nazi Germany*. 4th edition (Michigan, 2009).
———, ed. *Die BDM-Generation. Weibliche Jugendliche in Deutschland und Österreich im Nationalsozialismus* (Berlin, 2007).
Rellin, Martina, ed. *Klar bin ich eine Ost-Frau!: Frauen erzählen aus dem richtigen Leben* (Berlin, 2004).
Rocksloh-Papendieck, Barbara. *Verlust der kollektiven Bindung: Frauenalltag in der Wende* (Pfaffenweiler, 1995).
Roginskij, Arsenij, Frank Drauschke, and Anna Kaminsky, eds. *"Erschossen in Moskau . . .": Die deutschen Opfer des Stalinismus auf dem Moskauer Friedhof Donskoje 1950–1953* (Berlin, 2008).
Roseman, Mark. "Introduction: Generation Conflict and German History 1770–1968." In Roseman (1995).
———, ed. *Generations in Conflict: Youth Revolt and Generation Formation in Germany 1770–1968* (Cambridge, 1995).
Roth, Roland, and Dieter Rucht, eds. *Die sozialen Bewegungen in Deutschland seit 1945* (Frankfurt/Main, 2008).
Rublack, Ulinka, ed. *Gender in Early Modern German History* (Cambridge, 2002).
Rüdenauer, Erika, ed. *Dünne Haut: Tagebücher von Frauen* (Halle/Saale, 1987).

Rudolph, Jörg, Frank Drauschke, and Alexander Sachse. *Verurteilt zum Tode durch Erschießen. Opfer des Stalinismus aus Sachsen-Anhalt 1950–1953* (Magdeburg, 2006).
Rusch, Claudia. *Meine freie deutsche Jugend* (Frankfurt/Main, 2003).
Sachse, Carola. *Der Hausarbeitstag: Gerechtigkeit und Gleichberechtigung in Ost und West, 1939–1994* (Göttingen, 2002).
Schenk, Sabine. "On Employment Opportunities and Labour Market Exclusion: Towards a New Pattern of Gender Stratification?" In Kolinsky and Nickel (2003).
Schlosser, Horst Dieter. *Die deutsche Sprache in der DDR zwischen Stalinismus und Demokratie. Historische, politische und kommunikative Bedingungen* (Cologne, 1990).
Schmeidel, John C. *Stasi: Shield and Sword of the Party* (London, 2008).
Schmieding, Leonhard. *"Das ist unsere Party": HipHop in der DDR* (Stuttgart, 2014).
Schmidt, Sabine. *Frauenporträts und -protokolle aus der DDR: zur Subjektivität der Dokumentarliteratur* (Wiesbaden, 1999).
Schöne, Jens. *Das sozialistische Dorf. Bodenreform und Kollektivierung in der Sowjetzone und DDR* (Leipzig, 2008).
———. *Frühling auf dem Lande? Die Kollektivierung der DDR-Landwirtschaft* (Berlin, 2005).
Schroeder, Klaus. *Geschichte und Strukturen der DDR 1949–1990* (Cologne, 2013).
Schröter, Ursula. "Die DDR-Frauenorganisation im Rückblick." In Schröter, Ullrich, and Ferchland (2009).
Schröter, Ursula, Renate Ullrich, and Rainer Ferchland. *Patriarchat in der DDR: nachträgliche Entdeckungen in DFD-Dokumenten, DEFA-Dokumentarfilmen und soziologischen Befragungen* (Berlin, 2009).
Schulz, Kristina. "Studentische Bewegungen und Protestkampagnen." In Roth and Ruct (2008).
Schulze, Dietmar. *"Euthanasie" in Bernburg. Die Landes-Heil- und Pflegeanstalt Bernburg/Anhaltische Nervenklinik in der Zeit des Nationalsozialismus* (Essen, 1988).
Scott, Joan W. "Gender: A Useful Category of Historical Analysis." *American Historical Review* 91/5, 1986.
Sellier, André. *Histoire du camp de Dora* (Paris, 2010).
Sheffer, Edith. *Burned Bridge: How East and West Germans Made the Iron Curtain* (New York, 2011).
Sleifer, Jaap. *Planning Ahead and Falling Behind: The East German Economy in Comparison with West Germany 1936–2002* (Berlin, 2006).
Steege, Paul. *Black Market, Cold War: Everyday Life in Berlin, 1946–1949* (Cambridge, 2007).
Steiner, André. *The Plans That Failed: An Economic History of the GDR* (New York, 2010).
Steinert, Erika, and Hermann Müller. *Ein misslungener innerdeutscher Dialog: biografische Brüche ostdeutscher älterer Frauen in der Nachwendezeit* (Herbolzheim, 2007).
Steinhöfel, Dietlind. *"Wer bist du, fremde Schwester?" Lebenswege von Frauen in Deutschland—Ost und West* (Oberursel, 2001).
Stelling, Wiebke, and Wolfram Mallebrein. *Männer und Maiden: Leben und Wirken im Reichsarbeitsdienst in Wort und Bild* (Preußisch Oldendorf, 1979).
Stephenson, Jill. *Women in Nazi Germany* (London, 2001).
Stevenson, Patrick, *Language and German Disunity: A Sociolinguistic History of East and West in Germany, 1945–2000* (Oxford, 2002).
Strebel, Bernhard. *Das KZ Ravensbrück. Geschichte eines Lagerkomplexes* (Padeborn, 2003).

Strittmatter, Erwin. *Ole Bienkopp* (Berlin, 1965).
Suckut, Siegfried, ed. *Die DDR im Blick der Stasi 1976. Die geheimen Berichte an die SED-Führung* (Göttingen, 2009).
——, ed. *Volkes Stimmen: "ehrlich, aber deutlich": Privatbriefe an die DDR-Regierung* (Munich, 2016).
Tilly, Charles. *Big Structures, Large Processes, Huge Comparisons* (New York, 1984).
Timmermann, Heiner, ed. *Die DDR–Recht und Justiz als politisches Instrument* (Berlin, 2000).
Turp, Maggie. *Hidden Self-Harm: Narratives from Psychotherapy* (London, 2003).
——. *Narrative Repair in Psychotherapy* (New York, forthcoming).
Trappe, Heike. *Emanzipation oder Zwang? Frauen in der DDR zwischen Beruf, Familie und Sozialpolitik* (Berlin, 1995).
Uhl, Matthias. *Die Teilung Deutschlands. Niederlage, Ost-West Spaltung und Wiederaufbau 1945–1949* (Berlin-Brandenburg, 2009).
Vaizey, Hester. *Born in the GDR: Living in the Shadow of the Wall* (Oxford, 2014).
——. *Surviving Hitler's War: Family Life in Germany, 1939–1948* (Basingstoke, 2010).
Viebig, Michael, and Daniel Bohse. *Justiz im Nationalsozialismus. Über Verbrechen im Namen des Deutschen Volkes. Sachsen-Anhalt* (Magdeburg, 2013).
Vollnhals, Clemens. "Das Ministerium für Staatsicherheit." In Kaelble, Kocka, and Zwahr (1994).
Vonyó, Tamás. *The Economic Consequences of the War: West Germany's Growth Miracle after 1945* (Cambridge, 2018).
Wander, Maxie. *Guten Morgen, du Schöne. Protokolle nach Tonband* (Darmstadt, 1980).
——. *Leben wär' eine prima Alternativa. Tagebücher und Briefe, herausgegeben von Fred Wander* (Munich, 2004; first published in Berlin, 1979).
Weber, Hermann. *Die Sozialistische Einheitspartei Deutschlands 1946–1971* (Hanover, 1971).
——. *Dokumente zur Geschichte der Deutschen Demokratischen Republik 1945–1985* (Munich, 1986).
——. *Von der SBZ zur "DDR," 1945–1955* (Hanover, 1966).
——. *Von der SBZ zur "DDR," 1956–1967* (Hanover, 1967).
——, ed. *Der deutsche Kommunismus. Dokumente* (Cologne, 1963).
——, ed. *Die DDR 1945–1990*. 3rd edition (Munich, 2000).
Wehler, Hans Ulrich. *Deutsche Gesellschaftsgeschichte*. Vol. 5: *Bundesrepublik und DDR* (Munich, 2008).
Wentker, Hermann. "Justiz und Politik in der DDR." In Eppelmann, Faulenbach, and Mählert (2003).
Werkentin, Falco. *Politische Strafjustiz in der Ära Ulbricht* (Berlin, 1995).
Wierling, Dorothee. "Everyday Life and Gender Relations." In Lüdtke (1995).
——. *Geboren im Jahr Eins. Der Jahrgang 1949 in der DDR. Versuch einer Kollektivbiographie* (Berlin, 2002).
——. "How Do the 1929ers and the 1949ers Differ?" In Fulbrook (2009).
Wildt, Michael. *Generation des Unbedingten: Das Führungskorps des Reichsicherheitshauptamtes* (Hamburg, 2003).
Willner, Nina. *Forty Autumns: a Family's Story of Courage and Survival on Both Sides of the Berlin Wall* (New York, NY, 2016)
Winter, Alison. *Memory: Fragments of a Modern History* (Chicago, 2012).

Wolle, Stefan. *Der Große Plan. Alltag und Herrschaft in der DDR, 1949–1961* (Berlin, 2013).
———. *Der Traum von der Revolte: die DDR 1968* (Berlin, 2008).
———. *Die heile Welt der Diktatur. Alltag und Herrschaft in der DDR, 1971–1989* (Bonn, 1998).
Zachmann, Karin. *Mobilisierung der Frauen: Technik, Geschlecht und Kalter Krieg in der DDR* (Frankfurt/Main, 2004).
Zentrum für Interdisziplinäre Frauenforschung der Humboldt-Universität Berlin, ed. *Unter Hammer und Zirkel: Frauenbiographien vor dem Hintergrund ostdeutscher Sozialisationserfahrungen* (Pfaffenweiler, 1995).
Zetkin, Clara. *Die Arbeiterinnen- und Frauenfrage der Gegenwart* (Berlin, 1889).
———. *Zur Geschichte der proletarischen Frauenbewegung Deutschlands* (Moscow, 1928).
Zimmer, Dieter. *"Auferstanden aus Ruinen...": von der SBZ zur DDR* (Stuttgart, 1989).
Zwahr, Hartmut. "Die DDR auf dem Höhepunkt der Staatskrise 1989." In Kaelble, Kocka, and Zwahr (1994).

Index

1940s. *See* Nazi period; postwar period
1950s
  17 June 1953, 82, 85, 86, 89, 92–93, 106, 113, 145
  assessment, 116–19
  attitudes to women, 65, 66–69, 117–18
  border crossings, 115–16, 119
  children, 74–76
  collectivizations, 96, 105–10, 117
  disappearance in GDR, 83, 87–92, 125
  East/West politics, 81–85, 116–17
  economy, 82
  family ideology, 70–76
  GDR propaganda, 68–69
  GDR repression, 82–96
  gender and, 65–70, 75, 107, 117–18
  group tensions, 119
  grown-up years, 65–119
  housing, 78–81
  marriage, 71–72
  overview, 20
  refugees, 110–11
  reunification issue, 93–94
  role models, 96–111
  shaping attitudes, 71–74
  single parenthood, 77–78
  state interaction, 81–96
  travel/holidays and leisure, 111–16, 119
  voluntary work, 94–95, 109
  See also individual women
1960s
  1968, 131–34
  assessment, 163–66
  Berlin Wall, 115–16, 119, 125–26
  censorship, 141–43

  East/West politics, 134–35, 146
  families, 129, 130, 149–54
  GDR, 132–34
  GDR economy, 135
  GDR repression, 135, 141–43, 159–60
  generational differences, 150–54
  group solidarity, 163–66
  illness and death, 162–63
  lost book, 124–25, 176
  middle age, 135, 137, 162
  overview, 20–21, 124–25
  principal stories, 135–49
  social change, 127
  state interactions, 154–60
  travel/holidays and leisure, 146, 160–61
  voluntary work, 126
  weather, 130–31
  women and, 21, 126–30, 146, 149
  work and family, 153–54
  See also individual women
1970s
  assessment, 199–201
  censorship, 187–91, 192, 199
  consumer socialism, 169, 171, 196
  East/West relations, 170–71
  everyday oppression, 191
  group and group letters, 176–78
  illness and death, 198–99
  overview, 21, 169–71
  political attitudes, 177–78, 200
  politics and economy, 169–71, 195–96
  principal stories, 180–87
  social change, 178–80
  state interactions, 187–96
  terrorism, 178

travel/holidays and leisure, 196–98, 200
weather, 172–73
women and, 173–76, 200
See also individual women
1980s
  assessment, 241–42
  deaths, 213–21
  economy and politics, 203–05
  Erika Krämer and, 209–13, 242
  families and state, 231–34
  group strengthening, 207–8
  Jewish experience and, 235–41
  long-term consequences of humiliation, 209–13
  male members, 207, 216, 222–23
  overview, 21–22
  political attitudes, 208–9, 241–42
  principal stories, 223–29
  refugees to the West, 205
  SED loss of power. *See* reunification period
  state interactions, 229–34
  tensions and losses, 207–13
  travel/holidays and leisure, 234–41
  women and, 205–07
  See also individual women
1990s. *See* reunification period

abortions, 41, 44, 173
Abu Ghraib, 18
Adenauer, Konrad, 81
Afghanistan, Soviet invasion, 203
agency, 9, 294, 299–301
agriculture
  1950s collectivization, 105–11, 259, 286
  post-reunification, 263, 264
  potato harvest, 140
  Soviet Zone, 54–56
Albania, 149

Bauer, Kurt, 83
Baumann, Leni, ix
  1950s, 72–73, 75–76, 83, 97, 110–11, 117
  1960s, 153
  1970s, 186, 195
  1980s, 210–11, 226
  career, 110, 117, 153, 186, 195
  death, 289
  Erika Krämer and, 210–11
  GDR politics and, 83, 260–61
  on gender, 73
  handwriting, 165
  illness, 261
  move to West, 110–11
  politics, 296
  retirement, 261
  reunification period, 260–61, 264, 275–76, 281, 282
  role model, 97, 110–11, 294
BDM, 4, 5–6, 7, 28–30, 38–39, 48, 49, 286, 297
Bebel, August, 66, 174
Becker, Susanne, xi
  1980s, 219, 220
  death, 220
  lost book, 124–25
  move to FRG, 115
Bergen-Belsen, 33
Berger, Elfriede, ix
  1950s, 88, 97, 114–15
  1960s, 153
  1970s, 177, 187, 196–97
  on Anna Siebert, 97
  Erika Krämer and, 88
  insensitivity, 252, 253–54, 255, 258
  Nazi period, 56–57, 111
  postwar period, 111
  on reunification, 94
  reunification period, 252, 253–54, 255, 258, 273, 277, 279, 282
  travels, 57, 111, 114–15, 196–97, 277
  widow, 277
  work, 153, 277
Bergerson, Andrew, 8
Berlin Blockade, 53, 60, 292
Berlin Wall, 20, 115–16, 119, 124, 125–26, 137, 205, 300
Bernburg massacres, 40
Bessel, Richard, 6
Biafran War, 131
Biermann, Wolf, 171
Bloch, Ernst, 163
Brandt, Willy, 20, 134–35
Braun, Agnes, 198–99, 210
Brecht, Bertolt, 141
Brenner, Hilde, x
  1950s, 83–94, 114, 118

1960s, 153, 162–63, 164
  cosmopolitanism, 296–97
  death, 163, 164, 166, 296–97
  on reunification, 93–94
  travels, 114, 162
  work, 153
Brexit, 288
Brezhnev, Leonid, 188
Brunner, Carla, ix
  1950s farming, 108–9, 117
  group membership, 210
  Nazi period, 56, 57, 210
Buchenwald, 17, 34, 40, 57, 239
Bulgaria, 262

censorship
  1960s, 141–43
  1970s GDR, 187–91, 192, 199
  Nazi period, 29
  self-censorship, 14, 15, 187–91, 192, 199, 260, 293
China, 131, 149, 205
Cold War, 19, 53, 70, 113, 154, 170, 203
Comintern, 67
concentration camps, 37, 40, 44
consumer socialism, 20, 132, 169, 171, 196
consumerism, 126
continuity narrative, 292, 293, 297–99
Cowen, Stuart, 240
Cuba, 170, 234, 251
Czechoslovakia
  1980s, 208–9
  Nazi period, 57, 158
  Prague Spring (1968), 131, 132, 145
  refugees from, 40
  Soviet invasion, 131, 133, 134, 157–58, 205

death marches, 33, 37, 40, 44
denazification, 48
Dutschke, Rudi, 131

Ebel, Karl-Albert, 133
Elizabeth II, Queen, 146–47
end of war. *See* postwar period
Engels, Friedrich, 66
environmental damage, 143–45
environmental movement, 21, 204
European Economic Community, 82

family
  1950s attitudes, 118
  1960s, 129, 130, 149–54
  1980s, 231–34
  Nazi period, 28–29, 70, 74
  postwar period, 47–48
  reunification, 233
  state and, 231–34
  See also individual women
feminism, 21, 127, 173–74, 200, 206
Fettback, Wolfgang, 126
Fischer, Inge, x, 177
Fischer, Ruth, 66
floods, 145–46
Föllmer, Moritz, 294
forced labor, 33, 34–35, 36, 37, 40, 57
Fowkes, Ben, 66
France, 82, 156
Frevert, Ute, 5, 6, 206
Friebe, Edith, ix
  1980s, 235–36
  Denver, Colorado, 235–36
  on *Heimat*, 283
  on Jewish experience, 238, 253, 290, 296
  Lübschütz family and, 235–36, 296
  photo (1989), 236
  reunification period, 261–62, 273, 279, 282, 283
friendship myth, 19
Fulbrook, Mary, 7, 9, 174, 176, 207, 293

Gardelegen massacre, 33
Gebhardt, Miriam, 41, 42
gender. *See* women
generations, significance, 7–8
Gerhard, Ute, 173, 174
Goethe, Wolfgang von, 28
Gorbachev, Mikhail, 21, 205, 245
Gramsci, Antonio, 293
Greiswald, Astrid, ix
  1950s, 86, 88
  1970s, 177, 186
  1980s, 220, 221, 226, 233
  death, 275
  Erika Krämer and, 88
  group organizer, 282
  national service, 56
  Nazi period, 56
  postwar period, 56

religion, 253, 275
reunification period, 253, 275, 282
work, 56
Greiswald, Walter, 233, 273, 275, 280
Grüger, Christof, 101, 287
Guantanamo Bay, 18
guest workers, 169, 173
Gulf War, 252, 254, 256

Haase, Elly, x
  1950s, 76, 88, 111–12
  1970s, 191–92
  1980s, 208, 210, 224, 226, 231, 236
  carpenter, 58, 256, 295
  class, 58, 192
  Erika Krämer and, 88, 210
  GDR shadow, 280
  housing, 231
  humiliation, 295
  limits of optimism, 295–96
  on male members, 276
  marriage, 192
  politics and, 208, 256–58, 266
  postwar period, 58, 111–12
  reunification period, 256–58, 264, 266, 276, 277–78, 280
  state power and, 295–96
  travels, 111–12, 208, 236
Hacks, Peter, 141–42
Hager, Kurt, 174
Hansen, Brigitte, ix
  1960s, 147, 155
  1970s, 177, 186
  death, 177, 199, 227
  postwar period, 58
Harsch, Donna, 7, 8, 79, 80, 129, 170, 175–76, 204
Harz fortress, 32–33
Heimat
  Else Hermann and, 144, 274, 288
  GDR, 20, 200
  loss, 227, 249, 265
  loyalty to, 283
  myth, 11–12, 213, 284, 288
Heise, Katharina, 101
Helsinki Conference on Security and Cooperation (1975), 170
Helwig, Gisela, 8

Hermann, Else, x
  1950s, 74, 76, 81, 97, 100–105
  1960s, 126, 135, 137–45, 160, 162, 164
  1970s, 179, 180–84, 199
  1980s, 207, 223–26
  agency and power, 300
  on Anni Lange, 100
  assessment, 286–88
  on Berlin Wall, 126, 137
  career, 48–49, 100–102, 105, 117, 135, 137–39, 153–54, 180, 181, 221, 225
  censorship, 141–43
  death, 288
  divorce, 225, 272
  education, 31, 139–40, 145
  father, 139, 143–45
  friendships, 207
  on gender, 74
  group organizer, 273, 283
  health, 162, 164, 180, 273
  housing, 81, 138, 164, 181–82, 225, 274
  humiliation, 299
  interests, 274
  interviews, 16, 74, 101, 143, 145, 183, 225, 260, 286–89
  letters as fiction, 74
  lost book and, 124, 125
  on Magdeburg, 1–2
  marriage, 180–83, 199, 223, 287
  on marriage, 102, 118
  mother, 181–83
  moves, 272–73, 275
  national service, 35–38
  Nazi period, 29–30, 35–38, 269
  parents, 29–30
  photo (1950s), 103
  photo (1960s), 140
  photo (1998), 275
  on Poland, 161
  politics and, 100, 103–4, 141, 145, 160, 296, 299
  postwar, 37–38, 41, 48–49, 111
  potato harvest, 140
  principal story, 20, 286–88
  reunification period, 272–75, 283
  role model, 97, 100–105, 164, 294
  on Stasi informers, 260
  students, 287–88

travel/holidays, 139, 223, 224–25, 225–26, 272, 273
Herzig, Werner, 247
Heym, Stefan, 37, 79–80
Hitler, Adolf, 27, 32–33, 189
  See also Nazi period
Hitler Youth, 7, 27–28
  See also BDM
Hoffrogge, Ralf, 66
holidays
  1950s, 111–16, 119
  1960s, 160–61
  1970s, 196–98, 200
  1980s, 234–41
homosexuality, 183, 225, 287
Honecker, Erich
  1973 World Youth Games, 188
  accession to power, 20, 159
  consumer socialism, 169, 171
  economic and social policy, 170
  gender and, 206
  images, 14
  loss of power, 245–46
  photo, 230
  repression, 171
  Soviet support, 135
honeycomb state, 9
Höpfner, Gerda, x
  1950s, 84, 95, 231, 292
  1980s, 222–23, 231
  employment, 58–59
  GDR politics and, 84, 231, 292, 299
  postwar period, 58–59
  reunification period, 254–55, 275, 282
  taken off group list, 275, 282
  voluntary work, 95
housing
  1950s, 78–81
  1960s, 132
  1980s, 230–31
humiliation
  1950s, 77–78, 90–92
  1960s, 21
  1960s GDR censorship, 141–43
  1980s, 209–13, 228
  Elly Haase, 295
  Erika Krämer, 90–92, 209–13, 298
  long-term consequences, 209–13

moment of rupture, 298–99
significance, 17–18
state power, 300
Hungary, 145, 205, 245

International Women's Day, 206
interviews
  description, 284–90
  impact, 288–90
  procedures, 15–17
Iraq, Abu Ghraib, 18

Jäger, Ernst, 233, 276
Jäger, Martha, xi
  1950s, 81, 85–87, 113
  1960s, 151–52, 161, 162
  1970s, 192–95
  1980s, 230, 232–34
  death, 250–51, 261, 262, 275
  family, 151–52, 232–34
  family reunification, 233
  GDR politics and, 85–87, 192–95
  housing, 81, 234
  Nazi period, 111
  reunification period, 250
  reunion organizer, 230
  travel/holidays, 113, 233
Jäker, Vikar, 39
Jaruzelski, Wojciech, 204–05
Jews
  1989 anti-Semitism, 247
  attacks on, 4
  humiliation, 18
  Lübschütz family, 235–41, 296
  massacres, 40
  Nazi period, 4, 22–23, 237–41, 253, 290
Jugendweihe, 136
Jung, Carl, 163
Junker, Wolfgang, 132
Junkers, 54, 66

Karpe, Walter, 4, 238
Kautsky, Karl, 67
Kempf, Heidi, x
  1950s, 81
  1960s, 145, 161, 163–64
  1970s, 178

1995 reunion, 276
Else Hermann and, 145, 163–64
housing, 81, 230–31
medical technician, 58, 178
postwar period, 58
reunification period, 253–54, 264, 276, 277, 283
Schönebeck group, 276
travel, 161, 277
widow, 81, 231
Kennedy, Robert, 131
Ketschendorf/Fürstenwalde camp, 83
Kindler, Irma, x
 1950s, 80, 89, 95, 97, 98–99, 114
 1960s, 147, 148–49, 153, 164
 1970s, 186–87, 198
 1980s, 207, 220, 222, 229, 230, 232, 236–37
 assessment, 285
 Erika Krämer and, 89
 family, 99, 148, 149, 187, 229, 232, 270–71
 friendships, 207
 group organizer, 207
 on *Heimat*, 283
 housing, 80, 95, 292
 husband, 51–52, 149, 270, 271
 interviews, 16, 260, 285, 288
 national service, 32–33, 285
 Nazi period, 27, 30, 32–33, 269, 270, 285
 Nazi politics and, 296
 photo (1950), 51
 photo (1994), 271
 postwar period, 49–52, 111
 principal story, 20, 285
 retirement, 229
 reunification period, 267, 268–72, 283, 285
 role model, 97, 98–99
 travel/holidays, 114, 148, 149, 187, 229, 268, 269, 270, 272
 unemployment and, 232
 widowhood, 270, 285
 work, 51, 148, 149, 153, 285
King, Martin Luther, 131
Kirsch, Sarah, 175
Kleber, Sabine, xi
 1950s, 95–96, 113–14
 1960s, 160–61, 163, 164
 1970s, 179, 195–96, 197
 1980s, 220–21, 234
 character, 297
 echo from Nazi period, 280–81, 297
 health, 163
 Nazi period, 29, 111
 pushed out of GDR, 95–96, 160
 retirement, 234
 reunification period, 264, 278–79, 280–81, 282
 reunification politics, 261
 reunion organizer, 253, 282
 social change and, 179
 travel/holidays, 111, 113–14, 160–61, 197, 234, 264, 278
Klein, Ilse, x
 1950s, 77–78, 86, 118
 1970s, 169, 197, 198–99
 1980s, 232
 agency and power, 299, 300
 avoiding humiliation, 77–78, 299
 divorce, 77, 299
 remarriage, 78
 single mother, 77–78, 299
 unemployment, 169, 232
Kleist, Heinrich von, 28
Kohl, Helmut, 204
Kolinsky, Eva, 206
Kott, Sandrine, 129
Krämer, Erika, x
 1950s, 87–92, 125, 212
 1960s, 134–35, 161
 1960s politics and, 134–35
 1970s, 197, 198, 210
 1980s, 209–13, 227, 242
 agency and power, 300
 family, 212
 GDR repression, 87–92, 125, 292
 humiliation, 90–92, 143, 209–13, 242, 298
 illness, 89, 210, 212
 missing fiancé, 87–92, 285
 national service, 33, 211
 Nazi period, 33, 211
 outsider, 209–13, 275
 remarriage, 89

reunification period, 261, 275
taken off group list, 275
travel, 161, 197
Krenz, Egon, 246
Kristallnacht (1938), 4, 237, 238–39, 240–41
Krüger, Charlotte, ix
  1960s, 157
  1970s, 177, 178–79, 196
  1980s, 221–22
  death, 273–74, 275
  Nazi period, 1–2
  on opera, 1–2
  orchid grower, 176, 221
  reunification period, 262
  social attitudes, 178–79
  travels, 221
  widow, 221–22
Khrushchev, Nikita, 79, 142
Kurella, Alfred, 142

land reform. *See* agriculture
Lange, Anni, ix
  1950s, 86, 97, 99–100, 117
  1960s, 152–53
  1970s, 187
  1980s, 218–19
  agency and power, 300
  death, 219, 222, 233
  family life, 152–53
  friends, 236
  opera singer, 86, 99–100, 269
  role model, 97, 99–100, 294
Lange, Inge, 174–75
Langhoff, Wolfgang, 142–43
language, use, 15, 246, 290, 295
leisure
  1950s, 111–16, 119
  1960s, 160–61
  1970s, 196–98
  1980s, 234–35
Lenin, Vladimir, 132, 138, 257
Leninism, 65, 68, 83, 125, 134, 248
Lessing, Gotthold, 28
Liebmann, Helmut, 220, 222, 224, 251, 260, 279, 280
Liebmann, Lisa, xi
  1950s, 76, 89, 112, 113

  1960s, 131, 147, 150, 158, 162, 163, 164
  1970s, 188, 198
  1980s, 210, 218, 219–20, 224, 234
  children, 150
  death, 220, 222, 226, 227
  Erika Krämer and, 89
  health, 198, 218, 219–20
  on Hilde Brenner, 163
  holidays, 112
  photo (1950s), 112
  politics and, 158, 188
  reunion organizer, 147
  travels, 113, 198, 234
loyalty, 12, 19, 283
Lübke, Heinrich, 155
Lübschütz family, 235–41, 253, 296
Luxemburg, Rosa, 66

Macdonald, A.J., 4
Magdeburg meeting (1950), 1–3, 71, 221, 296, 298
Magnússon, Sigurđur Gylfi, 3, 9
Malaysia, communist insurgency, 131
Mann, Thomas, 164
Mao Zedong, 149, 187
Marshall Plan, 80, 82
Marxism-Leninism, 65, 68, 83, 125, 134, 163, 248
Mayakovsky, Vladimir, 141
Meier, Barbara, ix
  1950s, 83–84, 94
  1960s, 150, 161, 162
  1970s, 176, 185, 186, 189–91, 197–98
  1980s, 209, 211, 220, 226–27, 228
  cherry picking, 161, 226, 292–93
  death, 262, 272, 275
  Erika Krämer and, 211
  family, 150, 189–91
  on group letters, 176
  health, 162
  leisure, 161, 197
  Nazi period, 189, 269
  Nazi politics and, 297
  politics and, 83–84, 189–91, 209, 297
  on reunification, 94
  reunification period, 250–51
  travel, 161, 197–98, 251
Meier, Heinz, 276

microhistory, 3, 9, 19
Modrow, Hans, 248
Möller, Frieda, x
  1950s, 76, 85, 113
  1960s, 149, 161
  1970s, 179
  1980s, 214, 215, 216, 219, 224, 230, 234–35
  employment, 149, 259
  farming, 259
  GDR politics and, 85, 230, 235, 258–60, 299
  group organizer, 224
  humiliation, 299
  last letter, 284
  Nazi echoes, 280–81, 297
  reunification period, 250, 258–60, 273, 280–81, 284
  travel/holidays, 113, 230, 234–35, 259, 260, 284
Morgner, Irmtraud, 174, 175
myths
  clash of, 19
  GDR, 11, 13, 22
  Heimat, 11–12, 144, 213, 274, 288
  innocence, 12
  loyalty, 12, 19, 283
  power and, 19, 297
  reunification, 269
  Schönebeck group, 11–12, 13, 289, 292
  unity, 3, 12, 13, 14, 23, 97, 126, 164, 208, 213, 216, 242, 282

Naimark, Norman, 41
Napoleon, 164
Nathan, Max, 240
NATO, 81, 116
Nazi period
  agency and, 299–300
  BDM. *See* BDM
  censorship, 29
  collapse of routine, 30–31
  communist defeat, 67–68
  echoes from, 280–81, 290, 297
  end of war, 6–7, 37–39
  everyday life, 5–6
  family, 28–29, 70, 74
  group silence on, 296–97
  growing up in, 27–39
  Jewish experience, 22–23, 237–41, 290
  legacy, 22–23, 56–58, 60, 290
  national service, 31–38, 59, 296
  overview, 19–20
  propaganda, 30, 35, 60, 70, 241, 290
  refugees, 35, 36, 37
  school, 27–29, 30
  women and, 5–6, 59, 294, 299–300
  working for Nazi state, 31–32
  See also individual women
neo-Nazis, 247
Neutsch, Erik, 39, 101, 274
New Economic System, 132
Nicaragua, 170
Niethammer, Lutz, 15
Nixon, Richard, 131
nuclear weapons, 203, 204, 205
Nussbaum, Martha, 293–94

oil price shock (1973/74), 170, 204
Ólafsson, David, 3, 9
Oldenburger, Hans, 274
Olympics (1936), 238
Olympics (1964), 136

patriarchy, 66–67, 70, 173, 206, 293–94
Paul, Georgina, 300
peace consensus, 44
peace movement, 21, 204, 216, 259
photos, 13–14
  See also individual women
Pieck, Wilhelm, 250, 255
Pieper, Hertha, x
  1950s, 97, 105–9
  1960s, 135–37, 161, 164
  1970s, 184–85, 186
  1980s, 210, 226–27
  assessment, 286
  BDM, 38–39, 286, 297
  character, 297
  collectivization of agriculture, 105–9
  family, 107, 108, 135–37, 184–85, 226–27, 265, 286
  farming, 53–56, 105–9, 117, 185, 227, 263, 264, 286
  health, 184, 226, 265
  interviews, 16, 286, 288

marriage, 53
Nazi period, 29, 38–39, 286
photo (1957), 108
photo (1970s), 185
politics and, 227
postwar period, 38–39, 53–56
principal story, 20, 286
reunification period, 263–65, 282, 286
reunion organizer, 264–65
role model, 97, 105–9
widow, 184
Poland
1970 Treaty with FRG, 135
1980s, 204–05, 208–9, 229–30, 231
1989 revolution, 245
holidays in, 139
new borders, 40, 156–57
Solidarity, 204, 205
pollution, 95, 143, 144, 196, 247
postwar period
1946/47 winter, 44–46, 48
assessment, 59–60
attitudes to women, 47–48, 50–51
cries for help, 43
disappearances, 125
economy, 46–47
family, 47–48
legacy of Nazi years, 56–58, 60
overview, 6–7, 19–20, 39–59
principal stories, 48–56
rape, 41–42, 50, 60
refugees, 40–41, 43–44, 47, 50, 57
Schönebeck, 39–40
starvation, 42–43
state interaction, 56–59
staying alive, 42–46
on the move, 39–41
women's leading role, 43–44
work, 46–47, 58–59
See also individual women
Prague Spring (1968), 131, 132, 145, 157–58
Priewe, Anneliese, 141
Pritchard, Gareth, 37

Rank Organisation, 98–99
rape, 41–42, 50, 60
Ravensbrück, 33

Reagan, Ronald, 203
Red Army Faction (RAF), 21, 178, 204
Reese, Dagmar, 6, 28–29
refugees, 35, 37, 40–41, 43–44, 47, 50, 55, 57, 78–79, 110, 115, 205, 239–40
Reimann, Brigitte, 175
religion, 13, 149, 253, 275
reunification period
1990 reunion photo, 254
1996 reunion photo, 267
currency reform, 256, 257, 258, 261
East/West tensions, 22, 252, 253, 261, 262, 282, 289–90, 298
Eastern attitudes, 250–60, 289–90
Eastern losses, 289–90
GDR shadow, 279–80, 282
gender and, 10, 22, 249
group decline, 275–84
group political responses, 248–50
group reunification, 289–90
male members, 249
moment of rupture, 298
overview, 22–23
pessimism, 281
principal stories, 263–75
Schönebeck changes, 246–48
SED loss of power, 245–46, 248
street names, 250
unemployment, 250, 253
Wende, 248
Western attitudes, 252, 260–63
See also individual women
Riedel, Gisela, x
1950s, 96, 112–13
1960s, 151, 161
1970s, 178
1980s, 230, 233
family, 151
GDR politics and, 96
holidays, 233
Nazi period, 111
religion and, 253
reunification period, 251–53
travels, 112–13
work, 178
role models, 20, 96–97, 164, 175, 294–95
Romania, 262
Roseman, Mark, 7

rubble women, 65
Rundbrief. See Schönebeck group
Russia, 288
  See also Soviet Union

Sachsenhausen, 33
Schenk, Sabine, 75
Schiller, Friedrich, 28
Schmidt, Helmut, 146
Schmieding, Leonard, 8
Schneider, Johannes, 72, 216, 222, 231, 232, 250, 255, 279–80
Schneider, Marianne, xi
  1950s, 71–72, 74, 86, 91, 97, 99, 110, 112
  1960s, 124–25, 154–58, 161, 162, 164–65
  1970s, 179–80, 187–89
  1980s, 208, 213–18, 232
  death, 215–16, 222, 226, 227
  energy, 99
  Erika Krämer and, 91
  family, 74, 150, 189, 213–15, 232
  group organizer, 119, 154–55, 172, 176, 177, 184, 199, 209, 216, 230
  health, 162, 214–16
  holidays, 112, 157, 158, 161, 215
  on Leni Baumann, 110
  on lost book, 124–25
  marriage, 71–72
  Nazi period, 57
  photo (1950), 72
  photo (1951), 75
  photo (1956), 57
  politics and, 154–58, 187–89, 208, 216, 296
  postwar period, 111
  role model, 97, 164–65
  shaping attitudes, 71–72
  social change and, 179–80
  state power and, 231–32
  Sybille letters, 216–18
  use of irony, 295
Schöne, Jens, 109
Schönebeck
  demography, 3
  end of war, 39–40, 46
  group. *See* Schönebeck group

politics, 3–4
postwar period, 6–7
reunification period, 246–48, 253, 280
spatial assessment, 16
Schönebeck group
  1937 photo, 28
  1950s divergences, 119
  1960s solidarity, 163–66
  1970s, 176–78, 199–201
  1980s tensions and losses, 207–13
  agency and power, 299–301
  assessment, 284–90
  belief in its power, 292–93
  changing nature, 275–79
  complying without noticing, 293–95
  continuity and rupture, 297–99
  continuity narrative, 292, 293
  decline, 275–84
  dissolution, 284
  divergence and differences, 12–13
  end of war, 6–7
  everyday life and power, 4–5
  group reunification, 289–90
  interviews. *See* interviews
  letters, 11–12
  Magdeburg meeting, 1–3, 298
  male members, 207, 216, 222–23, 249, 275, 276, 283
  optimism, 292–93, 295–96
  origins, 1–3
  overview, 3–4
  principal figures, 20, 284–90, 294
  reunification period, 275–84
  role models, 20, 96–97, 164, 294–95
  self-narratives, 297
  silence on Nazi period, 296–97
  slow group death, 282–84
  subgroups, 282
  See also specific periods
Schröter, Ursula, 44
Schubert, Franz, 30
Seghers, Anna, 142
self-censorship, 14, 15, 187–91, 192, 199, 260, 293
self-narratives, 297
sexual abuse, 18
  See also rape
show trials, 68, 82, 83

Siebert, Anna, ix
  1950s, 60, 73, 80–81, 87, 89, 97–98, 117
  1960s, 135, 145–48, 164
  1962 flood, 145–46
  1970s, 177, 185–86, 196
  1980s, 207, 211–12, 220, 227–28, 236
  agency and power, 299
  assessment, 284–85
  bereavements, 147, 198–99, 227–28, 267
  Berlin Blockade, 60, 292
  Buchenwald and, 57
  career, 135, 146, 148, 153, 185–86, 299
  education, 52
  engineering, 53, 97, 98, 117, 267
  Erika Krämer and, 87, 89, 211–12
  family, 267
  GDR repression, 228
  gender discrimination, 146, 285, 299
  group organizer, 207
  health, 228
  Heimat, 227
  housing, 80–81
  humiliation, 299
  interviews, 16, 57, 260, 284–85, 288
  male members and, 276
  marriage, 97
  on marriage, 73
  national service, 33–35, 211
  Nazi period, 33–35, 211
  postwar period, 41–42, 52–53
  principal story, 20, 284–85
  retirement, 228
  reunification period, 265–68, 276, 282
  role model, 97–98, 164, 294
  travel/holidays, 147, 186, 196, 266, 267, 268
social media, 18
social security, 204
Sommer, Käthe, xi
  1950s, 76, 84
  1960s, 158–60, 299
  1970s, 187, 194, 200
  1980s, 232, 233
  expulsion from GDR, 159–60, 166, 177, 187, 191, 200, 299
  family reunification, 232
  GDR politics and, 84, 159–60, 194
  on *Heimat*, 283
  humiliation, 299
  illness, 277
  postwar period, 111
  reunification period, 262–63, 277, 283
Soviet Union
  1950s, 67, 79, 82–83, 92–93, 110, 115
  1960s, 132, 135, 138, 142, 149, 156
  1970 Treaty with FRG, 135
  1970s GDR and, 169, 199
  1980s, 21, 204, 205, 245, 263
  Berlin and, 115
  China and, 149
  collectivization, 110
  Helsinki Conference and, 170
  housing, 79
  invasion of Afghanistan, 203
  oil production, 170
  Poland and, 156
  Prague Spring and, 131, 132–33, 134, 157–58
  Stalinism, 68, 70
  World War II, 31
Sparmann, Richard, 39
spatial assessment, 16
stagflation, 169
Stalin, Joseph, 79, 145
Stalingrad, 31, 251, 297
Stalinism, 68, 70, 248
starvation, 35, 36, 42–43, 46
Stasi
  1960s, 149, 176
  1970s, 171
  1980s, 21, 204
  1989, 245, 248
  artists and, 274
  informers. *See* Stasi informers
  lost book and, 176
  Prague Spring and, 133
  role, 258, 286
  strength, 293
Stasi informers, 14, 92, 106, 189, 260
Steege, Paul, 53
Stein, Maria, xi
  1980s, 211, 235–37
  Lübschütz family and, 235–37, 296
  Nazi period, 269

photo (1989), 236
  reunification period, 277, 279, 282
  travels, 235–37, 277, 279
Steiner, André, 169
Stoph, Willi, 134–35
Sybille letters, 216–18

Tchaikovsky, Pyotr, 31
terrorism, 21, 178
Thoms, Liselotte, 107
Tokyo Olympics (1964), 136
trade unions, 94, 104, 206, 224
trauma, 17–18
travel
  1950s, 111–16, 119
  1960s, 146, 160–61
  1970s, 196–98, 200
  1980s, 234–41

Ulbricht, Walter, 20, 41, 129, 132, 134, 135, 155, 171, 230
unemployment, 169, 204, 230, 232, 250, 253, 267
United Kingdom, Queen's visit to FRG, 146–47
United Nations, self-determination, 155
United States
  1968, 131, 132
  1975 Helsinki Conference, 170
  1980s politics, 203
  Denver, Colorado, 235–41
  education, 179
  FRG and, 116
  Guantanamo Bay, 18
  Iraq, 18
Urman, Ernst, 240

Vaizey, Hester, 7–8
Vietnam War, 131, 132
Viewig, Kurt, 106
voluntary work, 94–95, 109, 126
Vonyó, Tamás, 80

Waldheim Trials, 83
Walter, Erna, x, 177, 219, 262, 275
Wander, Maxie, 174, 175
weather, 44–46, 130–31, 172–73
Wedekind, Frank, 73

Weimar period, 66, 67, 70, 294
Wende. See reunification period
Wolf, Christa, 174, 175
Wolle, Stefan, 133
women
  1950s attitudes, 65–70, 75, 107, 117–18
  1960s attitudes, 21, 126–30, 146, 149
  1970s attitudes, 173–76, 200
  1980s attitudes, 205–07
  autobiographies, 175–76
  end of war period, 6–7, 43–44
  hegemonic beliefs and, 293–94
  history of everyday life and, 8–9
  Nazi period, 5–6, 59, 294, 299–300
  patriarchy, 66–67, 70, 173, 206, 293–94
  postwar and, 47–48, 50–51
  rape, 41–42, 50, 60
  reunification and, 10, 22, 249
  stories, 10
World War I, 66

Zeller, Carl, 100
Zetkin, Clara, 66, 250
Zwahr, Hartmut, 7, 241–42

www.ingramcontent.com/pod-product-compliance
Lightning Source LLC
Chambersburg PA
CBHW071332080526
44587CB00017B/2813